THE PRINCE OF TENNIS
VOL. 28
The SHONEN JUMP Manga Edition

STORY AND ART BY
TAKESHI KONOMI

Translation/Joe Yamazaki
Consultant/Michelle Pangilinan
Touch-up Art & Lettering/Vanessa Satone
Design/Sam Elzway
Editor/Leyla Aker

Editor in Chief, Books/Alvin Lu
Editor in Chief, Magazines/Marc Weidenbaum
VP, Publishing Licensing/Rika Inouye
VP, Sales and Product Marketing/Gonzalo Ferreyra
VP, Creative/Linda Espinosa
Publisher/Hyoe Narita

Printed in the U.S.A.

Published by VIZ Media, LLC
P.O. Box 77010
San Francisco, CA 94107

SHONEN JUMP Manga Edition
10 9 8 7 6 5 4 3 2 1
First printing, November 2008

PARENTAL ADVISORY
THE PRINCE OF TENNIS
is rated A and is suitable
for readers of all ages.
ratings.viz.com

THE WORLD'S
MOST POPULAR MANGA

www.viz.com

www.shonenjump.com

Yuta Yamazaki (Ryoga) and me

I ve had the character Ryoga Echizen* in mind since the start, so I m really happy I finally get to show him to everybody! Thanks to all of you, my dream of a theatrical release has come true. Thank you very much. Now what should I do next ?

- Takeshi Konomi, 2005

*Ryoga is Ryoma's adopted brother and appears in the movie The Prince of Tennis—The Two Samurai: The First Game—Ed.

About Takeshi Konomi

Takeshi Konomi exploded onto the manga scene with the incredible **THE PRINCE OF TENNIS**. His refined art style and sleek character designs proved popular with **Weekly Shonen Jump** readers, and **THE PRINCE OF TENNIS** became the number one sports manga in Japan almost overnight. Its cast of fascinating male tennis players attracted legions of female readers even though it was originally intended to be a boys' comic. The manga continues to be a success in Japan and has inspired a hit anime series, as well as several video games and mountains of merchandise.

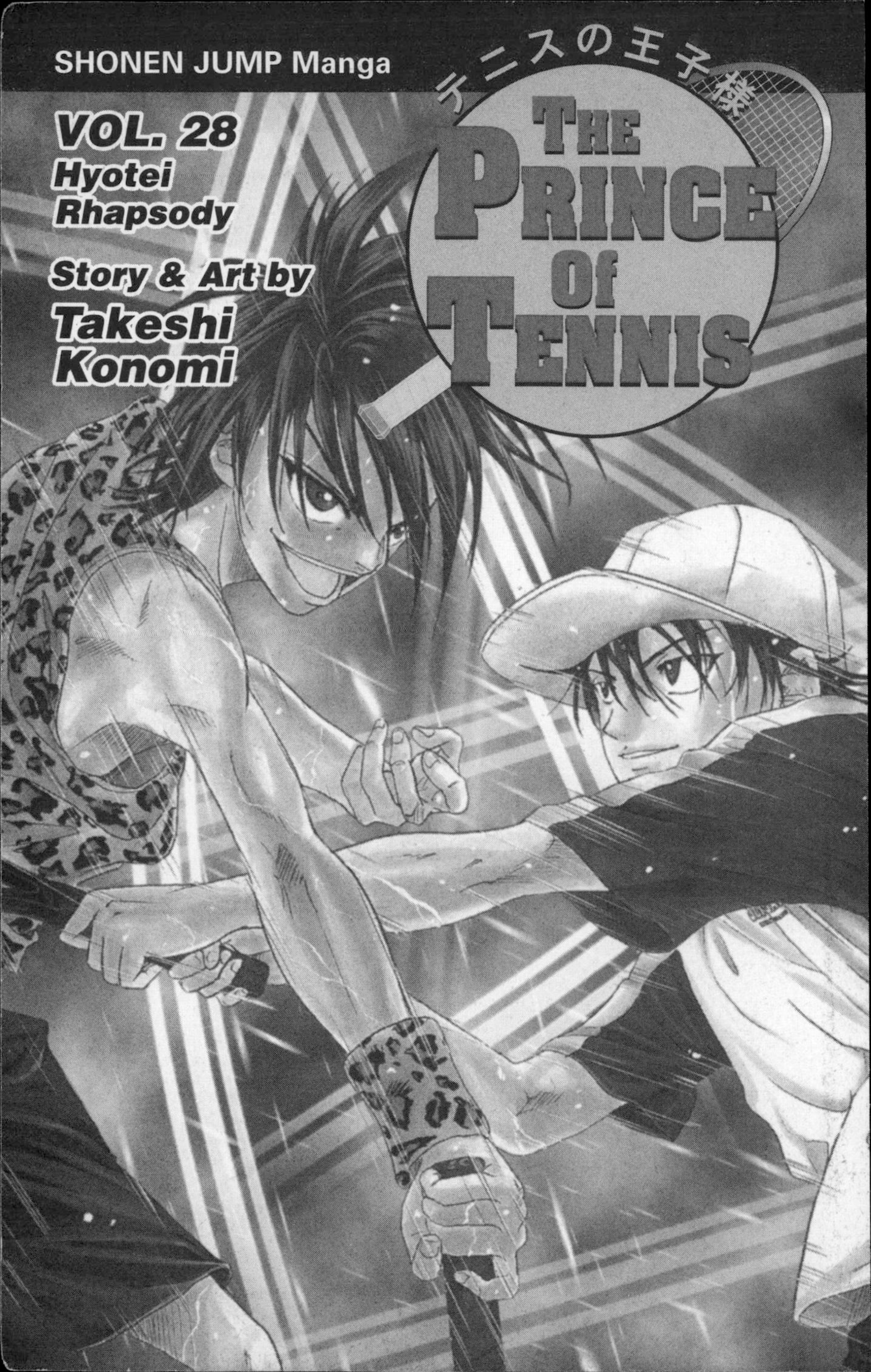
SHONEN JUMP Manga
VOL. 28
Hyotei Rhapsody
Story & Art by
Takeshi Konomi
テニスの王子様
THE PRINCE OF TENNIS

ENNIS CLUB

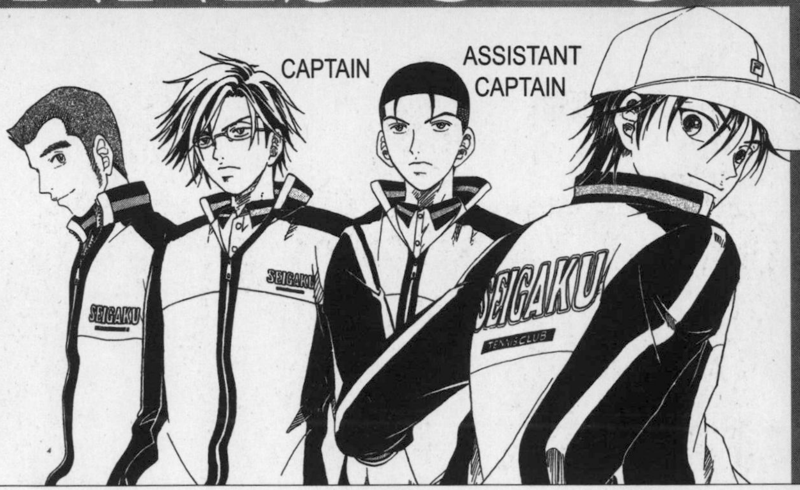
CAPTAIN
ASSISTANT CAPTAIN
SEIGAKU
SEIGAKU
SEIGAKU
TENNIS CLUB

• TAKASHI KAWAMURA • KUNIMITSU TEZUKA • SHUICHIRO OISHI • RYOMA ECHIZEN •

STORY & CHARACTERS

Seishun Academy student Ryoma Echizen is a tennis prodigy, with wins in four consecutive U.S. Junior Tennis Tournaments under his belt. He became a starter as a 7th grader and led his team to the District Preliminaries! Despite a few mishaps, Seishun won the District Prelims and the City Tournament, and earned a ticket to the Kanto Tournament. The team came away victorious from its first-round matches, but captain Kunimitsu injured his shoulder and went to Kyushu for treatment. Despite losing Kunimitsu and assistant captain Shuichiro to injury, Seishun pulled together as a team, not only reaching the finals of the tournament but also earning a slot at the Nationals!

In the finals against Rikkai, Seishun lost both doubles matches but won both singles matches to tie the teams at two each. In the final match, Ryoma struggled against Genichiro's Furin Kazan, but thanks to his Selfless State play he won! Now, with the Kanto Tournament championship in their hands, Seishun heads to the beach for a joint training camp with Rokkaku!

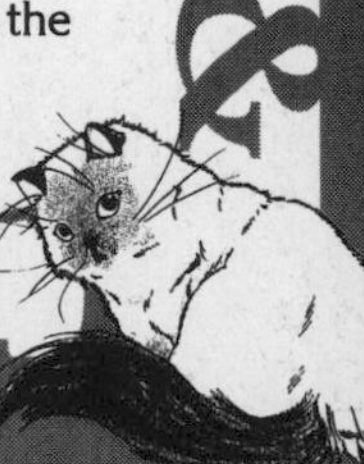

SEIGAKU T

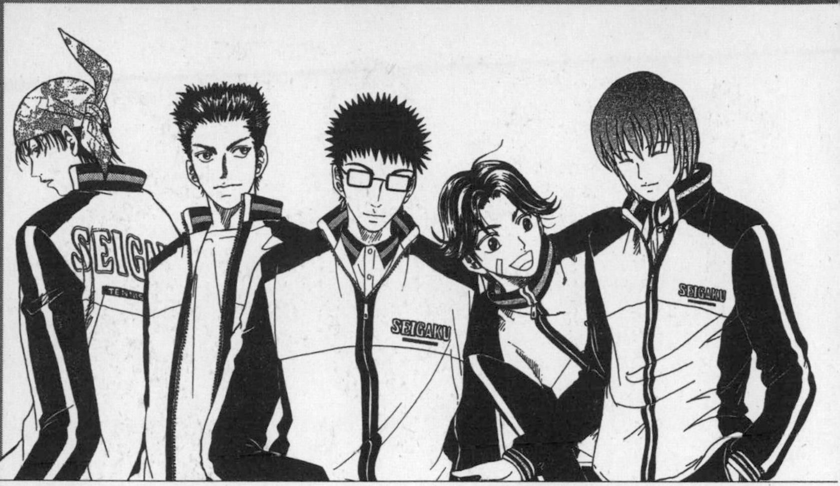

• KAORU KAIDO • TAKESHI MOMOSHIRO • SADAHARU INUI • EIJI KIKUMARU • SHUSUKE FUJI •

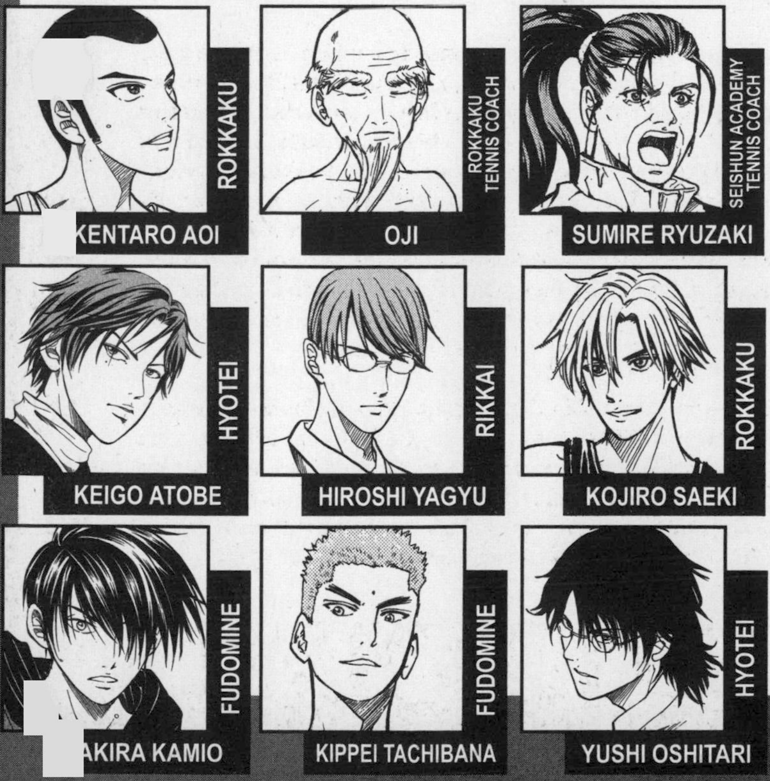

ROKKAKU
KENTARO AOI
ROKKAKU TENNIS COACH
OJI
SEISHUN ACADEMY TENNIS COACH
SUMIRE RYUZAKI
HYOTEI
KEIGO ATOBE
RIKKAI
HIROSHI YAGYU
ROKKAKU
KOJIRO SAEKI
FUDOMINE
AKIRA KAMIO
FUDOMINE
KIPPEI TACHIBANA
HYOTEI
YUSHI OSHITARI

CONTENTS Vol. 28
Hyotei Rhapsody

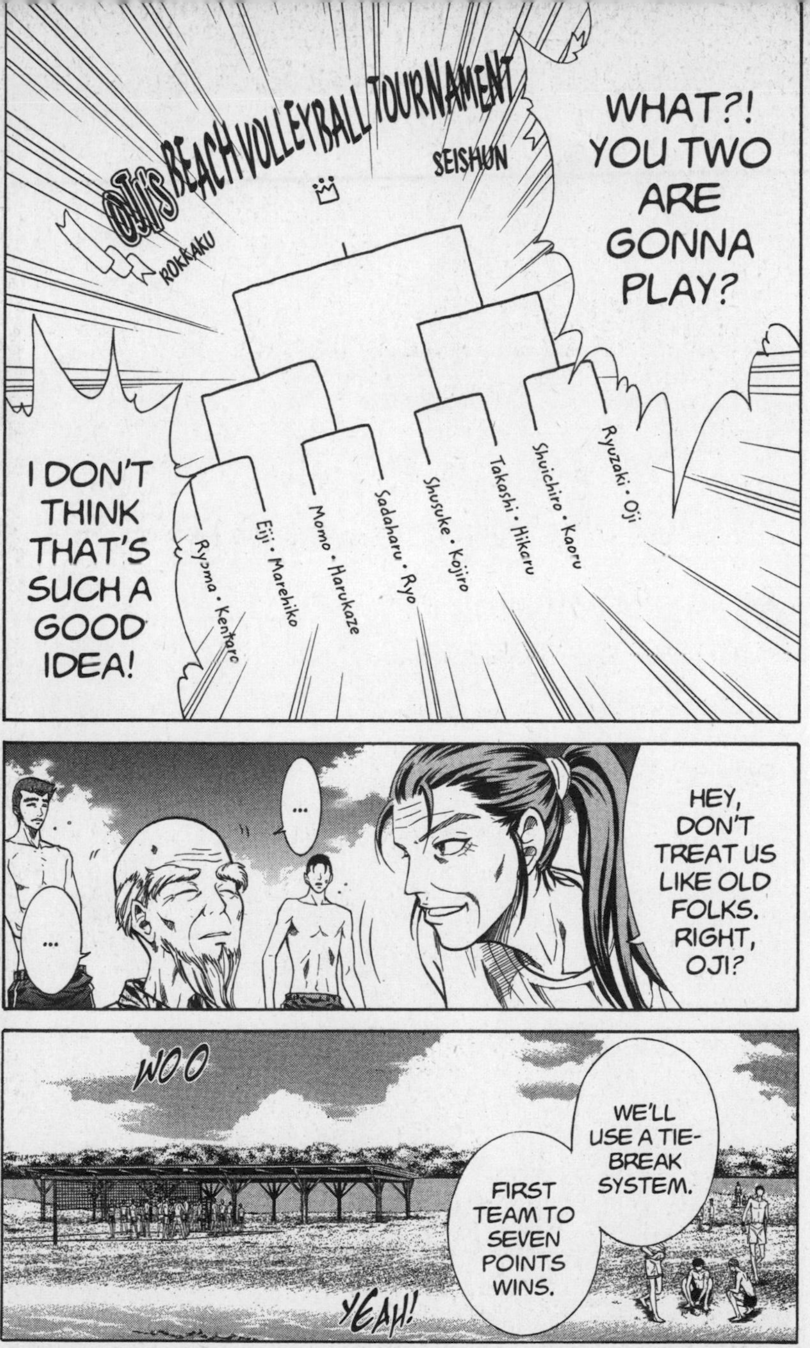
WHAT?! YOU TWO ARE GONNA PLAY?
OJI'S BEACH VOLLEYBALL TOURNAMENT
SEISHUN
ROKKAKU
Ryuzaki • Oji
Shuichiro • Kaoru
Takashi • Hikaru
Shusuke • Kojiro
Sadaharu • Ryo
Momo • Harukaze
Eiji • Marehiko
Ryoma • Kentaro
I DON'T THINK THAT'S SUCH A GOOD IDEA!
HEY, DON'T TREAT US LIKE OLD FOLKS. RIGHT, OJI?
...
...
WE'LL USE A TIE-BREAK SYSTEM.
FIRST TEAM TO SEVEN POINTS WINS.
WOO
YEAH!

GENIUS 238: THE WORLD'S GREATEST TERROR

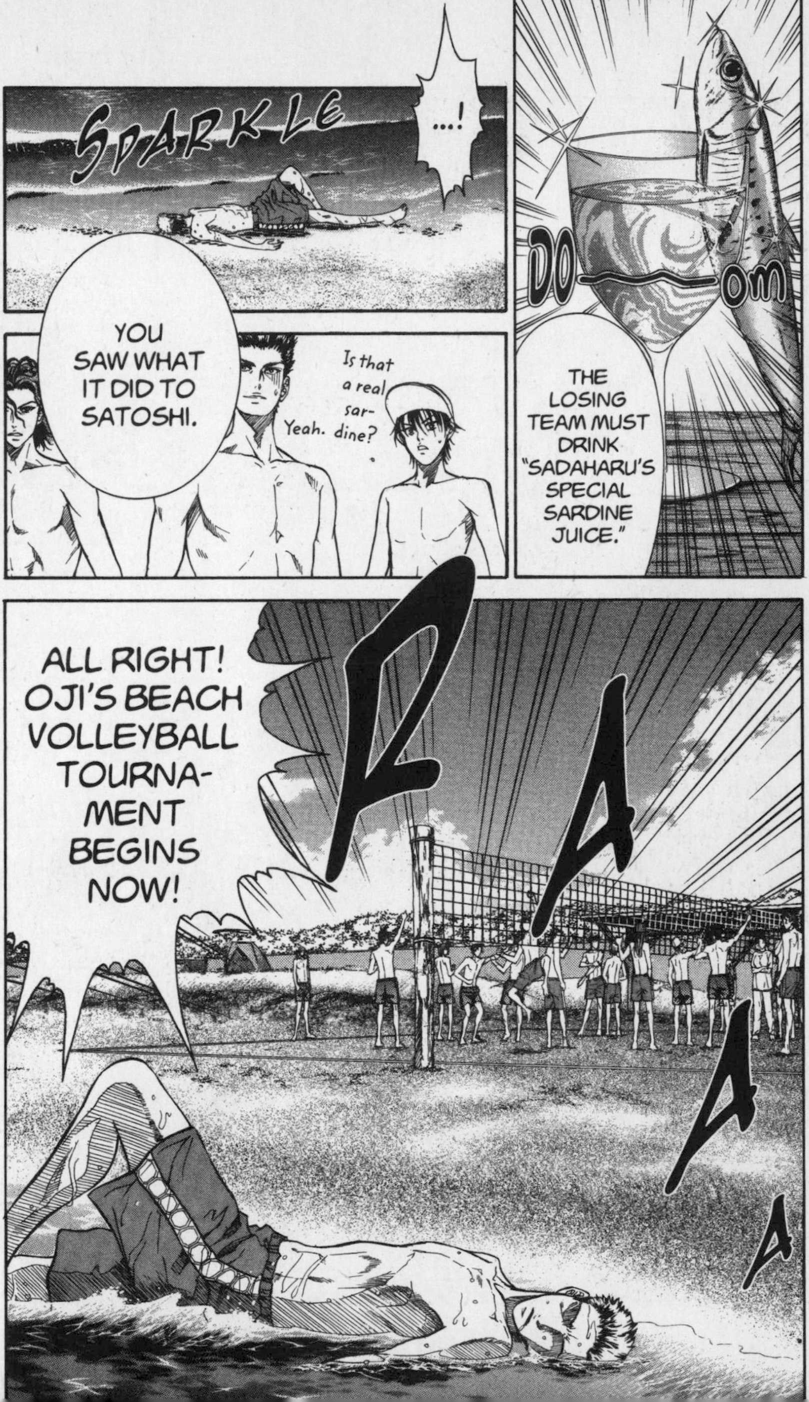
DO——om
THE LOSING TEAM MUST DRINK "SADAHARU'S SPECIAL SARDINE JUICE."
SPARKLE
...!
Is that a real sar-dine?
Yeah.
YOU SAW WHAT IT DID TO SATOSHI.
ALL RIGHT! OJI'S BEACH VOLLEYBALL TOURNA-MENT BEGINS NOW!
RAAAA

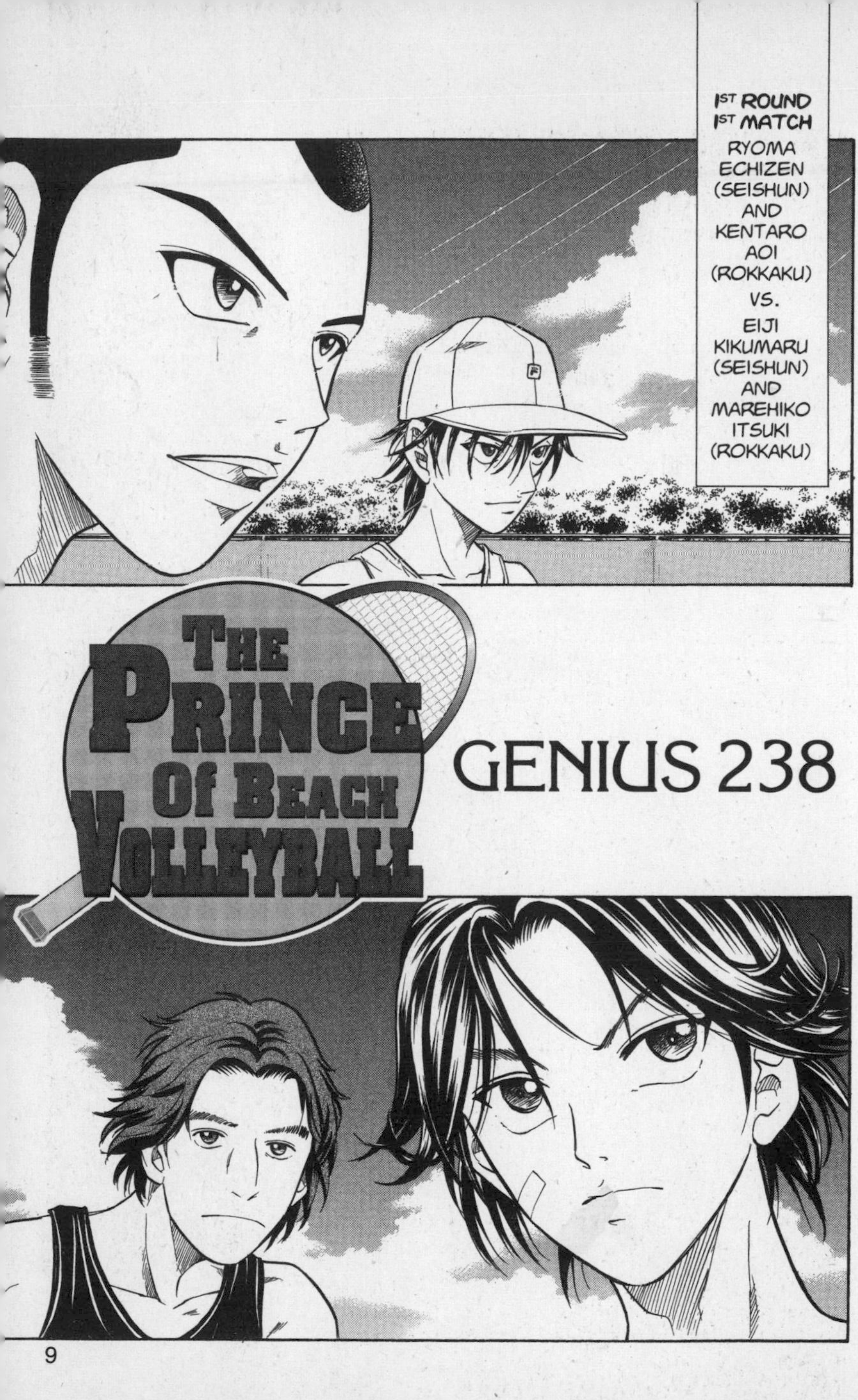
1ST ROUND
1ST MATCH
RYOMA ECHIZEN (SEISHUN) AND KENTARO AOI (ROKKAKU) VS. EIJI KIKUMARU (SEISHUN) AND MAREHIKO ITSUKI (ROKKAKU)
THE PRINCE OF BEACH VOLLEYBALL
GENIUS 238

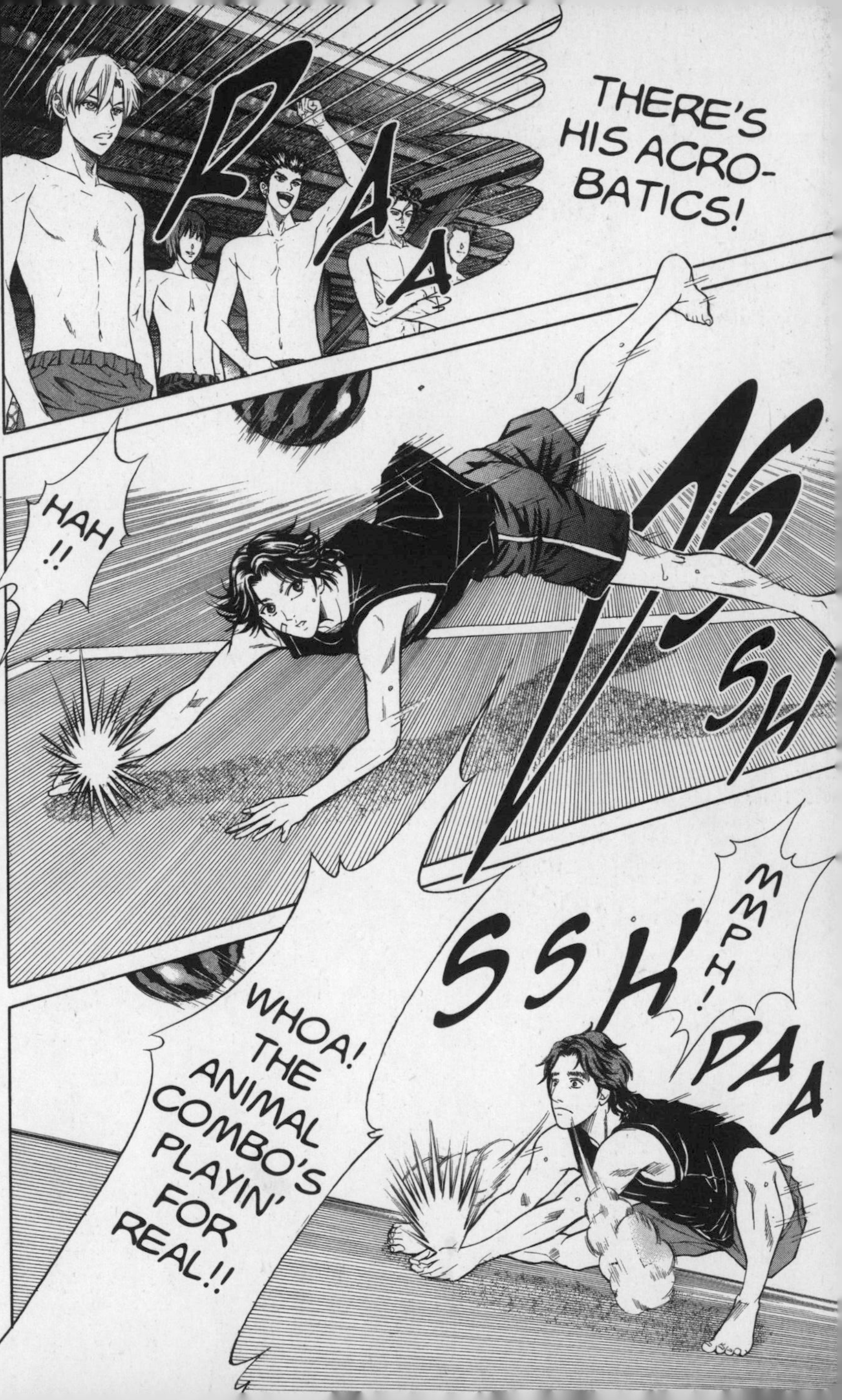
RAAA
THERE'S HIS ACRO-BATICS!
HAH!!
SSH
MMPH!
PAA
WHOA! THE ANIMAL COMBO'S PLAYIN' FOR REAL!!

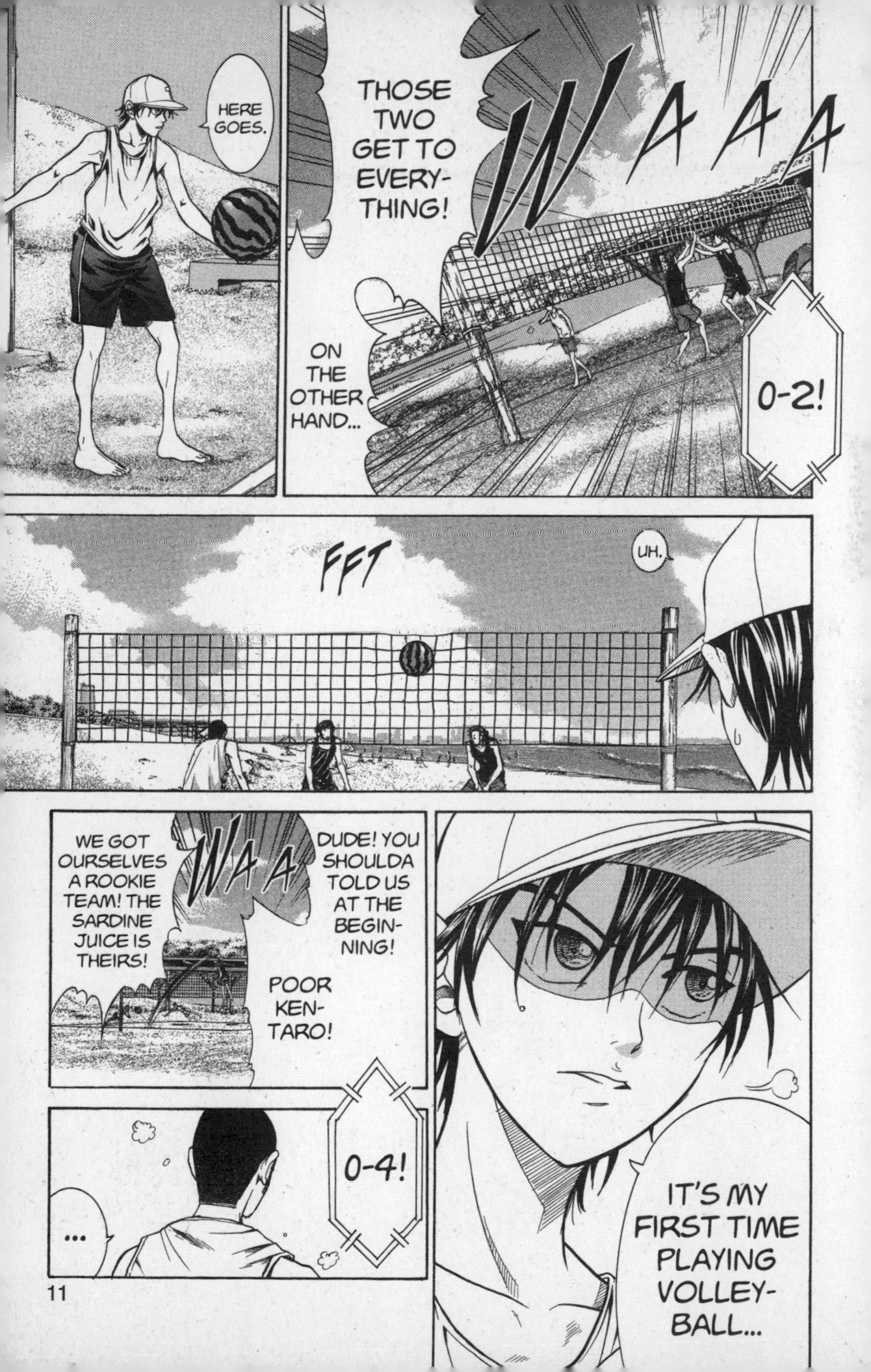
WAAA
THOSE TWO GET TO EVERY-THING!
0-2!
ON THE OTHER HAND...
HERE GOES.
UH.
FFT
IT'S MY FIRST TIME PLAYING VOLLEY-BALL...
DUDE! YOU SHOULDA TOLD US AT THE BEGIN-NING!
WAA
WE GOT OURSELVES A ROOKIE TEAM! THE SARDINE JUICE IS THEIRS!
POOR KEN-TARO!
0-4!
...

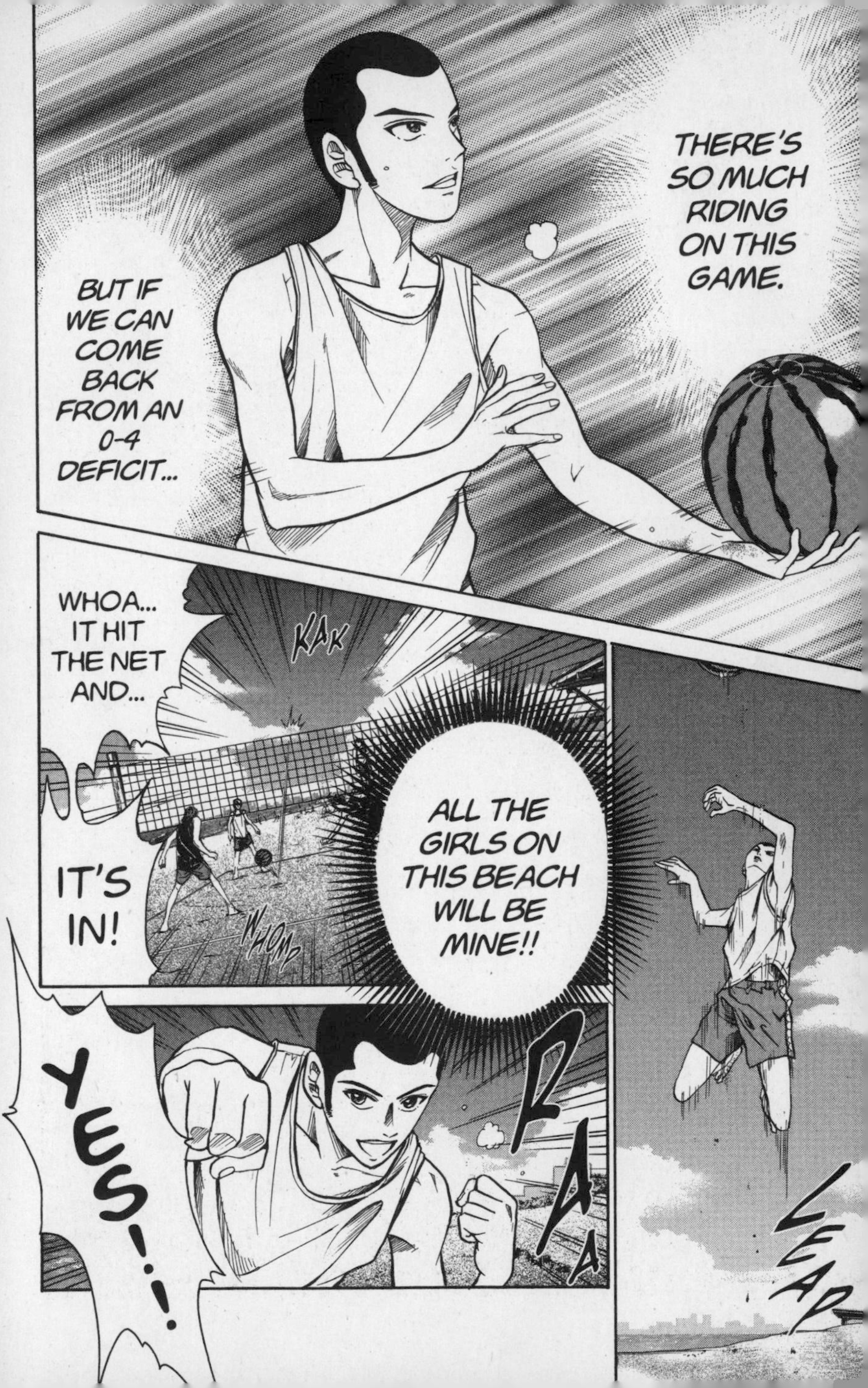
THERE'S SO MUCH RIDING ON THIS GAME.
BUT IF WE CAN COME BACK FROM AN 0-4 DEFICIT...
LEAP
KAK
WHOA... IT HIT THE NET AND...
WHOMP
IT'S IN!
ALL THE GIRLS ON THIS BEACH WILL BE MINE!!
RAA
YES-!!

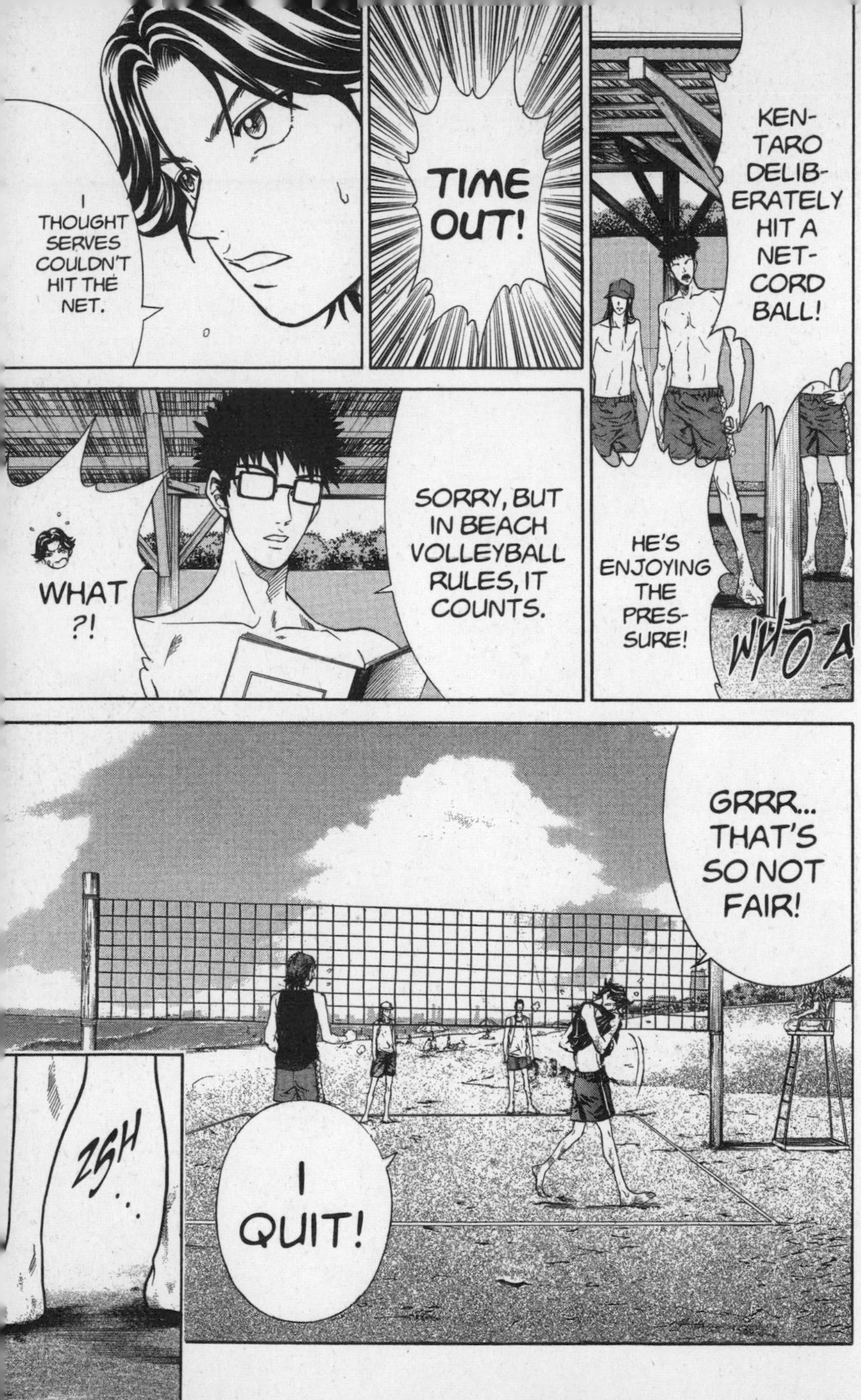
KEN-TARO DELIB-ERATELY HIT A NET-CORD BALL!
HE'S ENJOYING THE PRES-SURE!
WHOA
TIME OUT!
I THOUGHT SERVES COULDN'T HIT THE NET.
SORRY, BUT IN BEACH VOLLEYBALL RULES, IT COUNTS.
WHAT?!
GRRR... THAT'S SO NOT FAIR!
I QUIT!
ZSH...

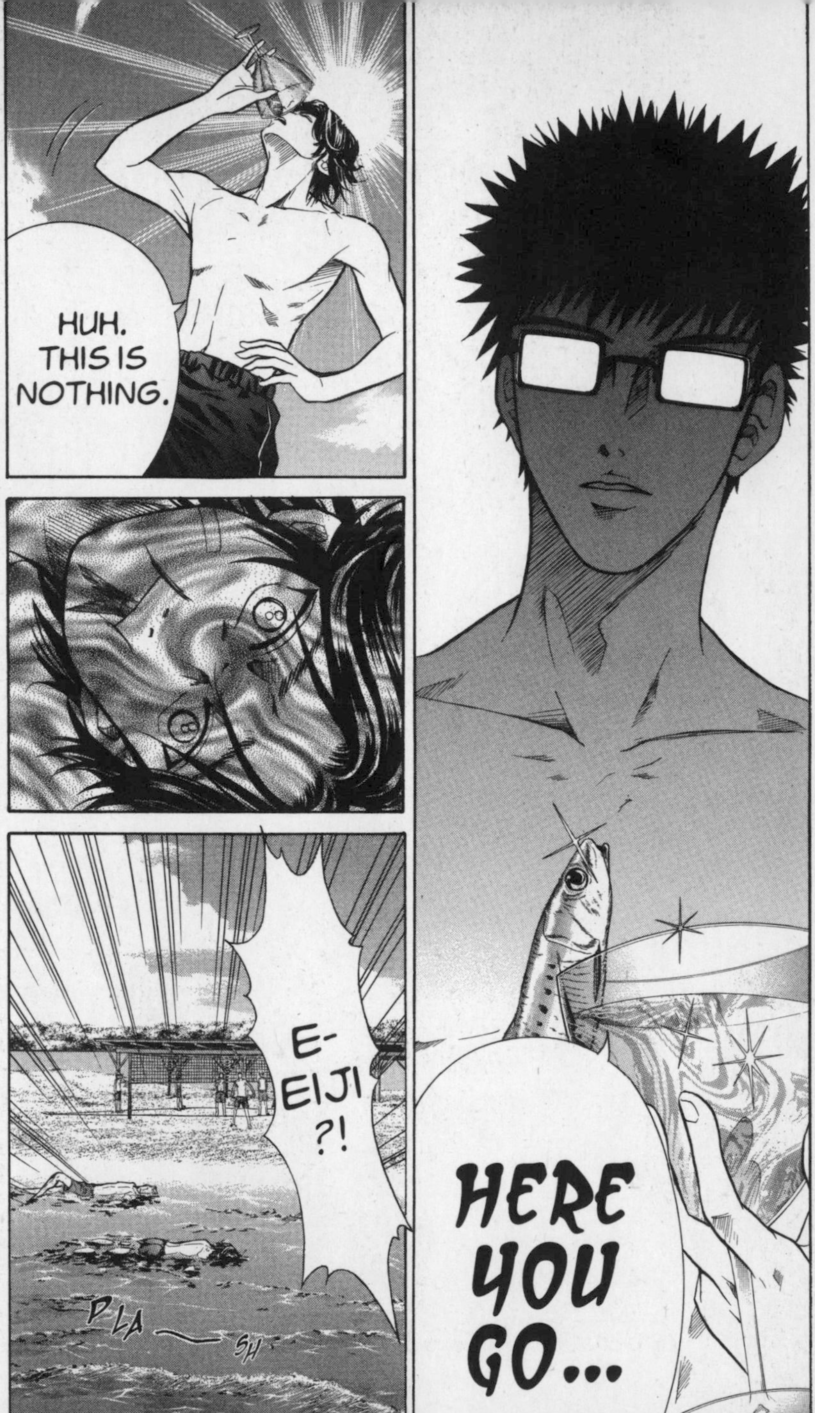
HERE YOU GO...
HUH. THIS IS NOTHING.
E- EIJI ?!
PLA—SH

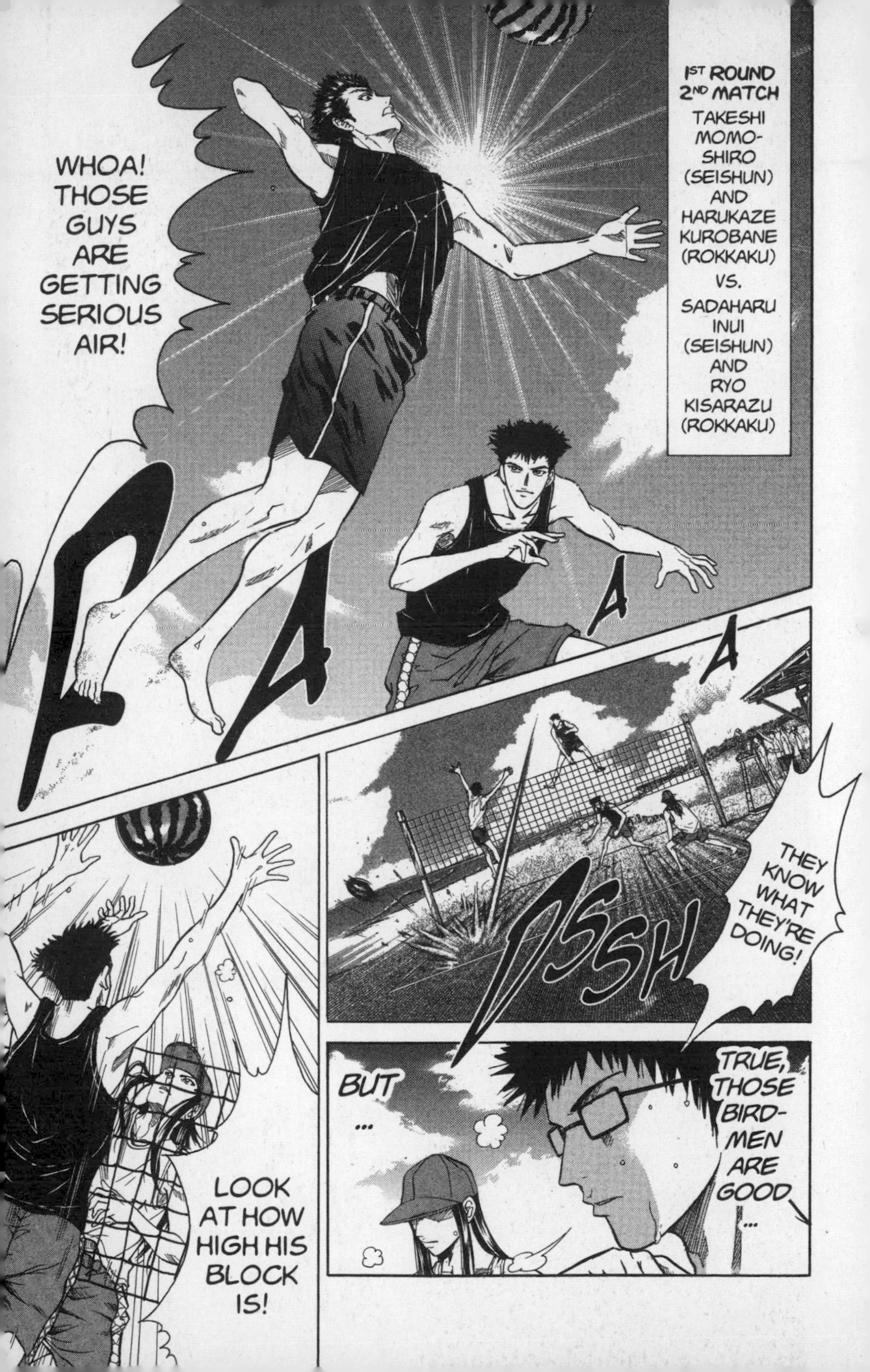
1ST ROUND 2ND MATCH
TAKESHI MOMOSHIRO (SEISHUN) AND HARUKAZE KUROBANE (ROKKAKU) VS. SADAHARU INUI (SEISHUN) AND RYO KISARAZU (ROKKAKU)
WHOA! THOSE GUYS ARE GETTING SERIOUS AIR!
FAAA
THEY KNOW WHAT THEY'RE DOING!
ASSH
TRUE, THOSE BIRD-MEN ARE GOOD...
BUT ...
LOOK AT HOW HIGH HIS BLOCK IS!

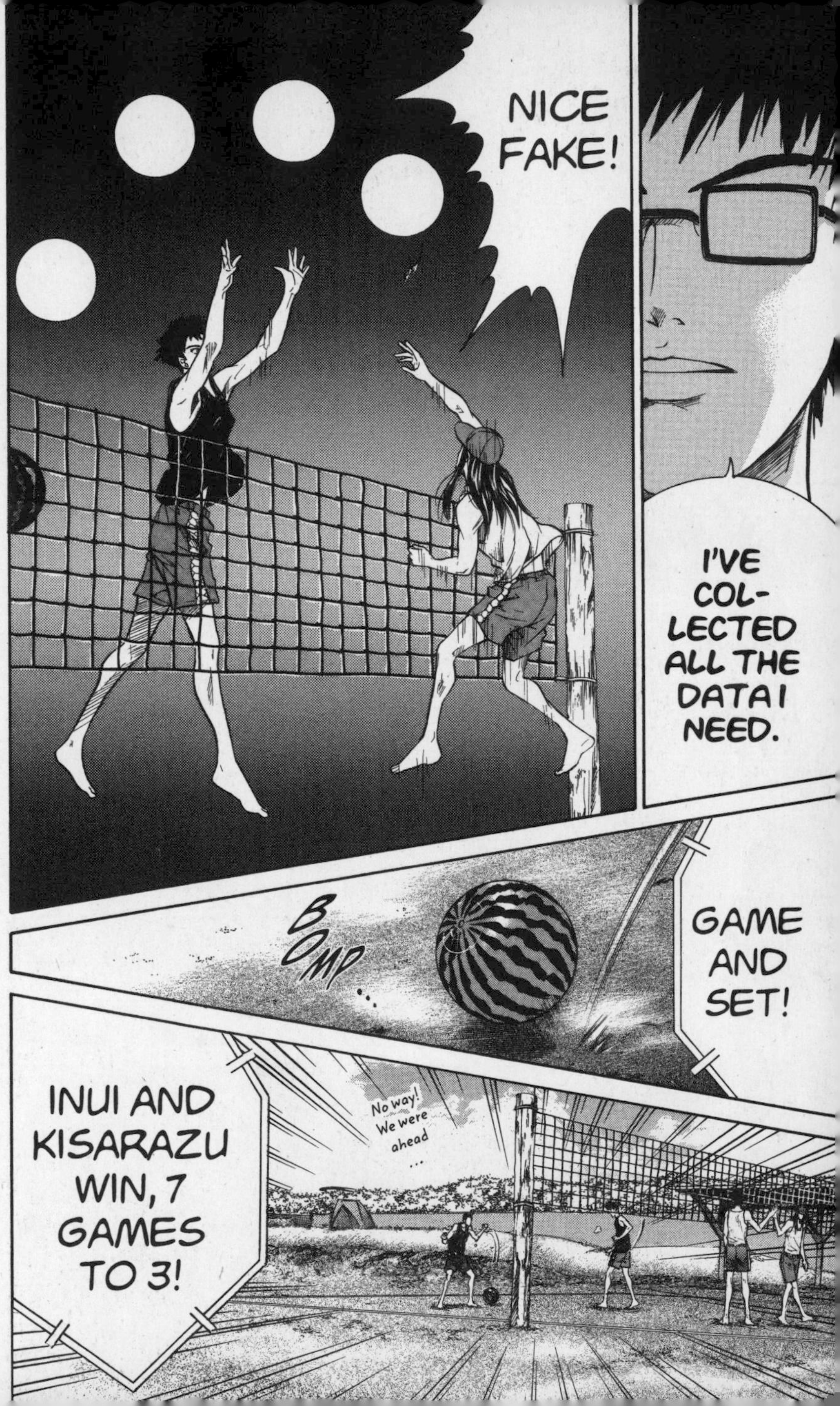
I'VE COL-LECTED ALL THE DATA I NEED.
NICE FAKE!
GAME AND SET!
BOMP
INUI AND KISARAZU WIN, 7 GAMES TO 3!
No way! We were ahead ...

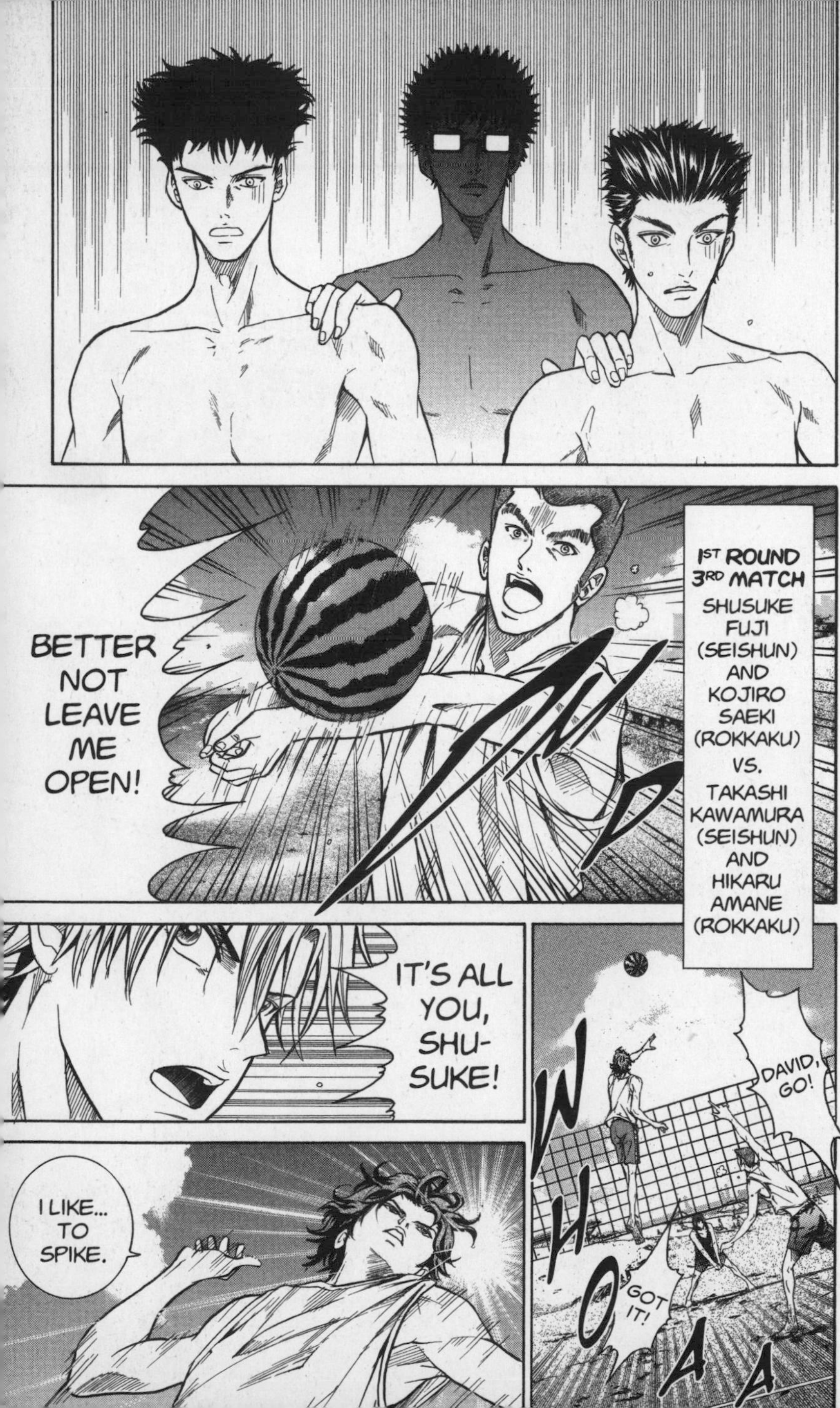
1ST ROUND 3RD MATCH
SHUSUKE FUJI (SEISHUN) AND KOJIRO SAEKI (ROKKAKU) VS. TAKASHI KAWAMURA (SEISHUN) AND HIKARU AMANE (ROKKAKU)
BETTER NOT LEAVE ME OPEN!
DAVID, GO!
GOT IT!
WHOAA
IT'S ALL YOU, SHU-SUKE!
I LIKE... TO SPIKE.

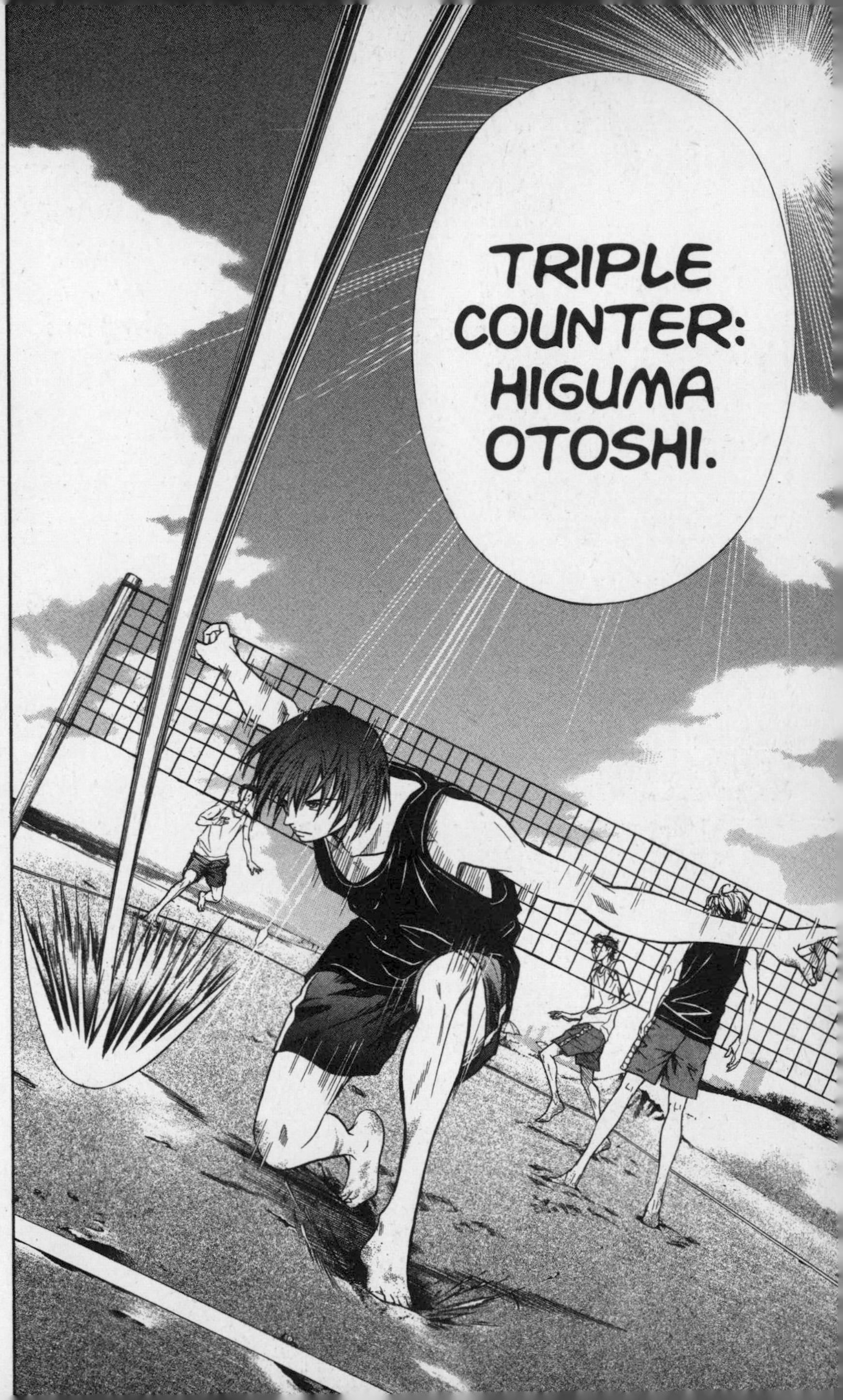
TRIPLE COUNTER: HIGUMA OTOSHI.

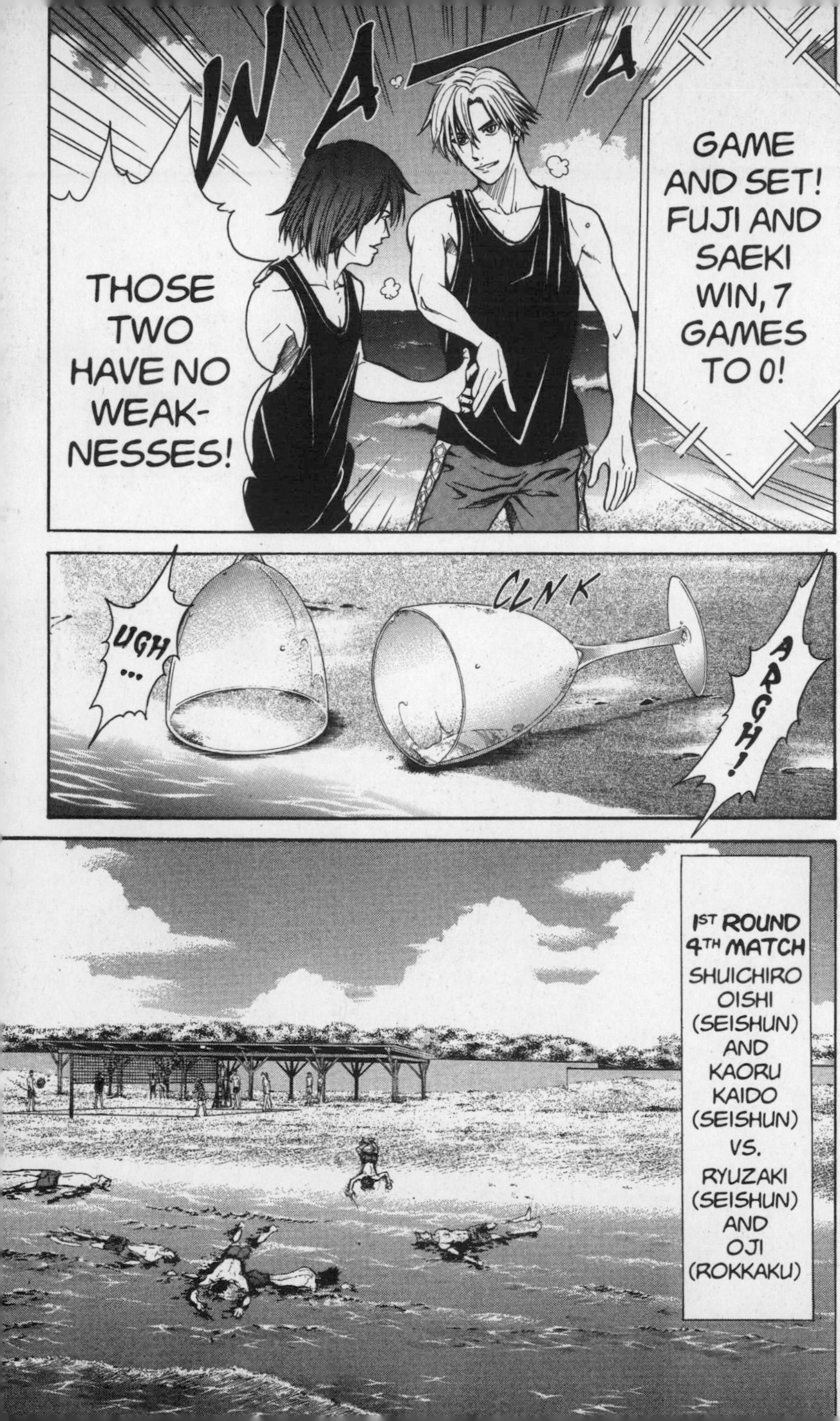
GAME AND SET! FUJI AND SAEKI WIN, 7 GAMES TO 0!
WA—A
THOSE TWO HAVE NO WEAK-NESSES!
ARGH!
CLNK
UGH...
1ST ROUND 4TH MATCH
SHUICHIRO OISHI (SEISHUN) AND KAORU KAIDO (SEISHUN) VS. RYUZAKI (SEISHUN) AND OJI (ROKKAKU)

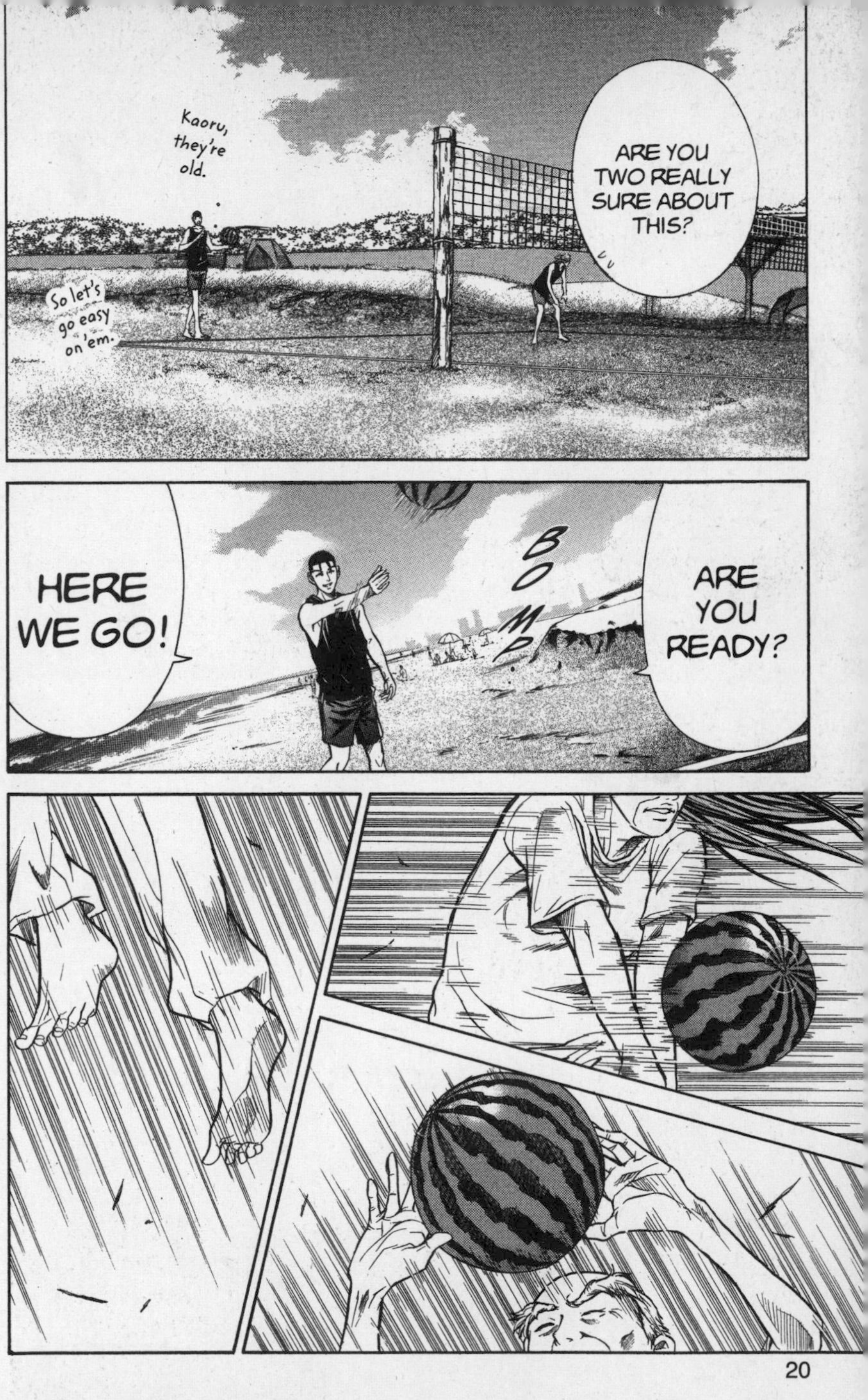
ARE YOU TWO REALLY SURE ABOUT THIS?
Kaoru, they're old.
So let's go easy on 'em.
ARE YOU READY?
BOMP
HERE WE GO!

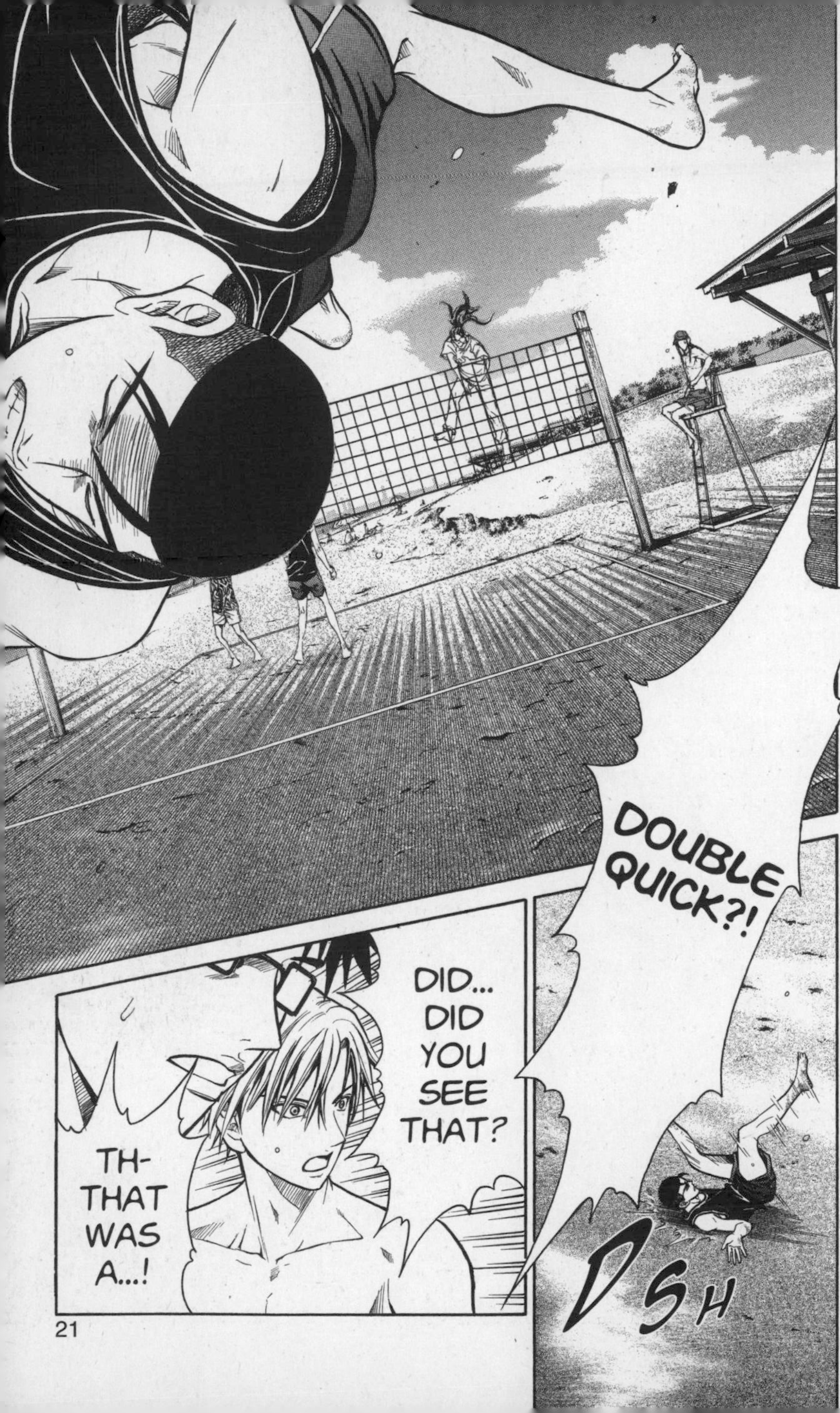
DOUBLE QUICK?!
DSH
DID... DID YOU SEE THAT?
TH- THAT WAS A...!

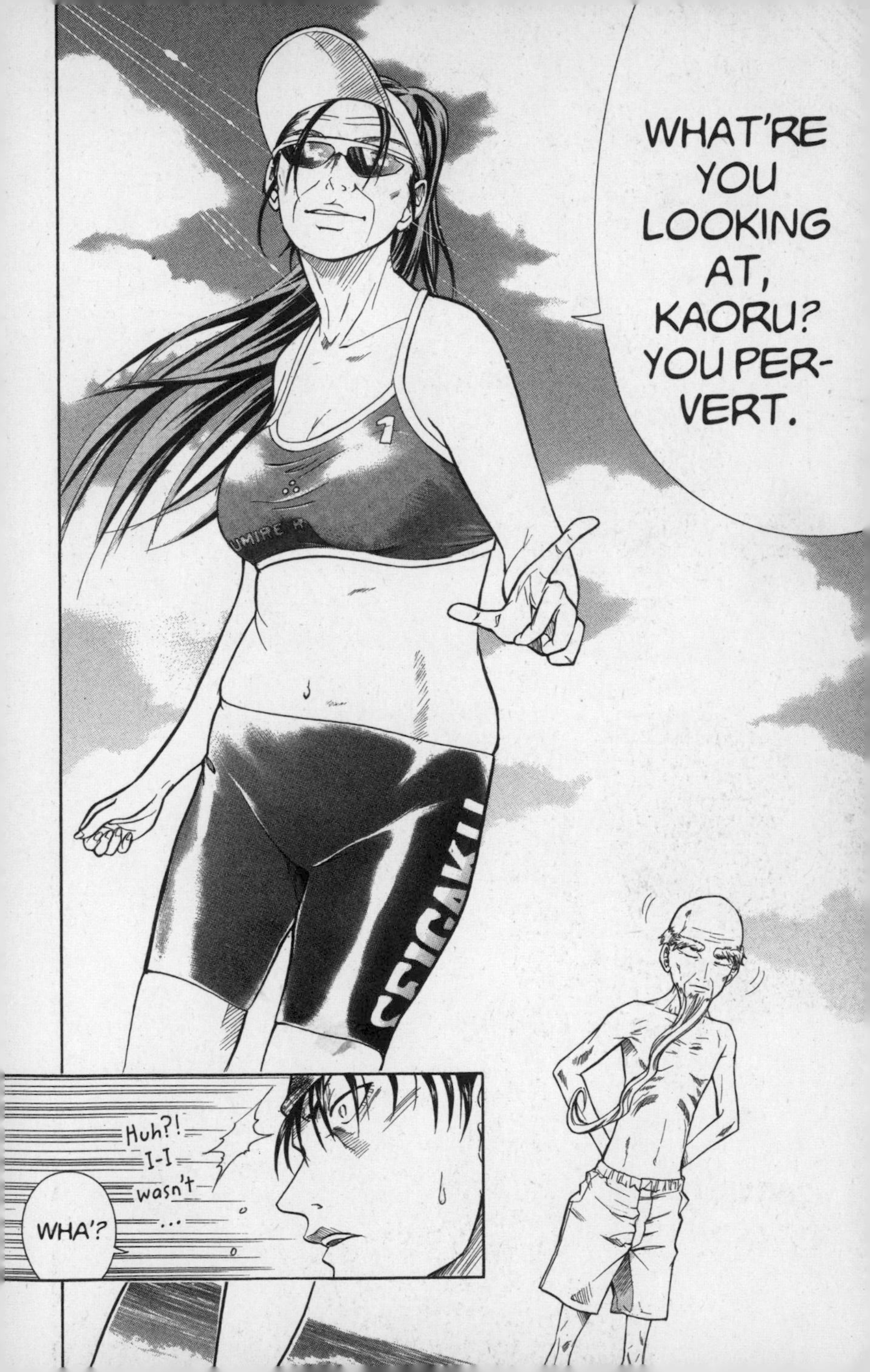
WHAT'RE YOU LOOKING AT, KAORU? YOU PER-VERT.
Huh?! I-I wasn't ...
WHA'?

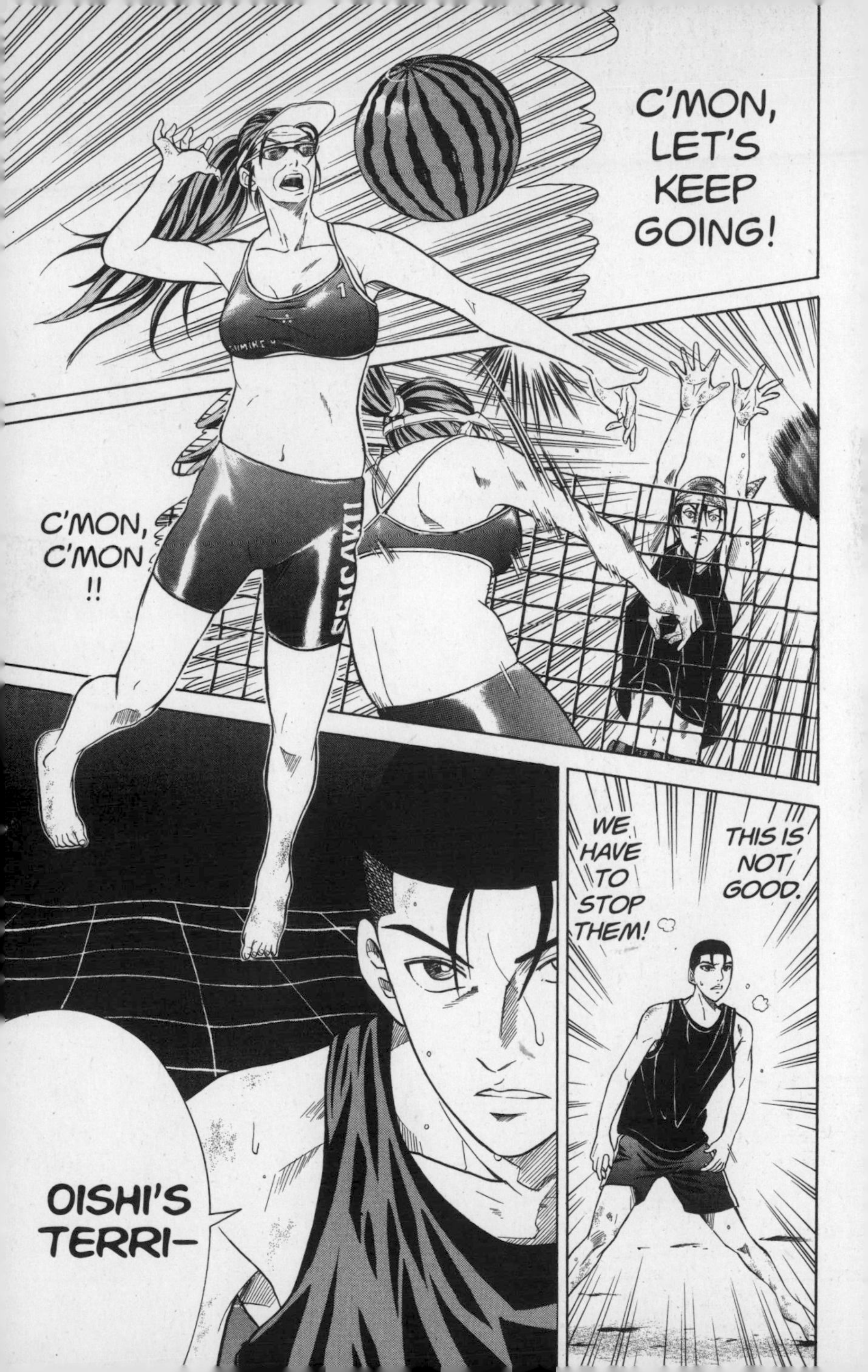
C'MON, LET'S KEEP GOING!
C'MON, C'MON !!
THIS IS NOT GOOD.
WE HAVE TO STOP THEM!
OISHI'S TERRI-

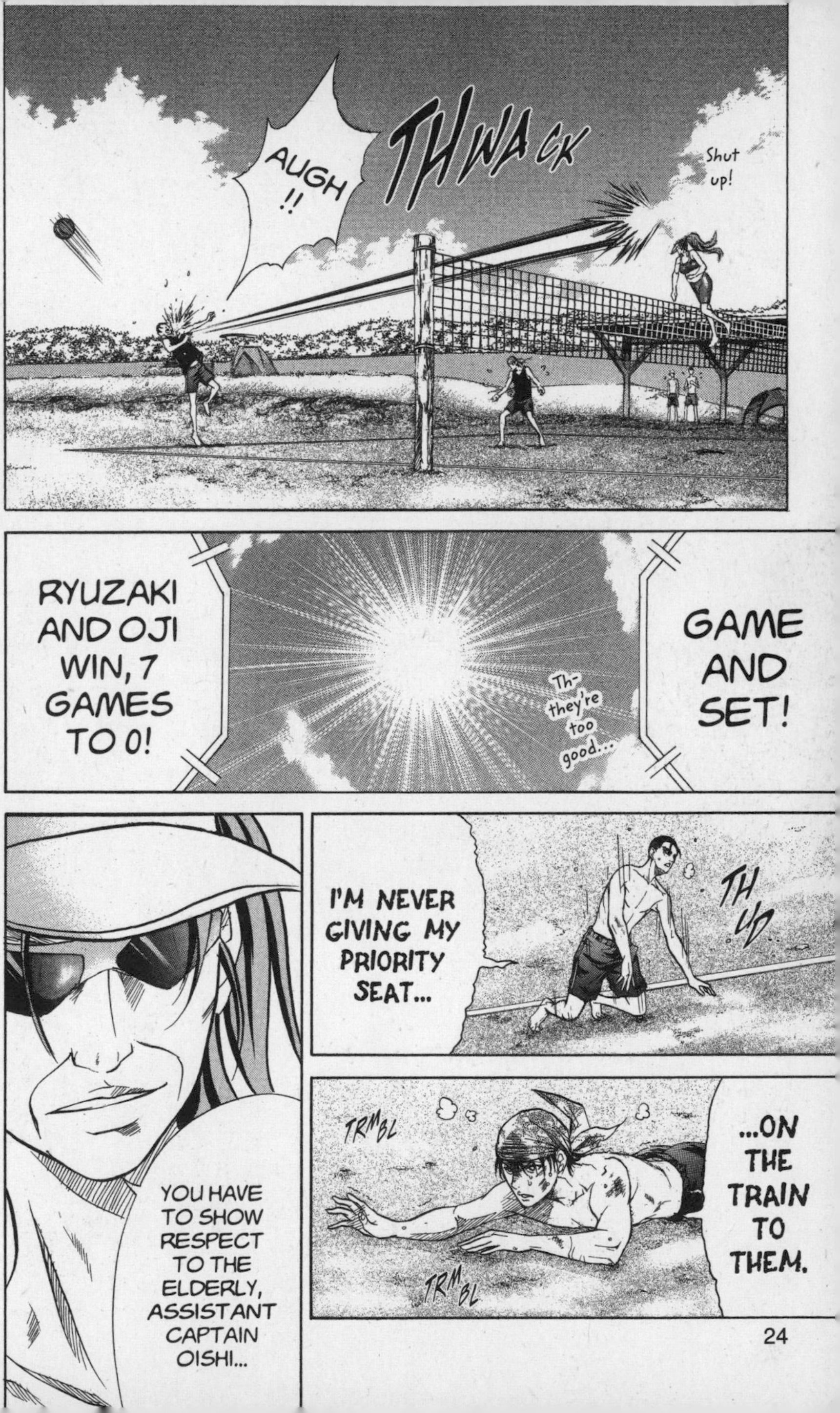
Shut up!
THWACK
AUGH!!
GAME AND SET!
Th-they're too good...
RYUZAKI AND OJI WIN, 7 GAMES TO 0!
THUD
I'M NEVER GIVING MY PRIORITY SEAT...
...ON THE TRAIN TO THEM.
TRMBL
TRMBL
YOU HAVE TO SHOW RESPECT TO THE ELDERLY, ASSISTANT CAPTAIN OISHI...

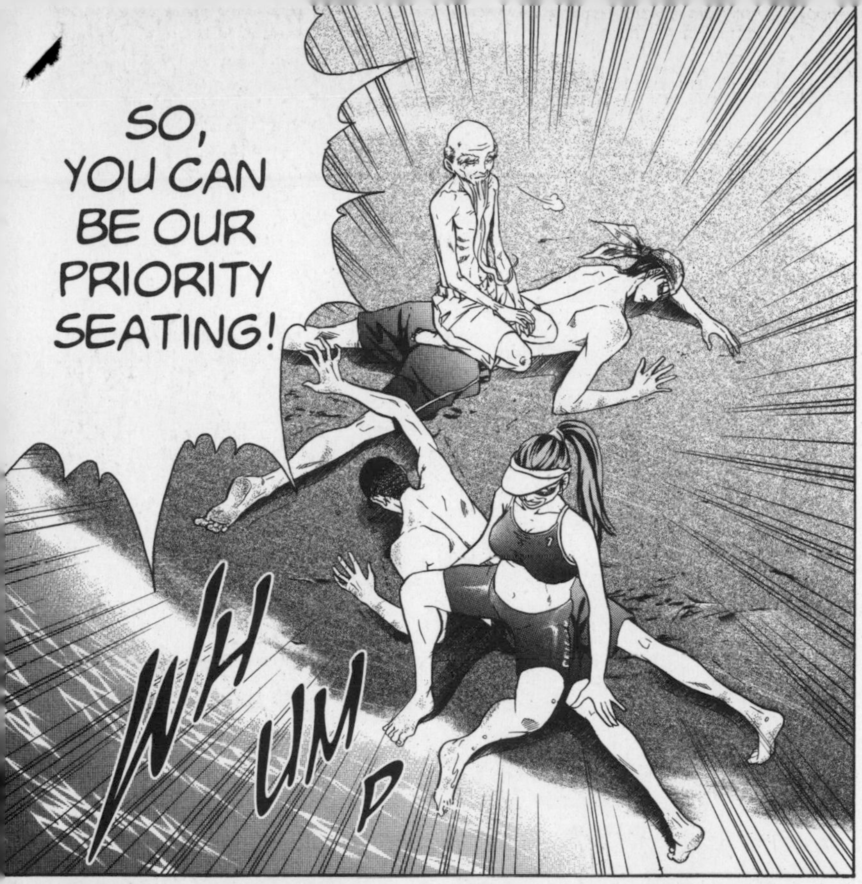
SO, YOU CAN BE OUR PRIORITY SEATING!
WHUMP
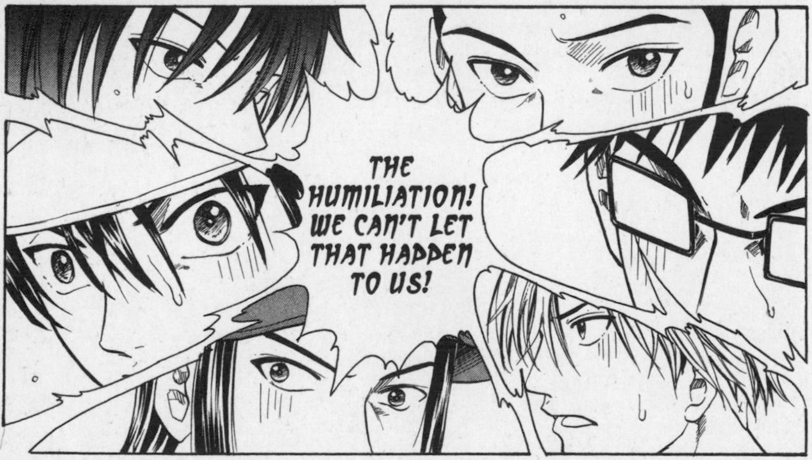
THE HUMILIATION! WE CAN'T LET THAT HAPPEN TO US!

The Prince of Beach Volleyball

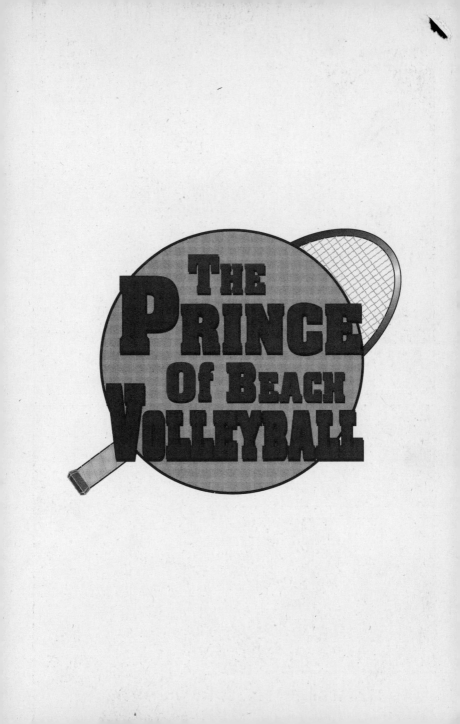

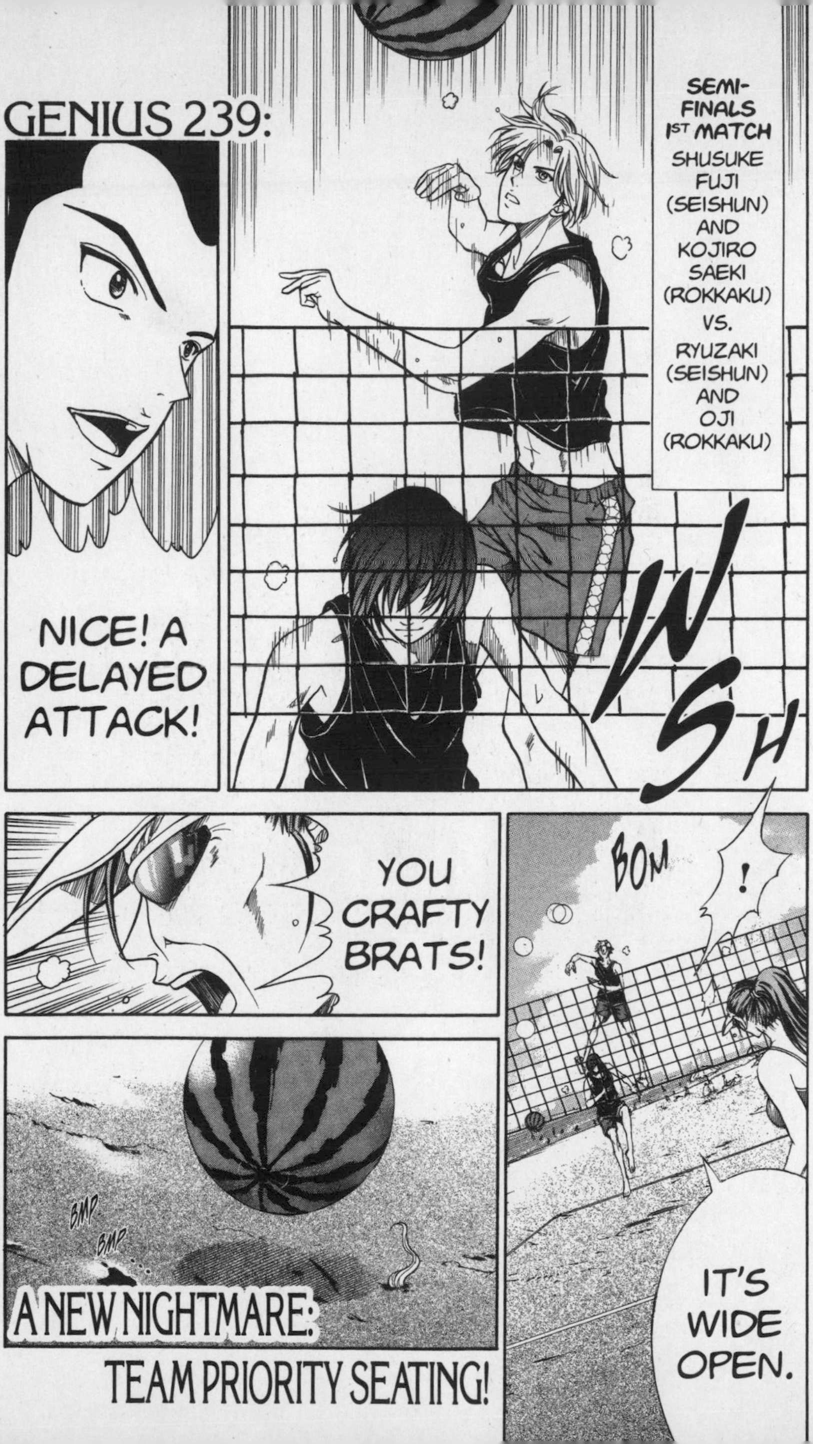
GENIUS 239:
SEMI-FINALS 1ST MATCH SHUSUKE FUJI (SEISHUN) AND KOJIRO SAEKI (ROKKAKU) VS. RYUZAKI (SEISHUN) AND OJI (ROKKAKU)
WSH
NICE! A DELAYED ATTACK!
BOM
!
IT'S WIDE OPEN.
YOU CRAFTY BRATS!
BMP BMP
A NEW NIGHTMARE: TEAM PRIORITY SEATING!

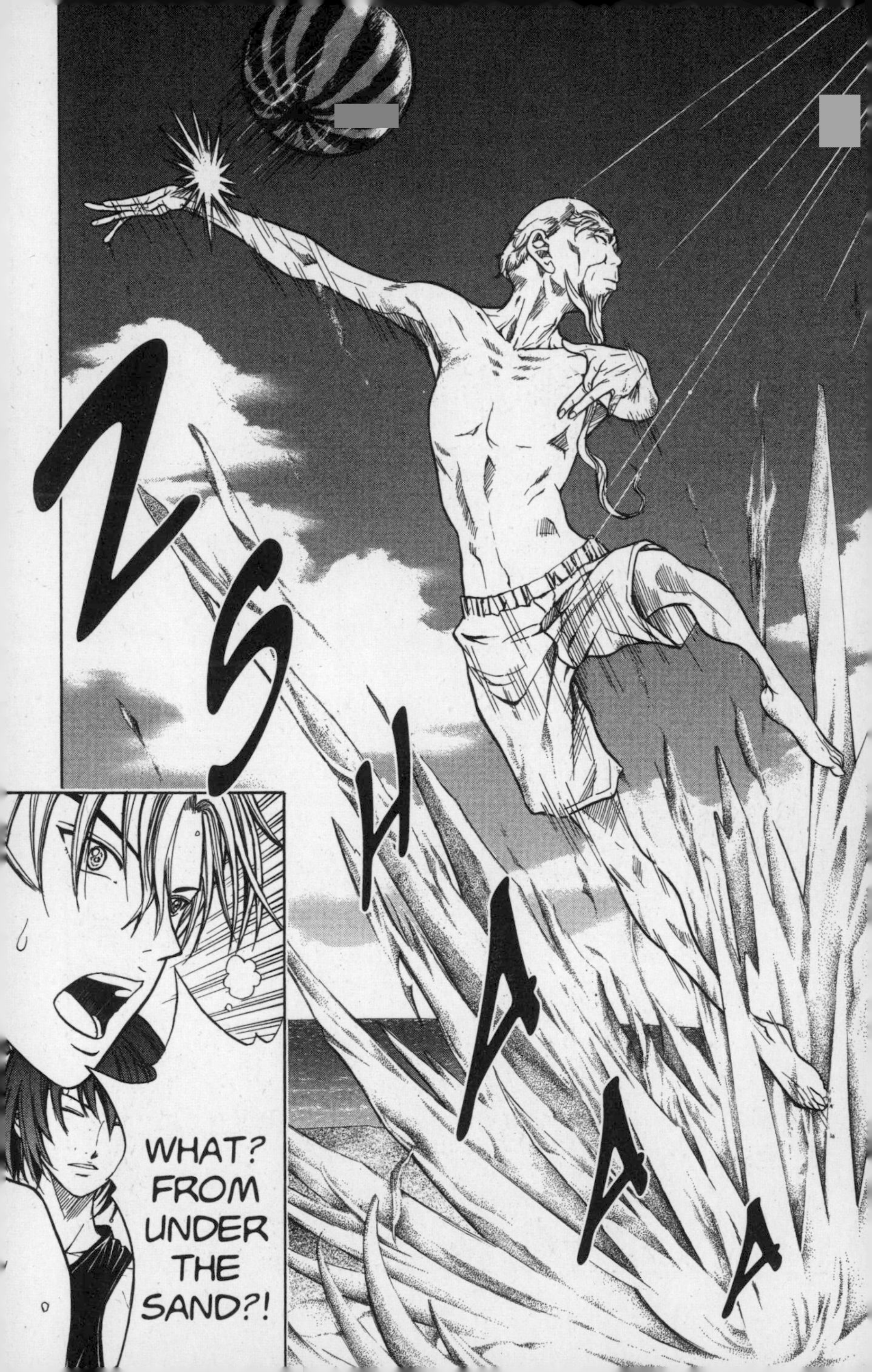
ZSHAAAA
WHAT? FROM UNDER THE SAND?!

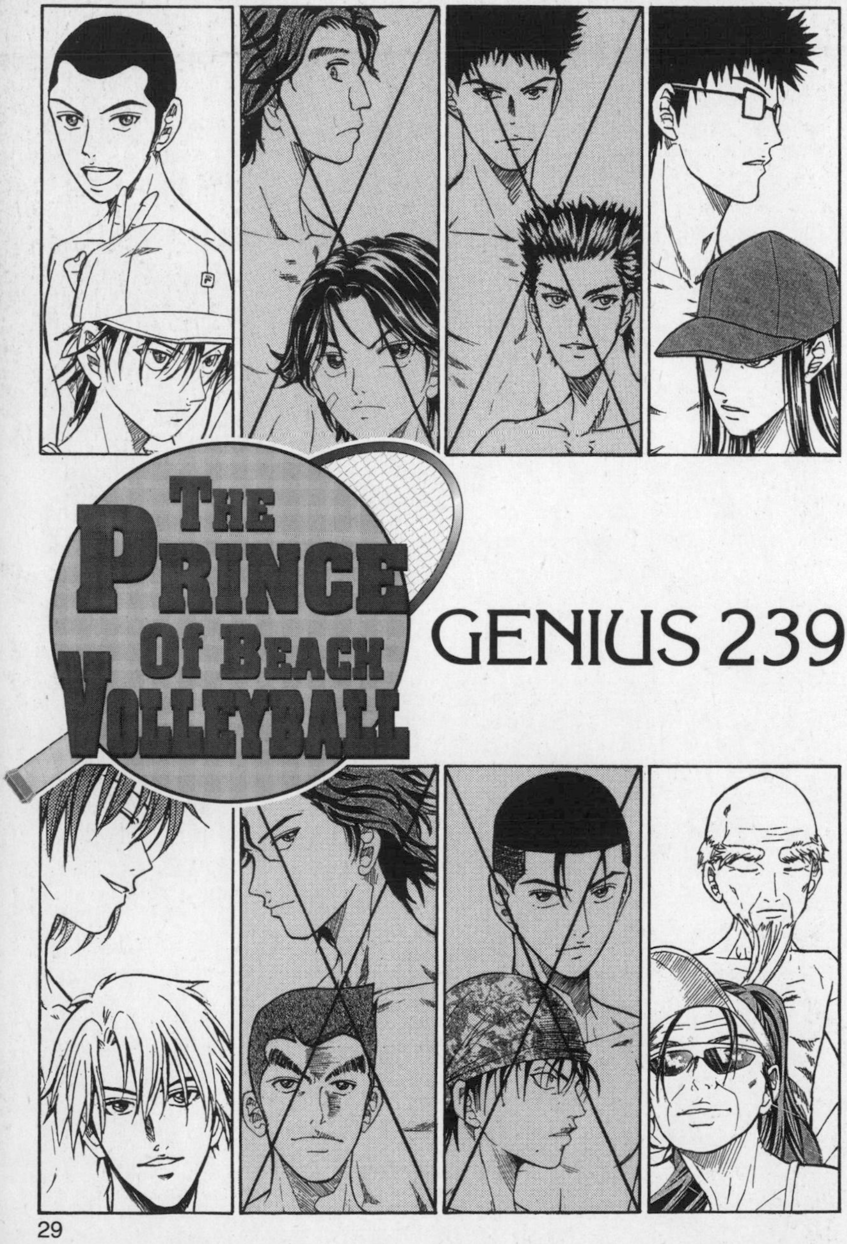
THE PRINCE Of BEACH VOLLEYBALL

GENIUS 239

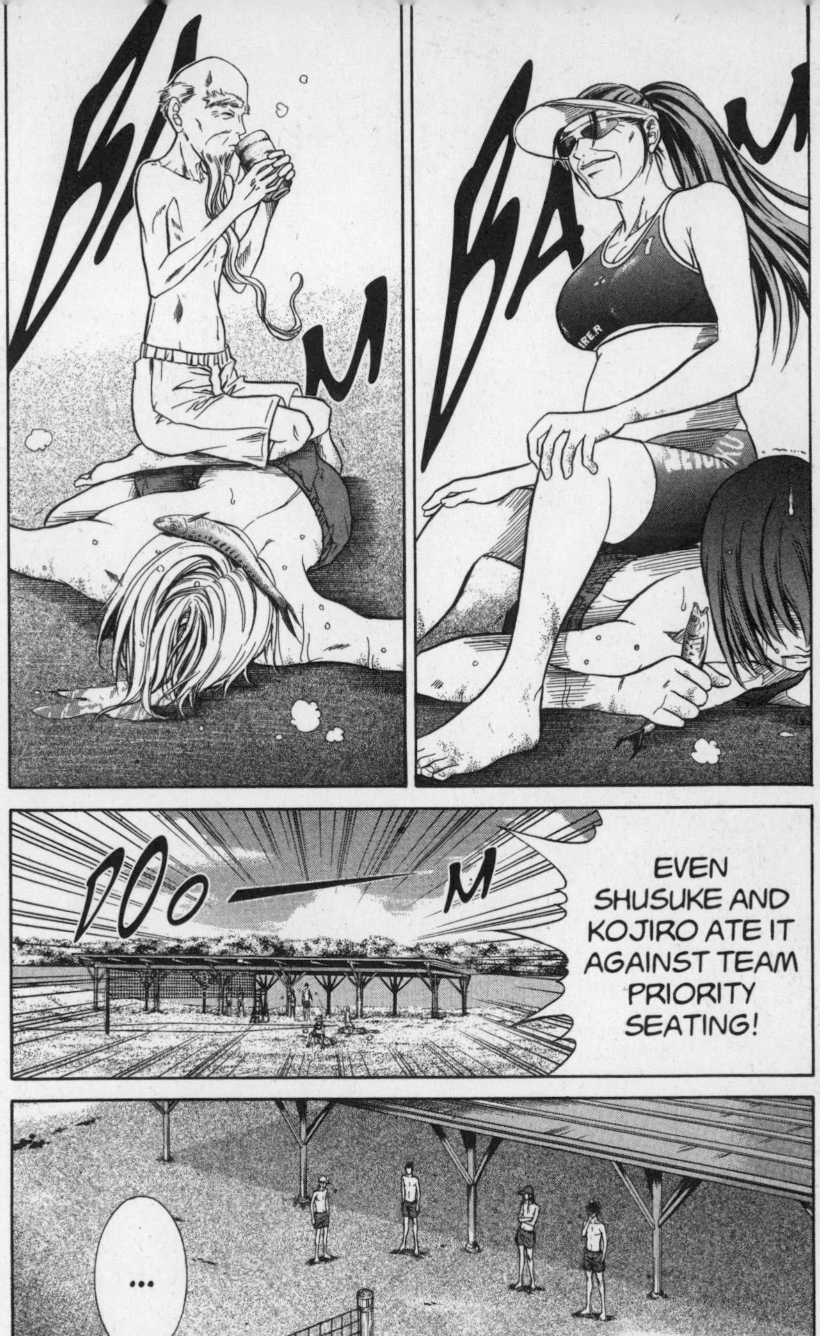
DOo—M
EVEN SHUSUKE AND KOJIRO ATE IT AGAINST TEAM PRIORITY SEATING!
...

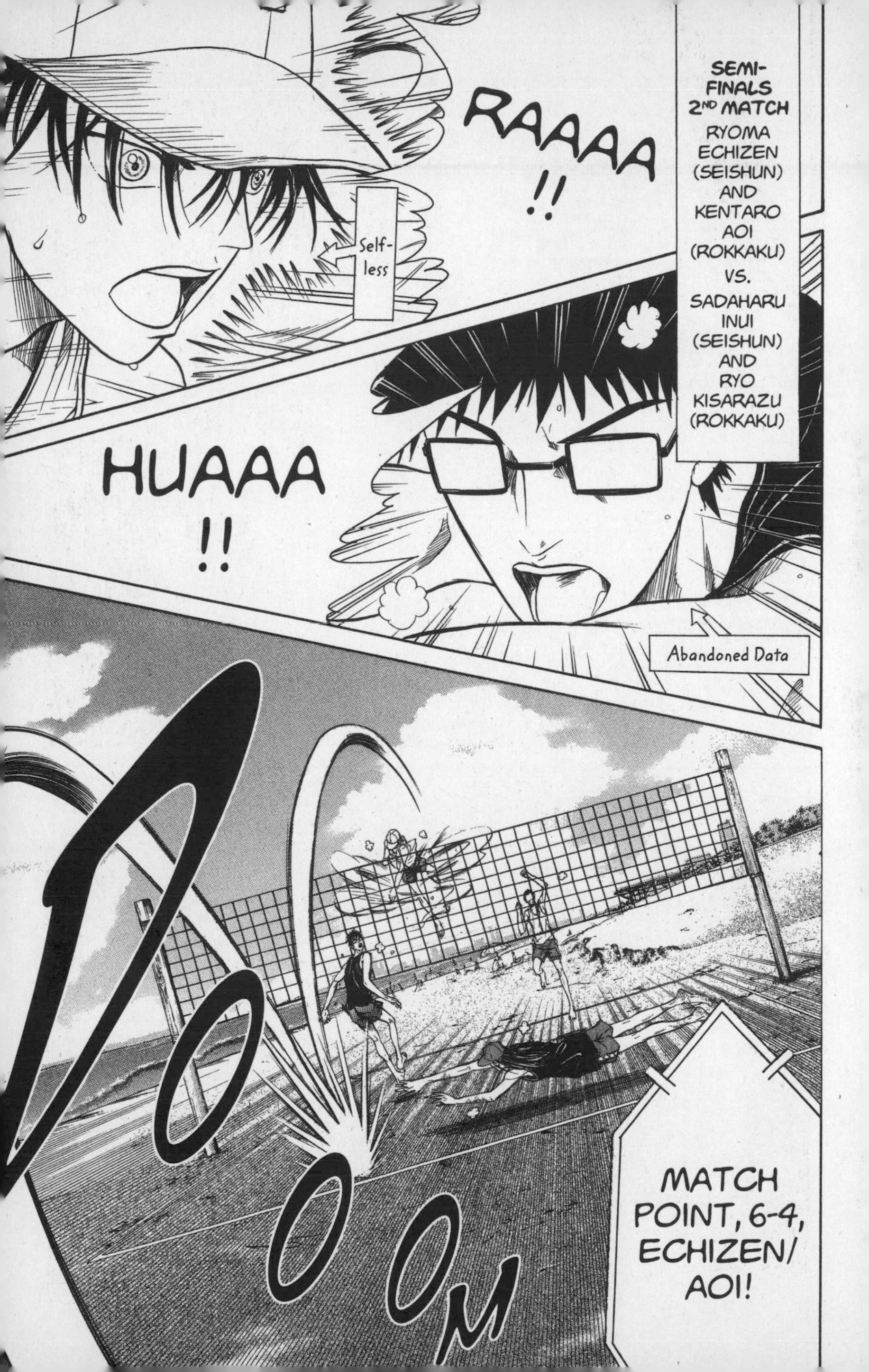
SEMI-FINALS 2ND MATCH RYOMA ECHIZEN (SEISHUN) AND KENTARO AOI (ROKKAKU) VS. SADAHARU INUI (SEISHUN) AND RYO KISARAZU (ROKKAKU)
RAAAA!!
Self-less
HUAAA!!
Abandoned Data
MATCH POINT, 6-4, ECHIZEN/AOI!
DOOOOM

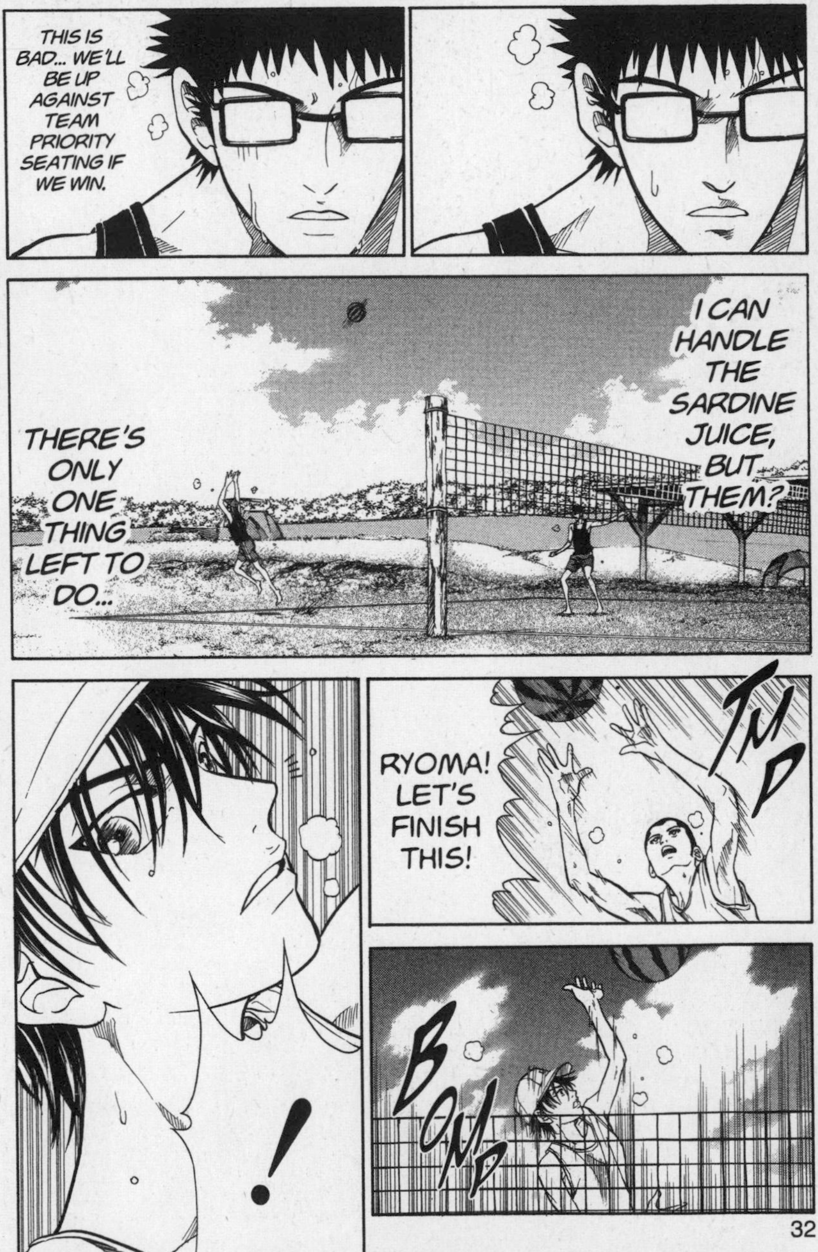
THIS IS BAD... WE'LL BE UP AGAINST TEAM PRIORITY SEATING IF WE WIN.
I CAN HANDLE THE SARDINE JUICE, BUT THEM?
THERE'S ONLY ONE THING LEFT TO DO...
TMD
RYOMA! LET'S FINISH THIS!
BOMD
!

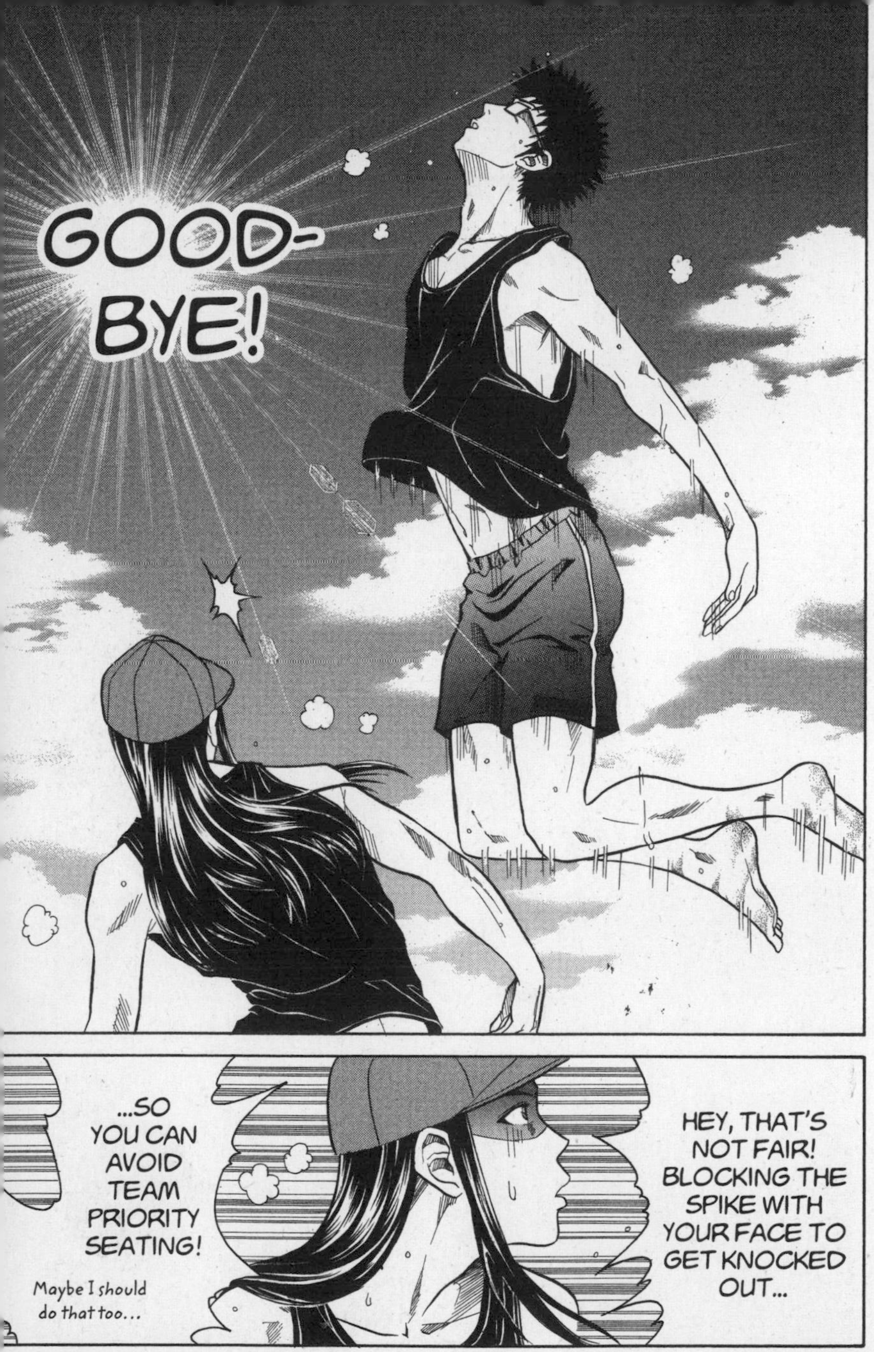
GOOD-BYE!
HEY, THAT'S NOT FAIR! BLOCKING THE SPIKE WITH YOUR FACE TO GET KNOCKED OUT...
...SO YOU CAN AVOID TEAM PRIORITY SEATING!
Maybe I should do that too...

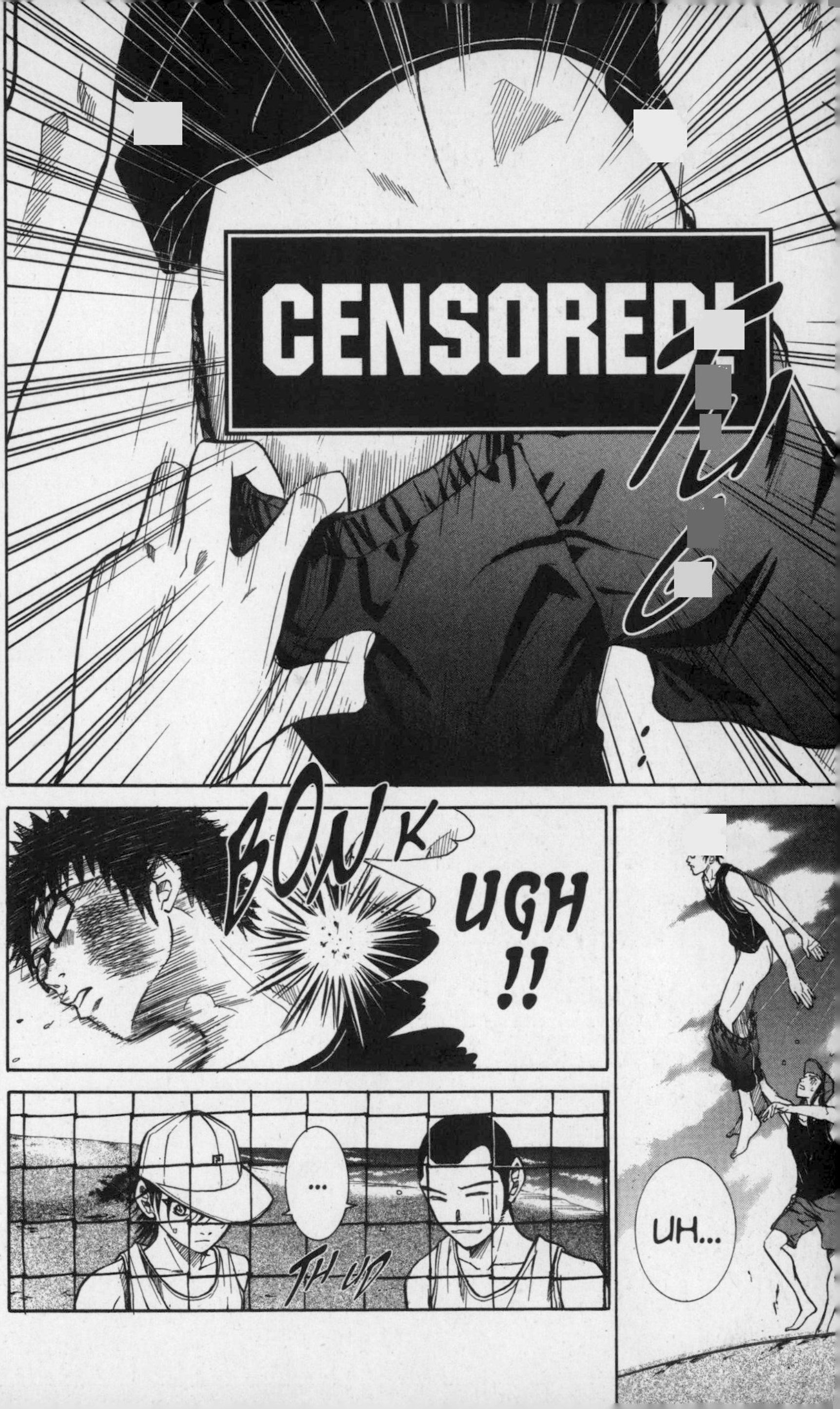
CENSORED!
UH...
BONK
UGH !!
...
THUD

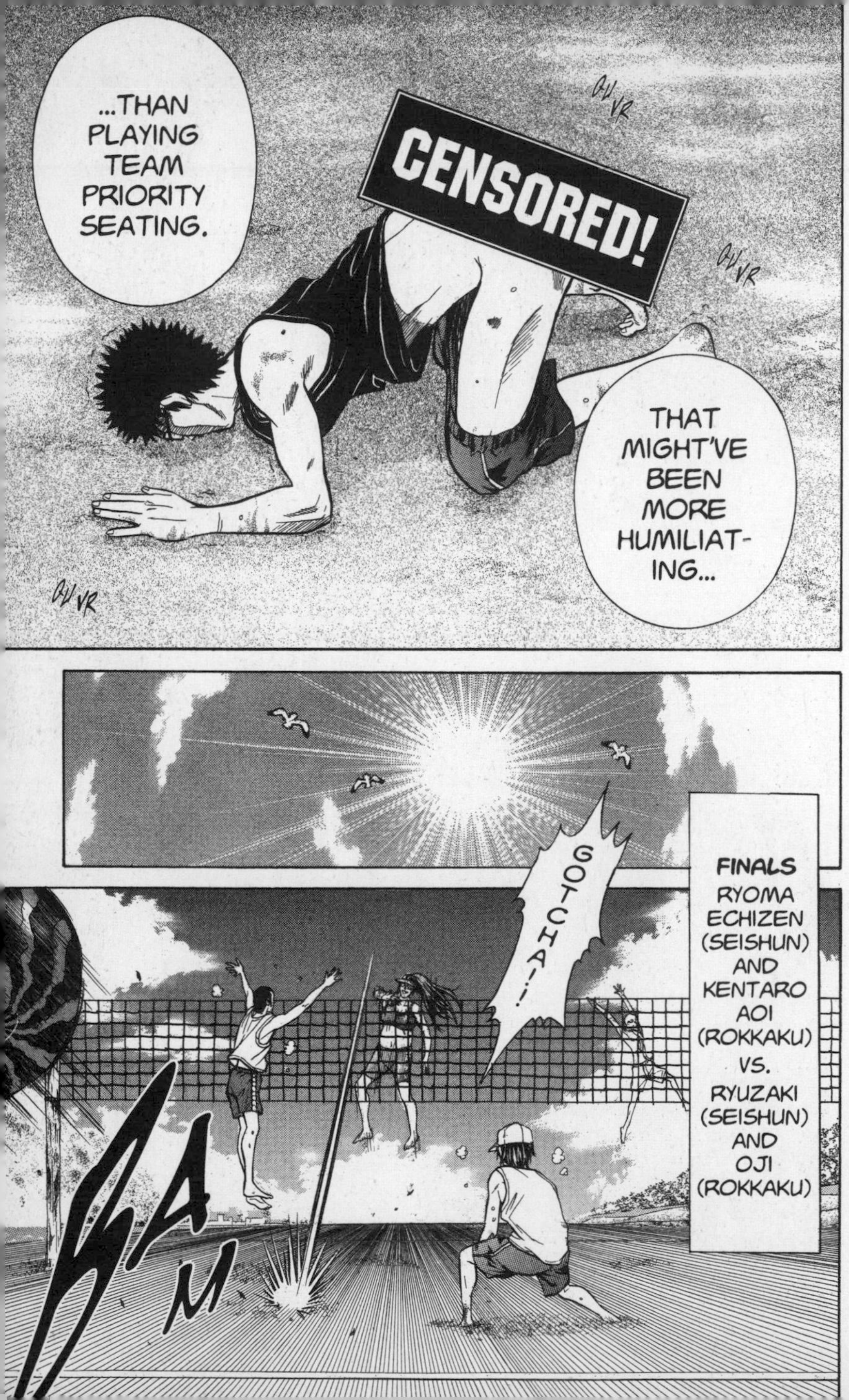
CENSORED!
THAT MIGHT'VE BEEN MORE HUMILIAT-ING...
...THAN PLAYING TEAM PRIORITY SEATING.
FINALS RYOMA ECHIZEN (SEISHUN) AND KENTARO AOI (ROKKAKU) VS. RYUZAKI (SEISHUN) AND OJI (ROKKAKU)
GOTCHA!!
BAM

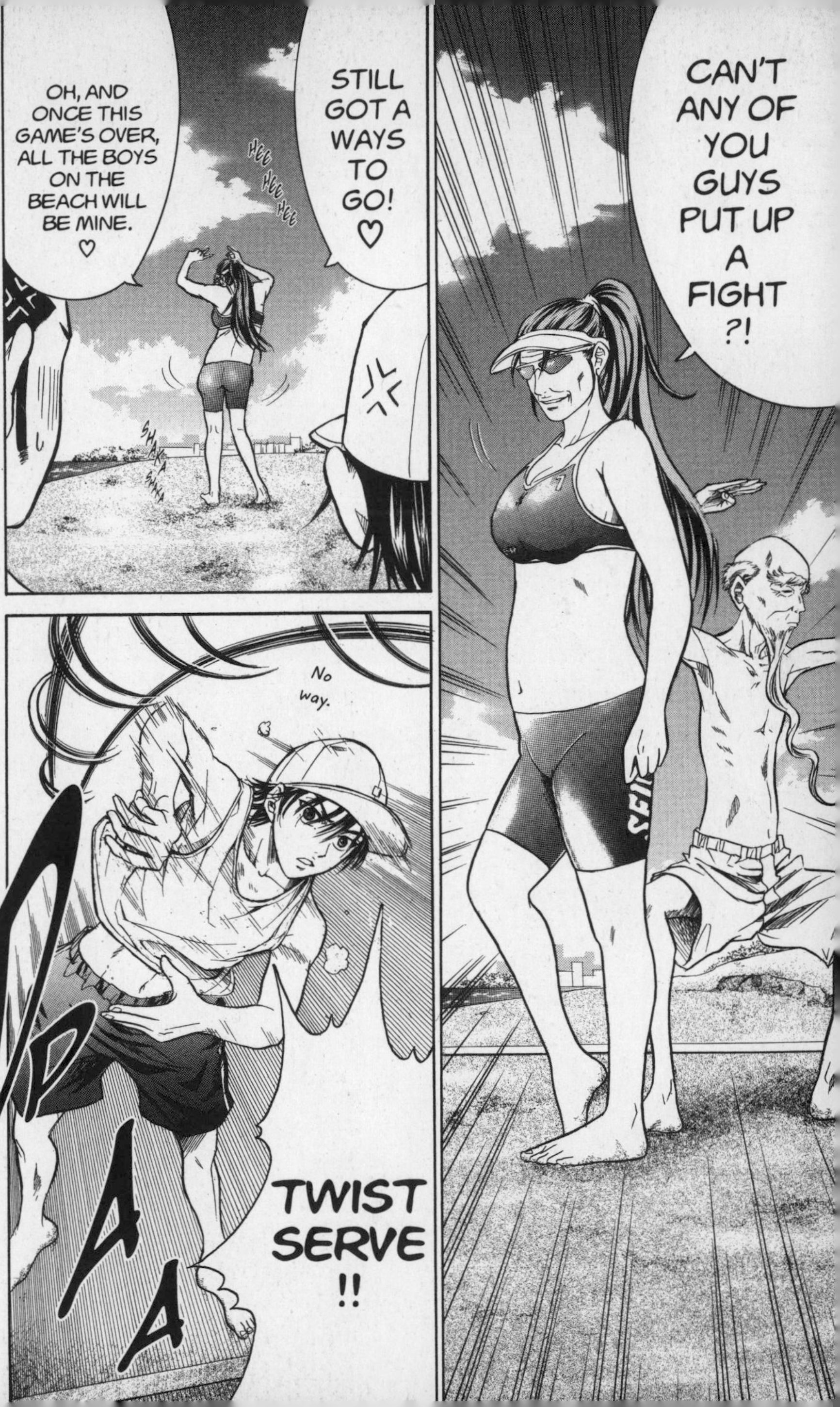
CAN'T ANY OF YOU GUYS PUT UP A FIGHT ?!
STILL GOT A WAYS TO GO! ♡
OH, AND ONCE THIS GAME'S OVER, ALL THE BOYS ON THE BEACH WILL BE MINE. ♡
HEE HEE HEE
SHAKA SHAKA
No way.
TWIST SERVE !!
DAAA

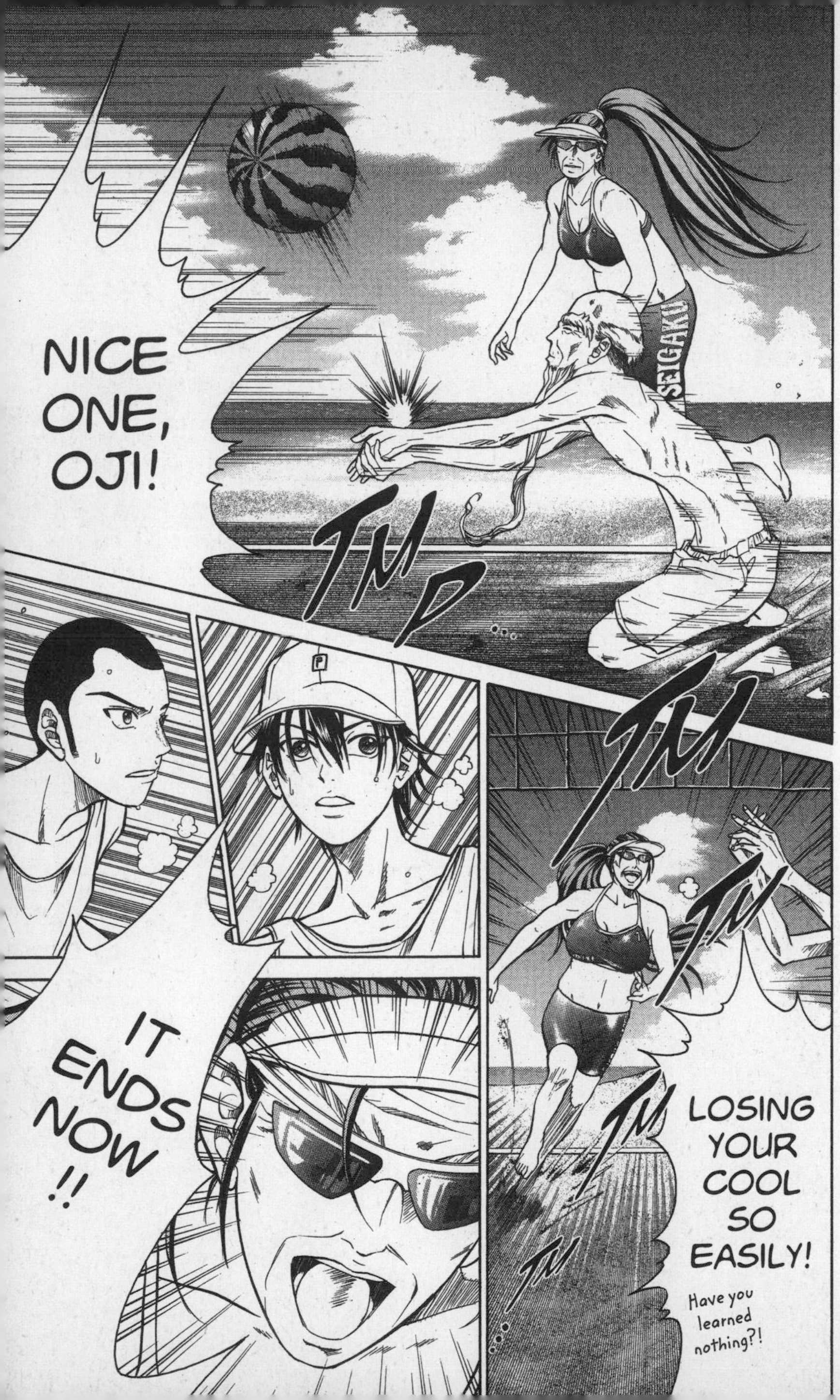
NICE ONE, OJI!
TMP
TM
TM
TM
LOSING YOUR COOL SO EASILY!
Have you learned nothing?!
TM
IT ENDS NOW!!

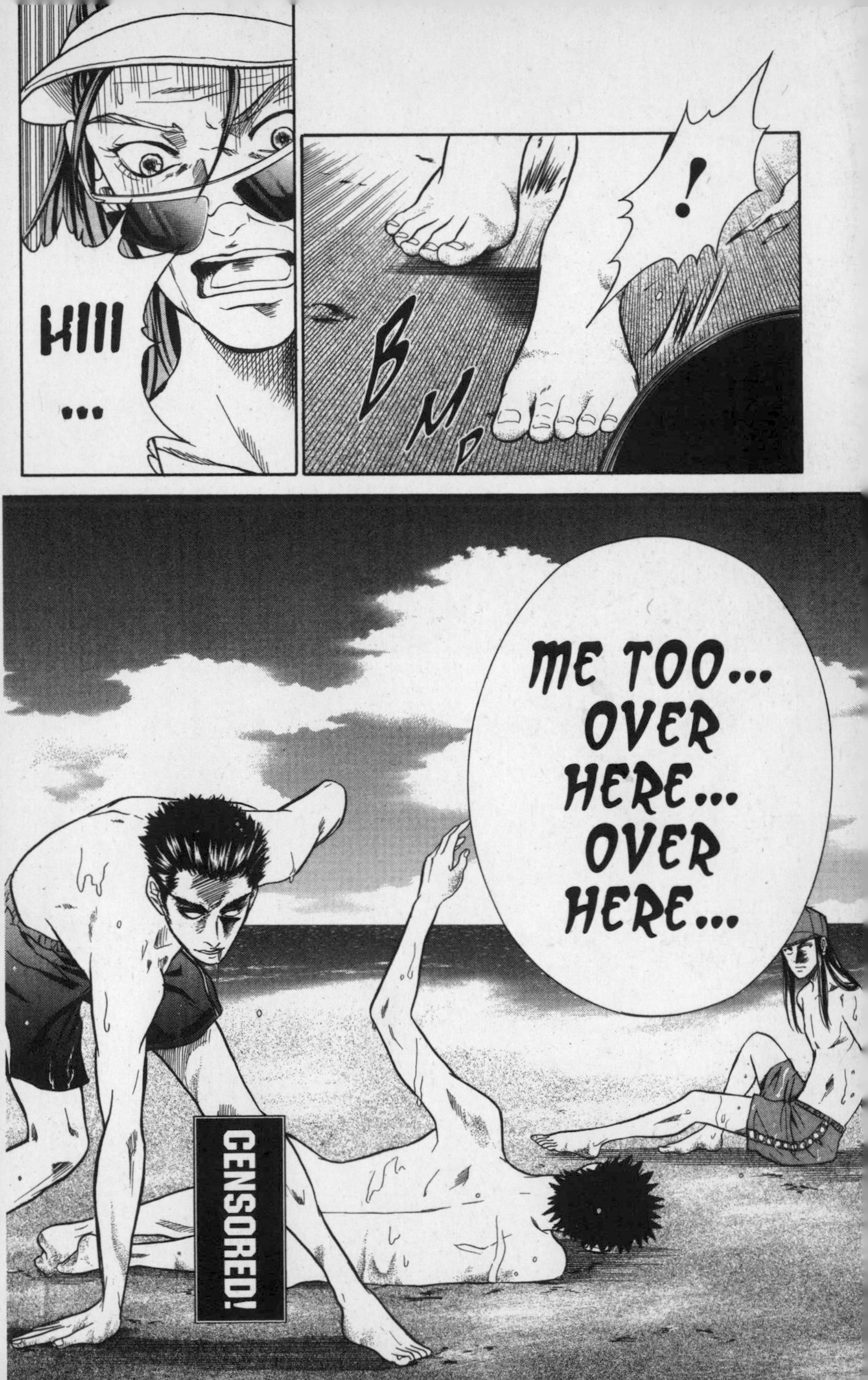
!
BMP
HIII
...
ME TOO... OVER HERE... OVER HERE...
CENSORED!

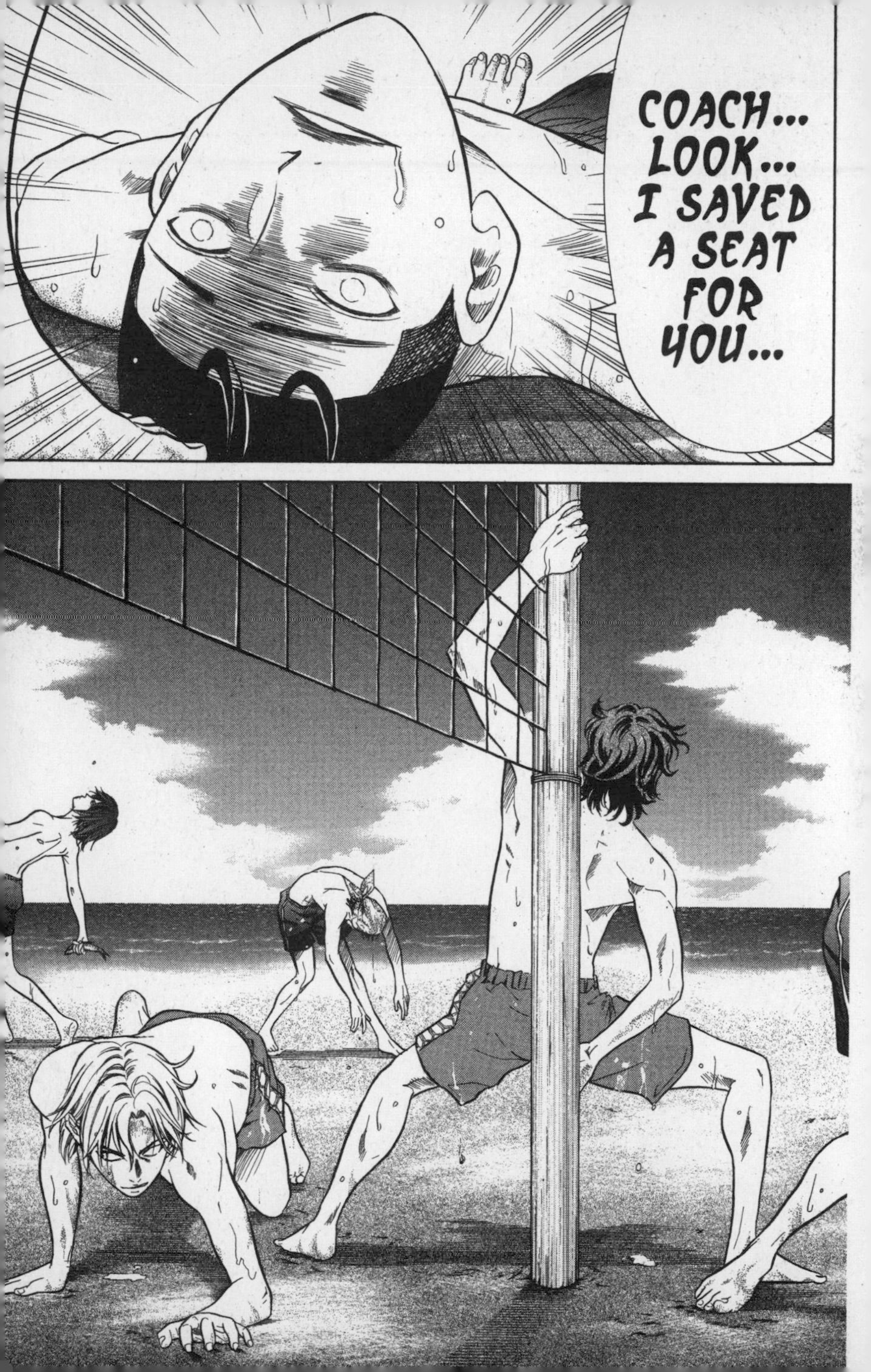
COACH... LOOK... I SAVED A SEAT FOR YOU...

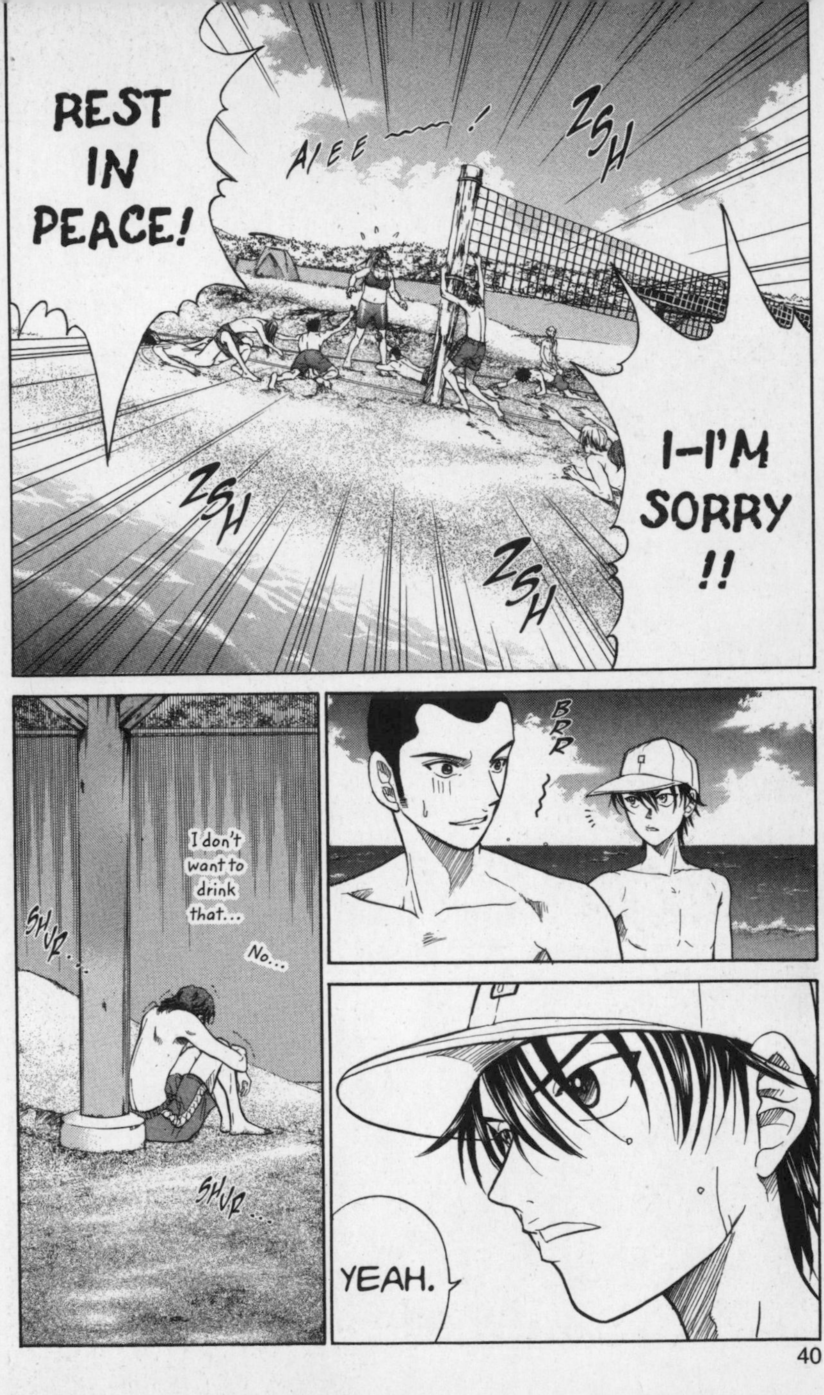
ZSH
AIEE~~!
REST IN PEACE!
I-I'M SORRY!!
ZSH
ZSH
BRR
YEAH.
I don't want to drink that...
No...
SHJR...
SHJR...

READ THIS WAY

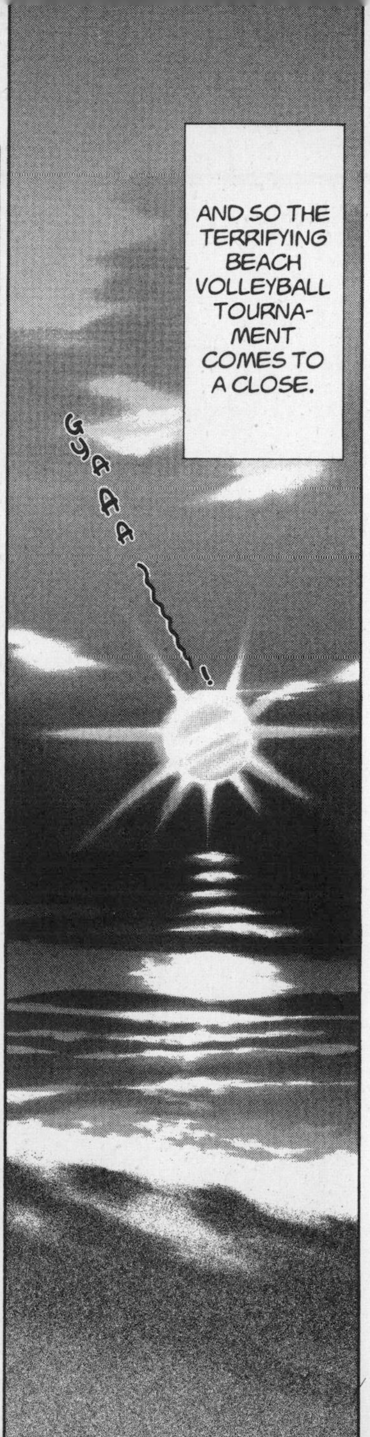
AND SO THE TERRIFYING BEACH VOLLEYBALL TOURNAMENT COMES TO A CLOSE.
GYAAAA~~~!

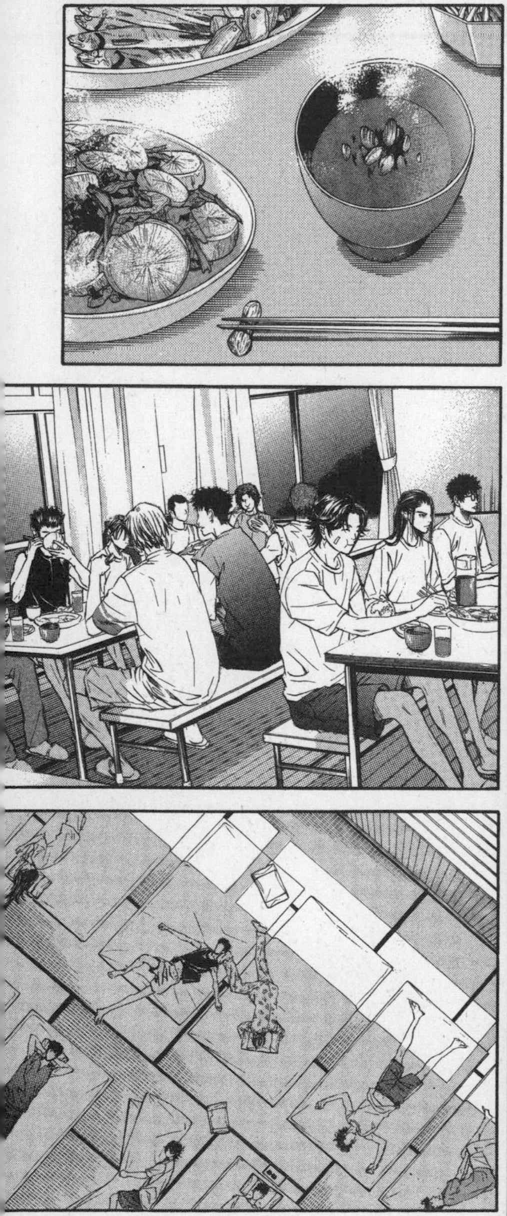

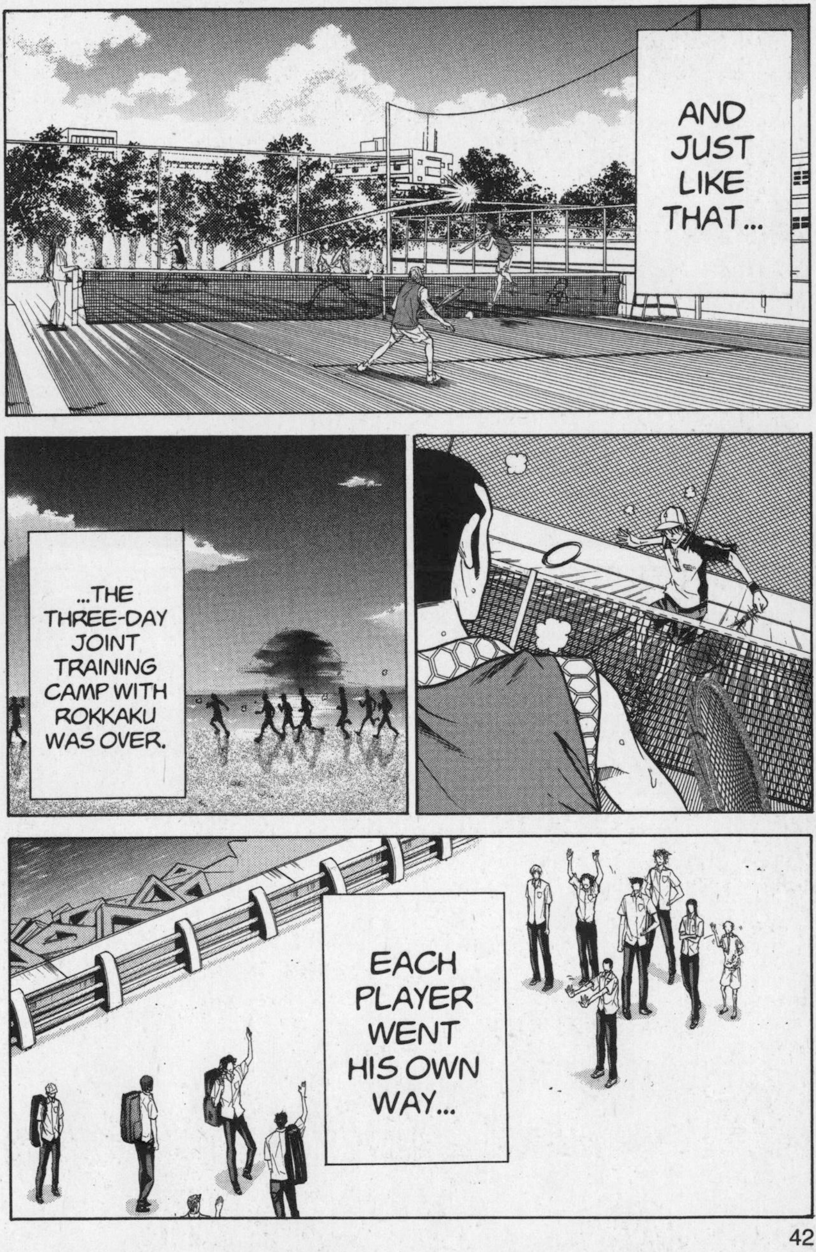
AND JUST LIKE THAT...
...THE THREE-DAY JOINT TRAINING CAMP WITH ROKKAKU WAS OVER.
EACH PLAYER WENT HIS OWN WAY...

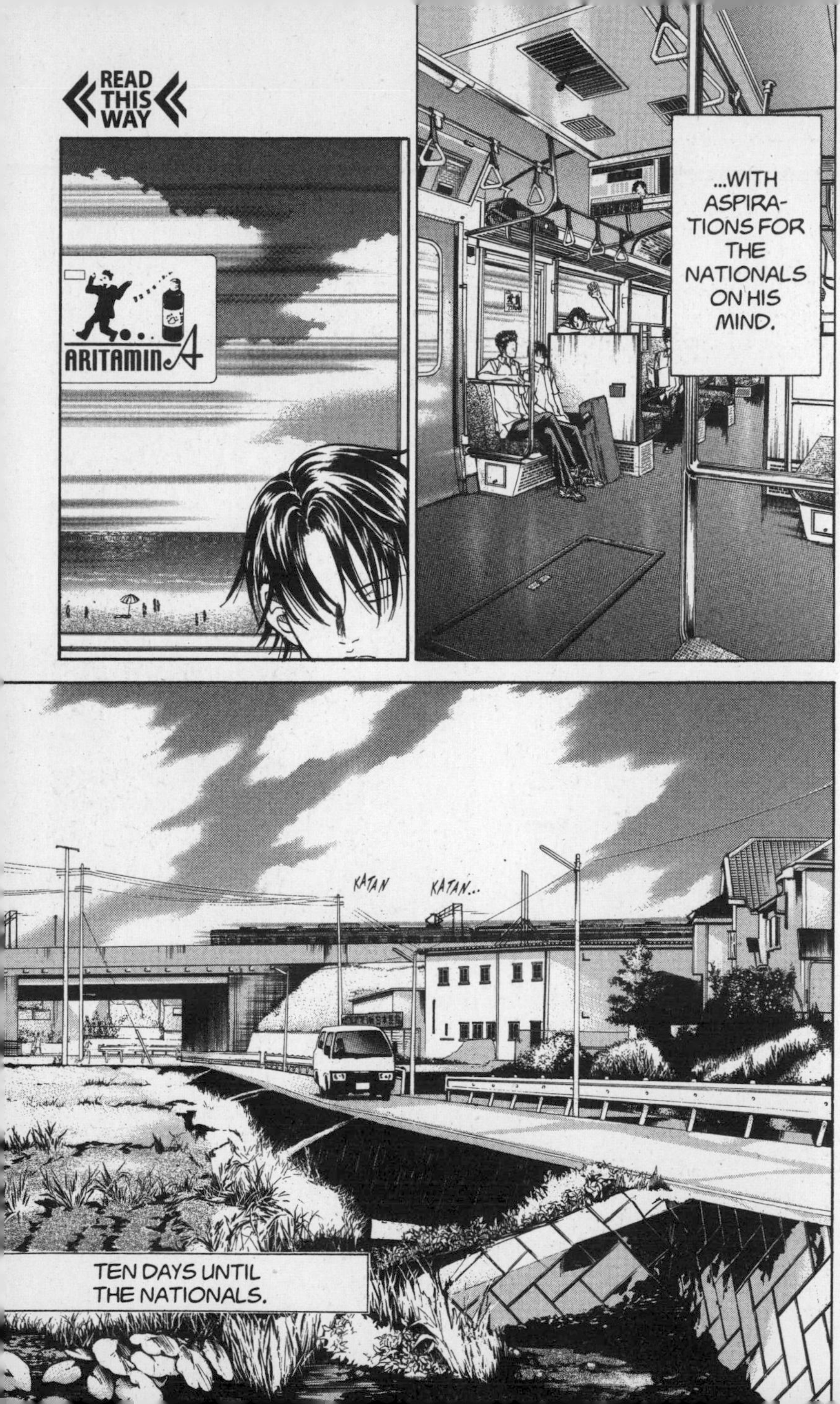
READ THIS WAY
...WITH ASPIRATIONS FOR THE NATIONALS ON HIS MIND.
ARITAMIN A
KATAN
KATAN...
TEN DAYS UNTIL THE NATIONALS.

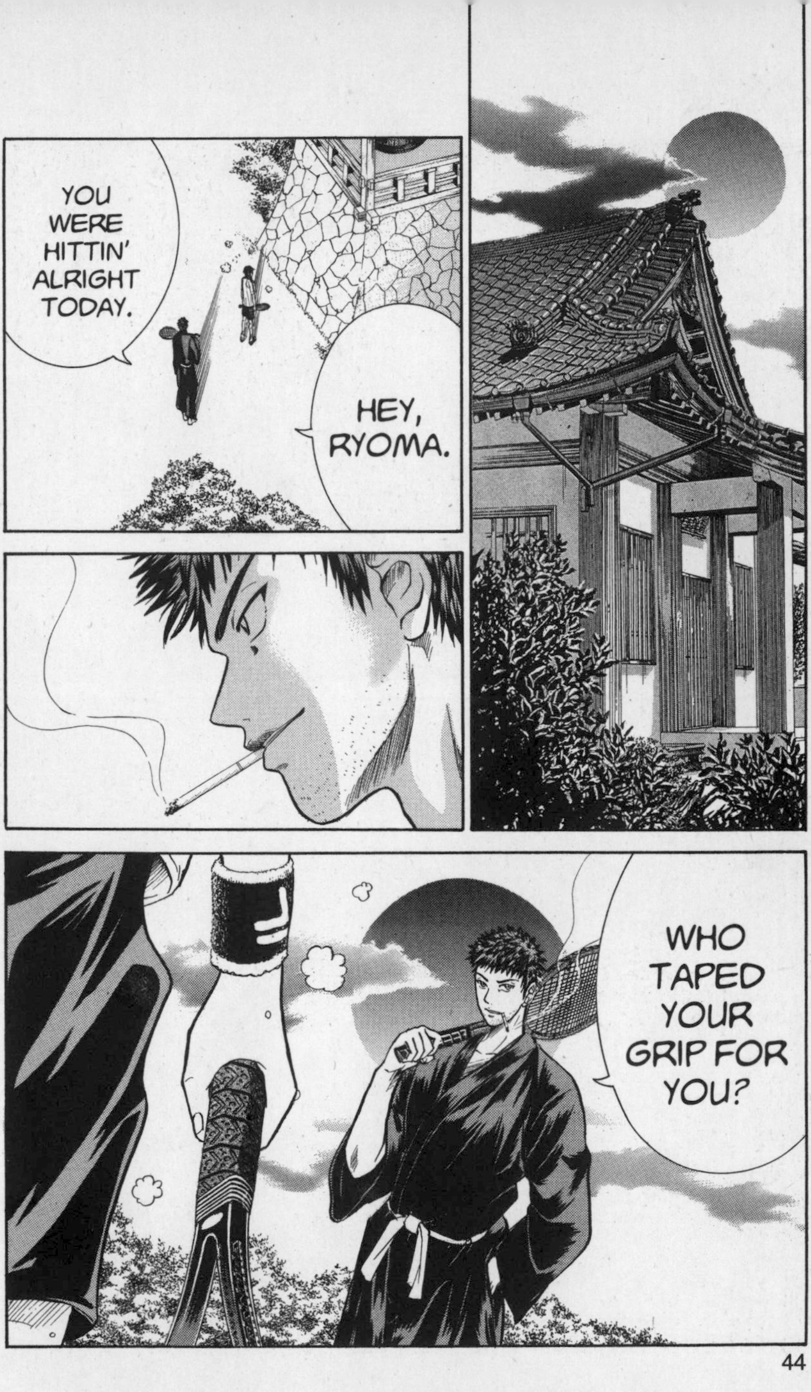
HEY, RYOMA.
YOU WERE HITTIN' ALRIGHT TODAY.
WHO TAPED YOUR GRIP FOR YOU?

READ THIS WAY

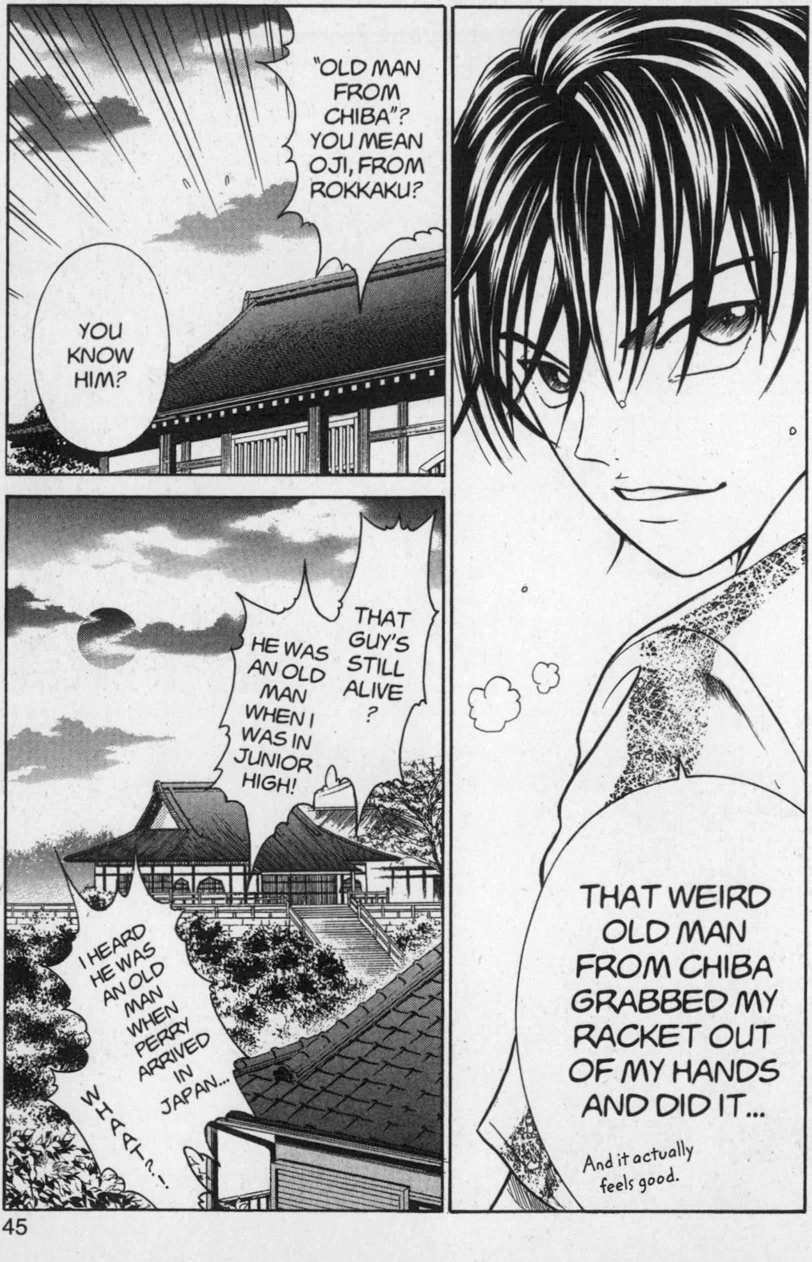
THAT WEIRD OLD MAN FROM CHIBA GRABBED MY RACKET OUT OF MY HANDS AND DID IT...
And it actually feels good.
"OLD MAN FROM CHIBA"? YOU MEAN OJI, FROM ROKKAKU?
YOU KNOW HIM?
THAT GUY'S STILL ALIVE?
HE WAS AN OLD MAN WHEN I WAS IN JUNIOR HIGH!
I HEARD HE WAS AN OLD MAN WHEN PERRY ARRIVED IN JAPAN...
WHAAT?!

The Prince of Beach Volleyball

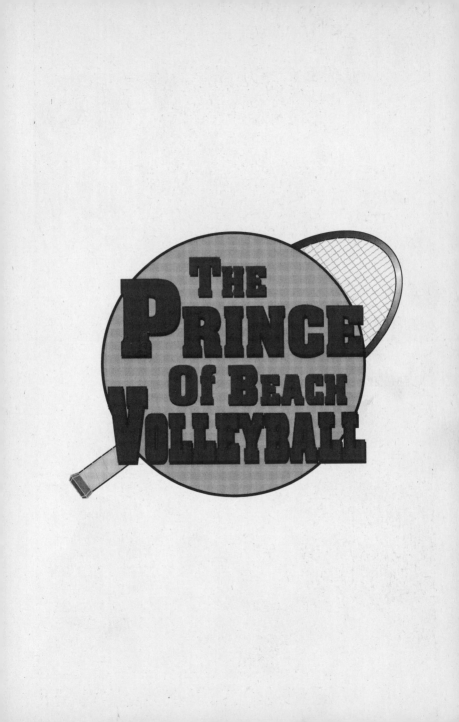

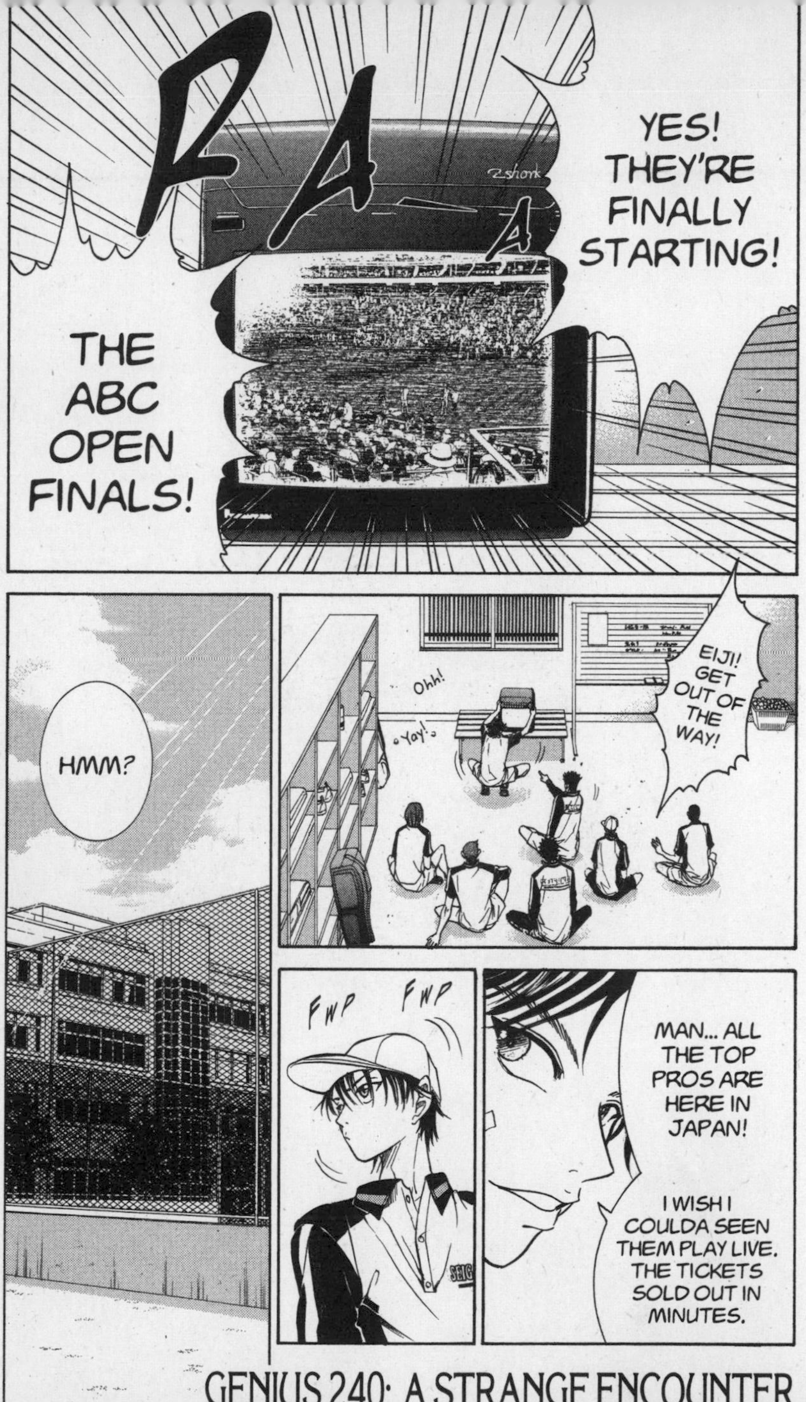
RAA
YES! THEY'RE FINALLY STARTING!
2shork
THE ABC OPEN FINALS!
EIJI! GET OUT OF THE WAY!
Ohh!
Yay!
MAN... ALL THE TOP PROS ARE HERE IN JAPAN!
I WISH I COULDA SEEN THEM PLAY LIVE. THE TICKETS SOLD OUT IN MINUTES.
FWP FWP
HMM?

GENIUS 240: A STRANGE ENCOUNTER

GENIUS 240: A STRANGE ENCOUNTER

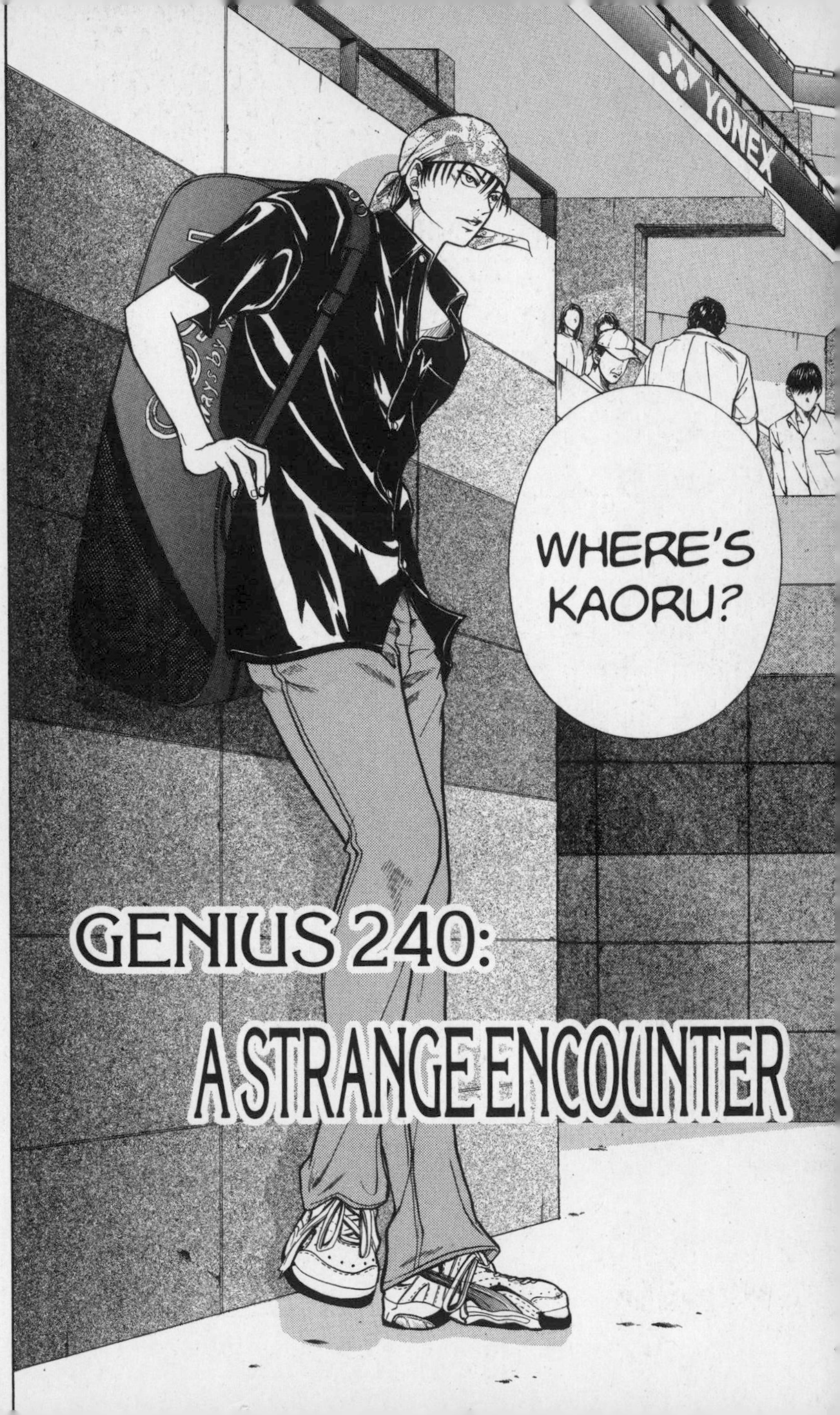
YONEX
WHERE'S KAORU?

READ THIS WAY

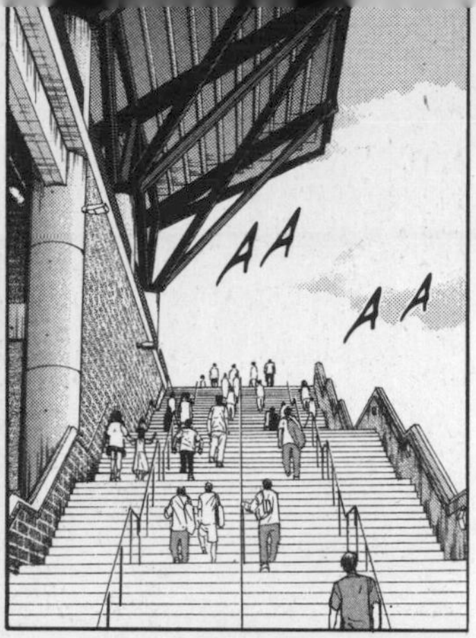
AA
AA

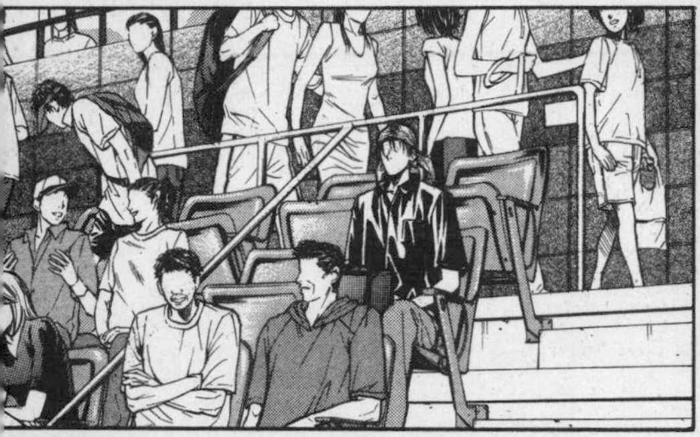

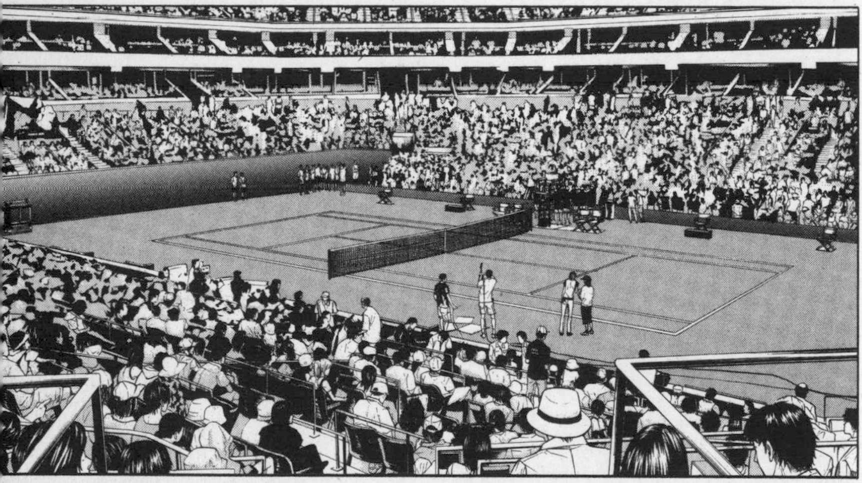

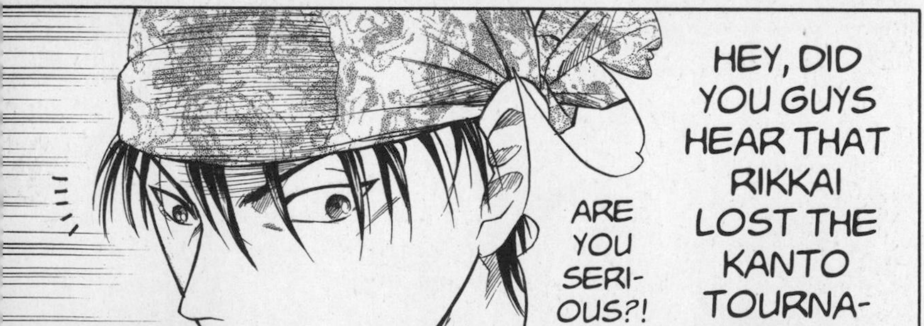
HEY, DID YOU GUYS HEAR THAT RIKKAI LOST THE KANTO TOURNAMENT?
ARE YOU SERIOUS?! AHA HA HA!

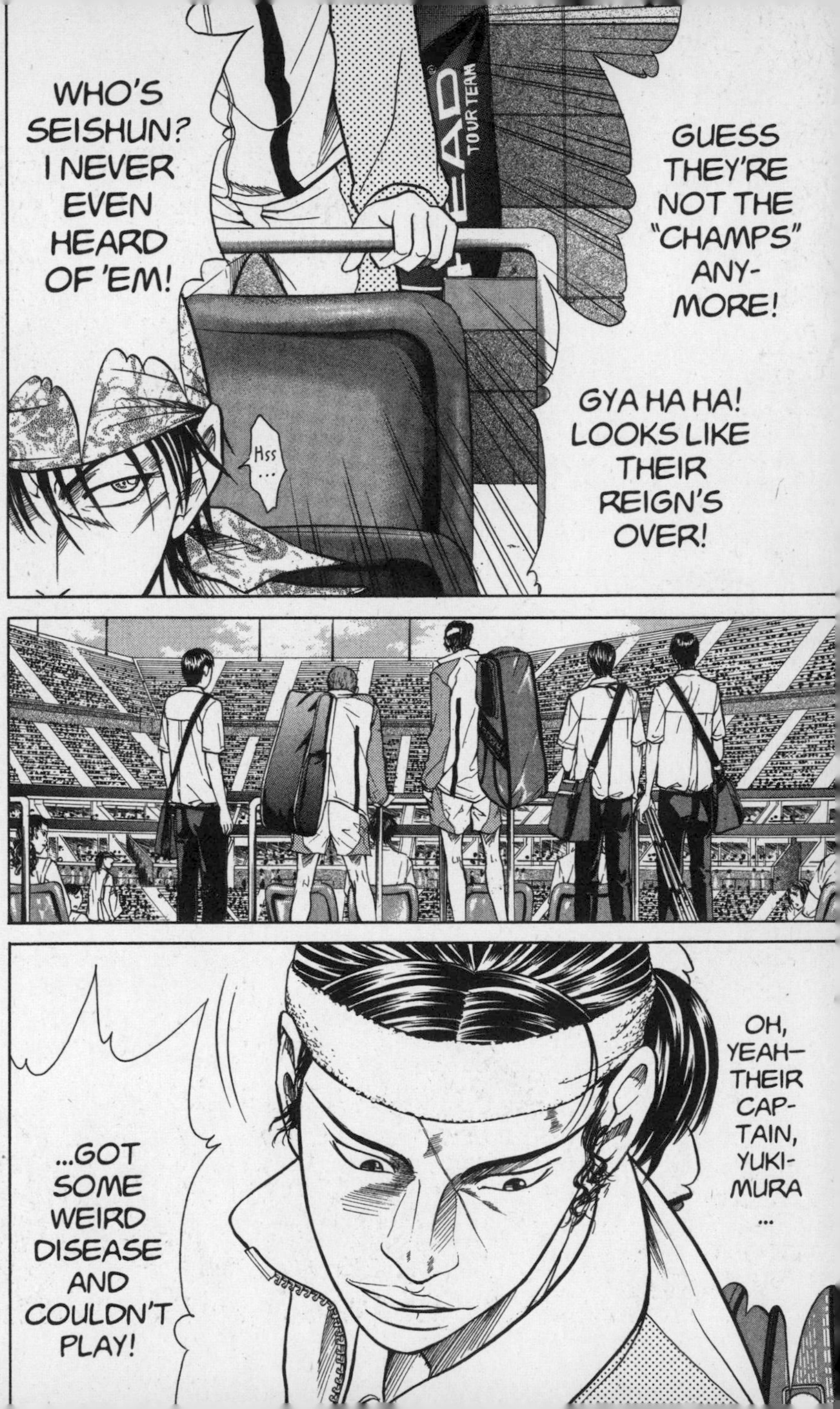
GUESS THEY'RE NOT THE "CHAMPS" ANY-MORE!
WHO'S SEISHUN? I NEVER EVEN HEARD OF 'EM!
GYA HA HA! LOOKS LIKE THEIR REIGN'S OVER!
Hss ...
OH, YEAH— THEIR CAP-TAIN, YUKI-MURA ...
...GOT SOME WEIRD DISEASE AND COULDN'T PLAY!

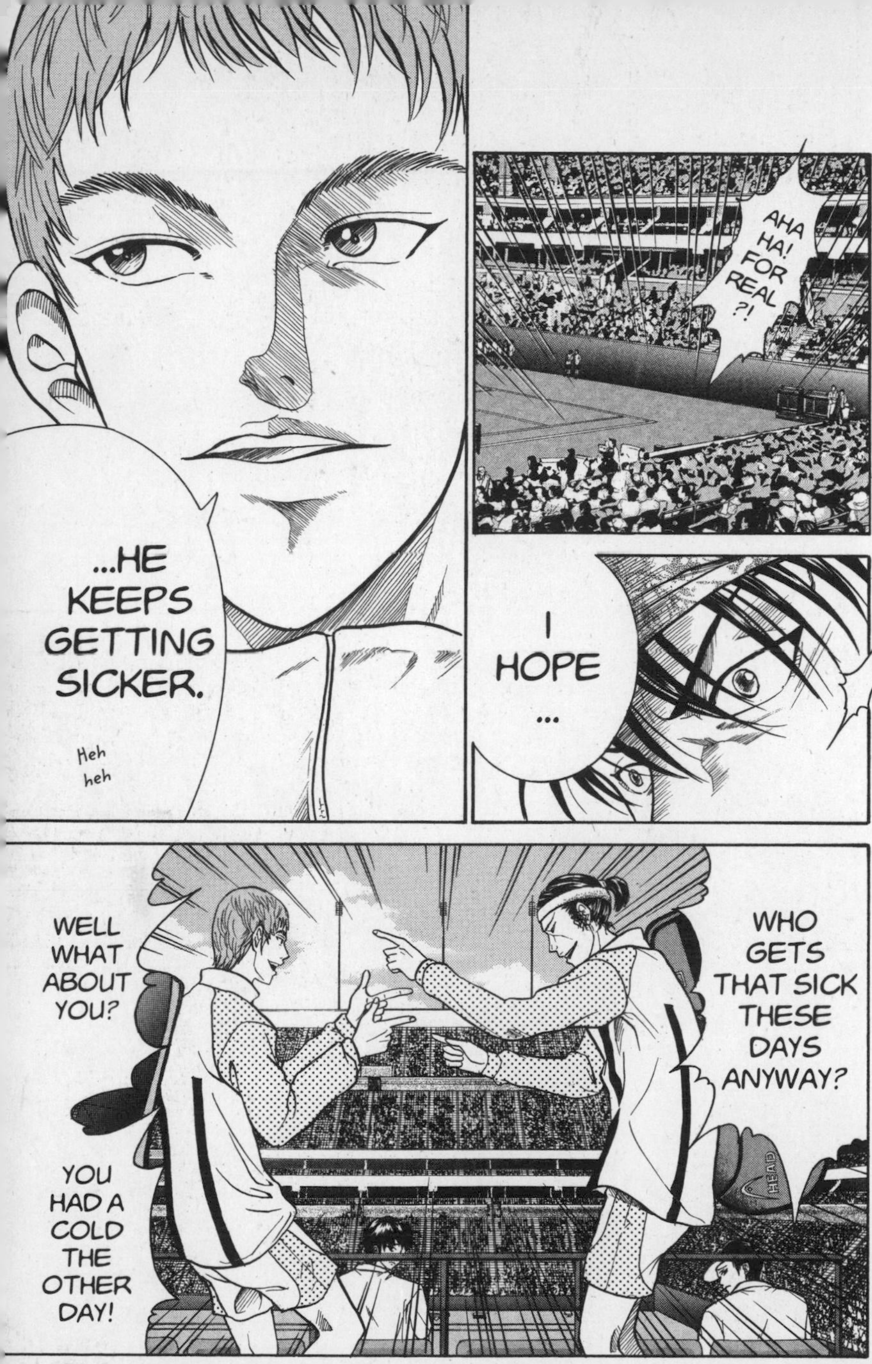
AHA HA! FOR REAL?!
I HOPE ...
...HE KEEPS GETTING SICKER.
Heh heh
WHO GETS THAT SICK THESE DAYS ANYWAY?
HEAD
WELL WHAT ABOUT YOU?
YOU HAD A COLD THE OTHER DAY!

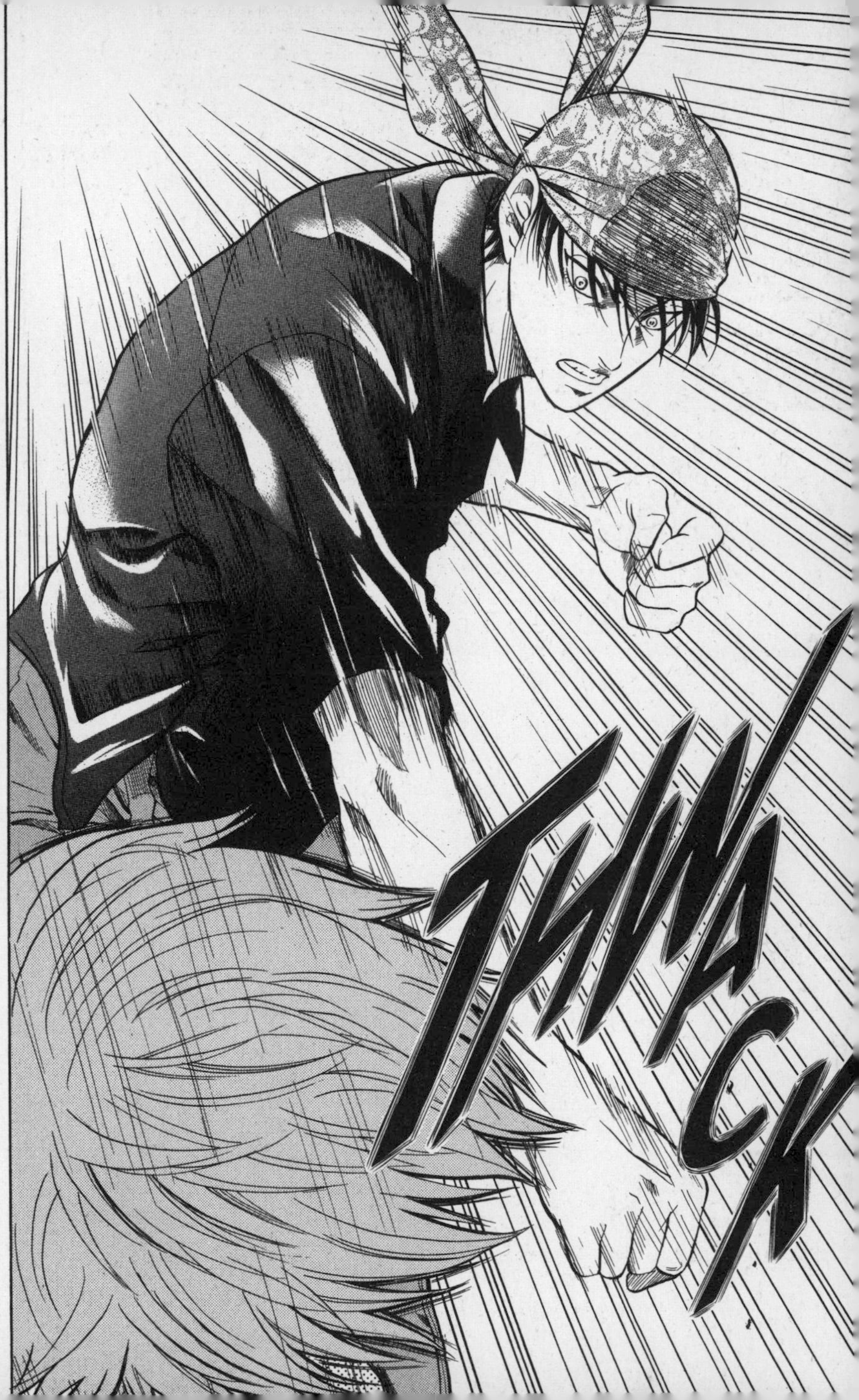
THWACK

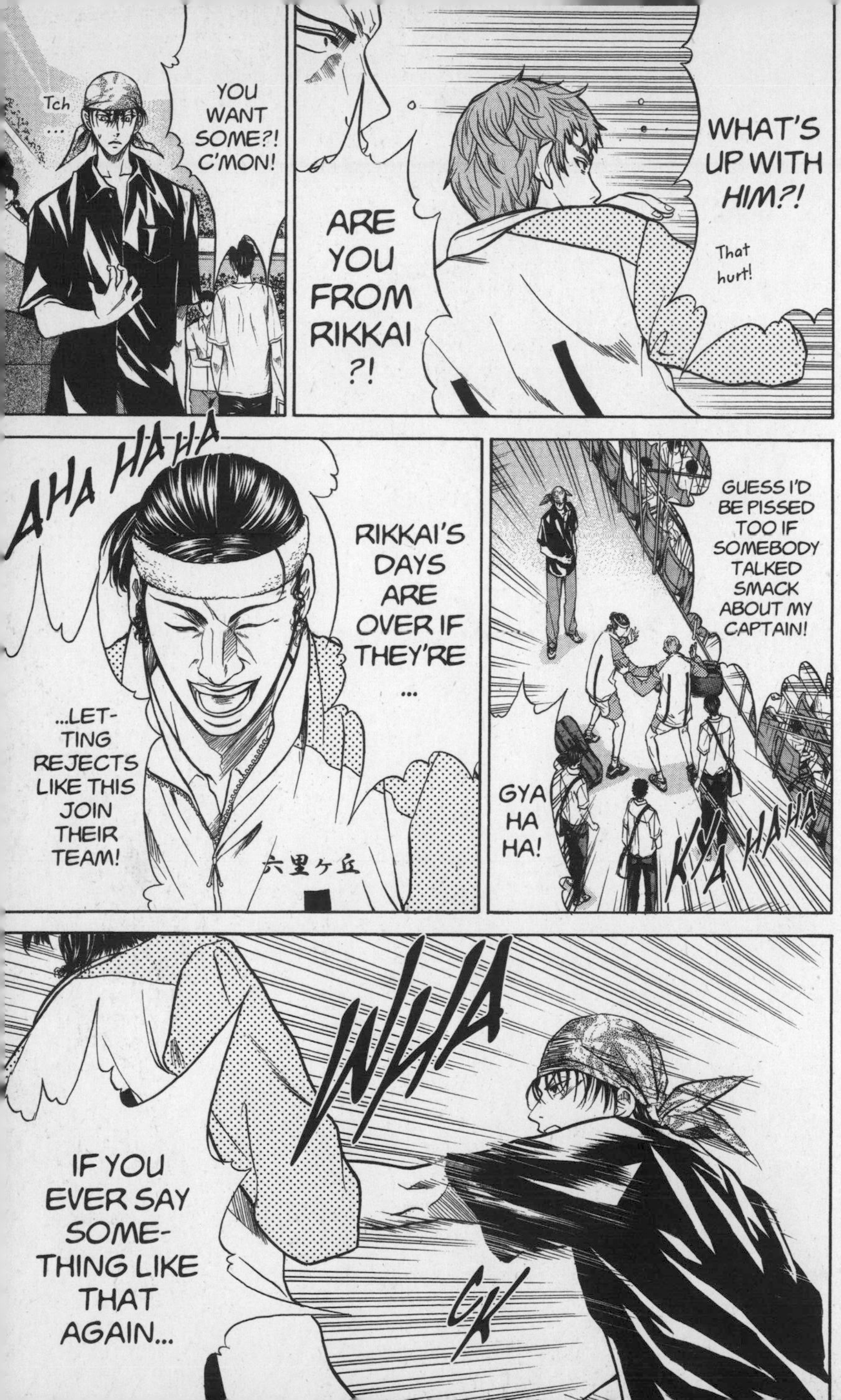
WHAT'S UP WITH HIM?!
That hurt!
ARE YOU FROM RIKKAI ?!
YOU WANT SOME?! C'MON!
Tch ...
GUESS I'D BE PISSED TOO IF SOMEBODY TALKED SMACK ABOUT MY CAPTAIN!
GYA HA HA!
KYA HAHA
AHA HAHA
RIKKAI'S DAYS ARE OVER IF THEY'RE ...
...LET-TING REJECTS LIKE THIS JOIN THEIR TEAM!
六里ケ丘
WHA
IF YOU EVER SAY SOME-THING LIKE THAT AGAIN...
GK

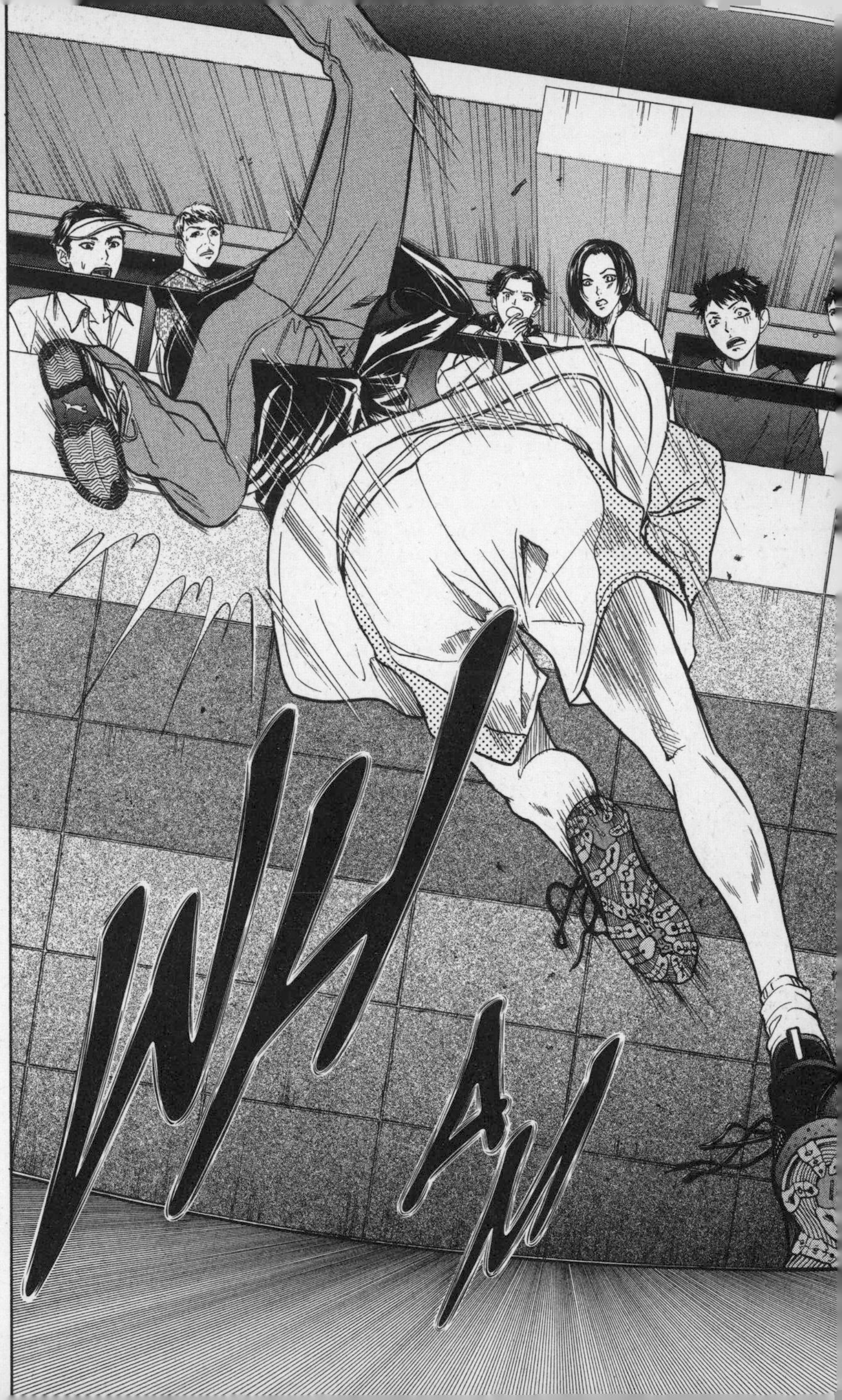
WHAM

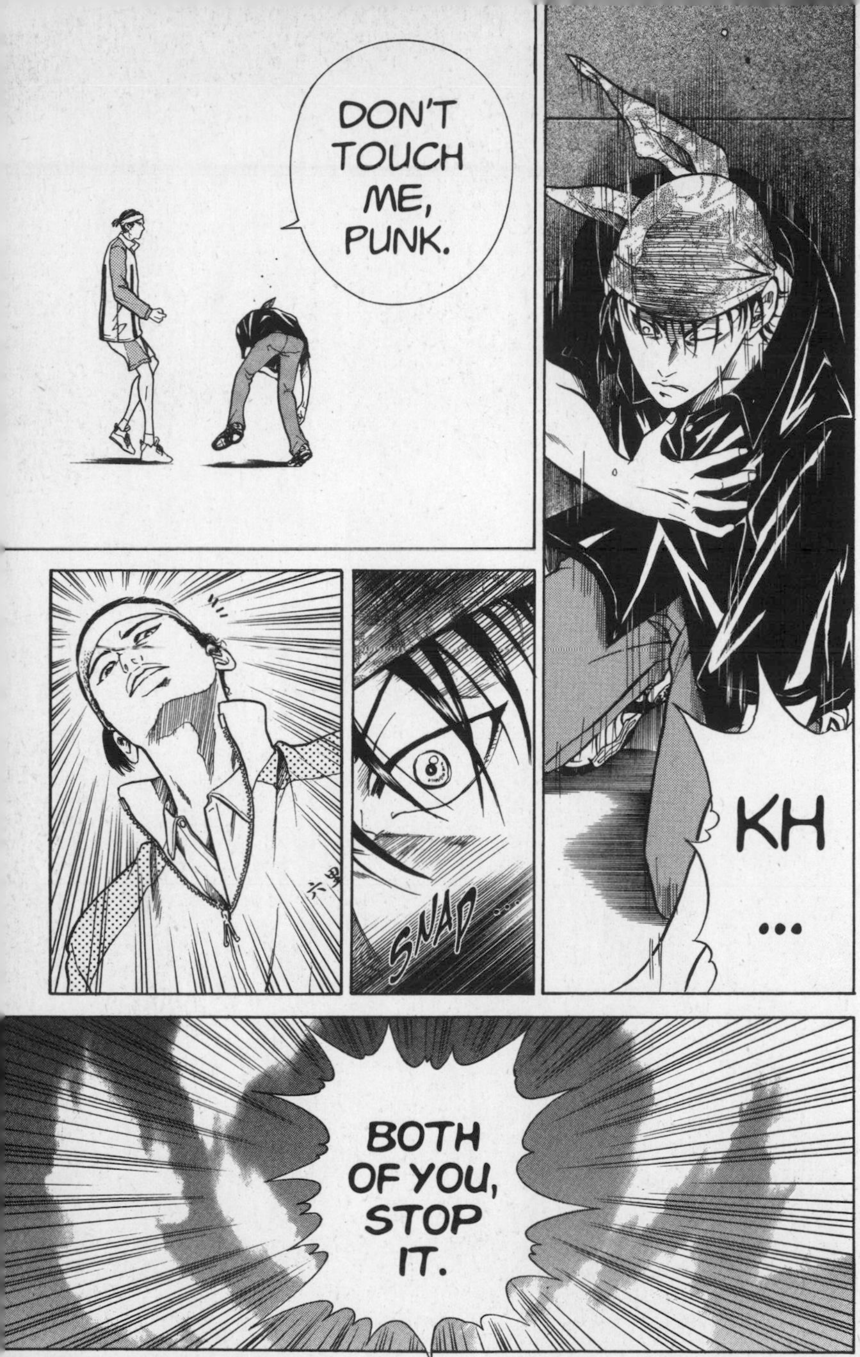
KH ...
DON'T TOUCH ME, PUNK.
SNAP
BOTH OF YOU, STOP IT.

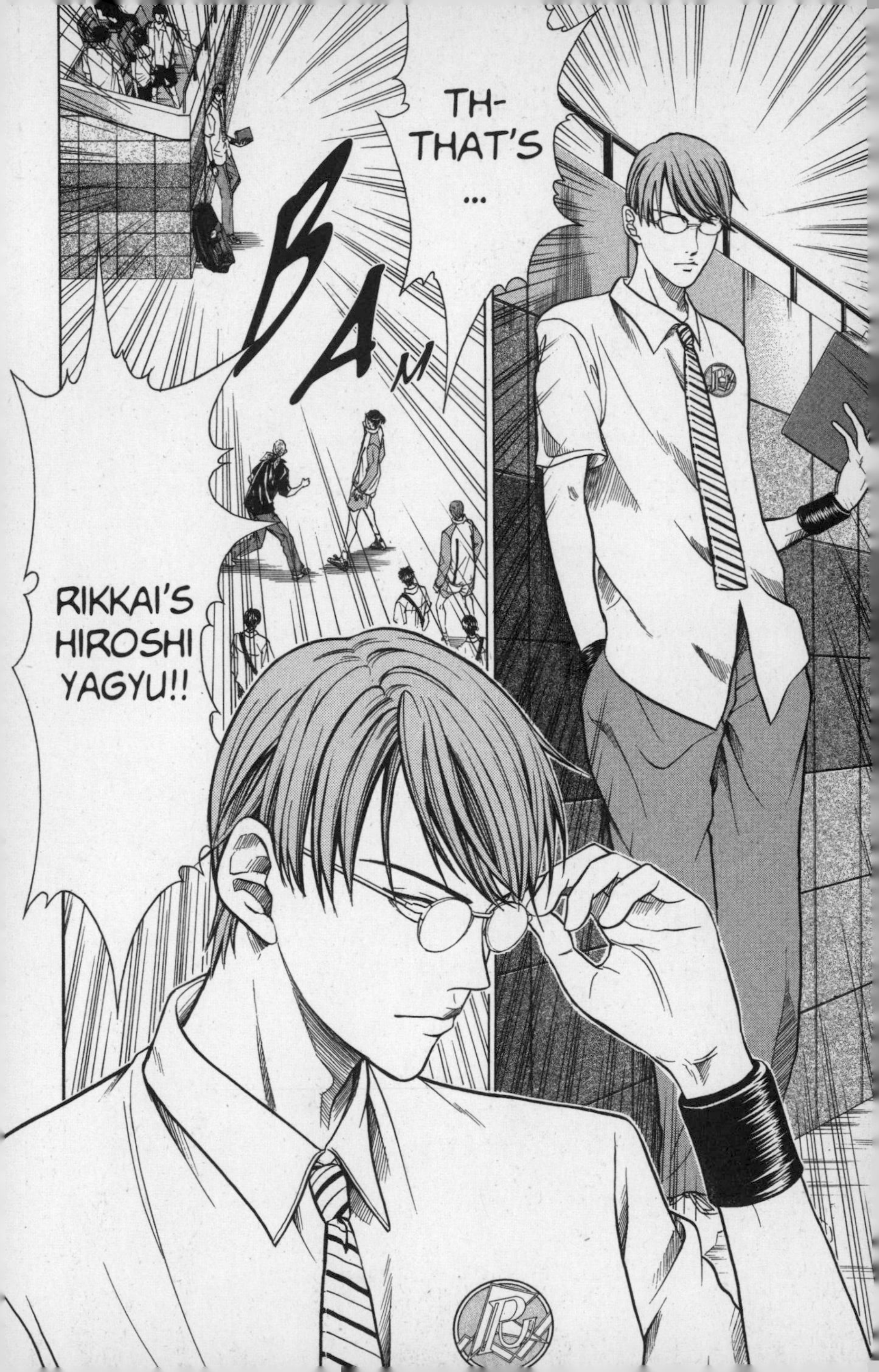
TH- THAT'S ...
BAM
RIKKAI'S HIROSHI YAGYU!!

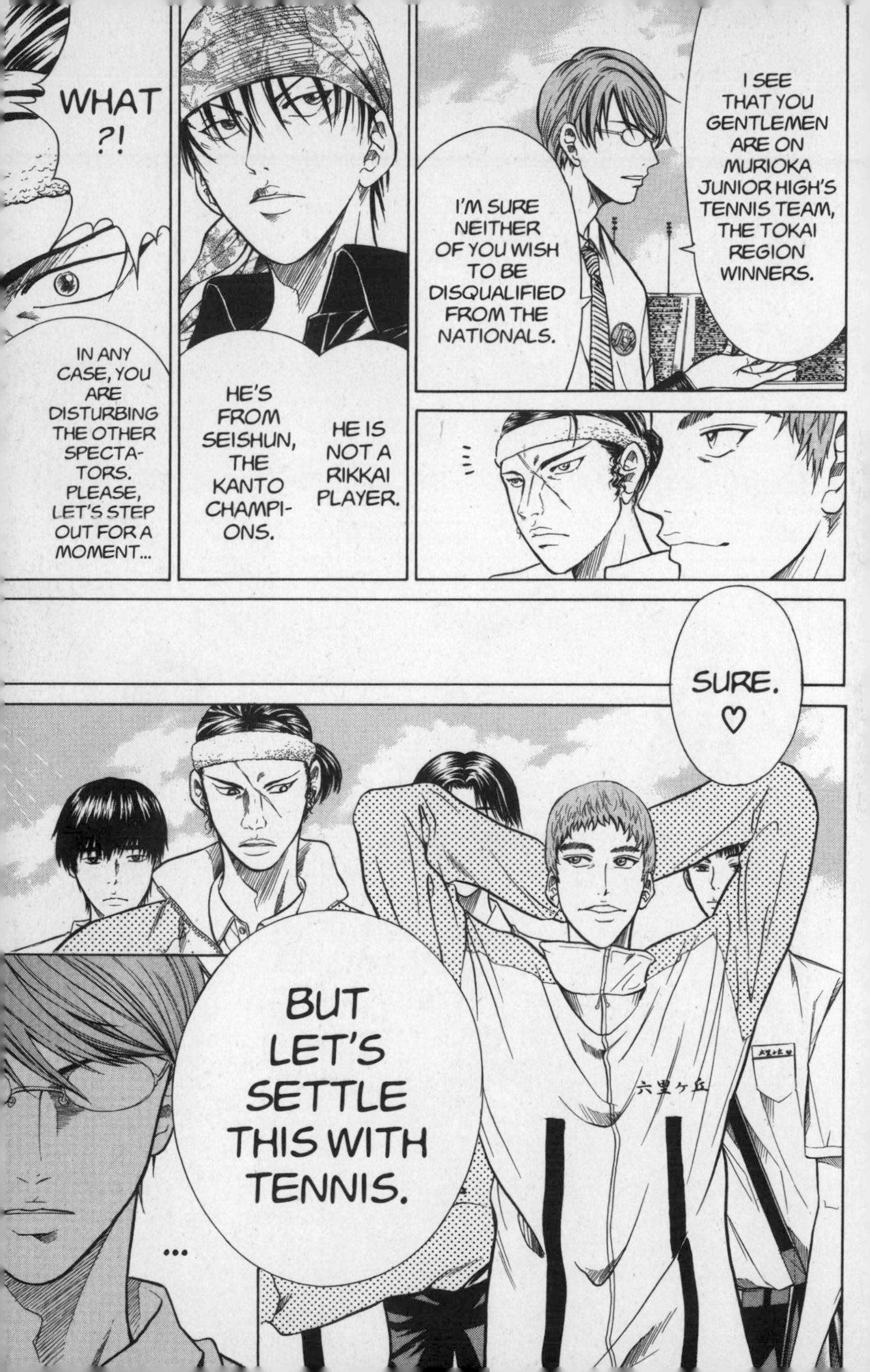
I SEE THAT YOU GENTLEMEN ARE ON MURIOKA JUNIOR HIGH'S TENNIS TEAM, THE TOKAI REGION WINNERS.
I'M SURE NEITHER OF YOU WISH TO BE DISQUALIFIED FROM THE NATIONALS.
HE IS NOT A RIKKAI PLAYER.
HE'S FROM SEISHUN, THE KANTO CHAMPIONS.
WHAT ?!
IN ANY CASE, YOU ARE DISTURBING THE OTHER SPECTATORS. PLEASE, LET'S STEP OUT FOR A MOMENT...
SURE. ♡
BUT LET'S SETTLE THIS WITH TENNIS.
六里ケ丘
...

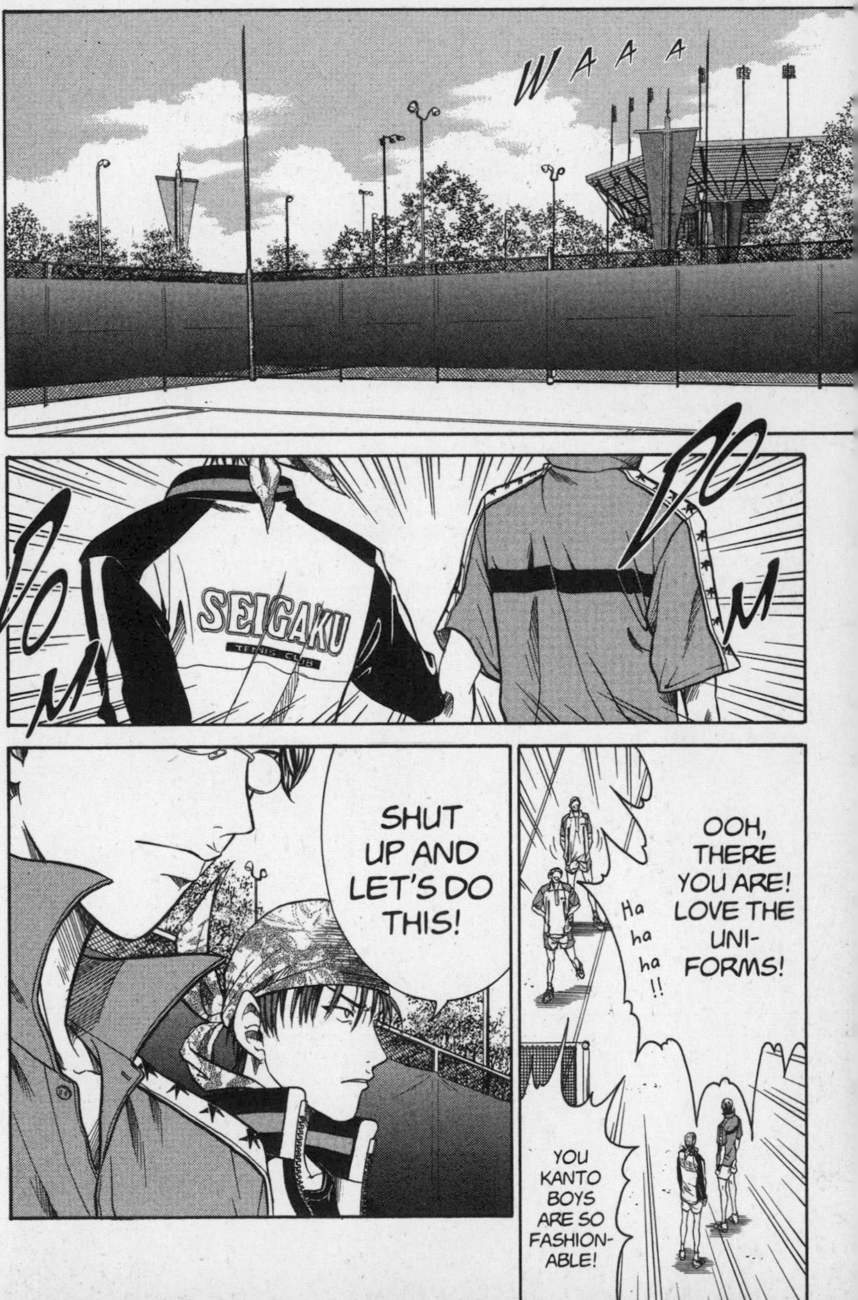
WAAA
DOM
DOM
SEIGAKU
TENNIS CLUB
OOH, THERE YOU ARE! LOVE THE UNI-FORMS!
Ha ha ha !!
YOU KANTO BOYS ARE SO FASHION-ABLE!
SHUT UP AND LET'S DO THIS!

READ THIS WAY

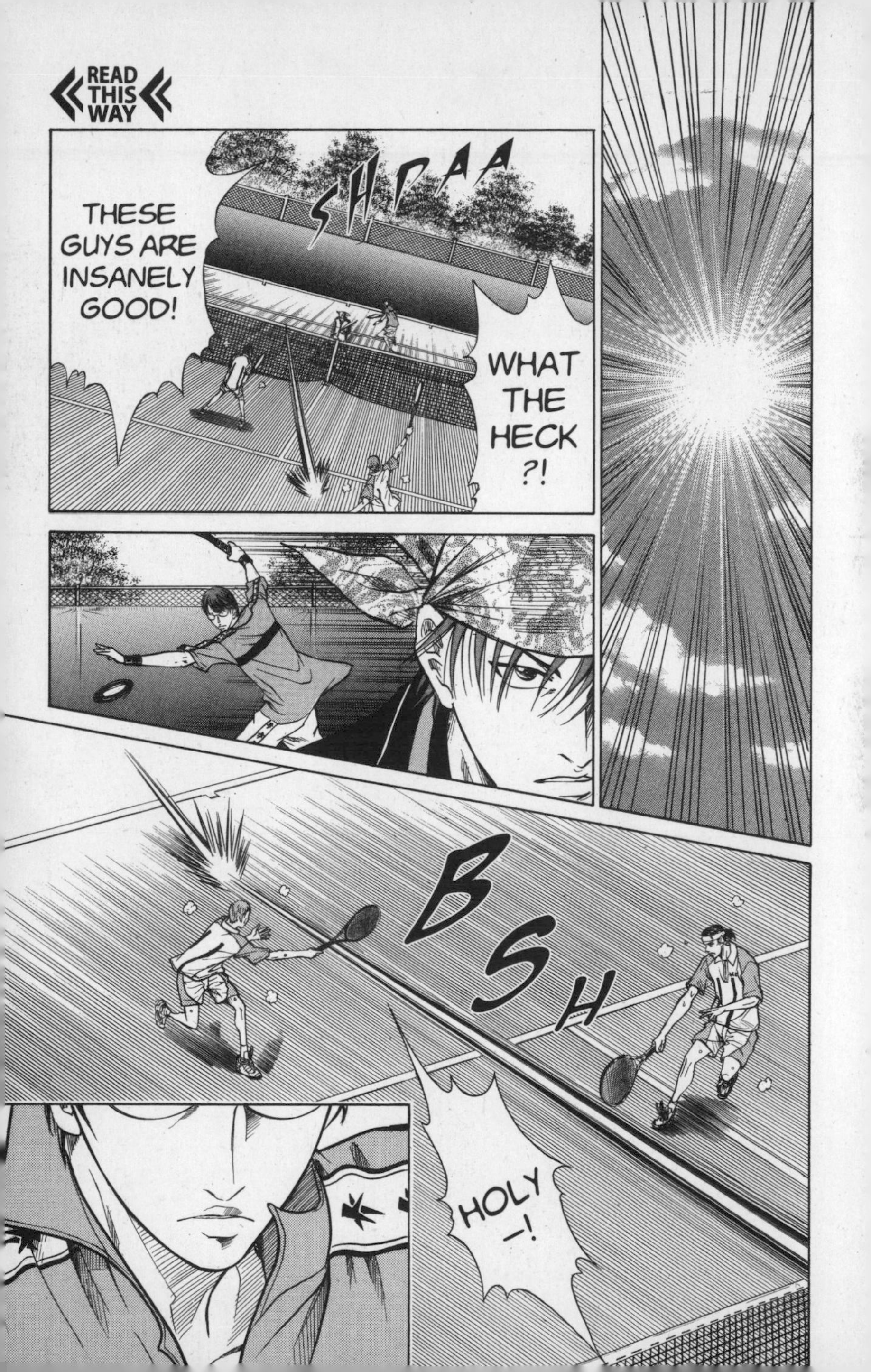
SHPAA
WHAT THE HECK ?!
THESE GUYS ARE INSANELY GOOD!
BSH
HOLY —!

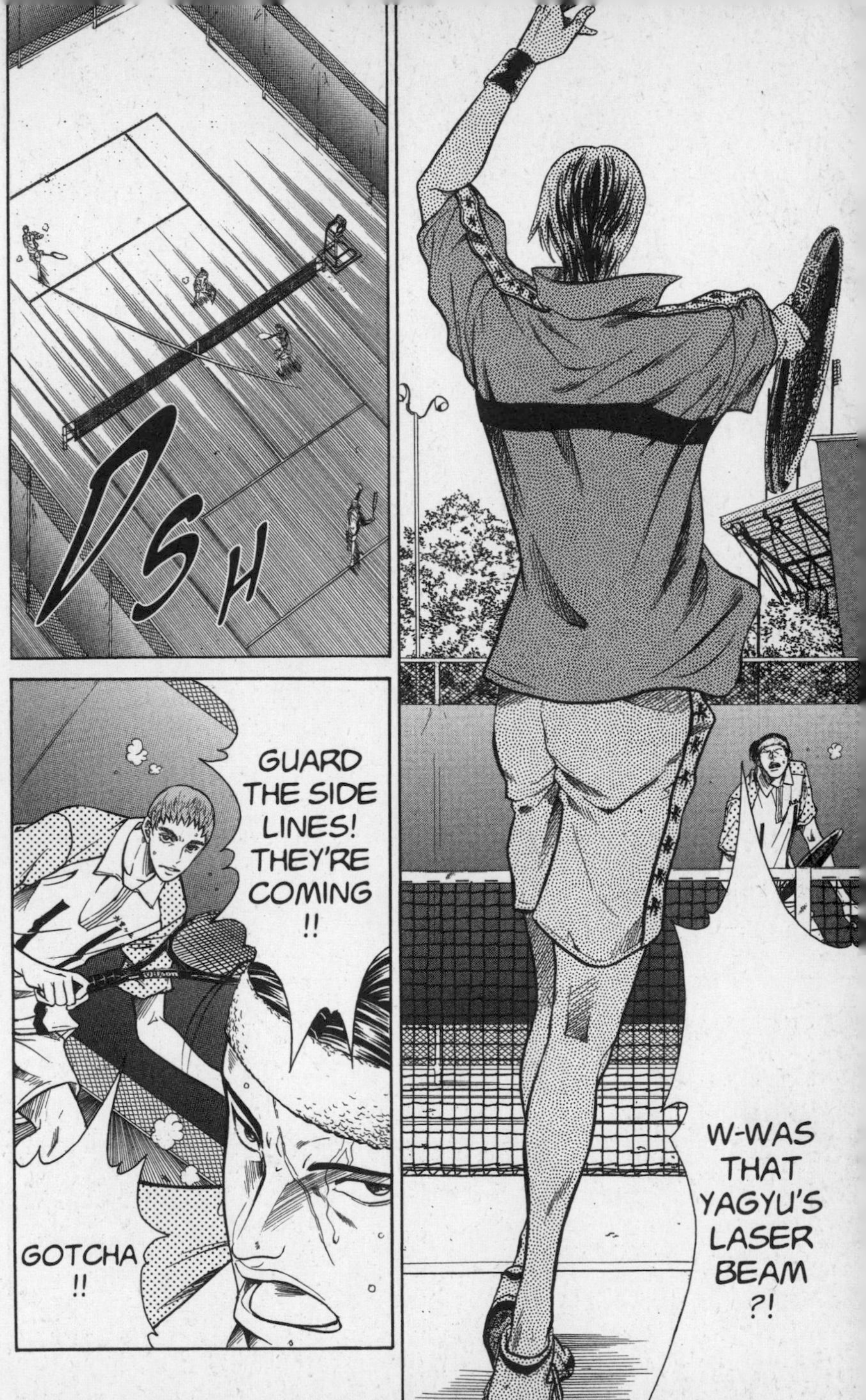
W-WAS THAT YAGYU'S LASER BEAM ?!
DSH
GUARD THE SIDE LINES! THEY'RE COMING !!
GOTCHA !!

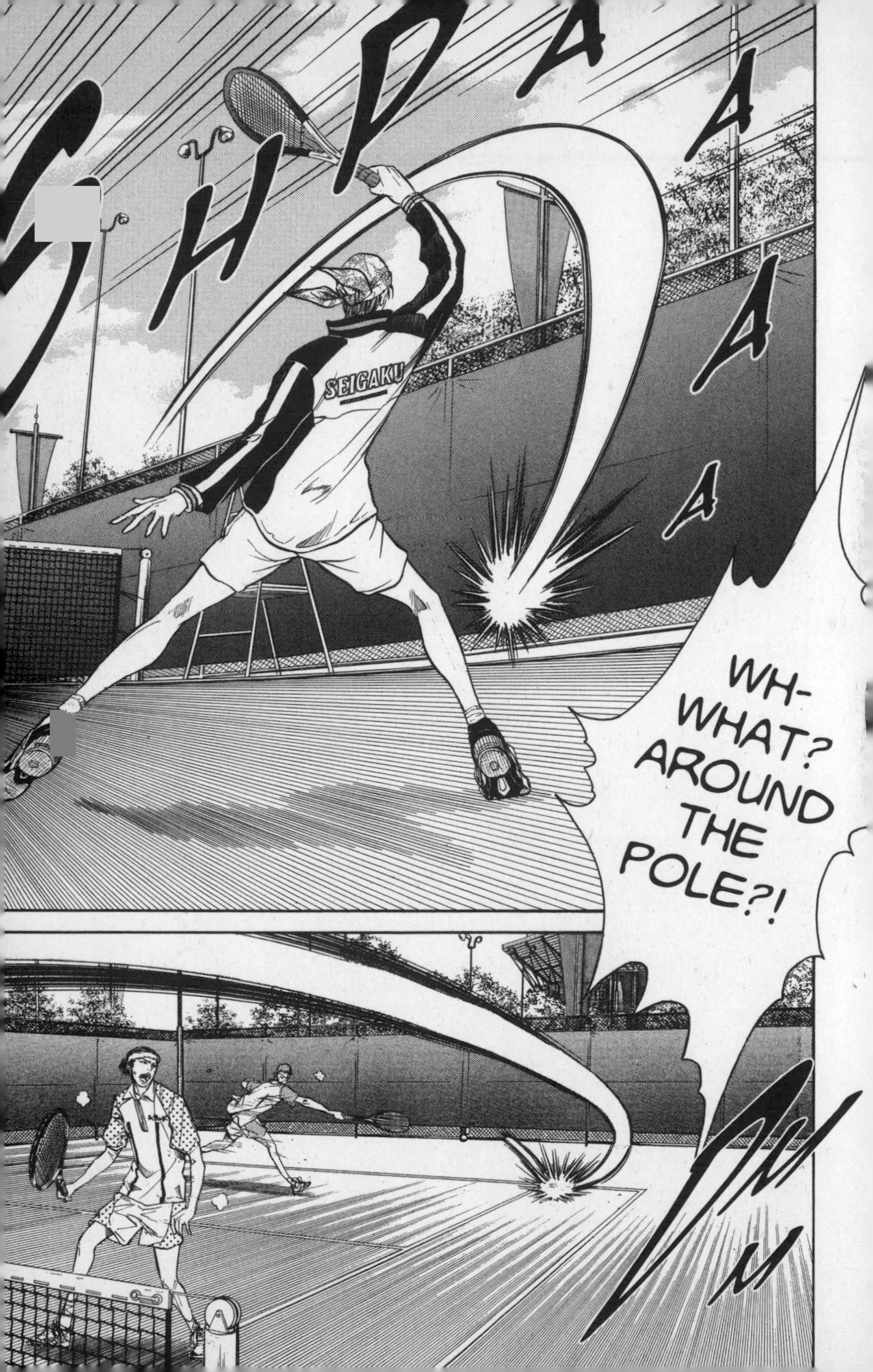
SHPAAAAA
SEIGAKU
WH-WHAT? AROUND THE POLE?!

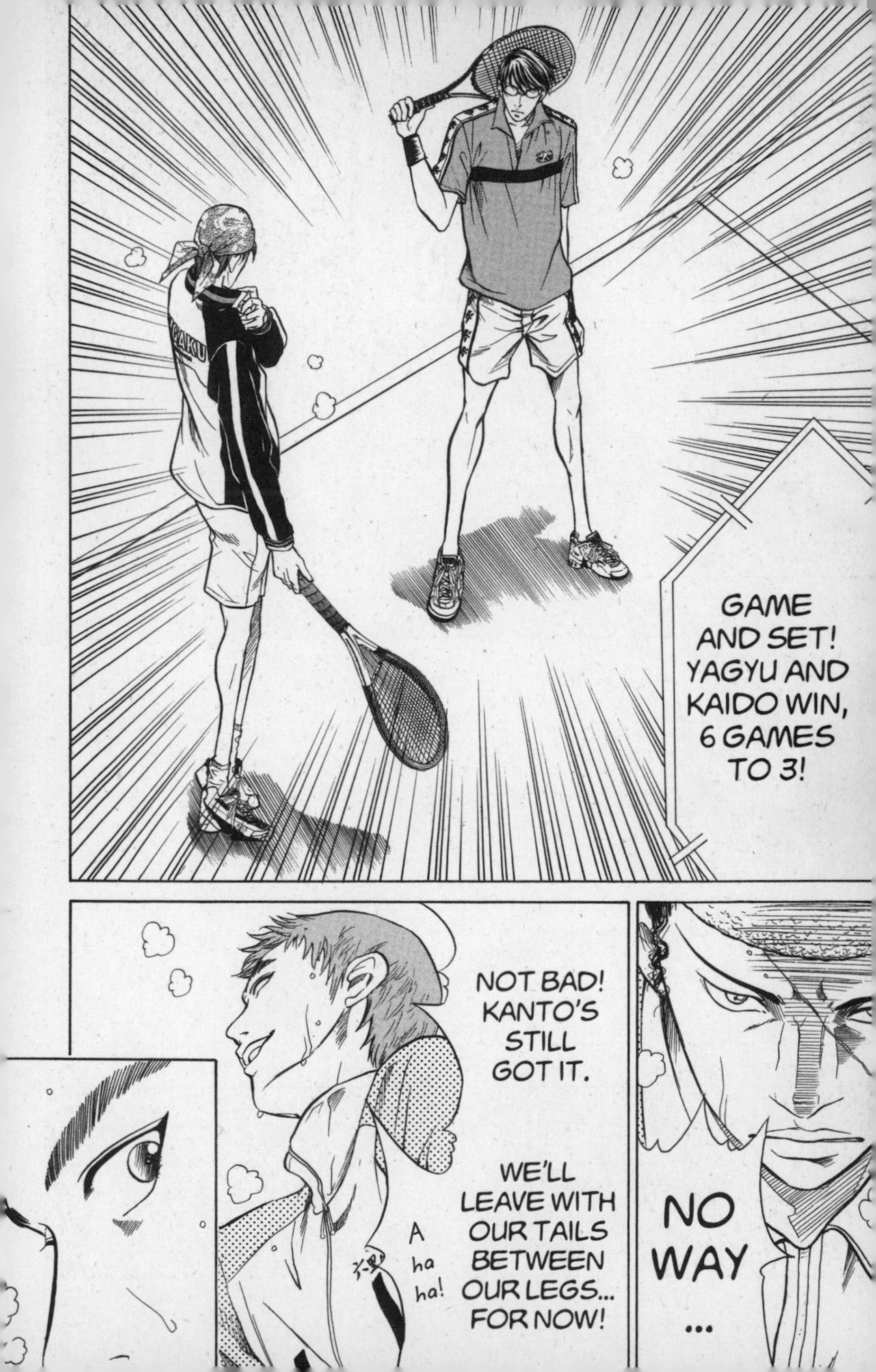
GAME AND SET! YAGYU AND KAIDO WIN, 6 GAMES TO 3!
NO WAY ...
NOT BAD! KANTO'S STILL GOT IT.
WE'LL LEAVE WITH OUR TAILS BETWEEN OUR LEGS... FOR NOW!
A ha ha!

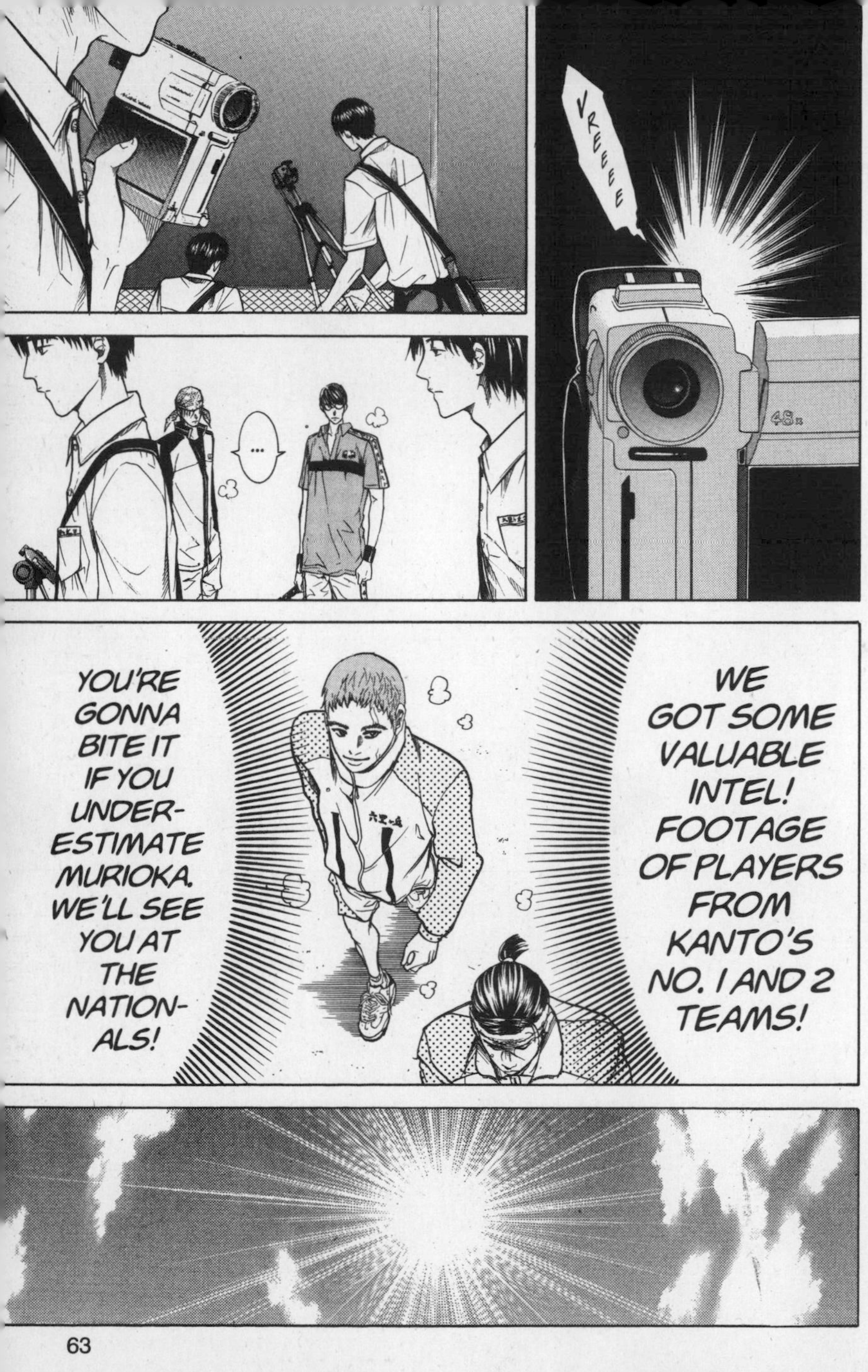
VREEEE
...
WE GOT SOME VALUABLE INTEL! FOOTAGE OF PLAYERS FROM KANTO'S NO. 1 AND 2 TEAMS!
YOU'RE GONNA BITE IT IF YOU UNDER-ESTIMATE MURIOKA. WE'LL SEE YOU AT THE NATION-ALS!

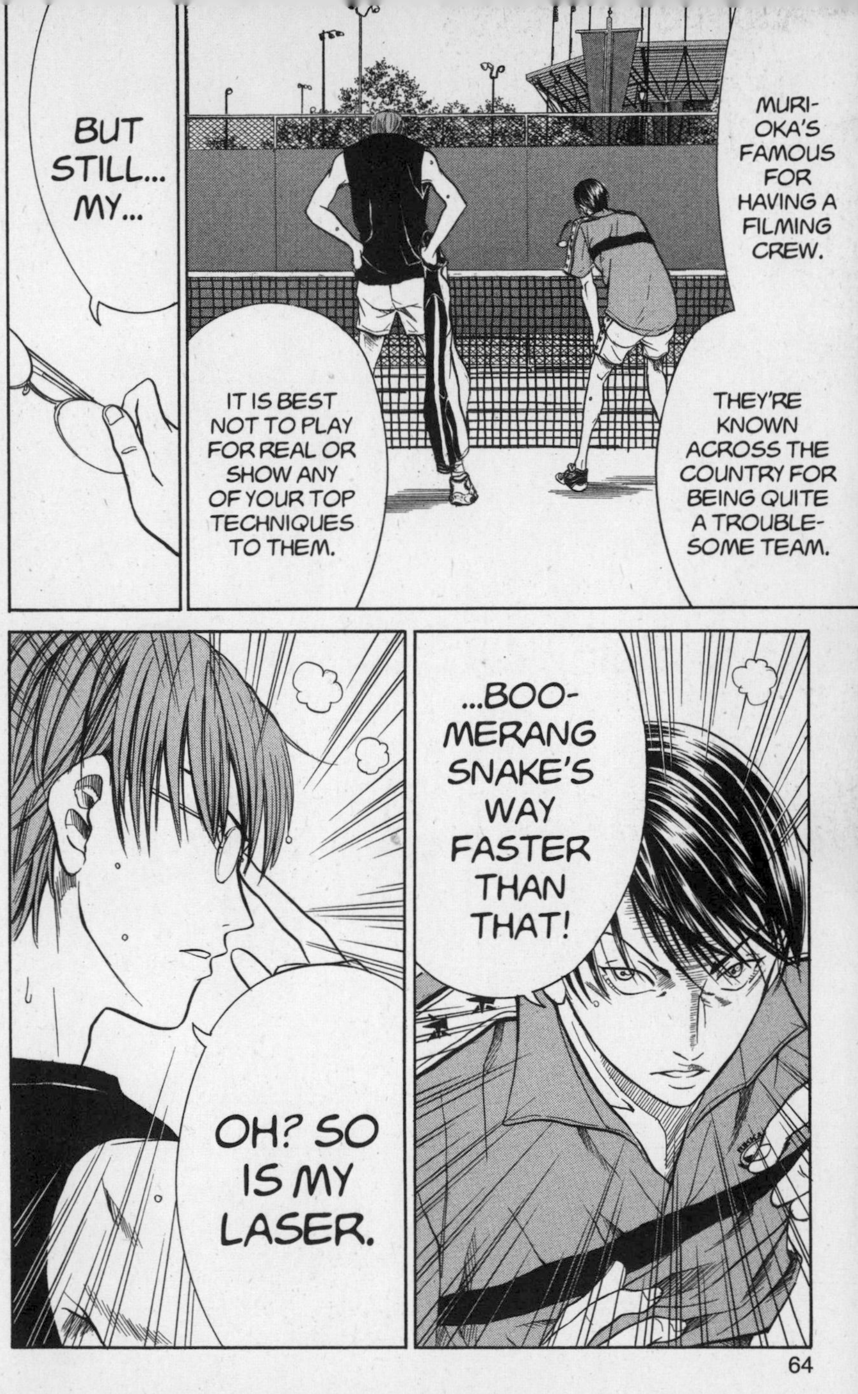
MURI-OKA'S FAMOUS FOR HAVING A FILMING CREW.
THEY'RE KNOWN ACROSS THE COUNTRY FOR BEING QUITE A TROUBLE-SOME TEAM.
IT IS BEST NOT TO PLAY FOR REAL OR SHOW ANY OF YOUR TOP TECHNIQUES TO THEM.
BUT STILL... MY...
...BOO-MERANG SNAKE'S WAY FASTER THAN THAT!
OH? SO IS MY LASER.

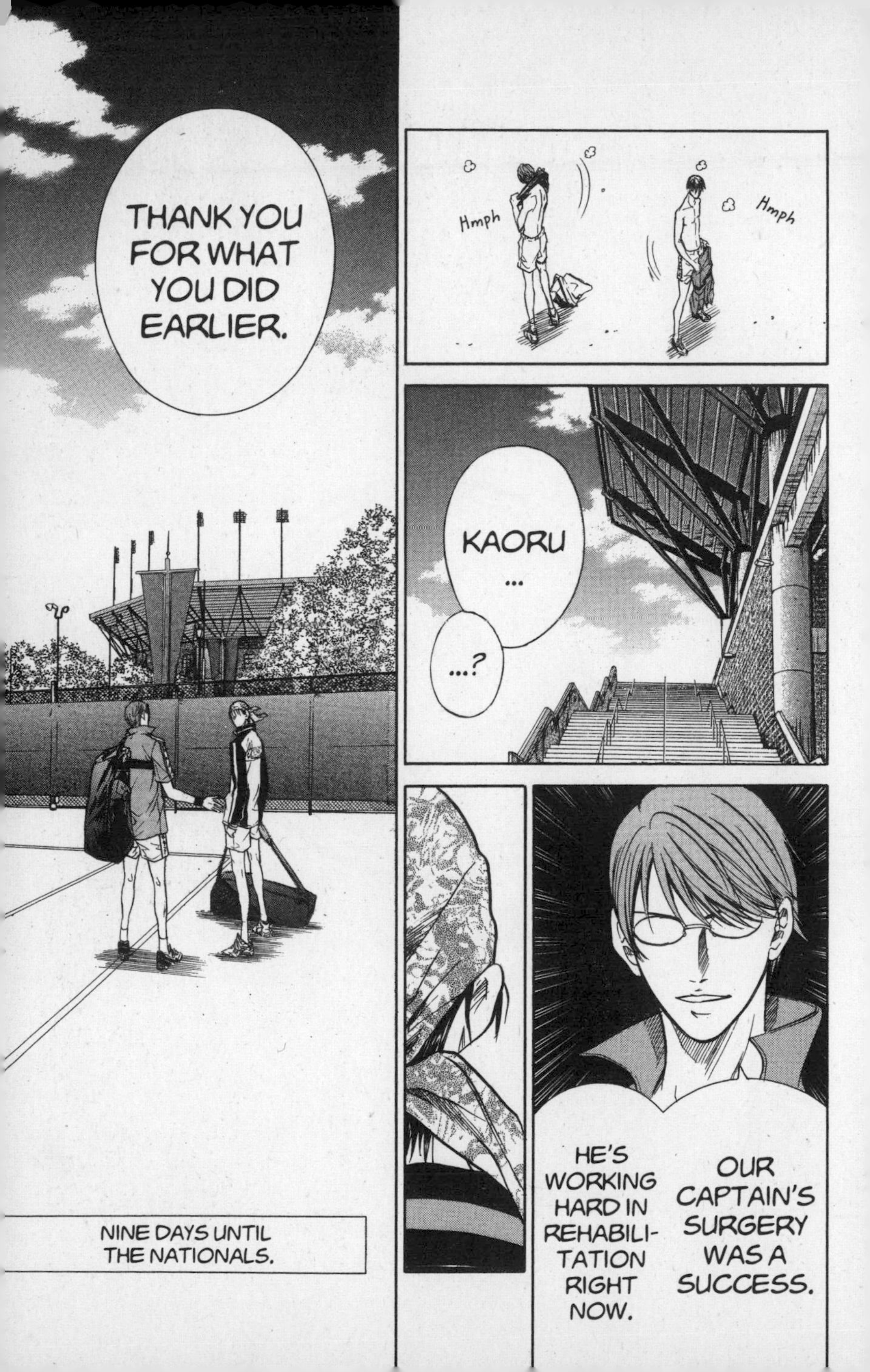
Hmph
Hmph
KAORU ...
...?
OUR CAPTAIN'S SURGERY WAS A SUCCESS.
HE'S WORKING HARD IN REHABILI-TATION RIGHT NOW.
THANK YOU FOR WHAT YOU DID EARLIER.
NINE DAYS UNTIL THE NATIONALS.

GENIUS 241: RYOMA'S GIRLFRIEND

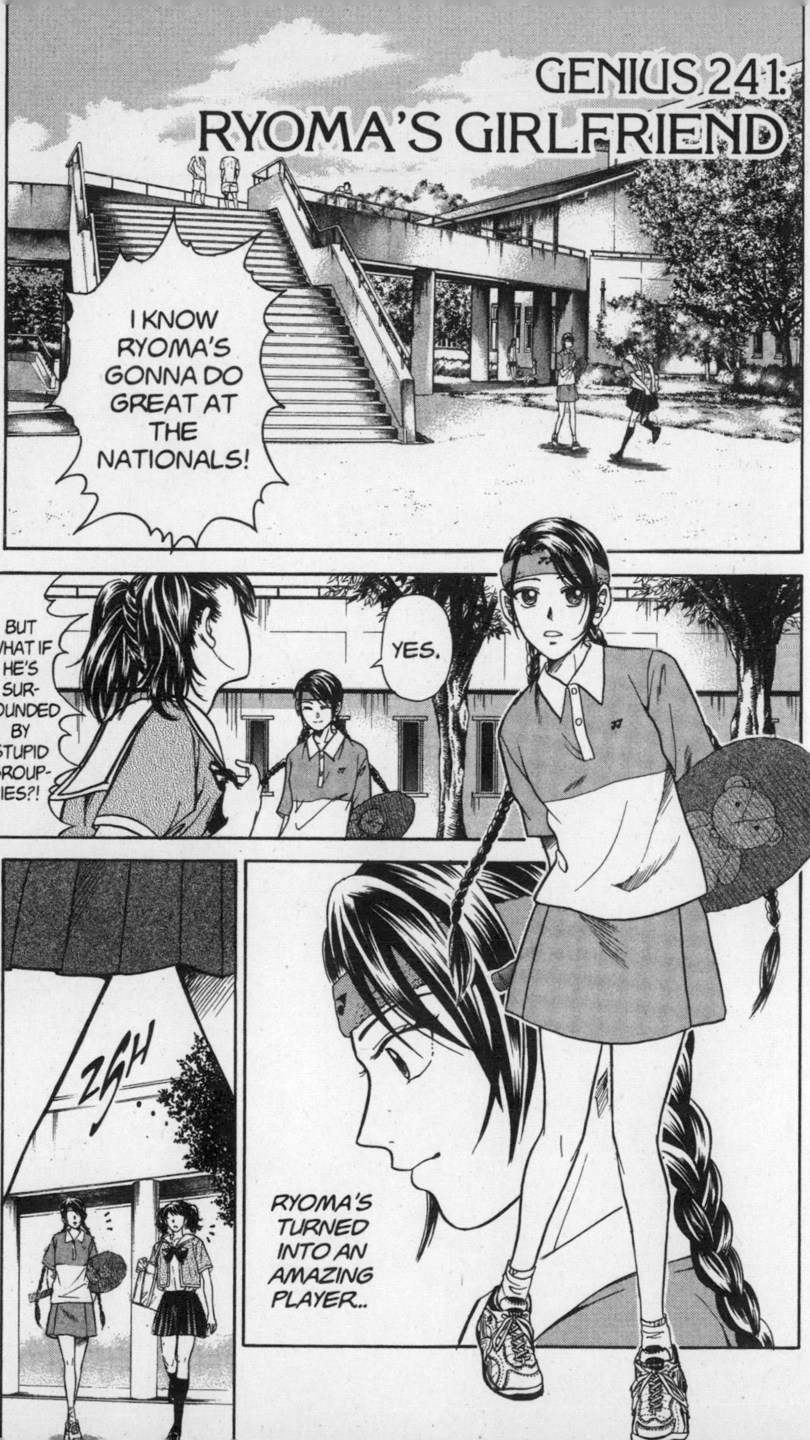
I KNOW RYOMA'S GONNA DO GREAT AT THE NATIONALS!
YES.
BUT WHAT IF HE'S SURROUNDED BY STUPID GROUPIES?!
RYOMA'S TURNED INTO AN AMAZING PLAYER...
ZSH

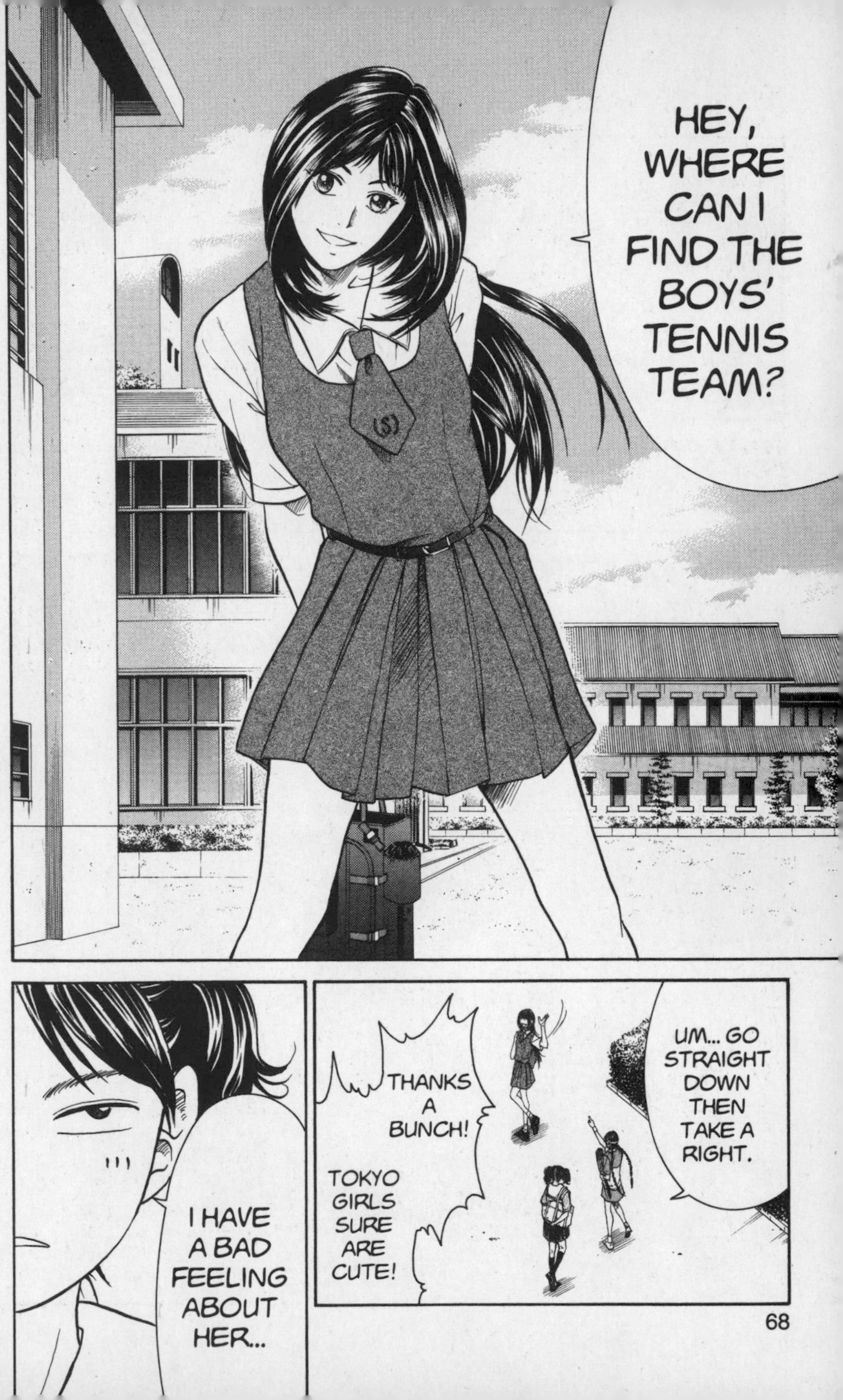
HEY, WHERE CAN I FIND THE BOYS' TENNIS TEAM?
UM... GO STRAIGHT DOWN THEN TAKE A RIGHT.
THANKS A BUNCH!
TOKYO GIRLS SURE ARE CUTE!
I HAVE A BAD FEELING ABOUT HER...

READ THIS WAY

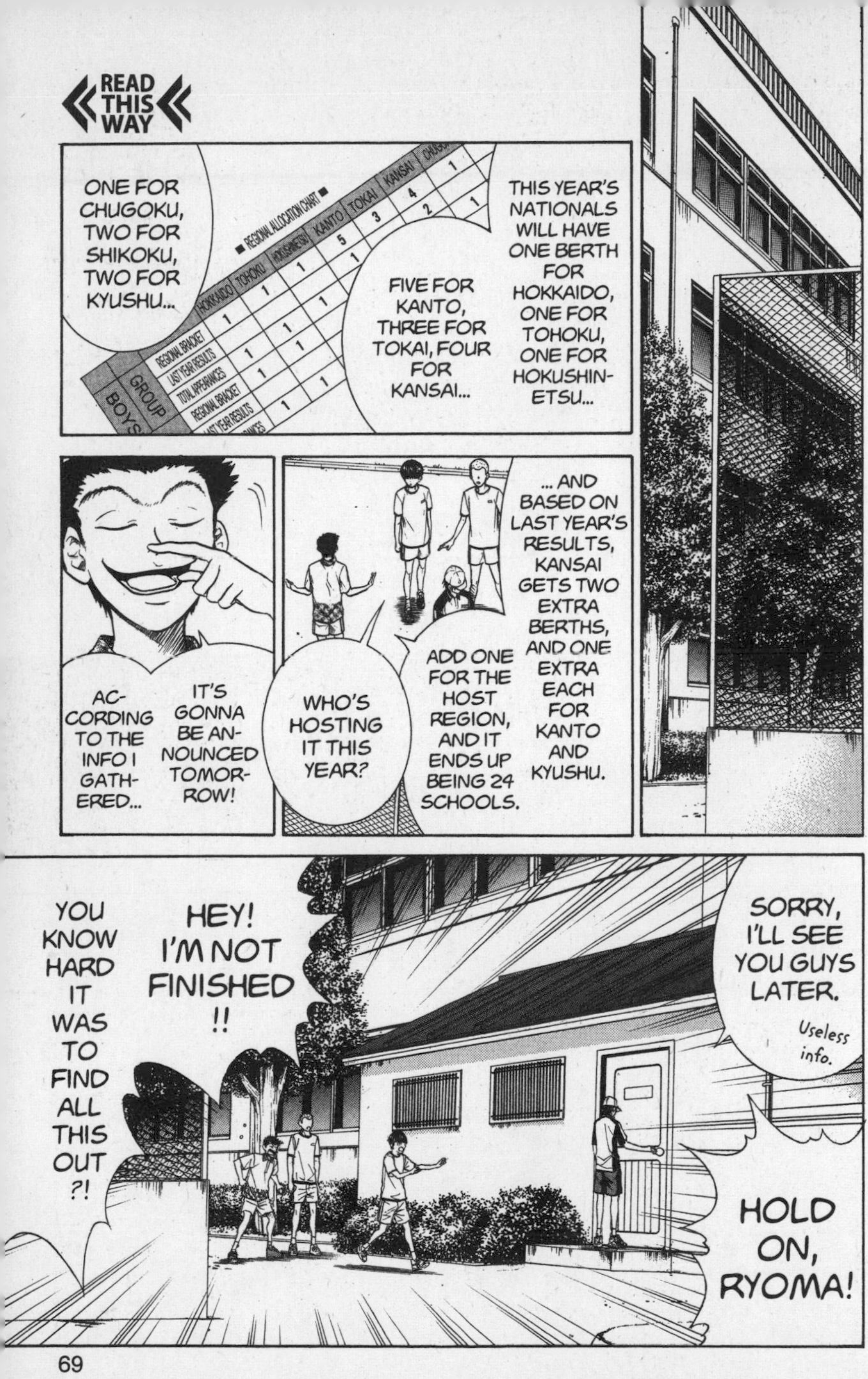
THIS YEAR'S NATIONALS WILL HAVE ONE BERTH FOR HOKKAIDO, ONE FOR TOHOKU, ONE FOR HOKUSHIN-ETSU...
FIVE FOR KANTO, THREE FOR TOKAI, FOUR FOR KANSAI...
ONE FOR CHUGOKU, TWO FOR SHIKOKU, TWO FOR KYUSHU...
REGIONAL ALLOCATION CHART
... AND BASED ON LAST YEAR'S RESULTS, KANSAI GETS TWO EXTRA BERTHS, AND ONE EXTRA EACH FOR KANTO AND KYUSHU.
ADD ONE FOR THE HOST REGION, AND IT ENDS UP BEING 24 SCHOOLS.
WHO'S HOSTING IT THIS YEAR?
IT'S GONNA BE ANNOUNCED TOMORROW!
ACCORDING TO THE INFO I GATHERED...
SORRY, I'LL SEE YOU GUYS LATER.
Useless info.
HOLD ON, RYOMA!
HEY! I'M NOT FINISHED!!
YOU KNOW HARD IT WAS TO FIND ALL THIS OUT?!

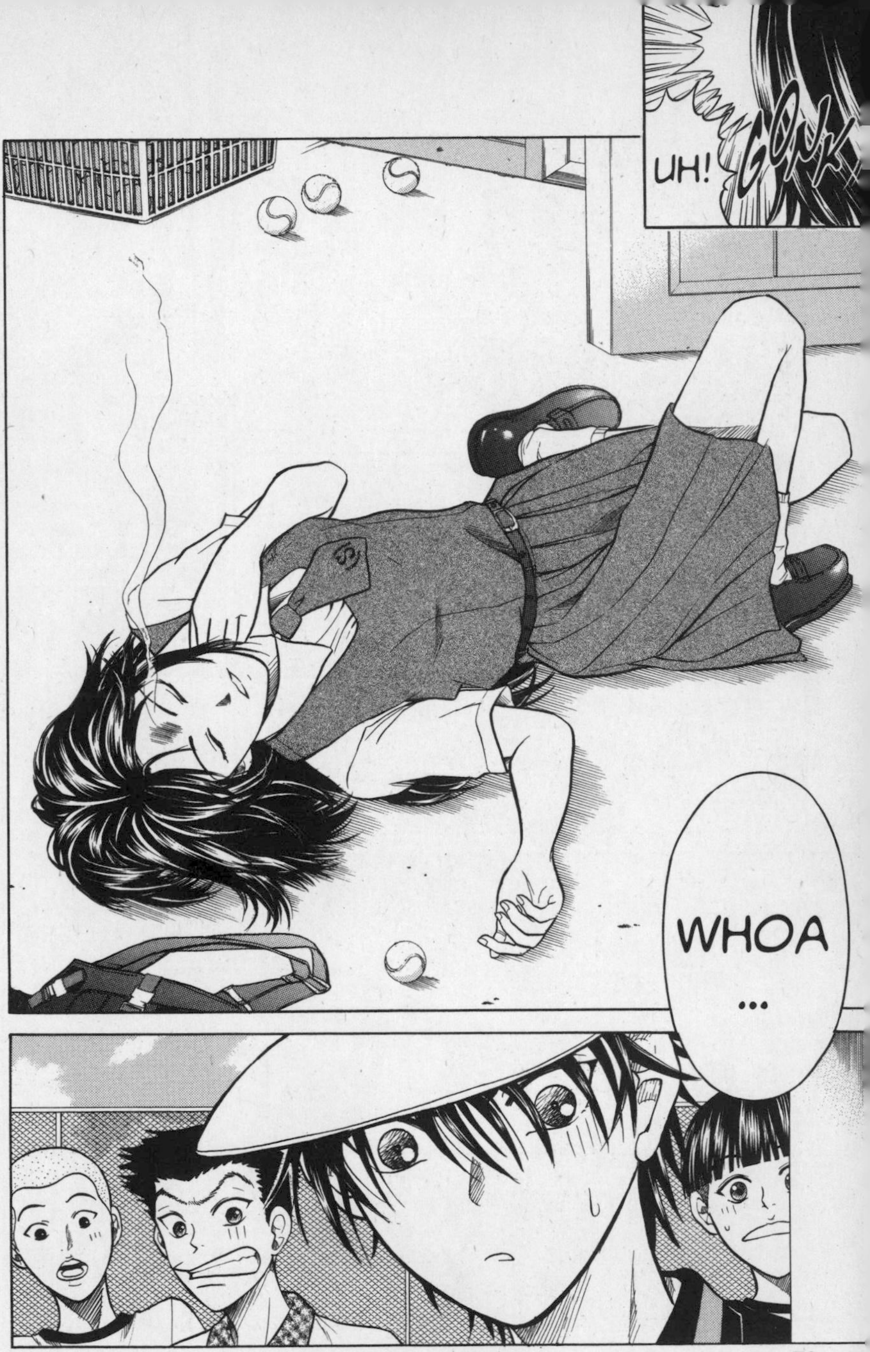
UH!
WHOA ...

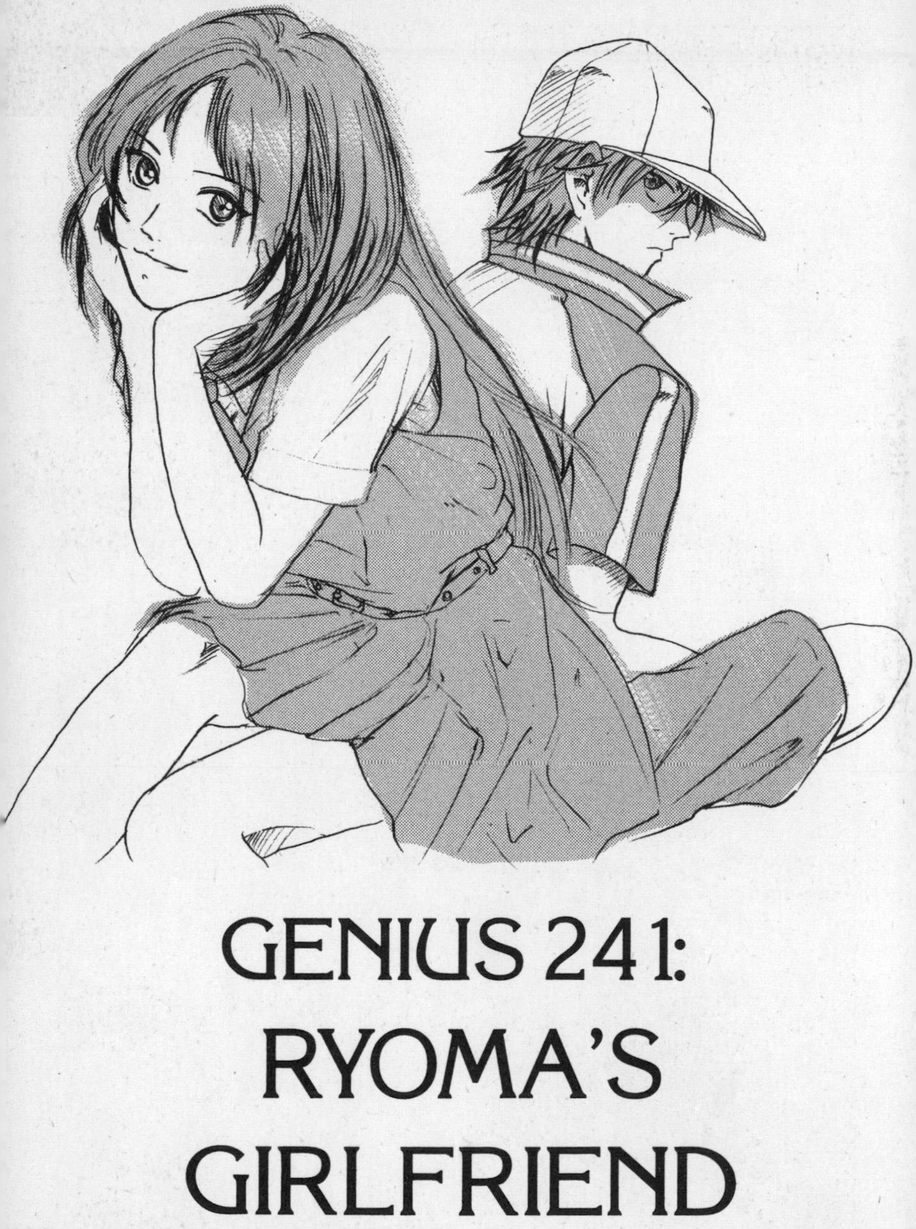

GENIUS 241: RYOMA'S GIRLFRIEND

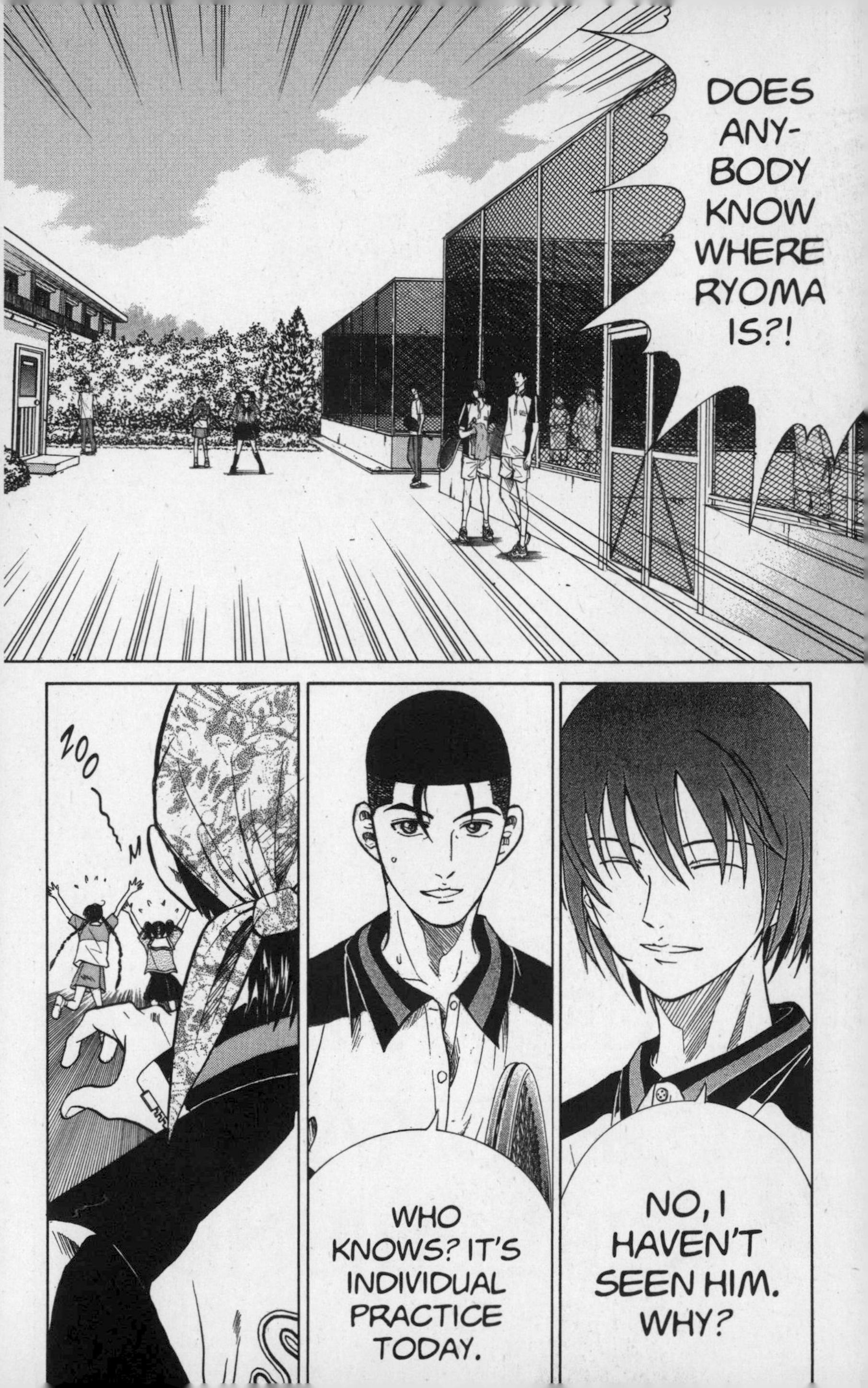
DOES ANYBODY KNOW WHERE RYOMA IS?!
NO, I HAVEN'T SEEN HIM. WHY?
WHO KNOWS? IT'S INDIVIDUAL PRACTICE TODAY.
ZOOM

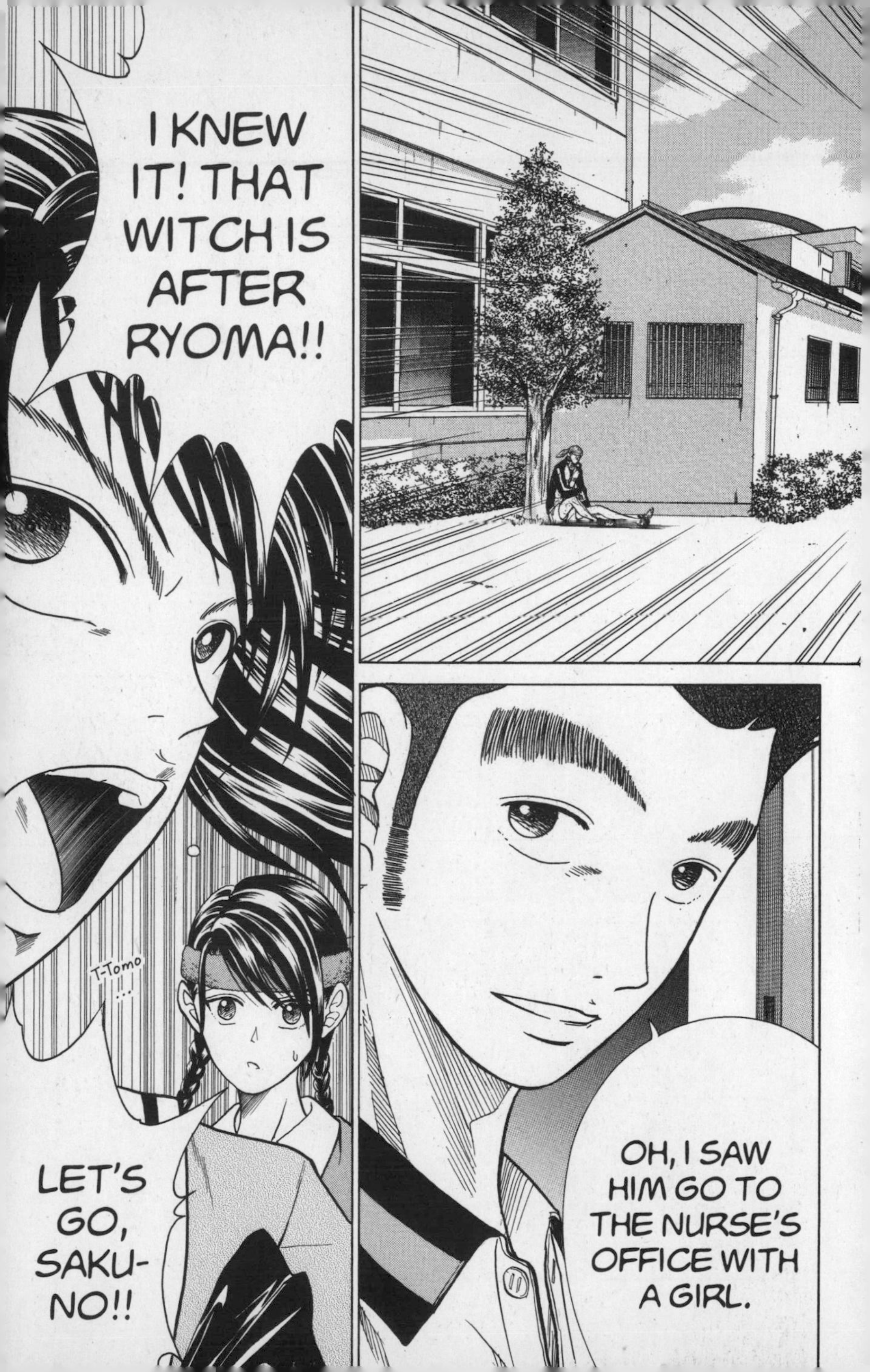
OH, I SAW HIM GO TO THE NURSE'S OFFICE WITH A GIRL.
I KNEW IT! THAT WITCH IS AFTER RYOMA!!
T-Tomo...
LET'S GO, SAKUNO!!

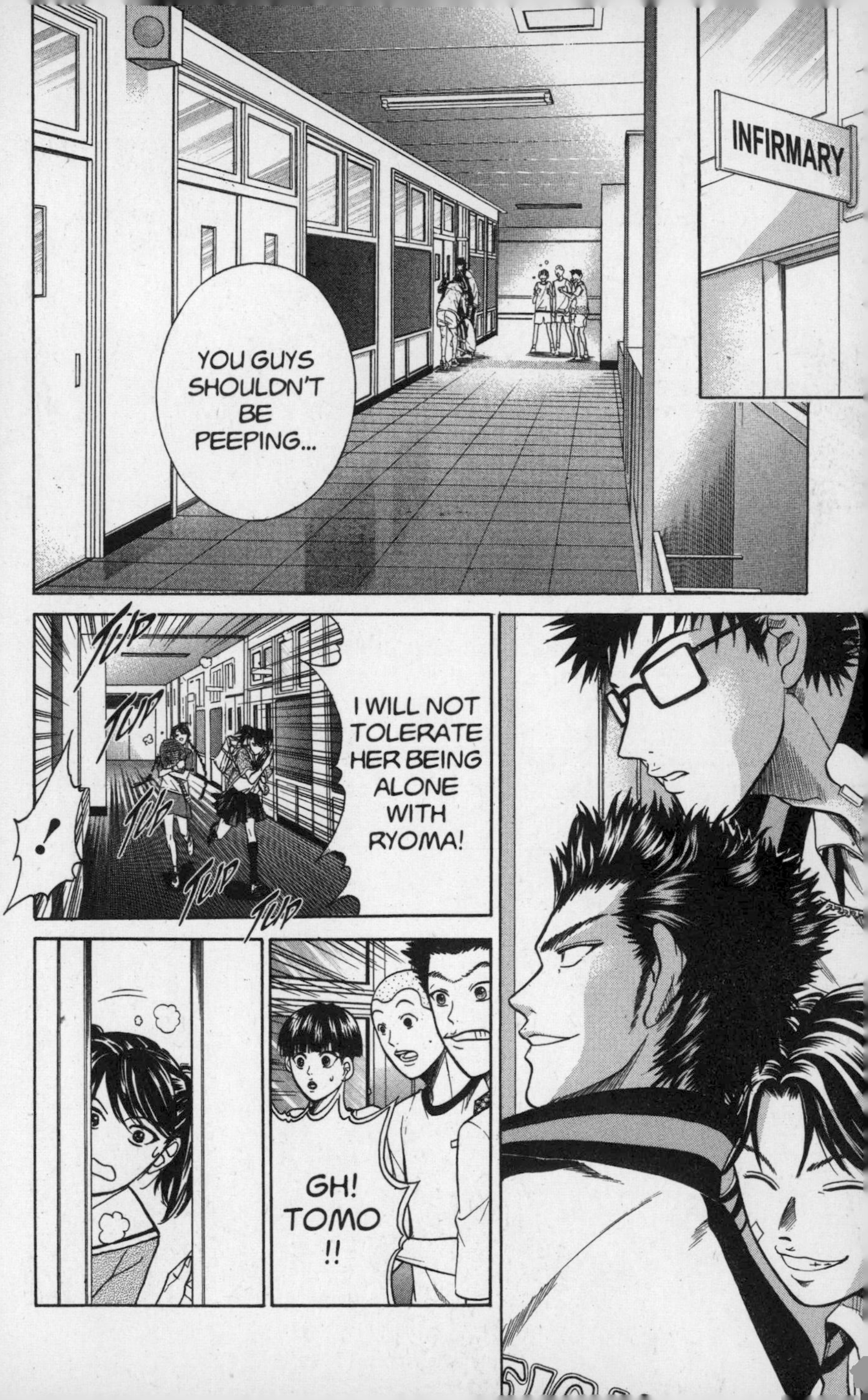
INFIRMARY
YOU GUYS SHOULDN'T BE PEEPING...
I WILL NOT TOLERATE HER BEING ALONE WITH RYOMA!
!
GH! TOMO !!

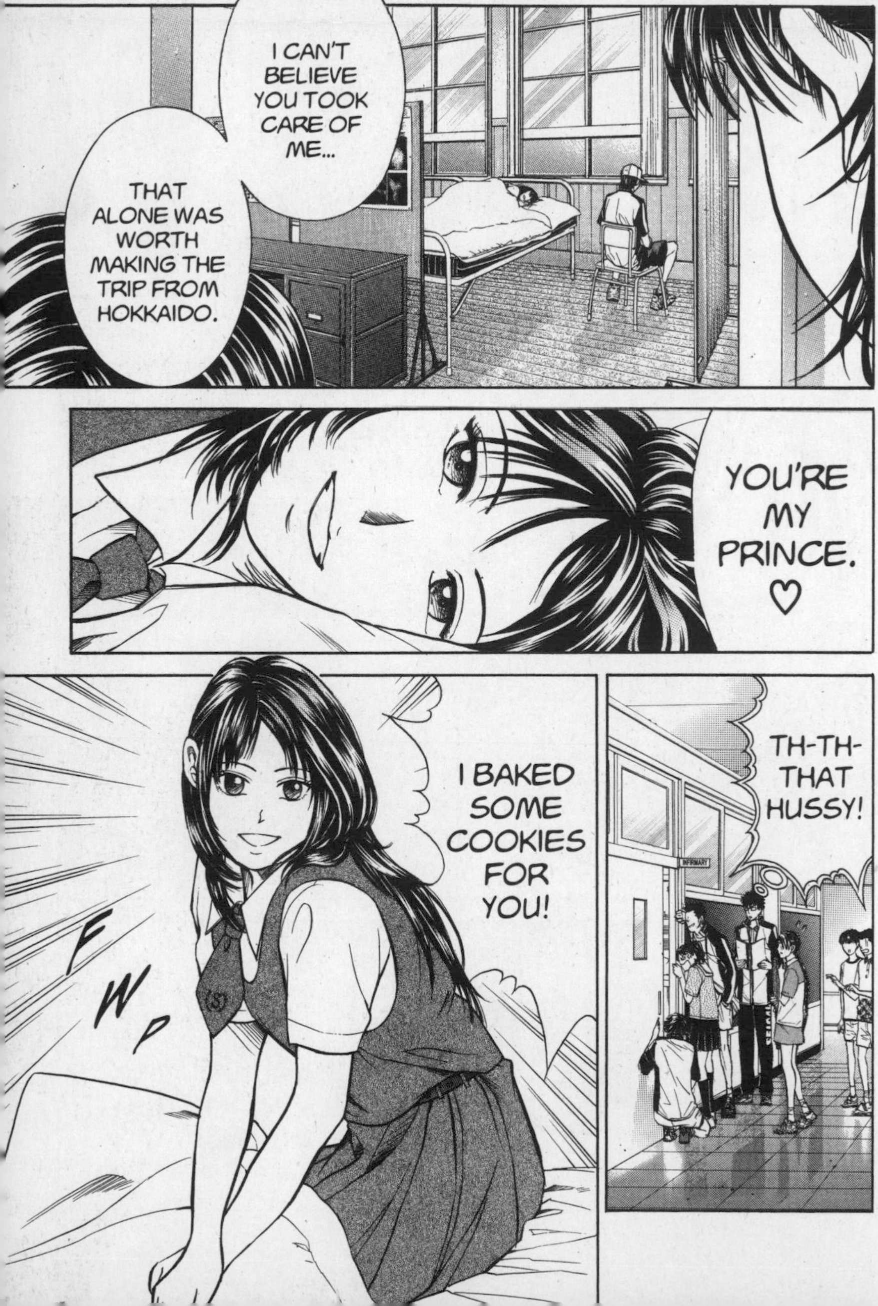
I CAN'T BELIEVE YOU TOOK CARE OF ME...
THAT ALONE WAS WORTH MAKING THE TRIP FROM HOKKAIDO.
YOU'RE MY PRINCE. ♡
TH-TH-THAT HUSSY!
INFIRMARY
I BAKED SOME COOKIES FOR YOU!
FWP

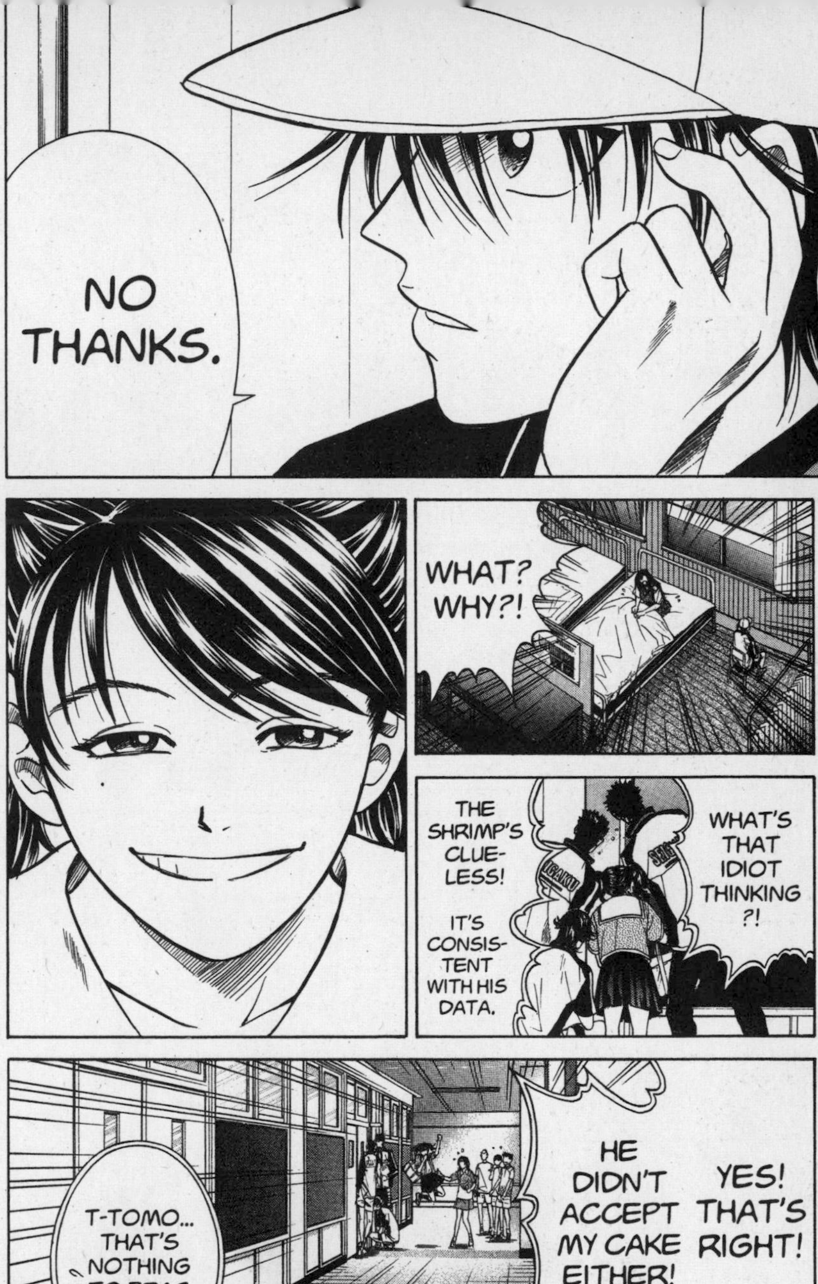
NO THANKS.
WHAT? WHY?!
WHAT'S THAT IDIOT THINKING?!
THE SHRIMP'S CLUELESS!
IT'S CONSISTENT WITH HIS DATA.
YES! THAT'S RIGHT!
HE DIDN'T ACCEPT MY CAKE EITHER!
Mua ha ha
T-TOMO... THAT'S NOTHING TO BRAG ABOUT...

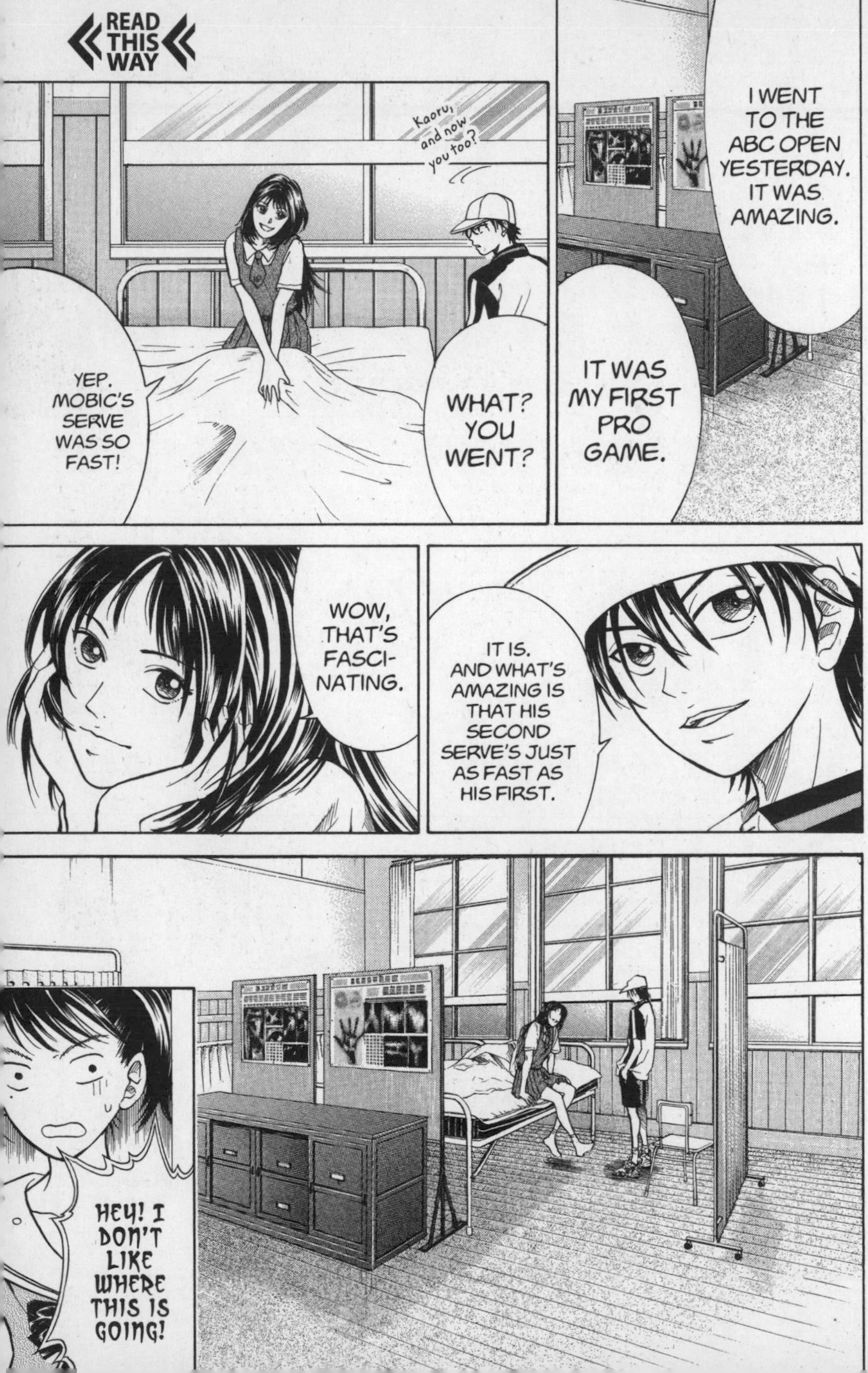
READ THIS WAY
I WENT TO THE ABC OPEN YESTERDAY. IT WAS AMAZING.
IT WAS MY FIRST PRO GAME.
Kaoru, and now you too?
WHAT? YOU WENT?
YEP. MOBIC'S SERVE WAS SO FAST!
IT IS. AND WHAT'S AMAZING IS THAT HIS SECOND SERVE'S JUST AS FAST AS HIS FIRST.
WOW, THAT'S FASCI-NATING.
HEY! I DON'T LIKE WHERE THIS IS GOING!

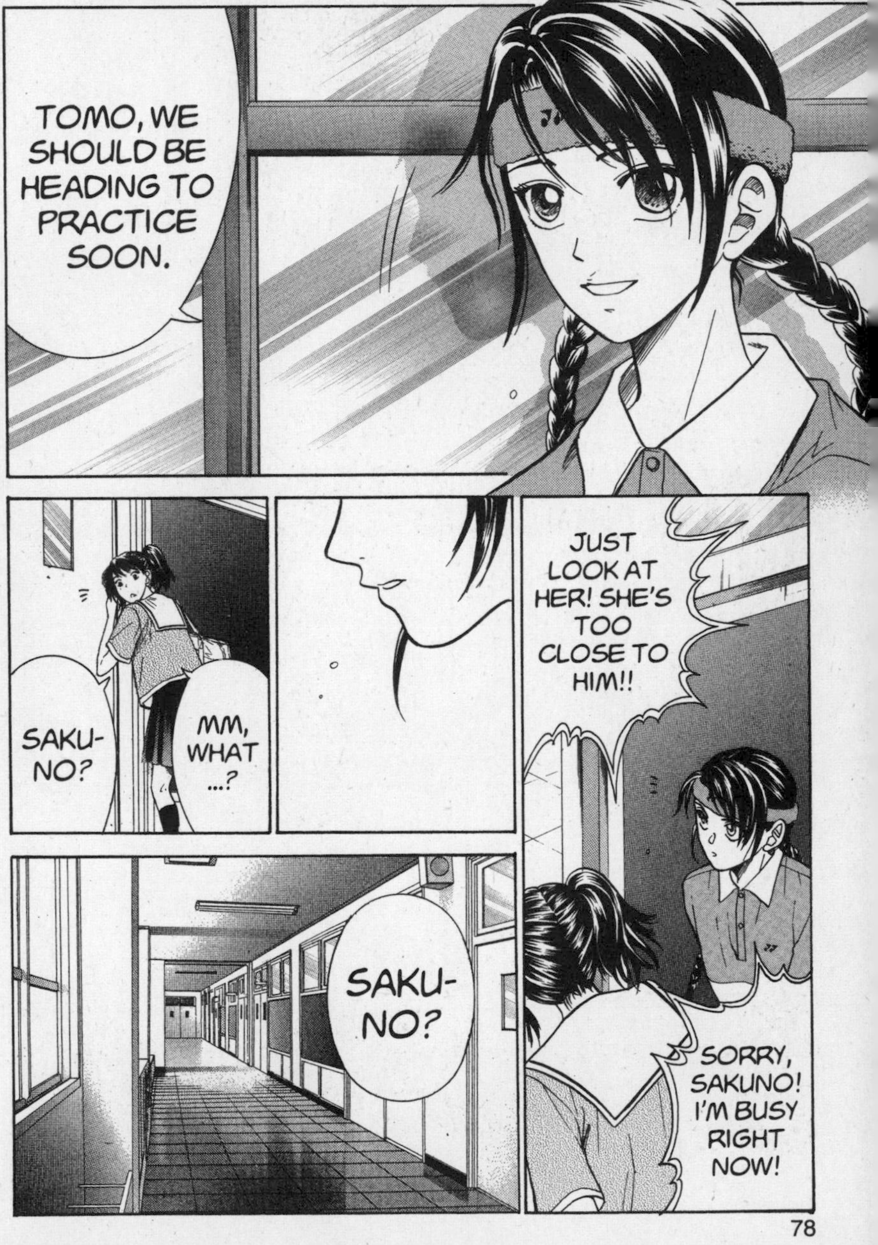
TOMO, WE SHOULD BE HEADING TO PRACTICE SOON.
JUST LOOK AT HER! SHE'S TOO CLOSE TO HIM!!
SORRY, SAKUNO! I'M BUSY RIGHT NOW!
MM, WHAT ...?
SAKU-NO?
SAKU-NO?

READ THIS WAY

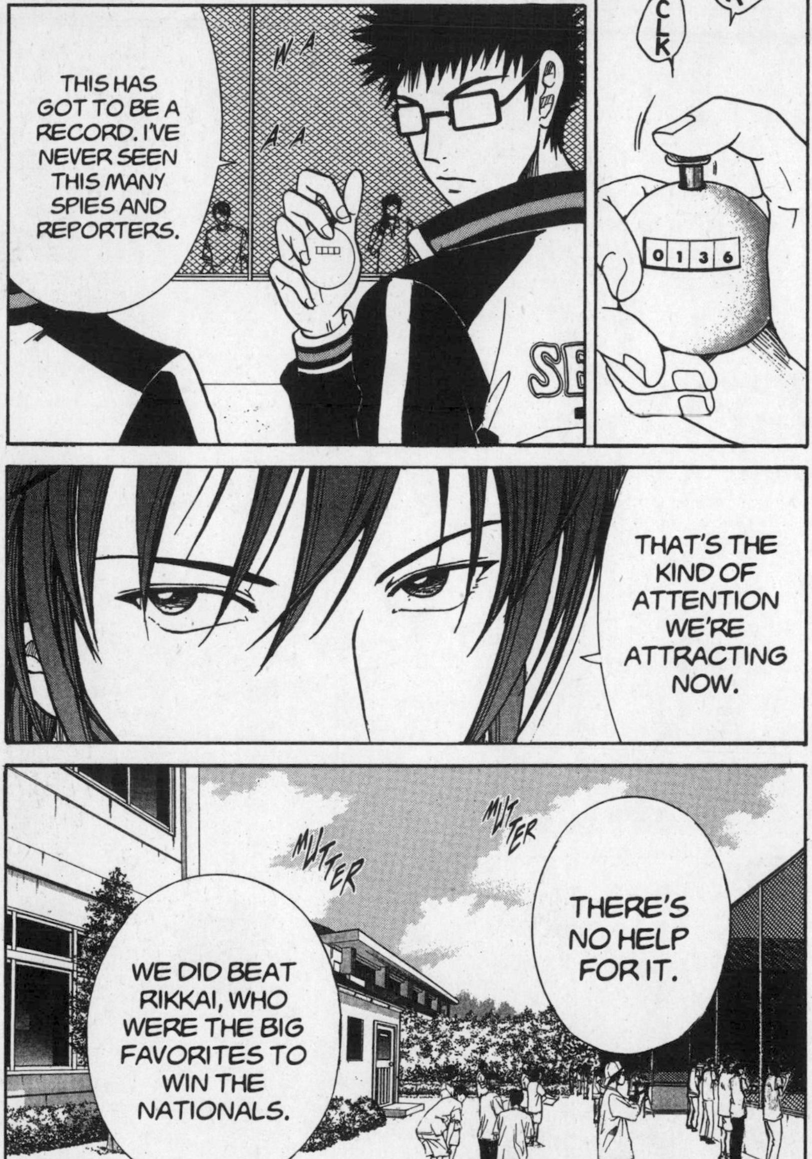
CLK
CLK
WA
AA
THIS HAS GOT TO BE A RECORD. I'VE NEVER SEEN THIS MANY SPIES AND REPORTERS.
THAT'S THE KIND OF ATTENTION WE'RE ATTRACTING NOW.
MUTTER
THERE'S NO HELP FOR IT.
MUTTER
WE DID BEAT RIKKAI, WHO WERE THE BIG FAVORITES TO WIN THE NATIONALS.

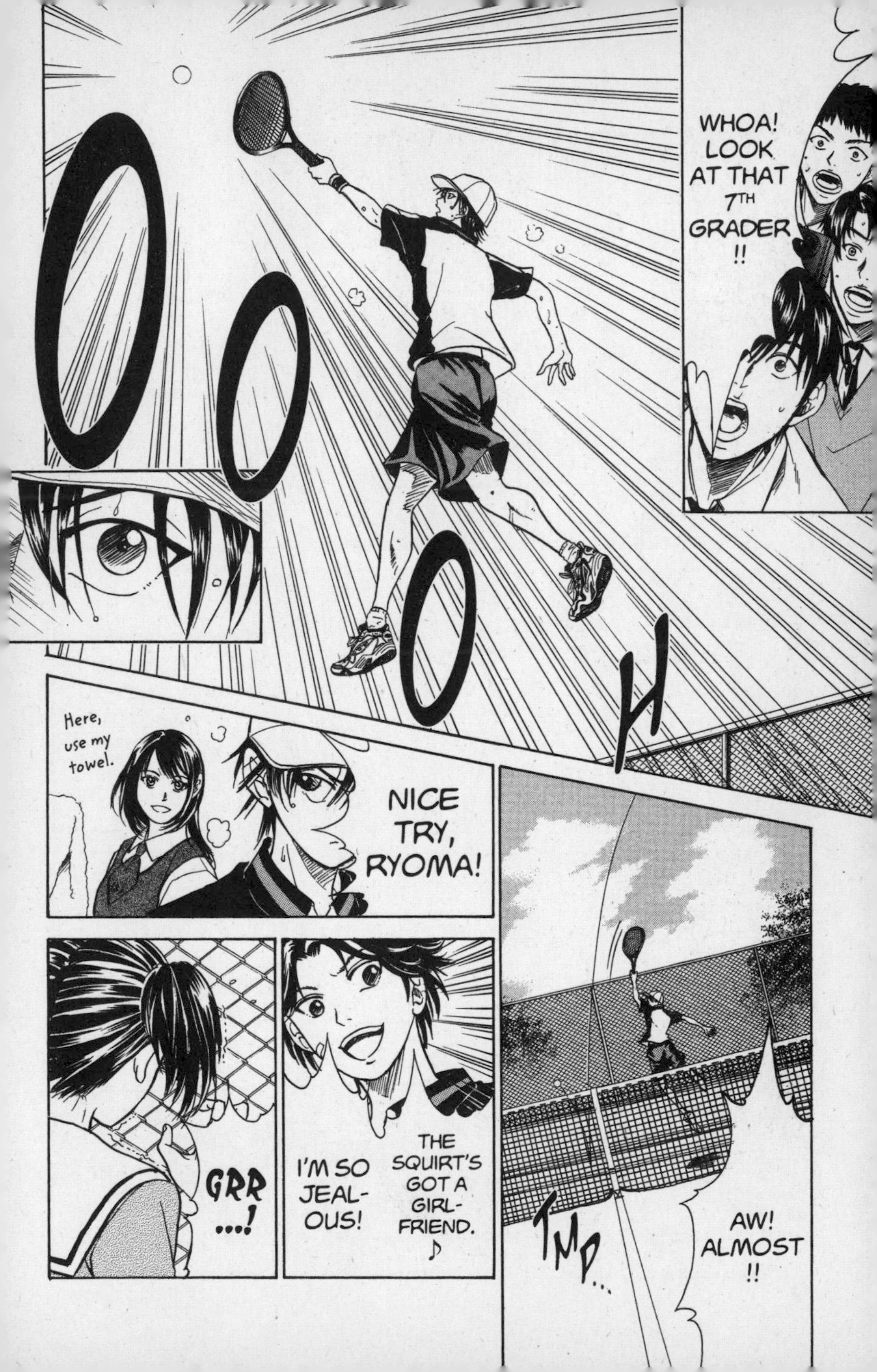
WHOA! LOOK AT THAT 7TH GRADER!!
OOOOH
AW! ALMOST!!
TMP...
NICE TRY, RYOMA!
Here, use my towel.
THE SQUIRT'S GOT A GIRLFRIEND. ♪
I'M SO JEALOUS!
GRR...!

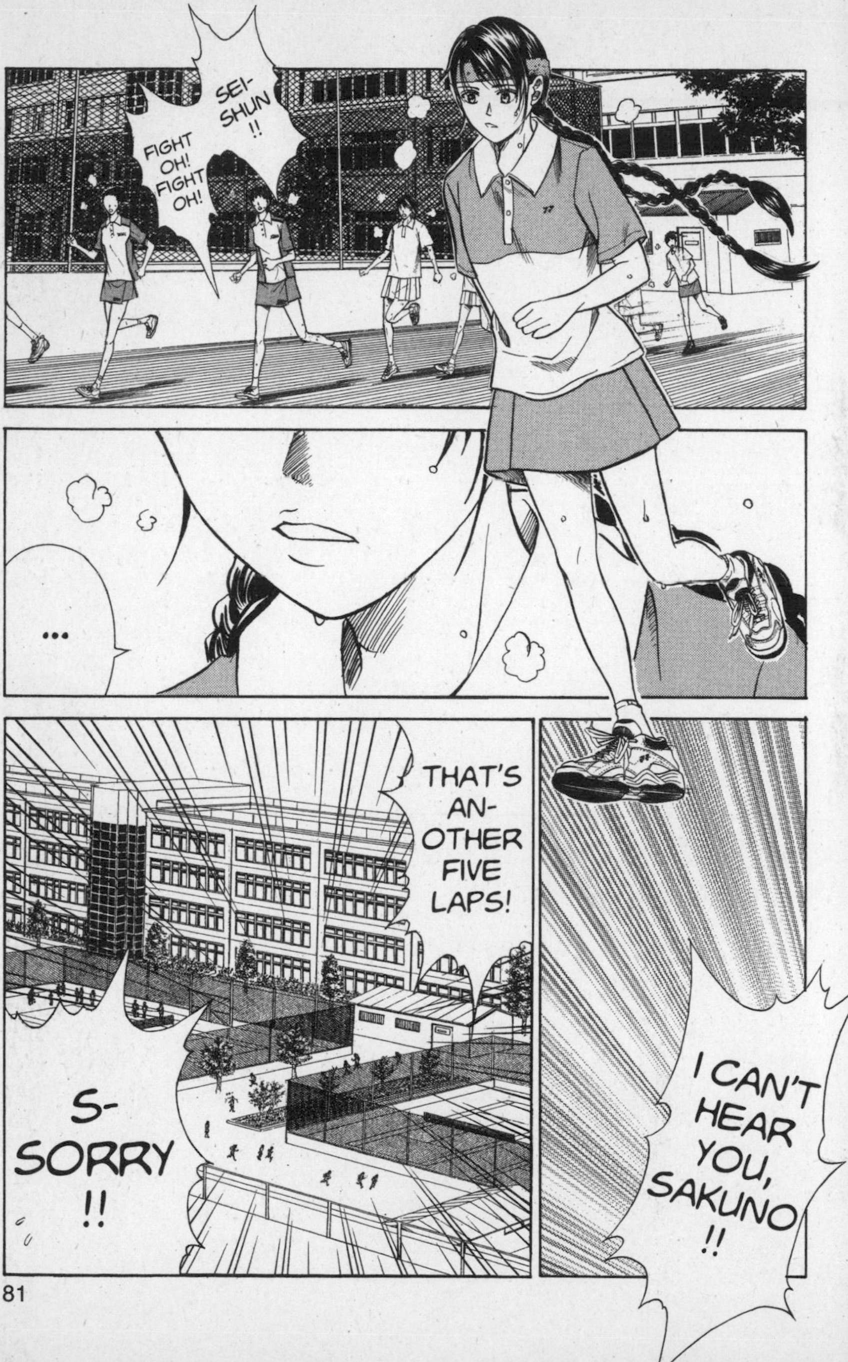
SEI-SHUN!!
FIGHT OH! FIGHT OH!
...
I CAN'T HEAR YOU, SAKUNO!!
THAT'S AN-OTHER FIVE LAPS!
S-SORRY!!

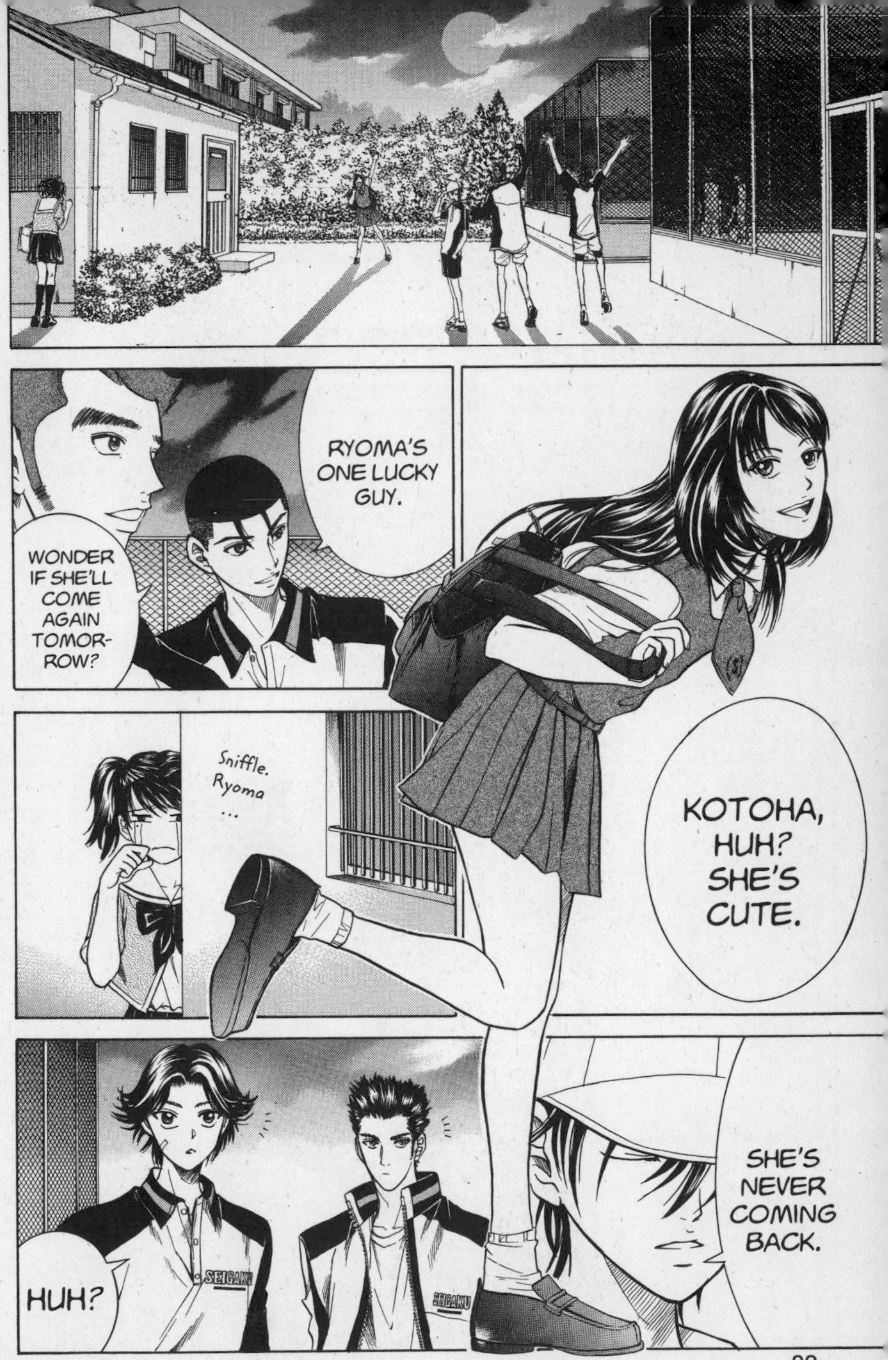
KOTOHA, HUH? SHE'S CUTE.
RYOMA'S ONE LUCKY GUY.
WONDER IF SHE'LL COME AGAIN TOMOR-ROW?
Sniffle. Ryoma ...
SHE'S NEVER COMING BACK.
SEIGAKU
SEIGAKU
HUH?

READ THIS WAY

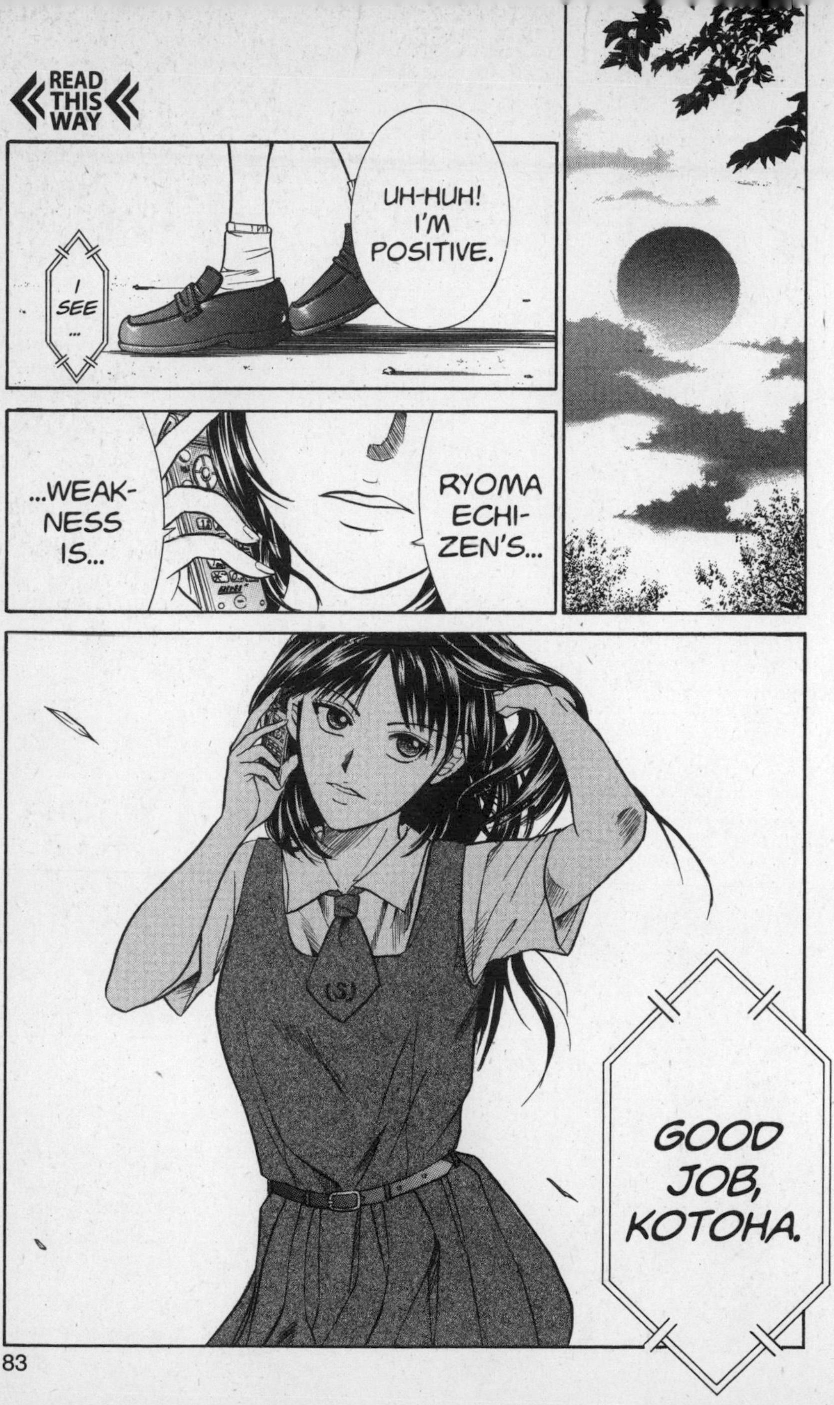
UH-HUH! I'M POSITIVE.
I SEE ...
RYOMA ECHI-ZEN'S...
...WEAK-NESS IS...
GOOD JOB, KOTOHA.

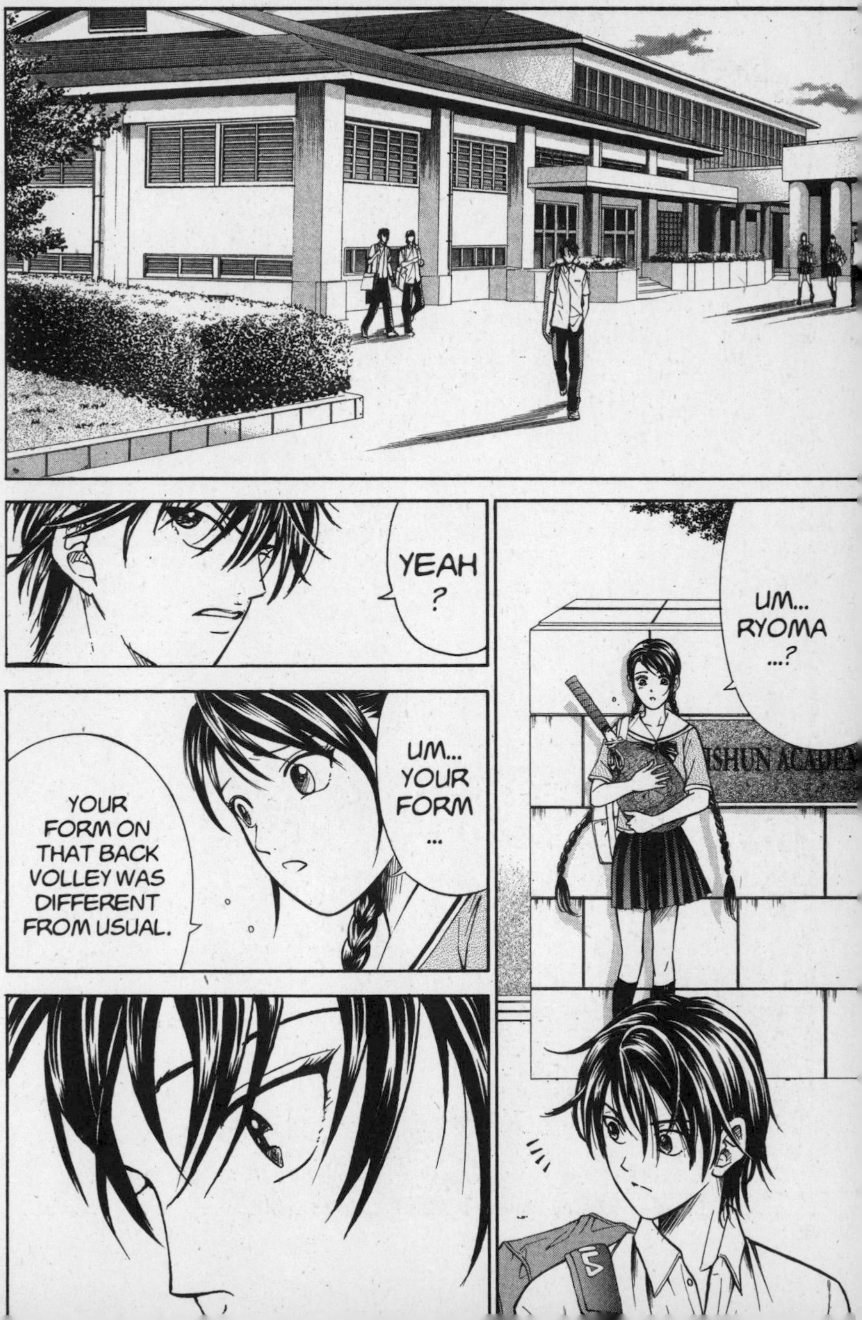
UM... RYOMA ...?
YEAH ?
UM... YOUR FORM ...
YOUR FORM ON THAT BACK VOLLEY WAS DIFFERENT FROM USUAL.

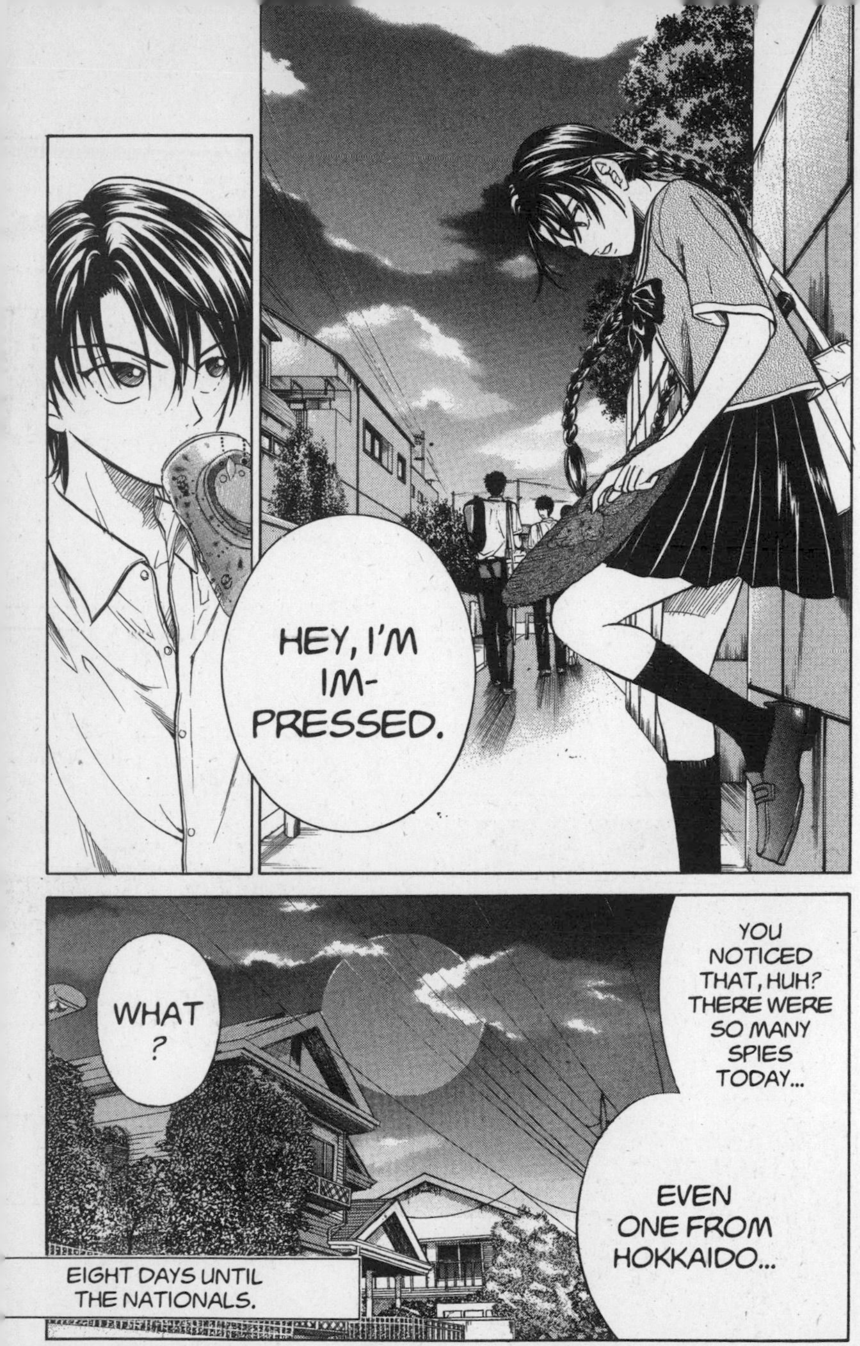
HEY, I'M IM-PRESSED.
WHAT?
YOU NOTICED THAT, HUH? THERE WERE SO MANY SPIES TODAY...
EVEN ONE FROM HOKKAIDO...
EIGHT DAYS UNTIL THE NATIONALS.

テニスの王子様

THE PRINCE OF TENNIS

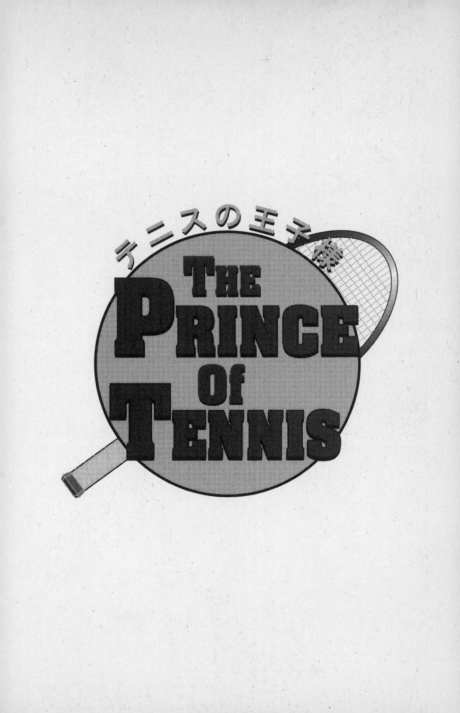

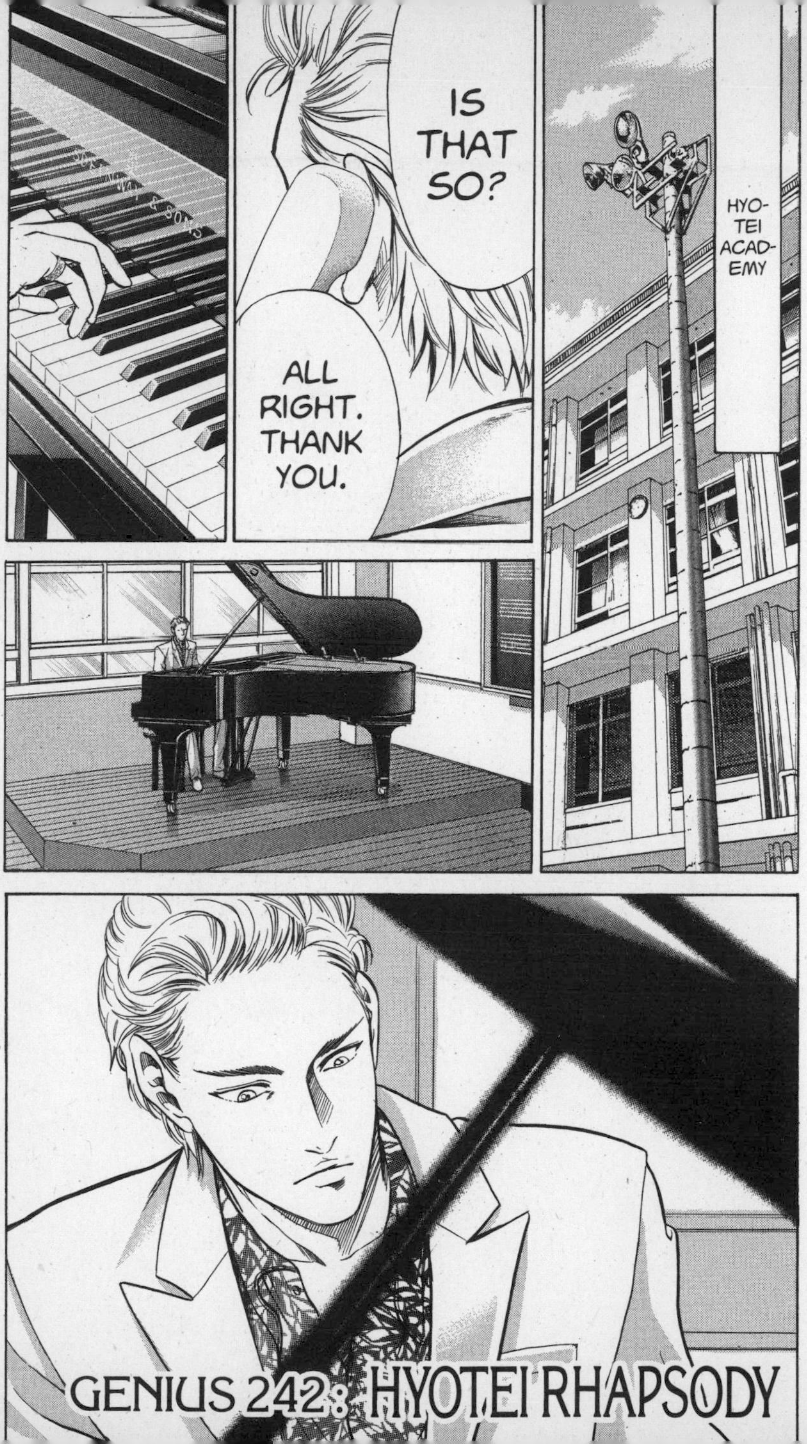
HYOTEI ACADEMY
IS THAT SO?
ALL RIGHT. THANK YOU.
GENIUS 242: HYOTEI RHAPSODY

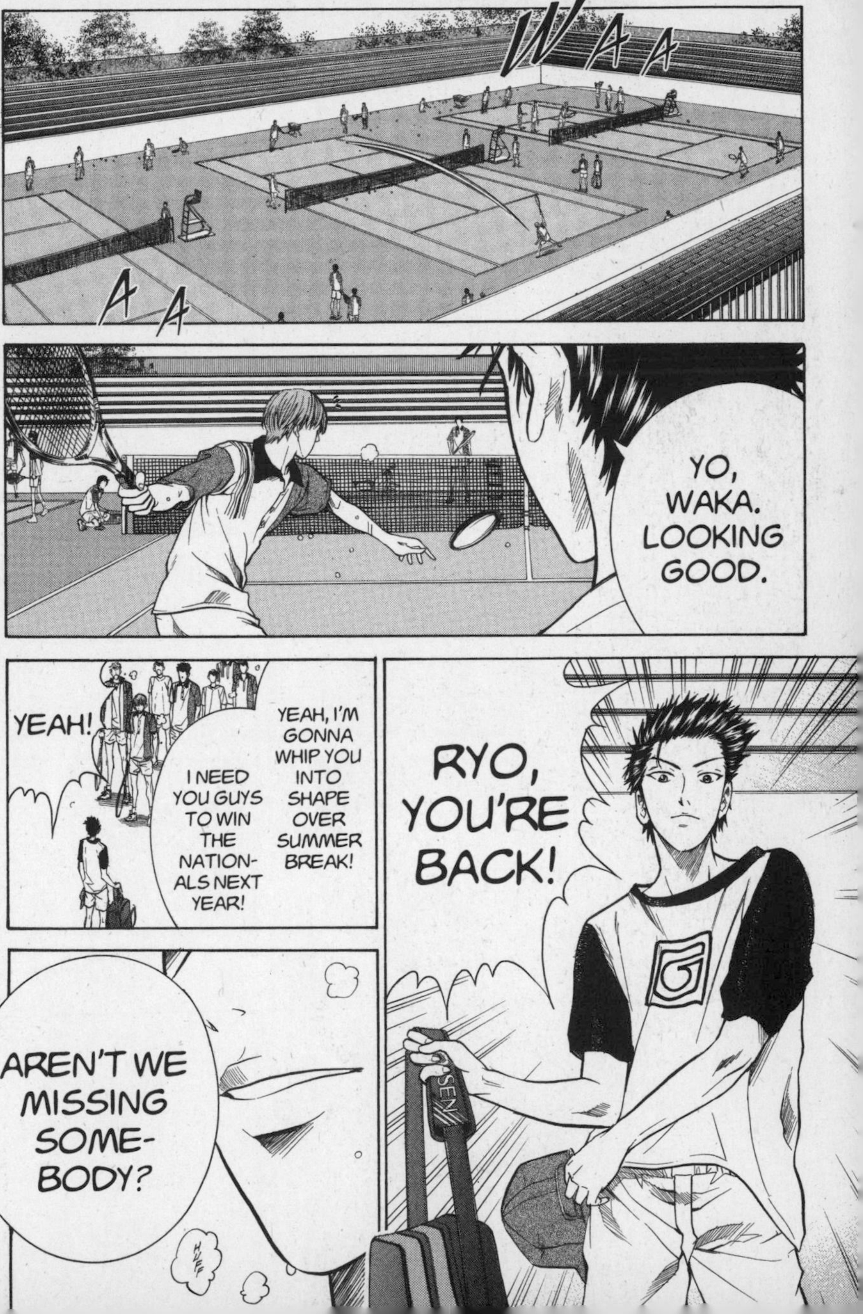
WAAAA
YO, WAKA. LOOKING GOOD.
RYO, YOU'RE BACK!
YEAH, I'M GONNA WHIP YOU INTO SHAPE OVER SUMMER BREAK!
I NEED YOU GUYS TO WIN THE NATION-ALS NEXT YEAR!
YEAH!
AREN'T WE MISSING SOME-BODY?

GENIUS 242: HYOTEI RHAPSODY

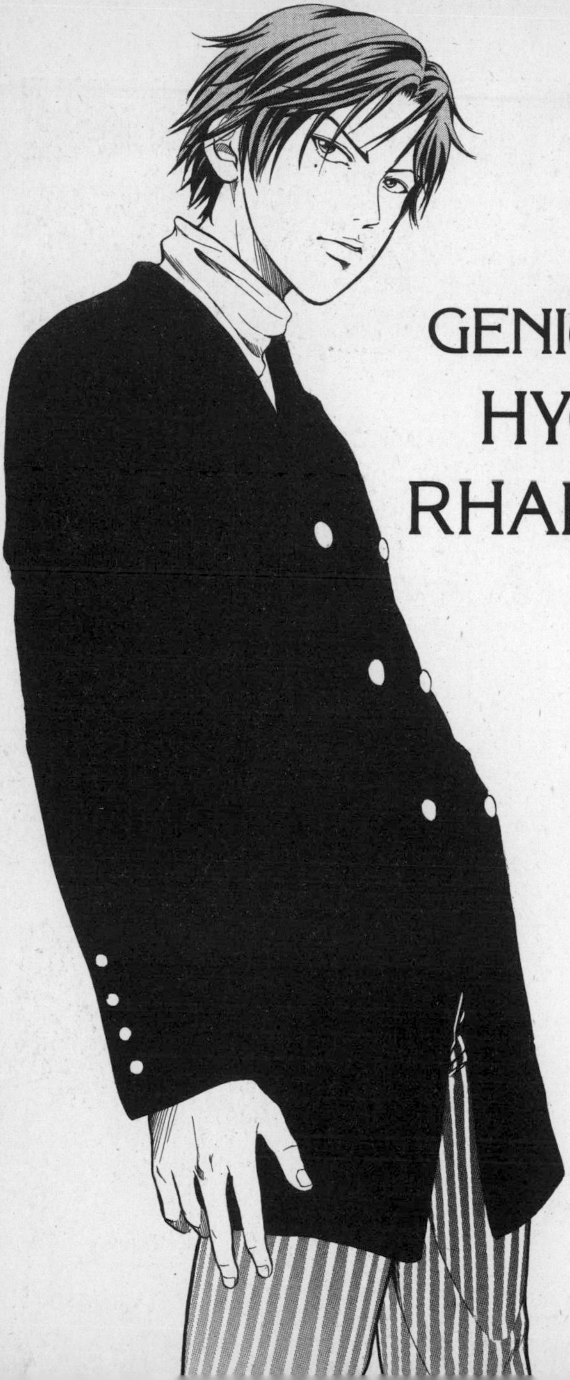

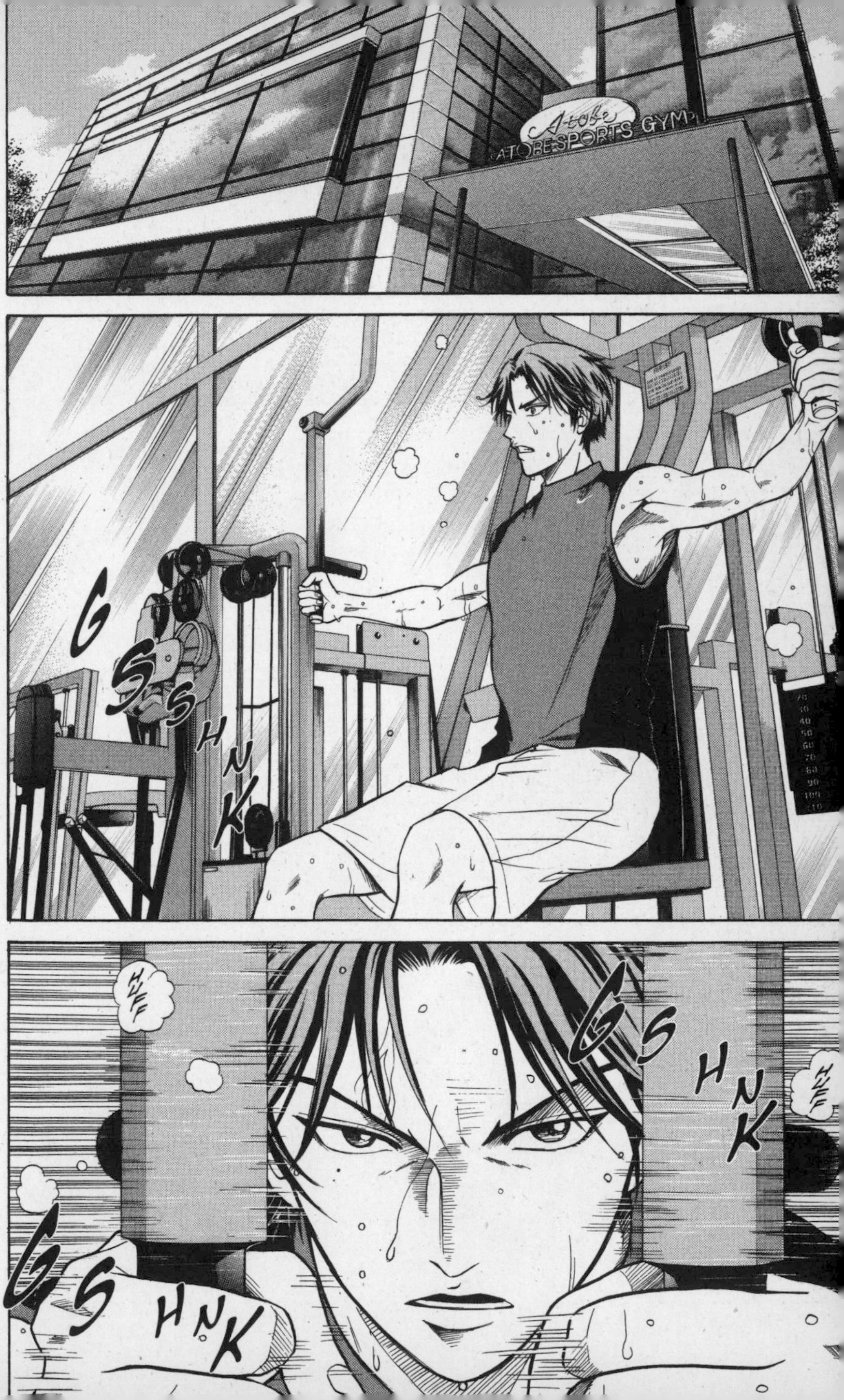

Atobe
ATOBE SPORTS GYM
GSHNK
HUFF
GSHNK
HUFF
GSHNK

READ THIS WAY

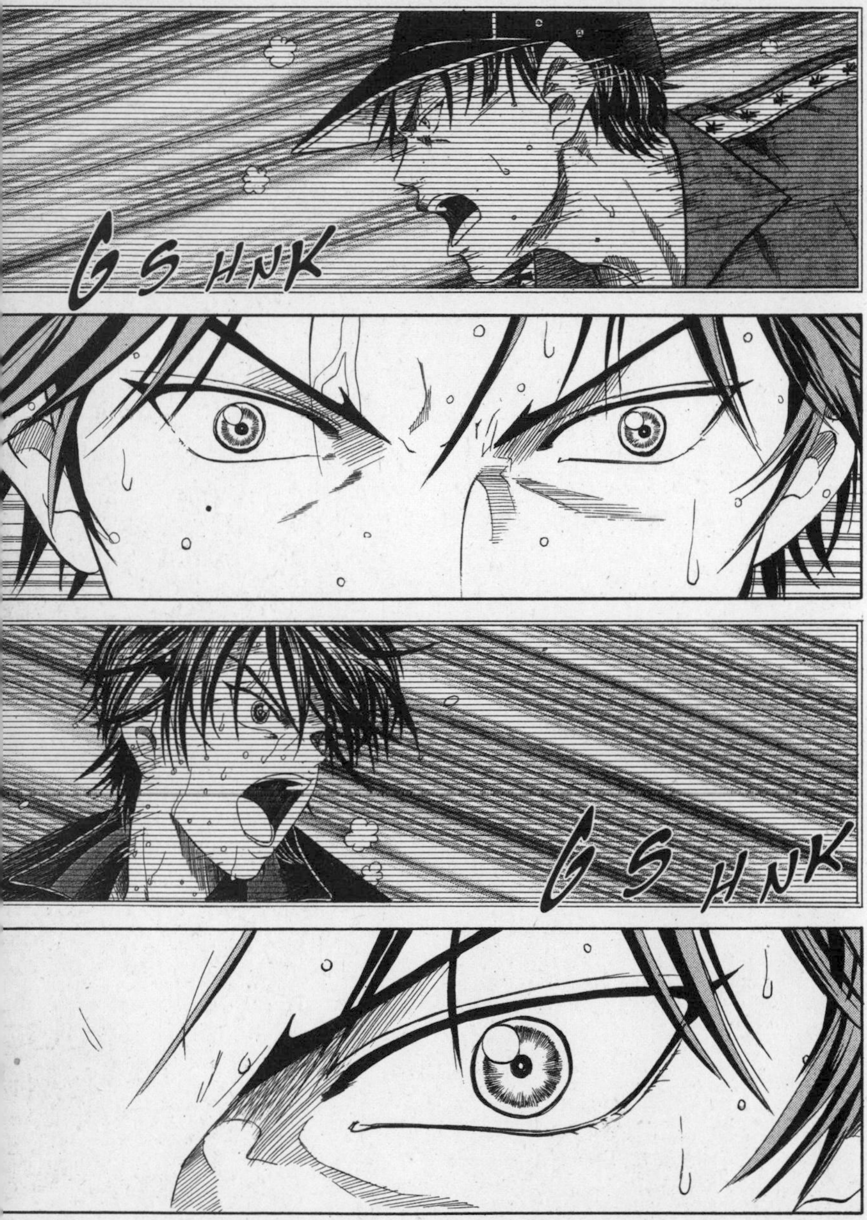
GSHNK
GSHNK

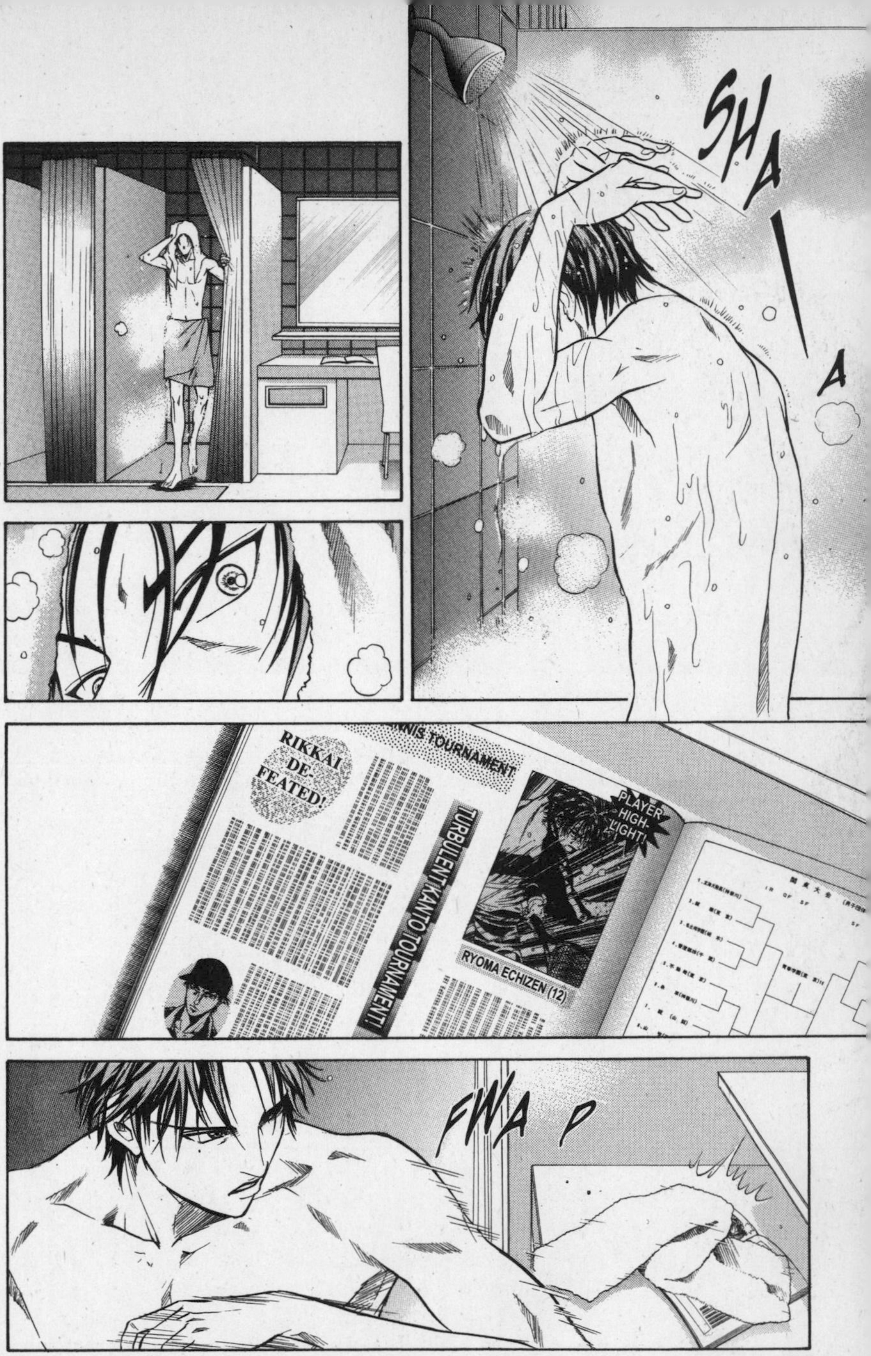
SHAA
NNIS TOURNAMENT
RIKKAI DE-FEATED!
TURBULENT KANTO TOURNAMENT!
PLAYER HIGH-LIGHT!
RYOMA ECHIZEN (12)
FWAP

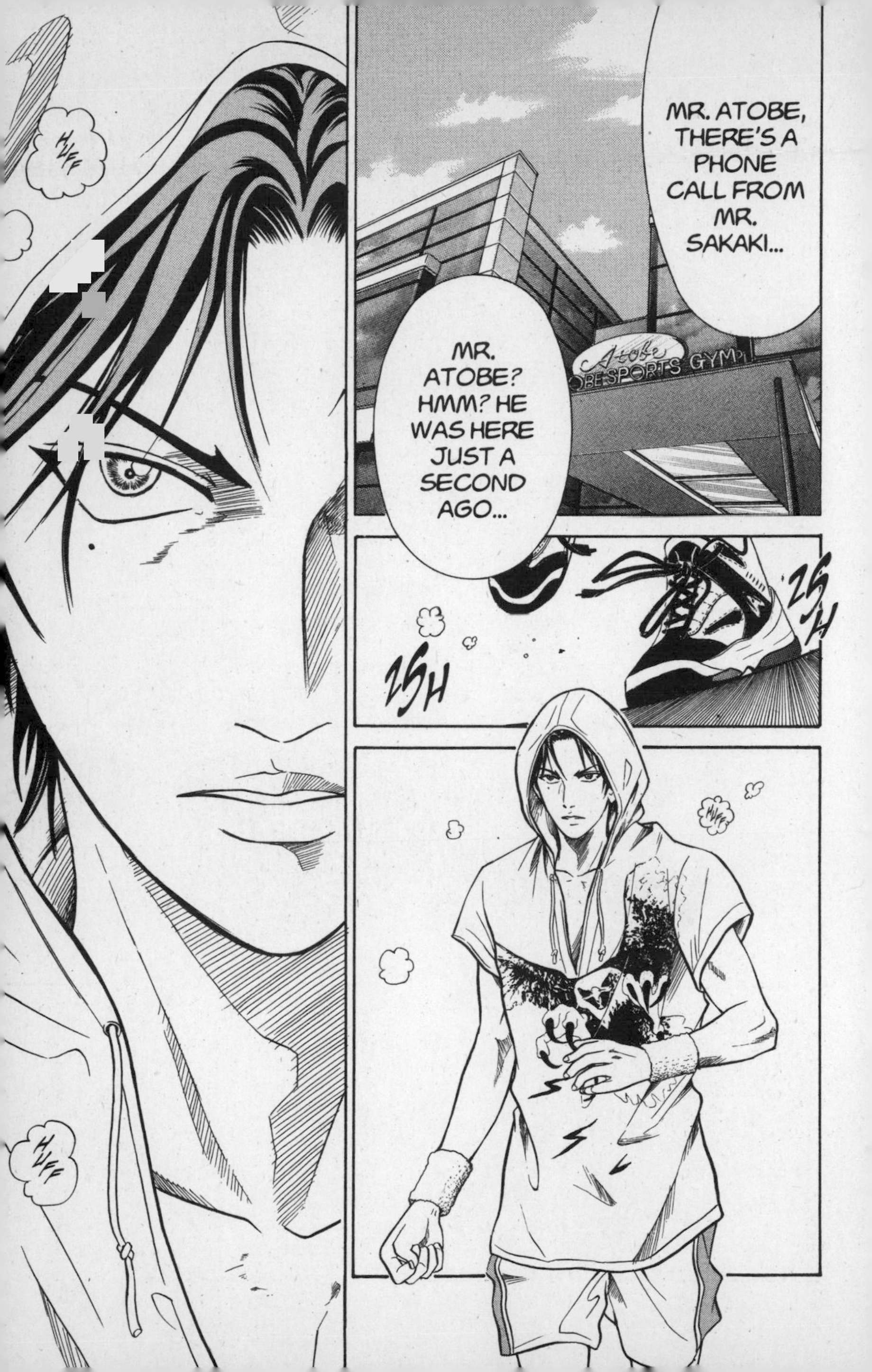
MR. ATOBE, THERE'S A PHONE CALL FROM MR. SAKAKI...
MR. ATOBE? HMM? HE WAS HERE JUST A SECOND AGO...
Atobe
OBE SPORTS GYM
ZSH
ZSH
HUFF
HUFF
HUFF

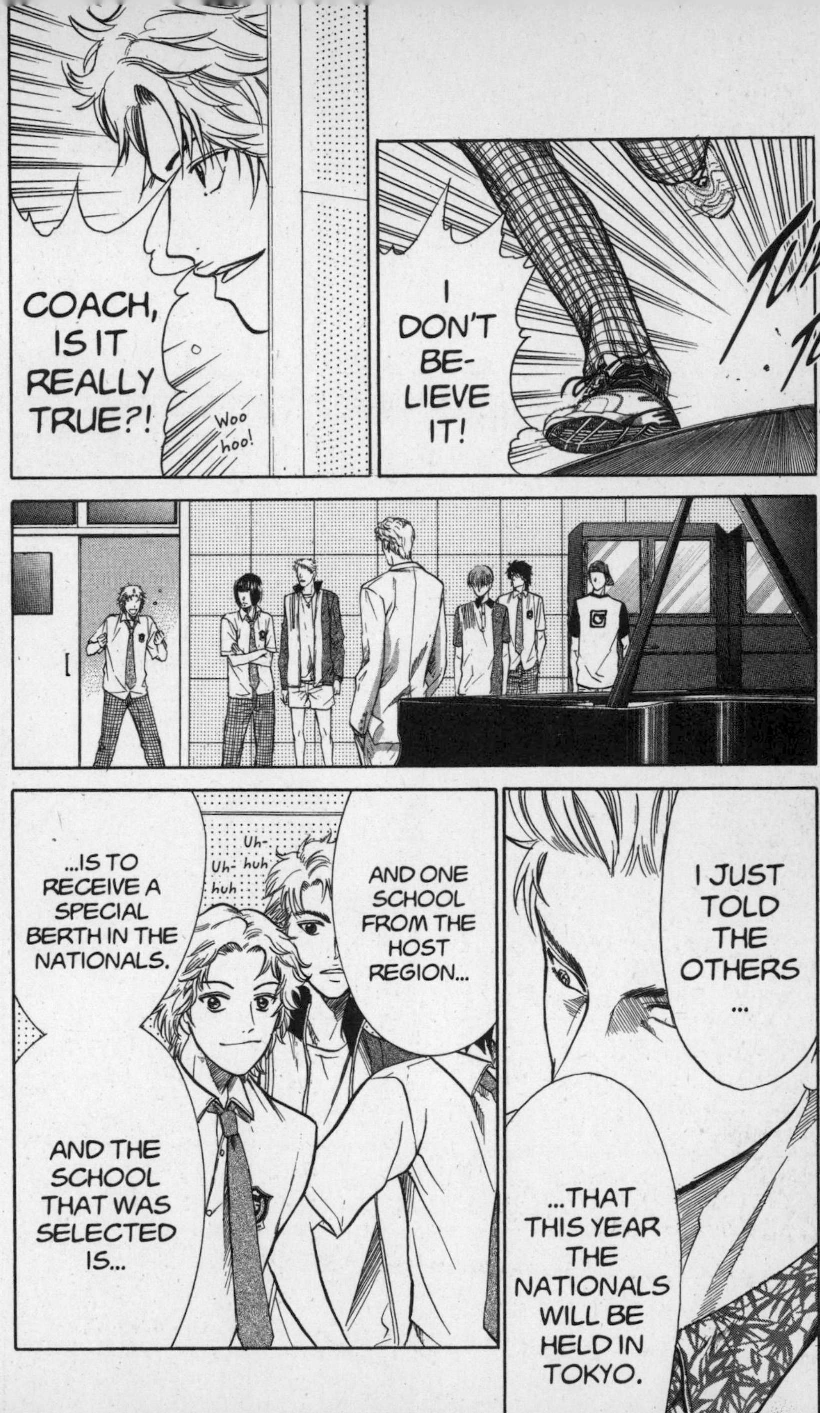
TUD TUD
I DON'T BE-LIEVE IT!
COACH, IS IT REALLY TRUE?!
Woo hoo!
I JUST TOLD THE OTHERS ...
...THAT THIS YEAR THE NATIONALS WILL BE HELD IN TOKYO.
AND ONE SCHOOL FROM THE HOST REGION...
Uh-huh Uh-huh
...IS TO RECEIVE A SPECIAL BERTH IN THE NATIONALS.
AND THE SCHOOL THAT WAS SELECTED IS...

READ THIS WAY

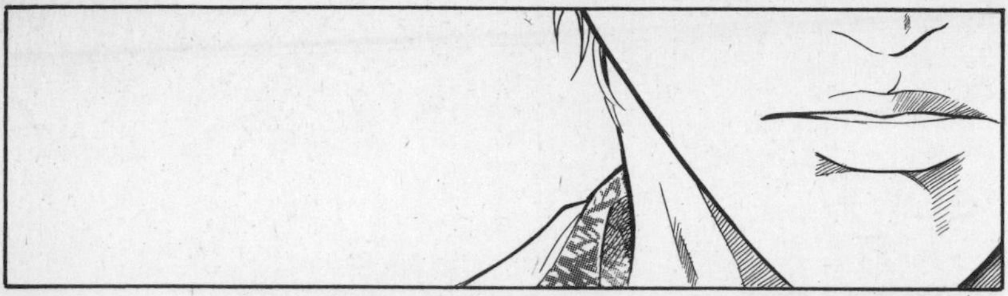

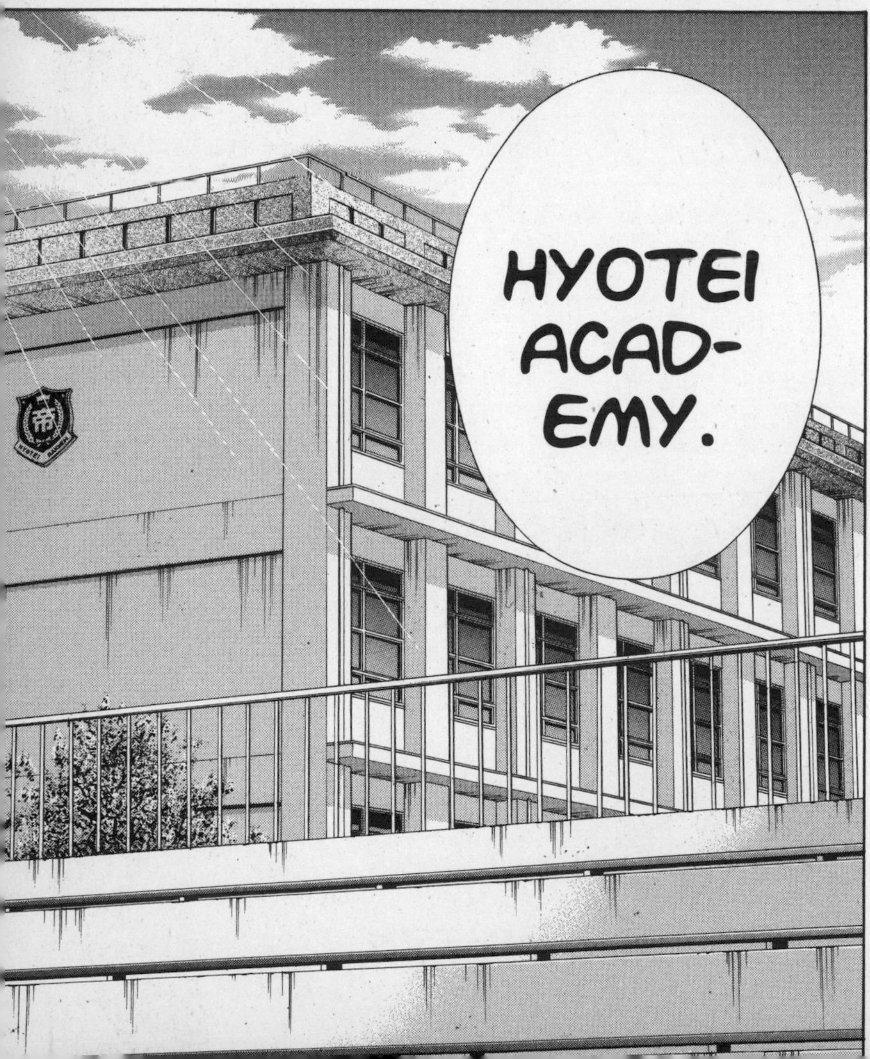
HYOTEI ACAD-EMY.

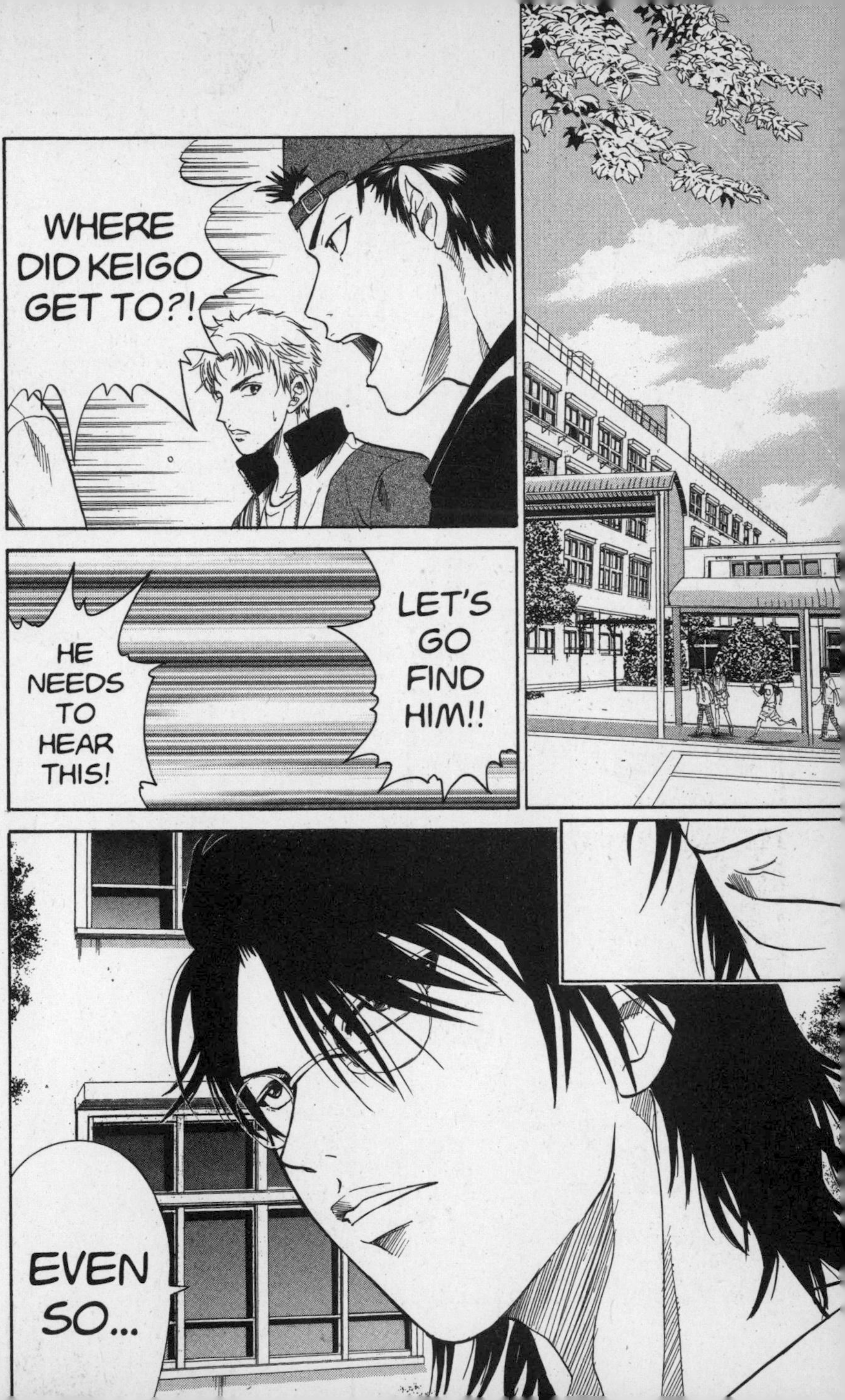
WHERE DID KEIGO GET TO?!
LET'S GO FIND HIM!!
HE NEEDS TO HEAR THIS!
EVEN SO...

READ THIS WAY

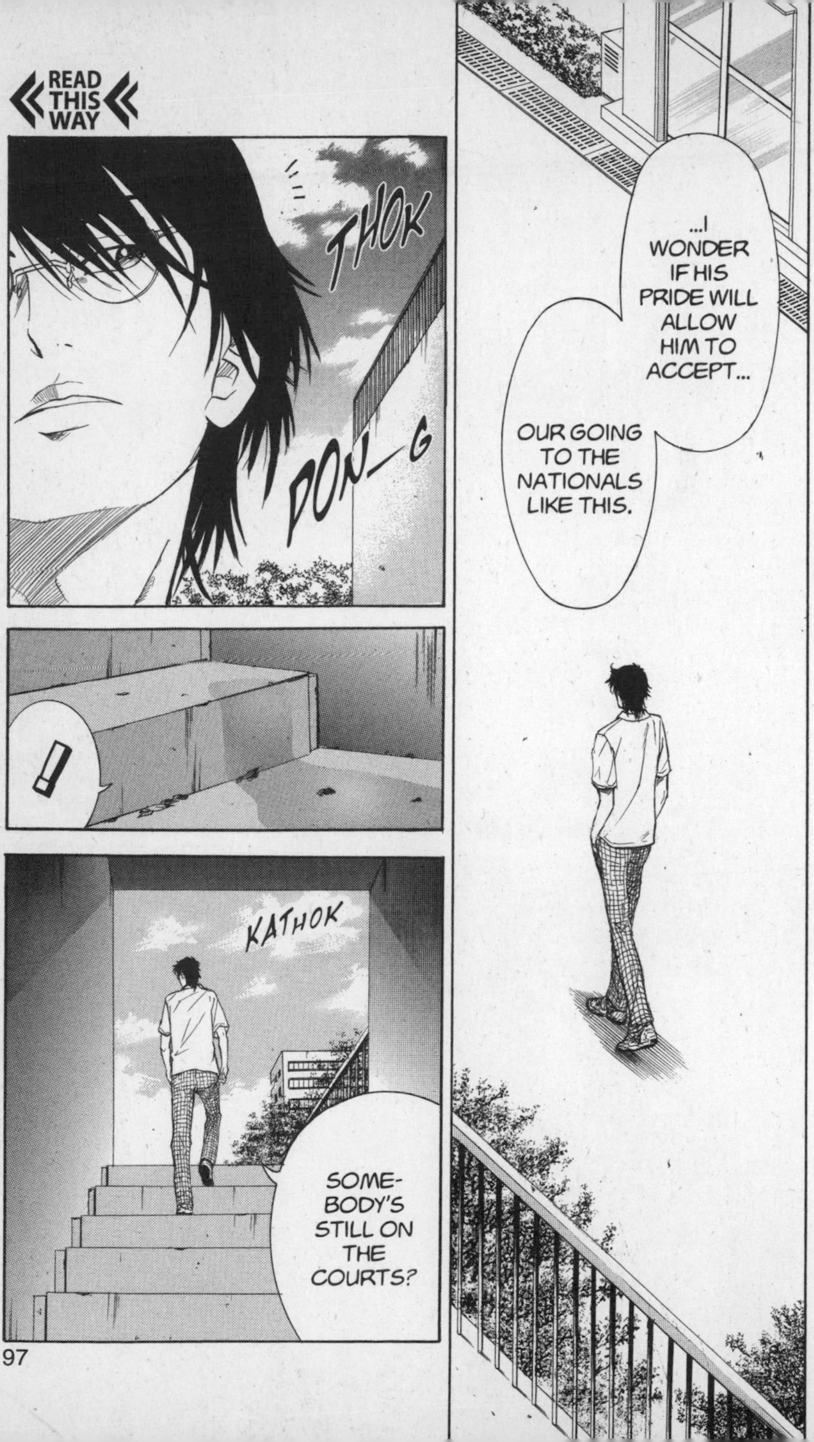
...I WONDER IF HIS PRIDE WILL ALLOW HIM TO ACCEPT...
OUR GOING TO THE NATIONALS LIKE THIS.
THOK
DON—G
!
KATHOK
SOME-BODY'S STILL ON THE COURTS?

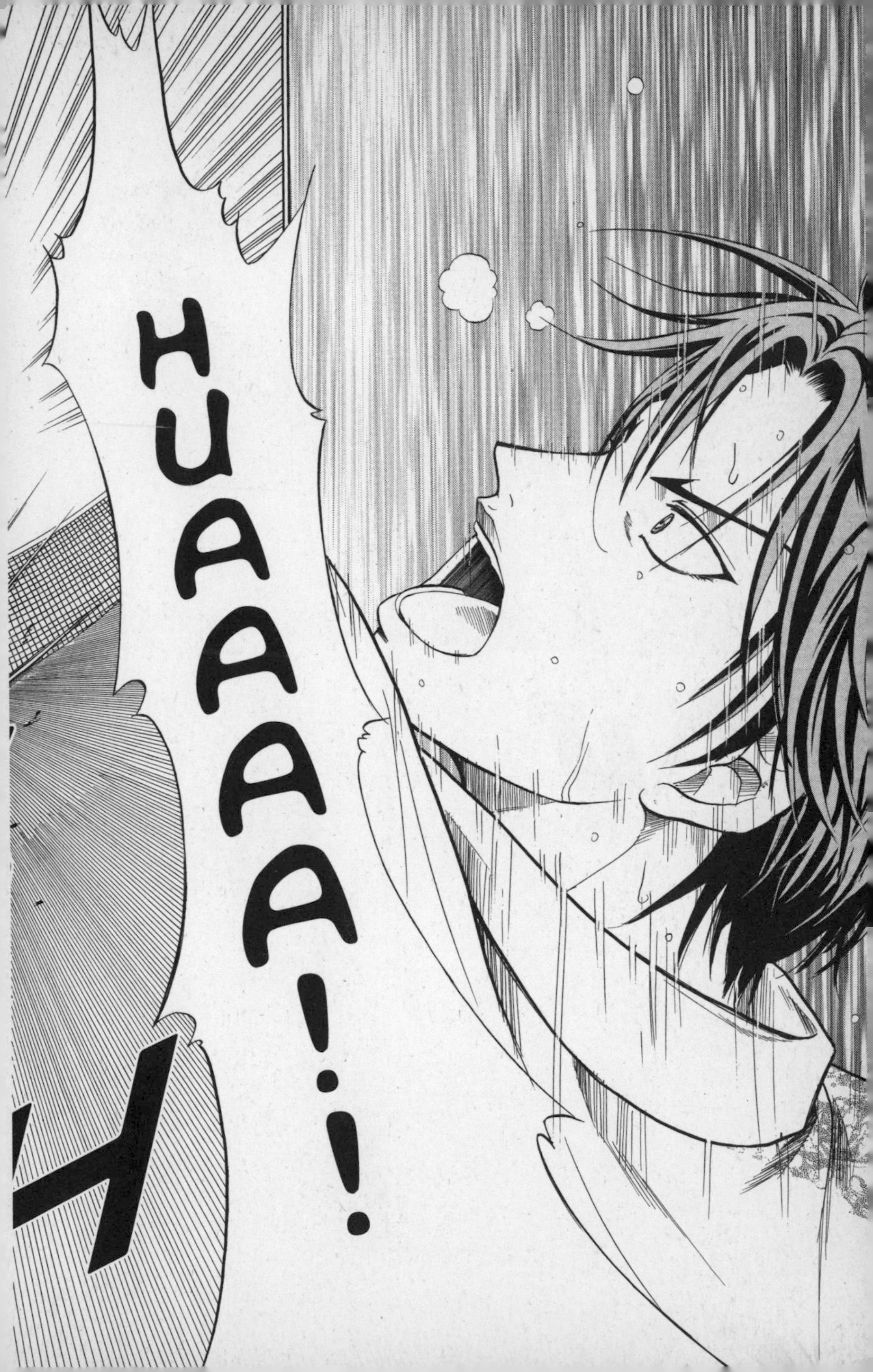
HUAAAA!!!

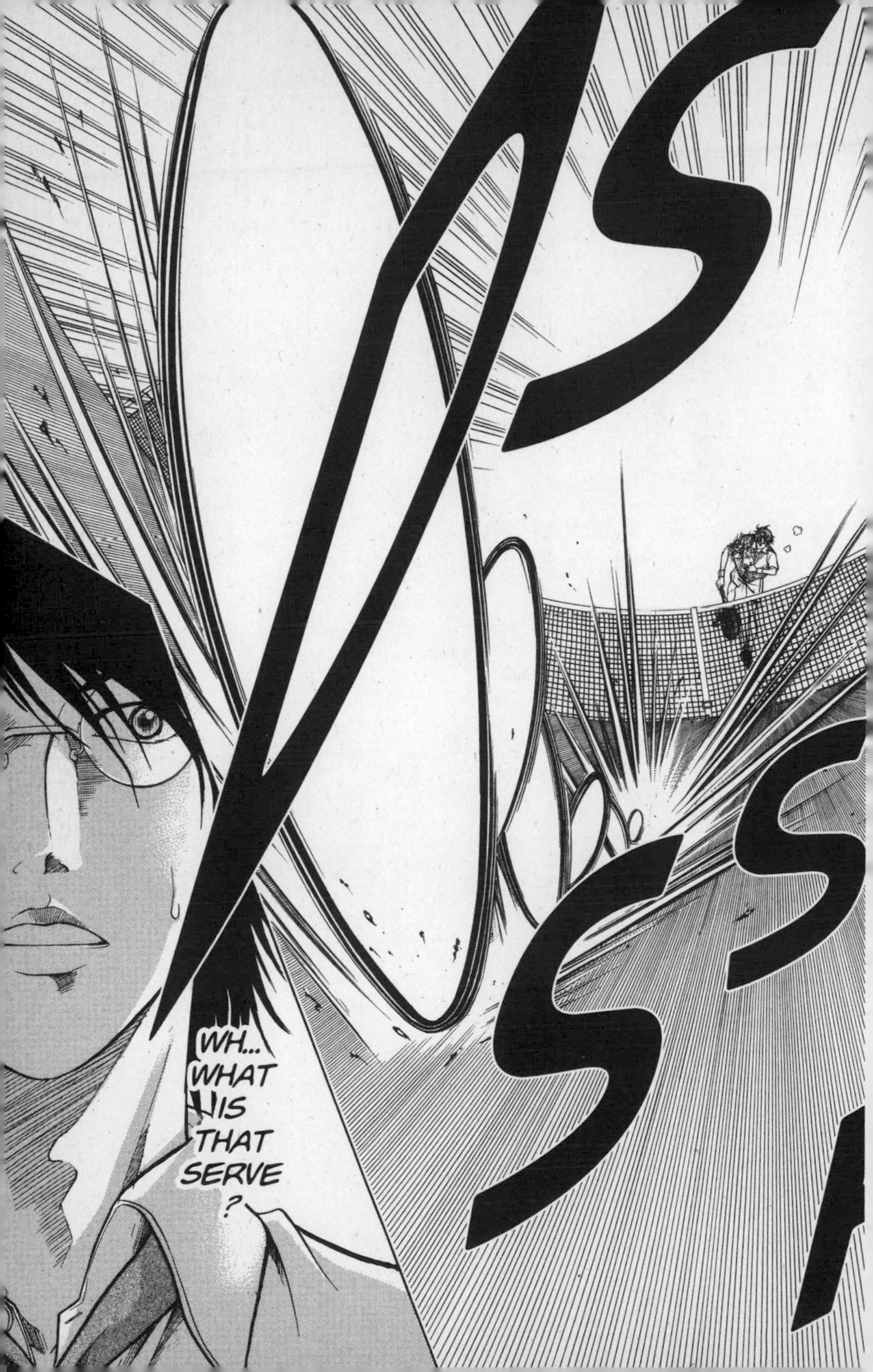
WH... WHAT IS THAT SERVE?

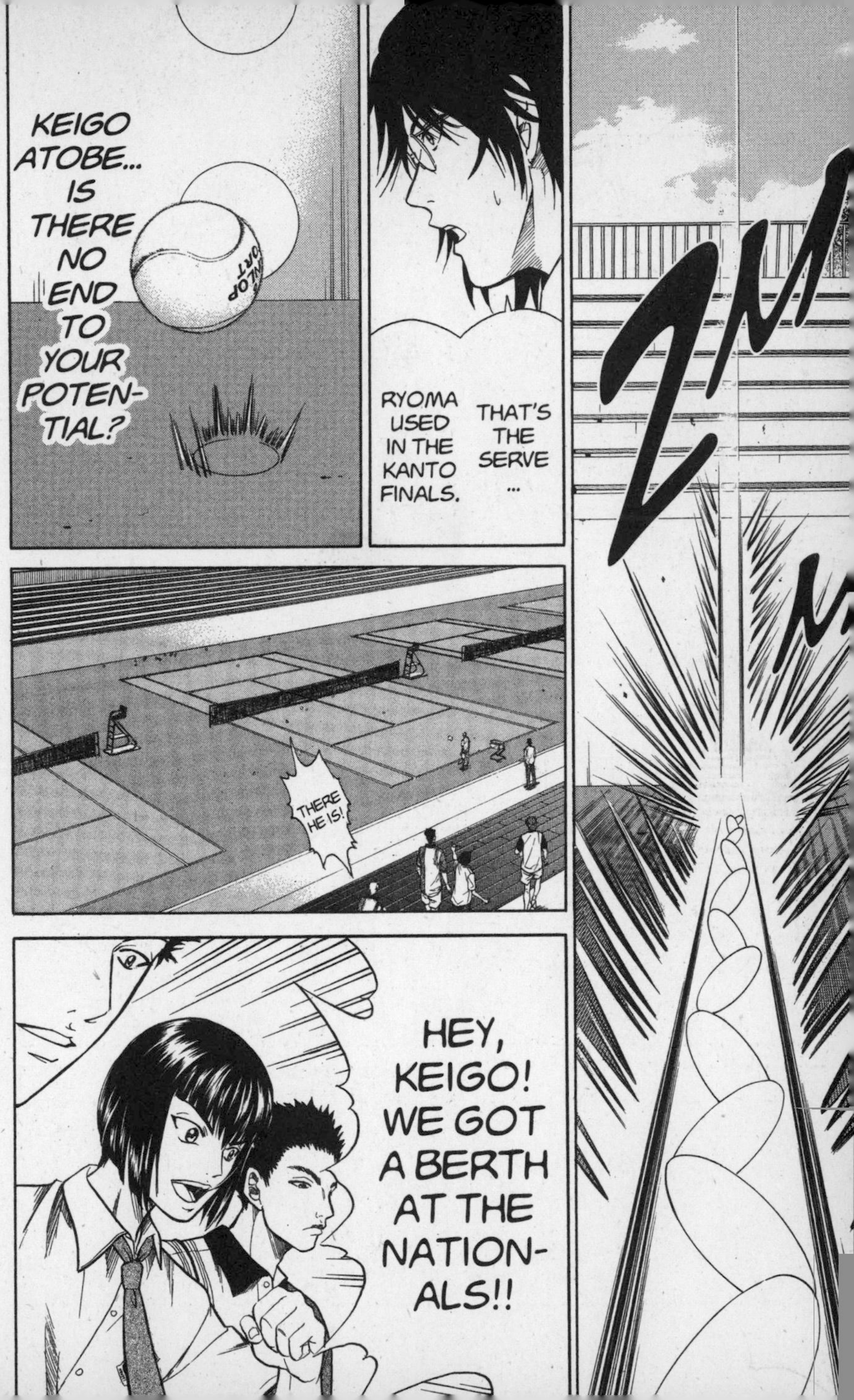

ZM
THAT'S THE SERVE ...
RYOMA USED IN THE KANTO FINALS.
KEIGO ATOBE... IS THERE NO END TO YOUR POTENTIAL?
THERE HE IS!
HEY, KEIGO! WE GOT A BERTH AT THE NATIONALS!!

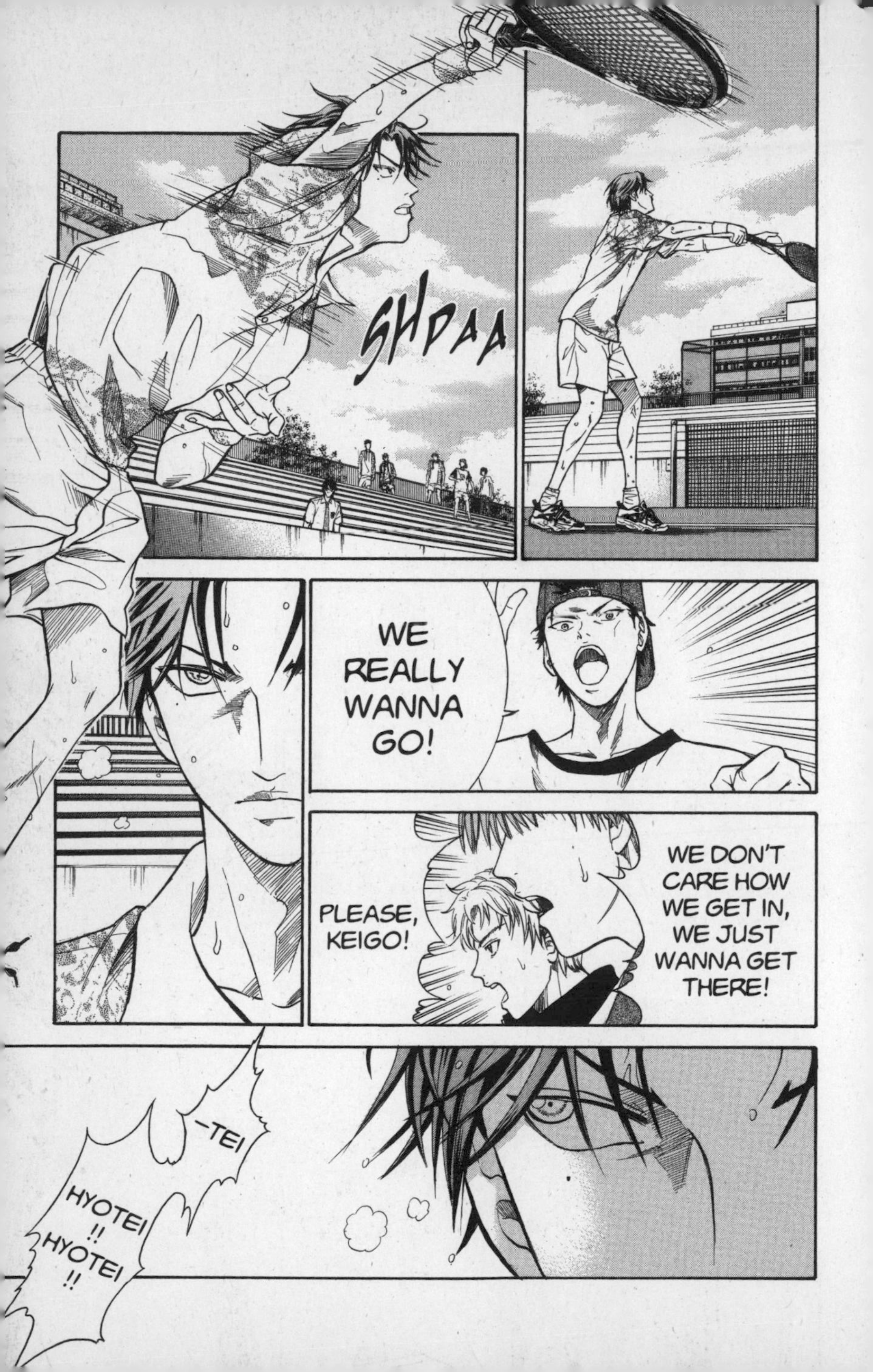
SHDAA
WE REALLY WANNA GO!
WE DON'T CARE HOW WE GET IN, WE JUST WANNA GET THERE!
PLEASE, KEIGO!
—TEI
HYOTEI!! HYOTEI!!

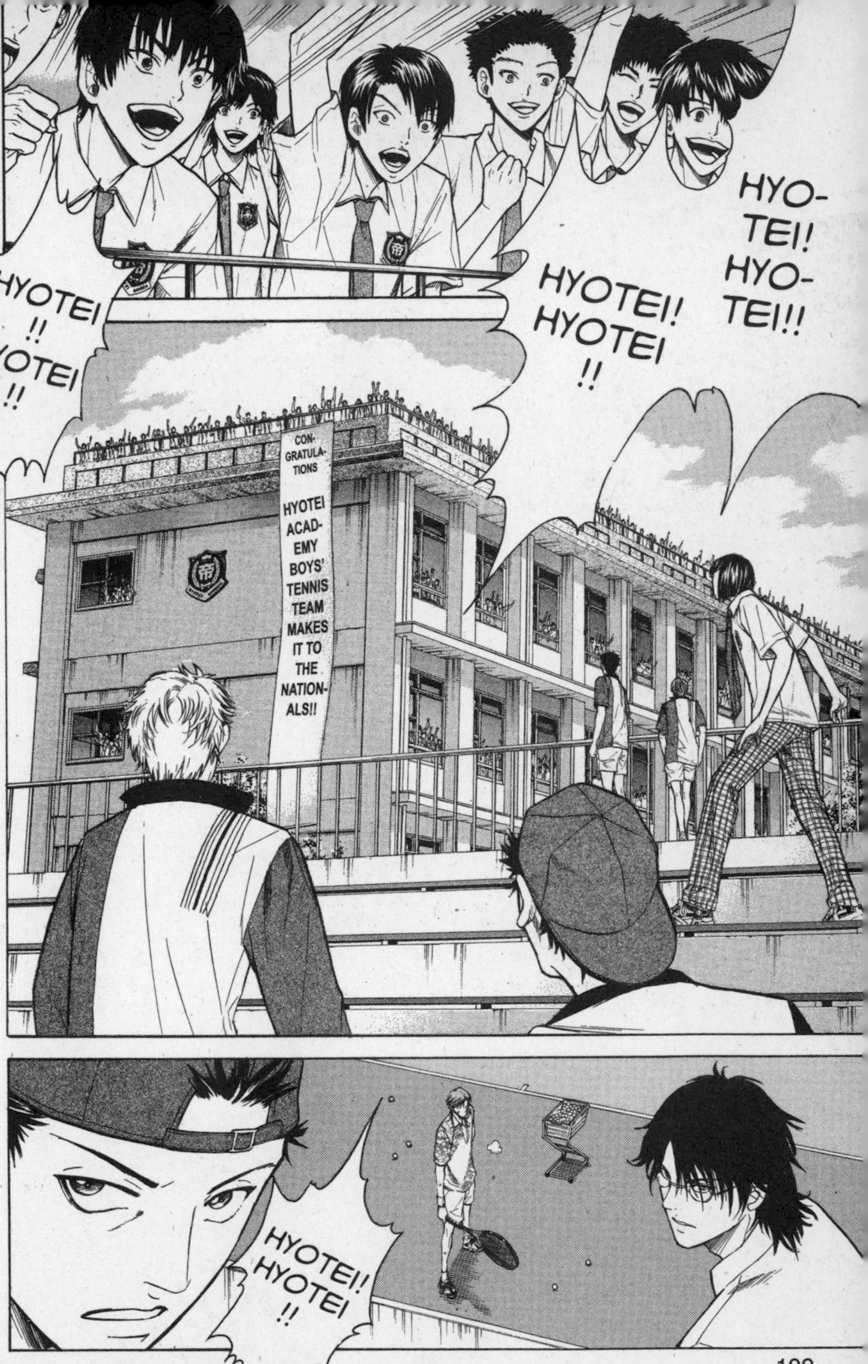
HYO-TEI! HYO-TEI!!
HYOTEI! HYOTEI !!
HYOTEI !! HYOTEI !!
CONGRATULATIONS
HYOTEI ACADEMY BOYS' TENNIS TEAM MAKES IT TO THE NATIONALS!!
HYOTEI! HYOTEI !!

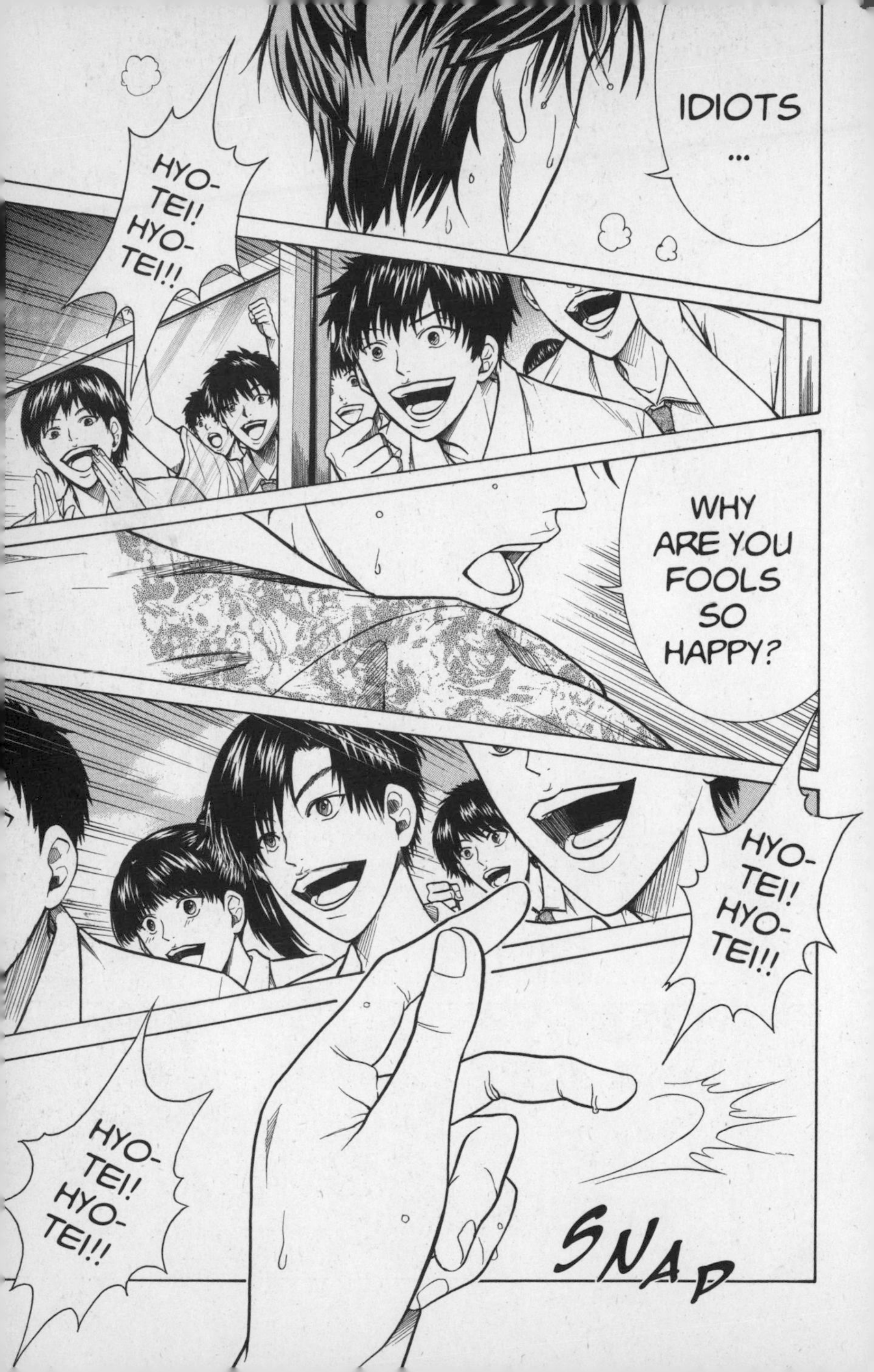

IDIOTS ...
HYO-TEI! HYO-TEI!!
WHY ARE YOU FOOLS SO HAPPY?
HYO-TEI! HYO-TEI!!
HYO-TEI! HYO-TEI!!
SNAP

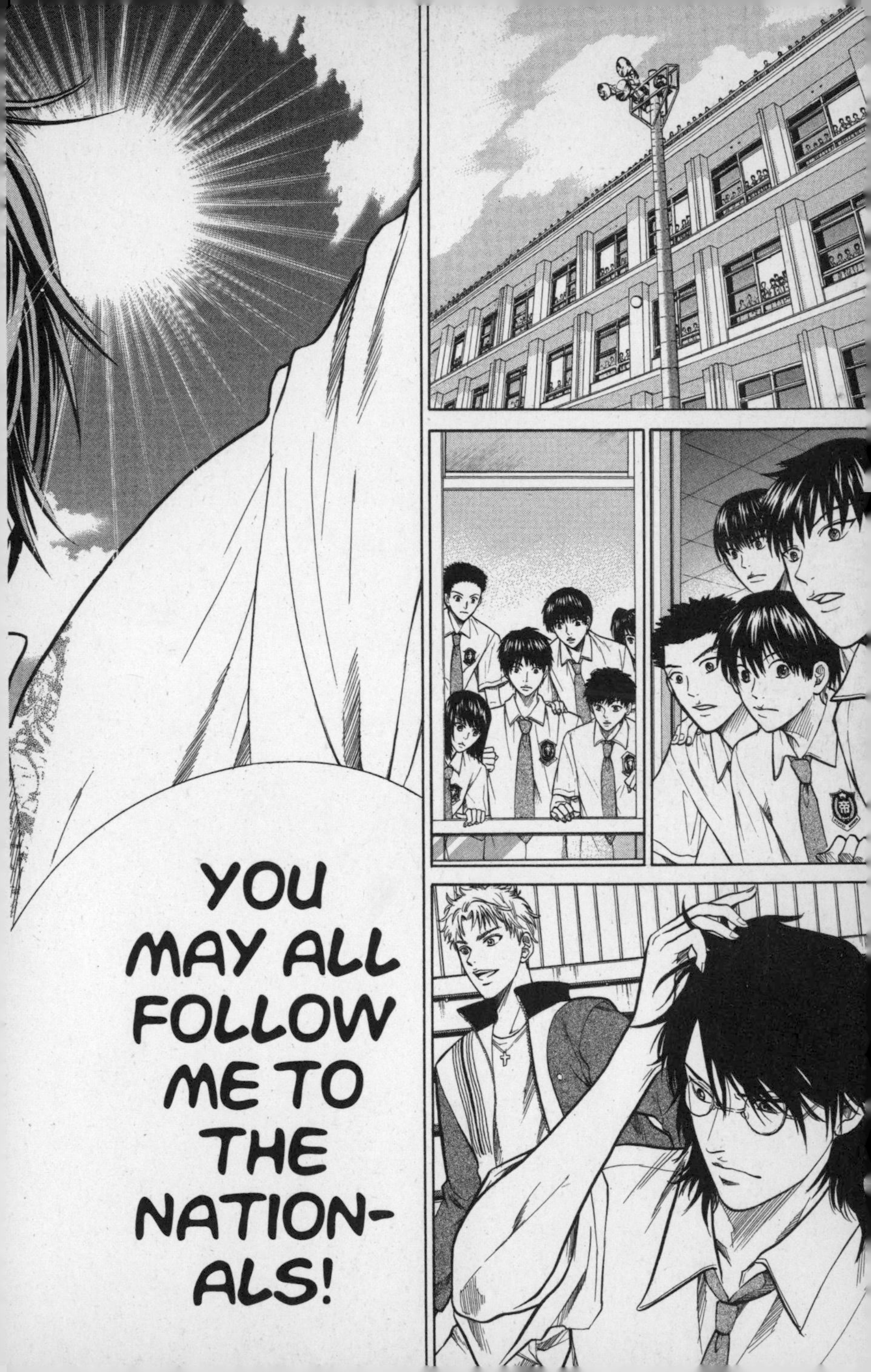
YOU MAY ALL FOLLOW ME TO THE NATION-ALS!

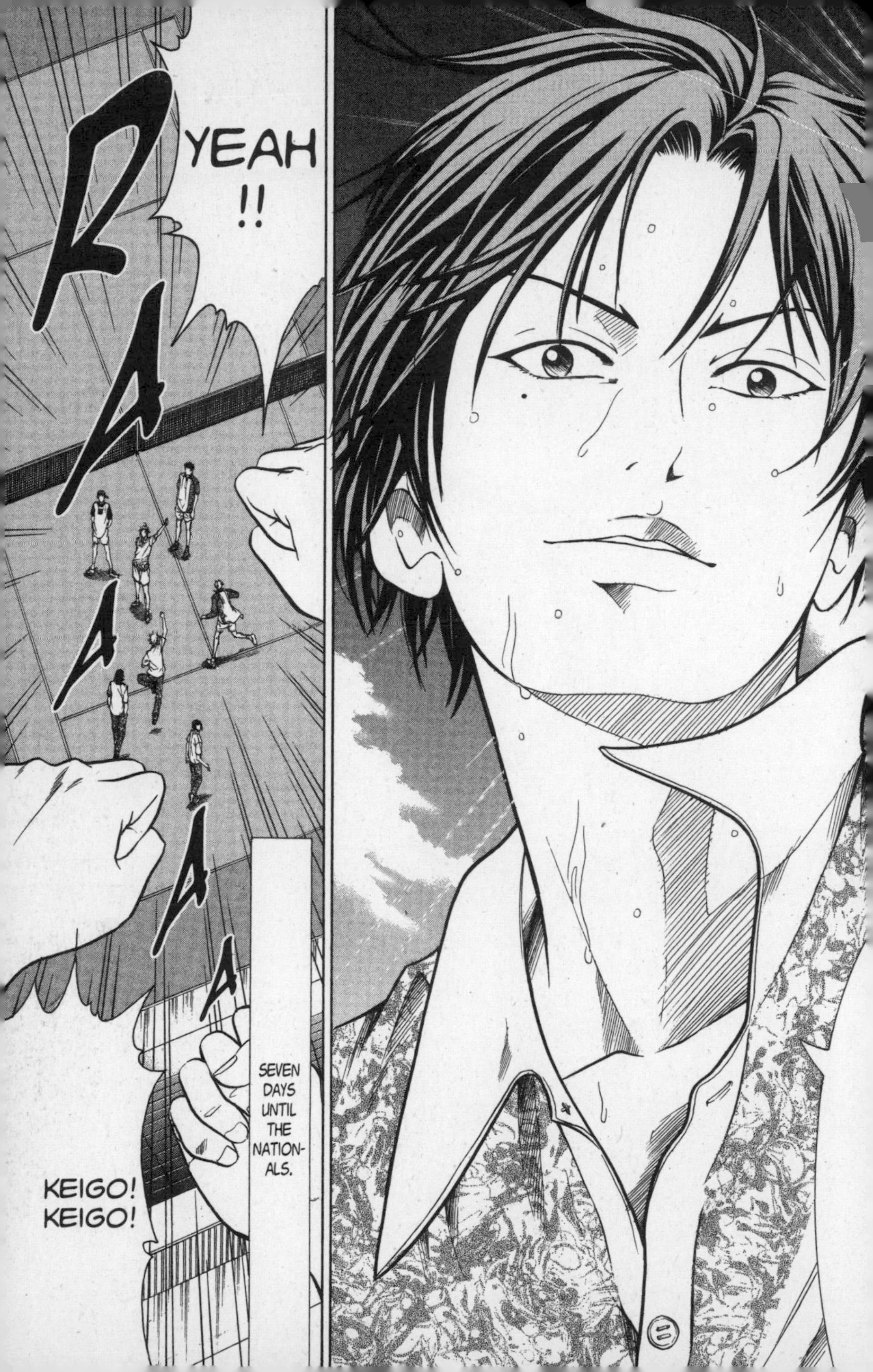
YEAH !!
SEVEN DAYS UNTIL THE NATION-ALS.
KEIGO! KEIGO!

帝

HYOTEI GAKUEN

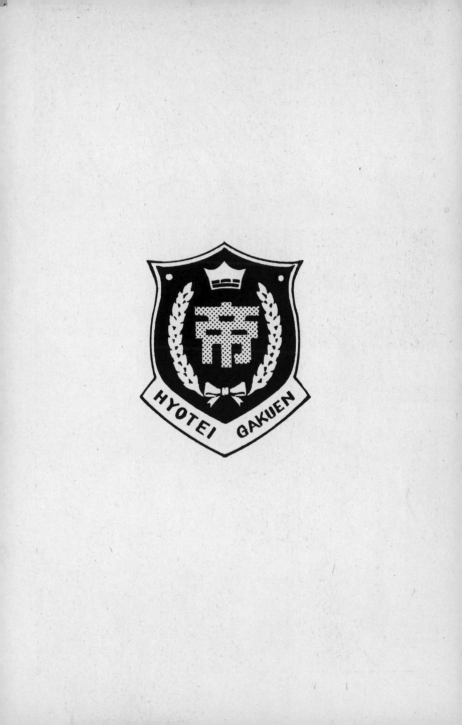

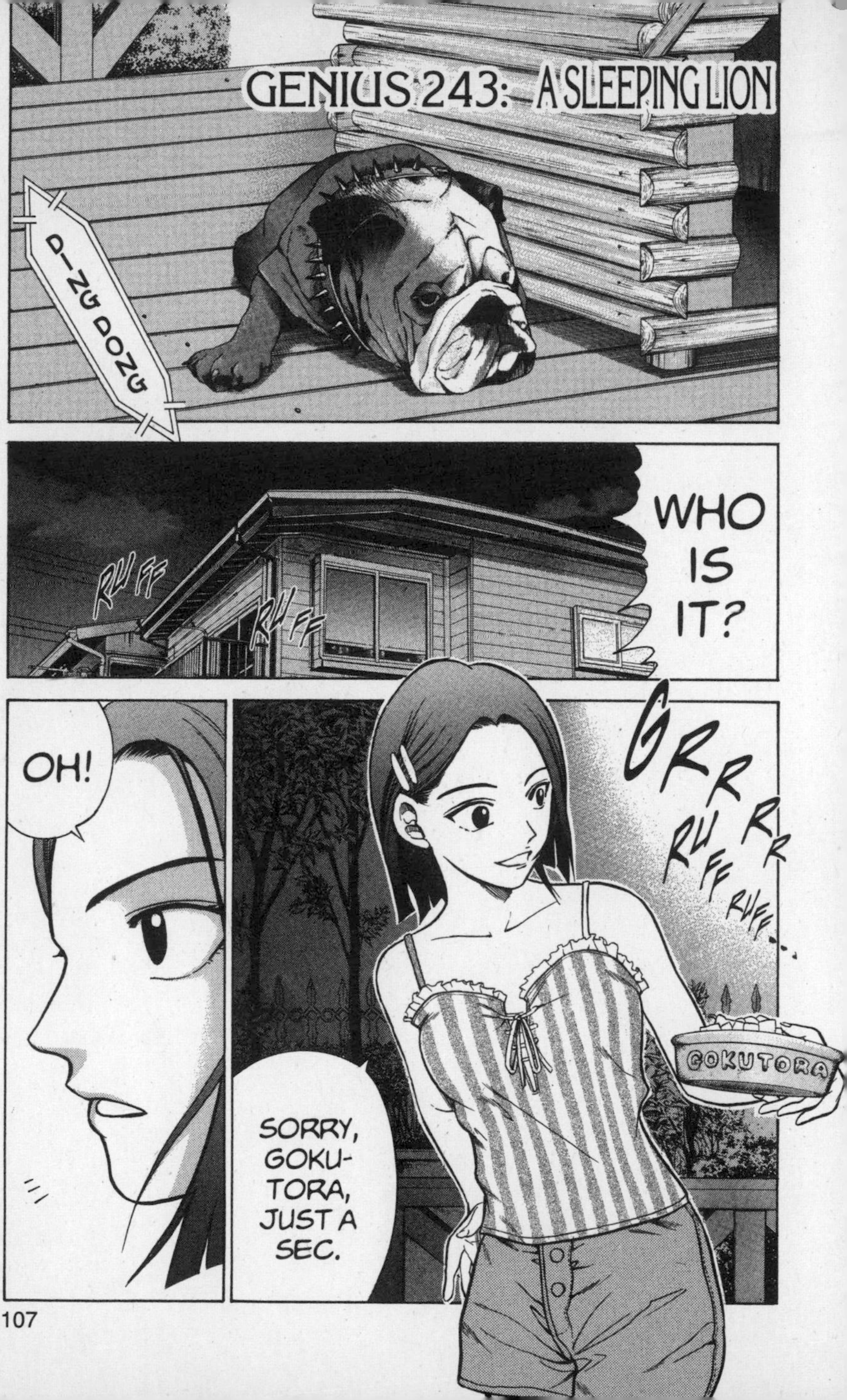
GENIUS 243: A SLEEPING LION
DING DONG
RUFF
RUFF
WHO IS IT?
GRRR RRR
RUFF RUFF RUFF...
GOKUTORA
SORRY, GOKU-TORA, JUST A SEC.
OH!

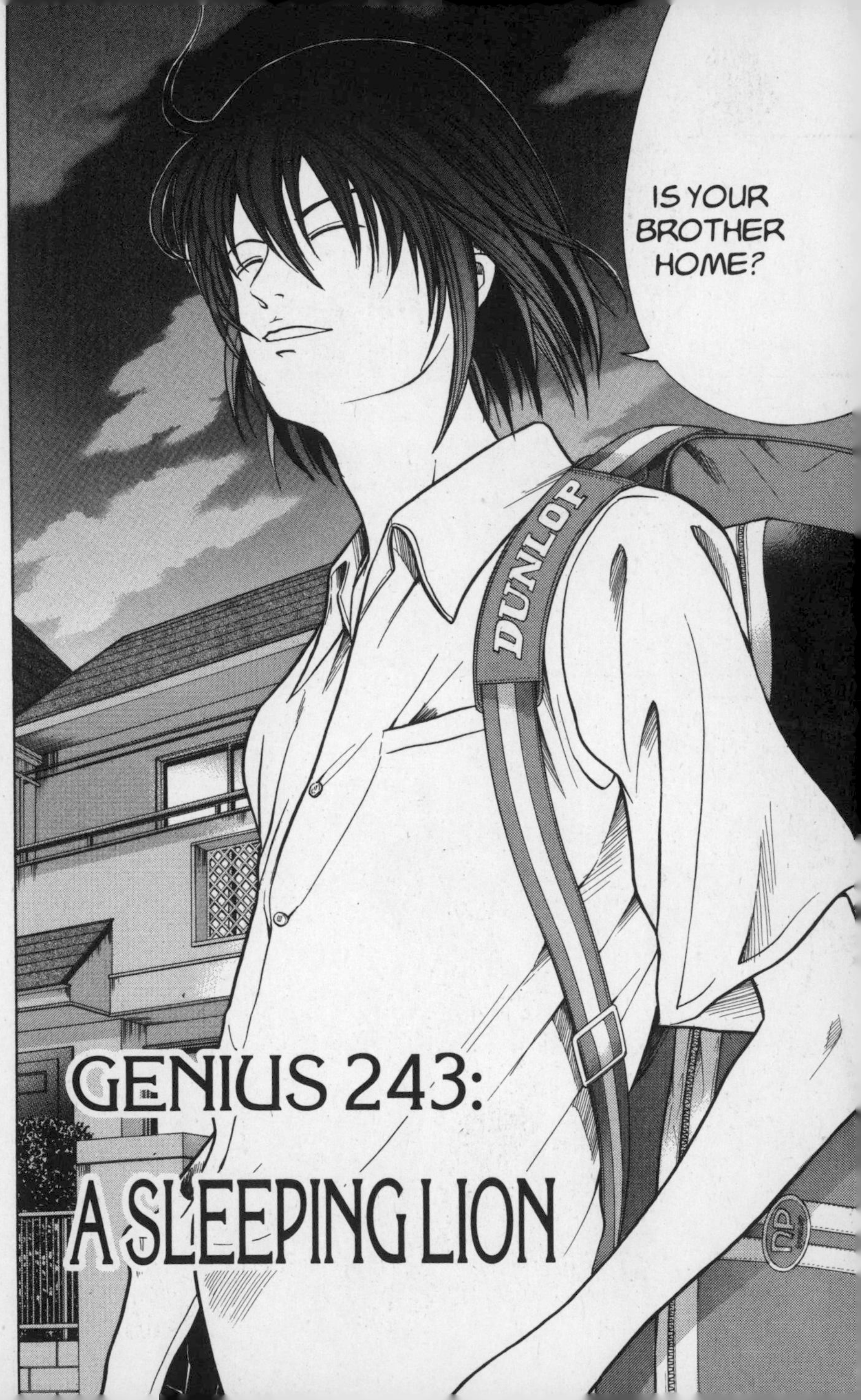
IS YOUR BROTHER HOME?
DUNLOP
GENIUS 243:
A SLEEPING LION

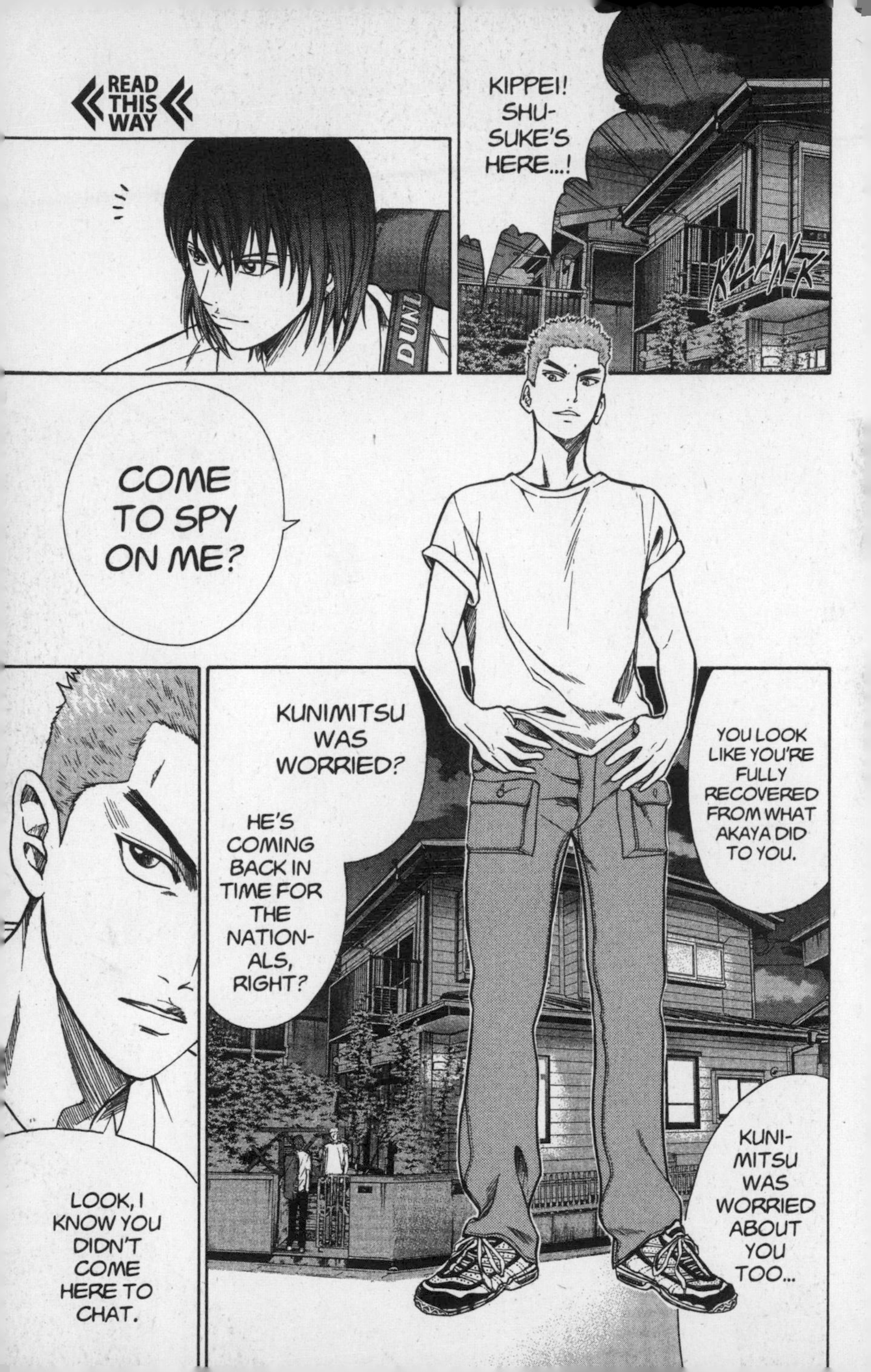
READ THIS WAY
KIPPEI! SHU-SUKE'S HERE...!
KLANK
COME TO SPY ON ME?
YOU LOOK LIKE YOU'RE FULLY RECOVERED FROM WHAT AKAYA DID TO YOU.
KUNI-MITSU WAS WORRIED ABOUT YOU TOO...
KUNIMITSU WAS WORRIED?
HE'S COMING BACK IN TIME FOR THE NATION-ALS, RIGHT?
LOOK, I KNOW YOU DIDN'T COME HERE TO CHAT.

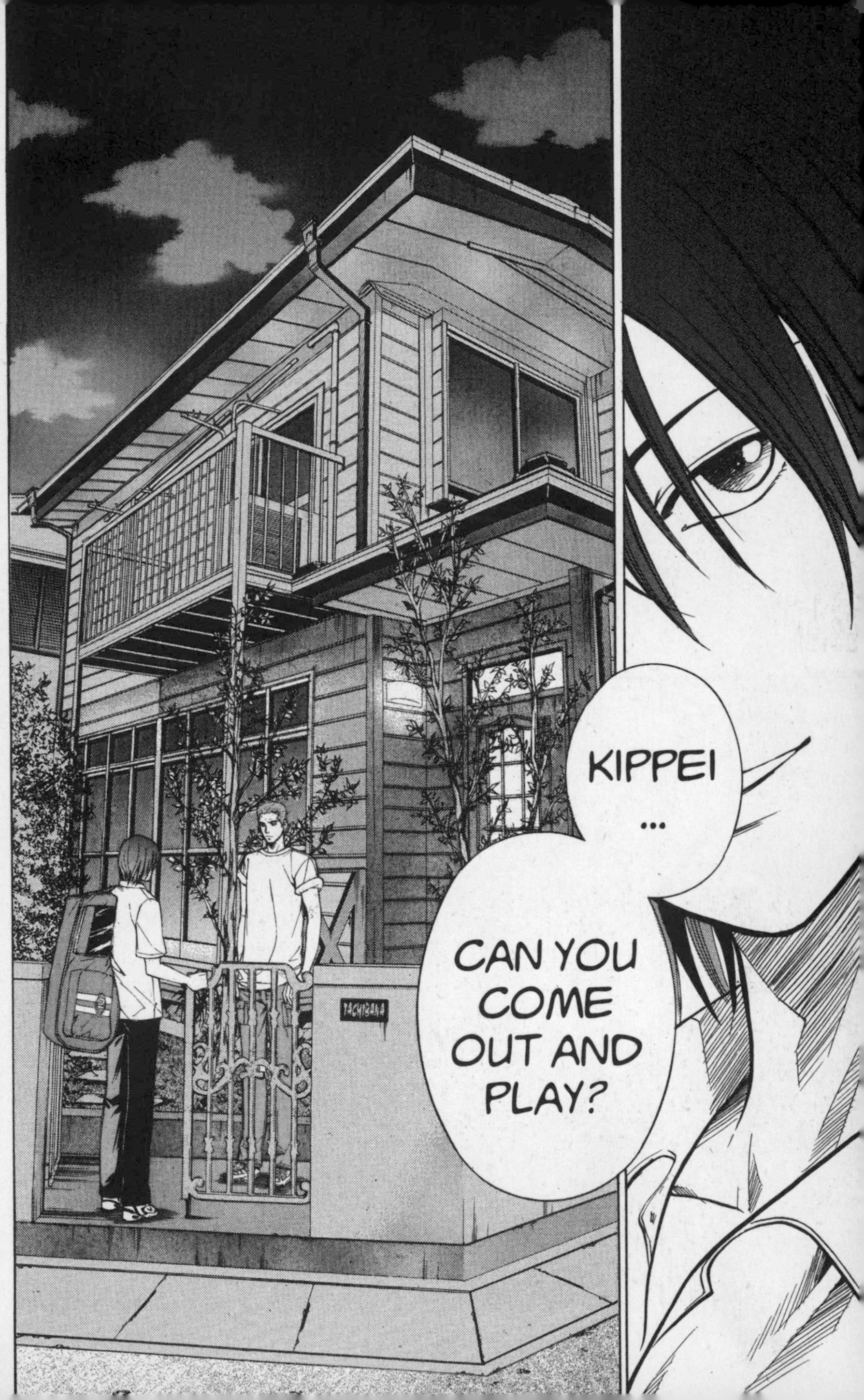
KIPPEI ...
CAN YOU COME OUT AND PLAY?
TACHIBANA

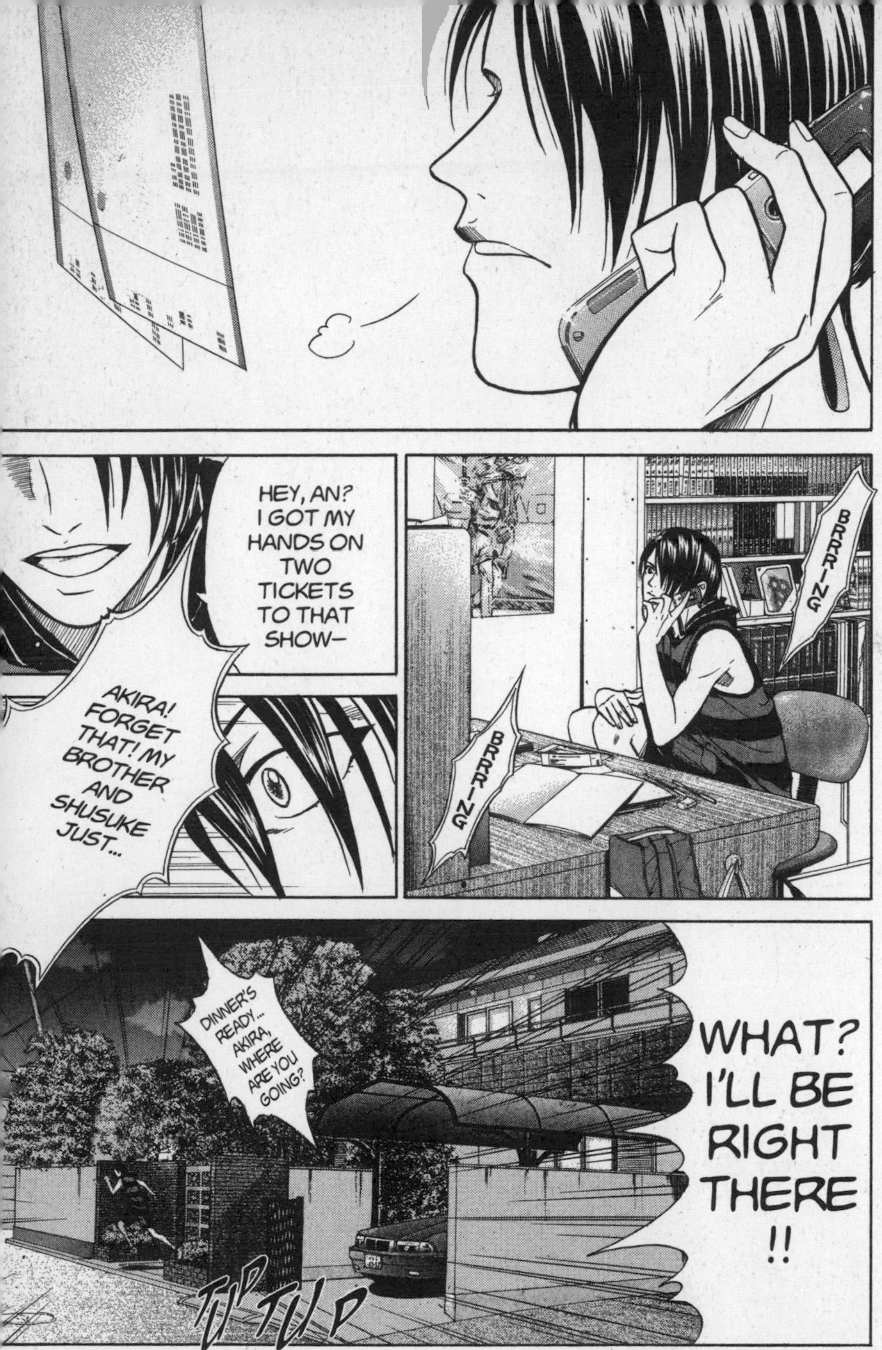
BRRRING
BRRRING
HEY, AN? I GOT MY HANDS ON TWO TICKETS TO THAT SHOW–
AKIRA! FORGET THAT! MY BROTHER AND SHUSUKE JUST...
WHAT? I'LL BE RIGHT THERE!!
DINNER'S READY... AKIRA, WHERE ARE YOU GOING?
TUD TUD

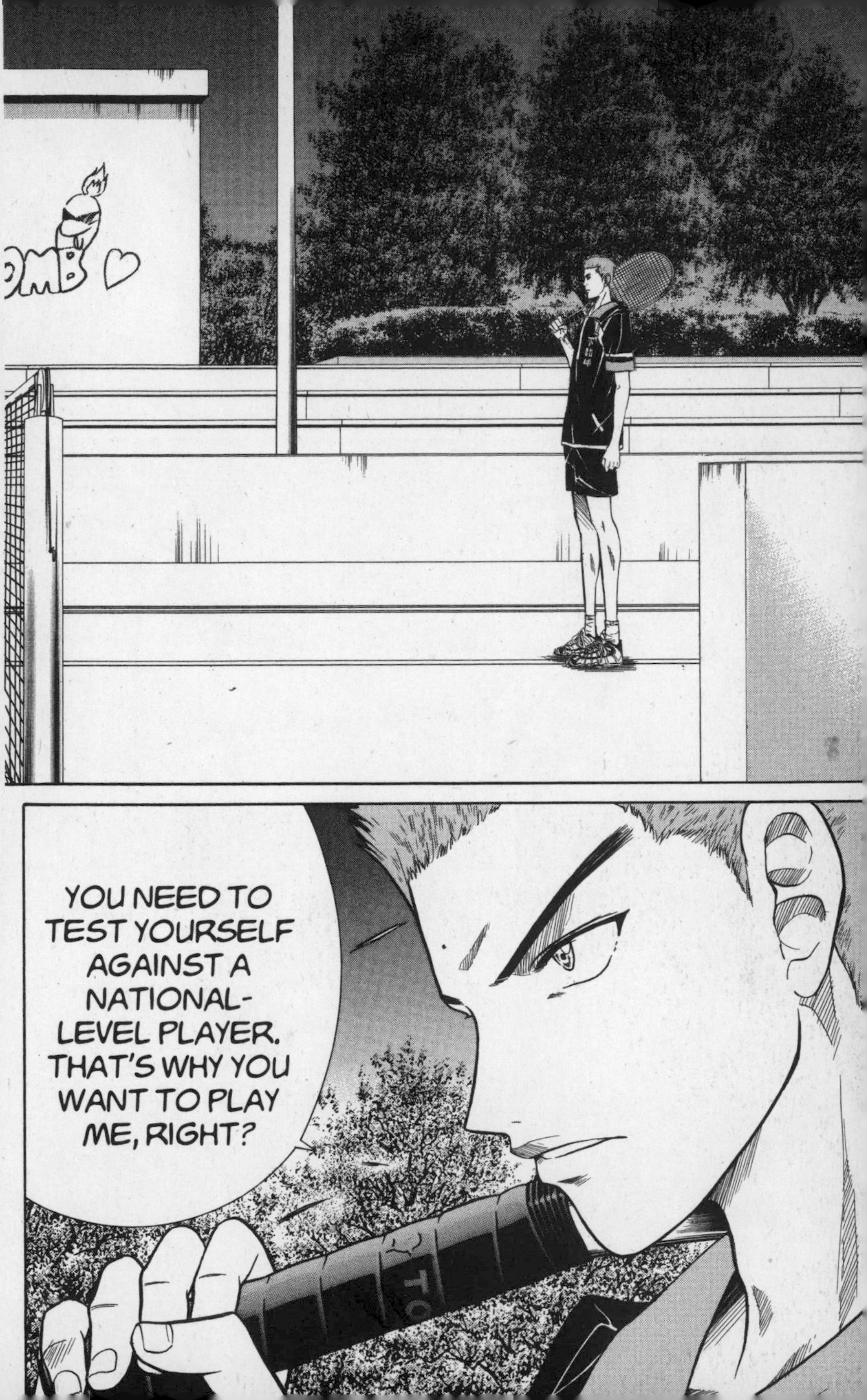
YOU NEED TO TEST YOURSELF AGAINST A NATIONAL-LEVEL PLAYER. THAT'S WHY YOU WANT TO PLAY ME, RIGHT?

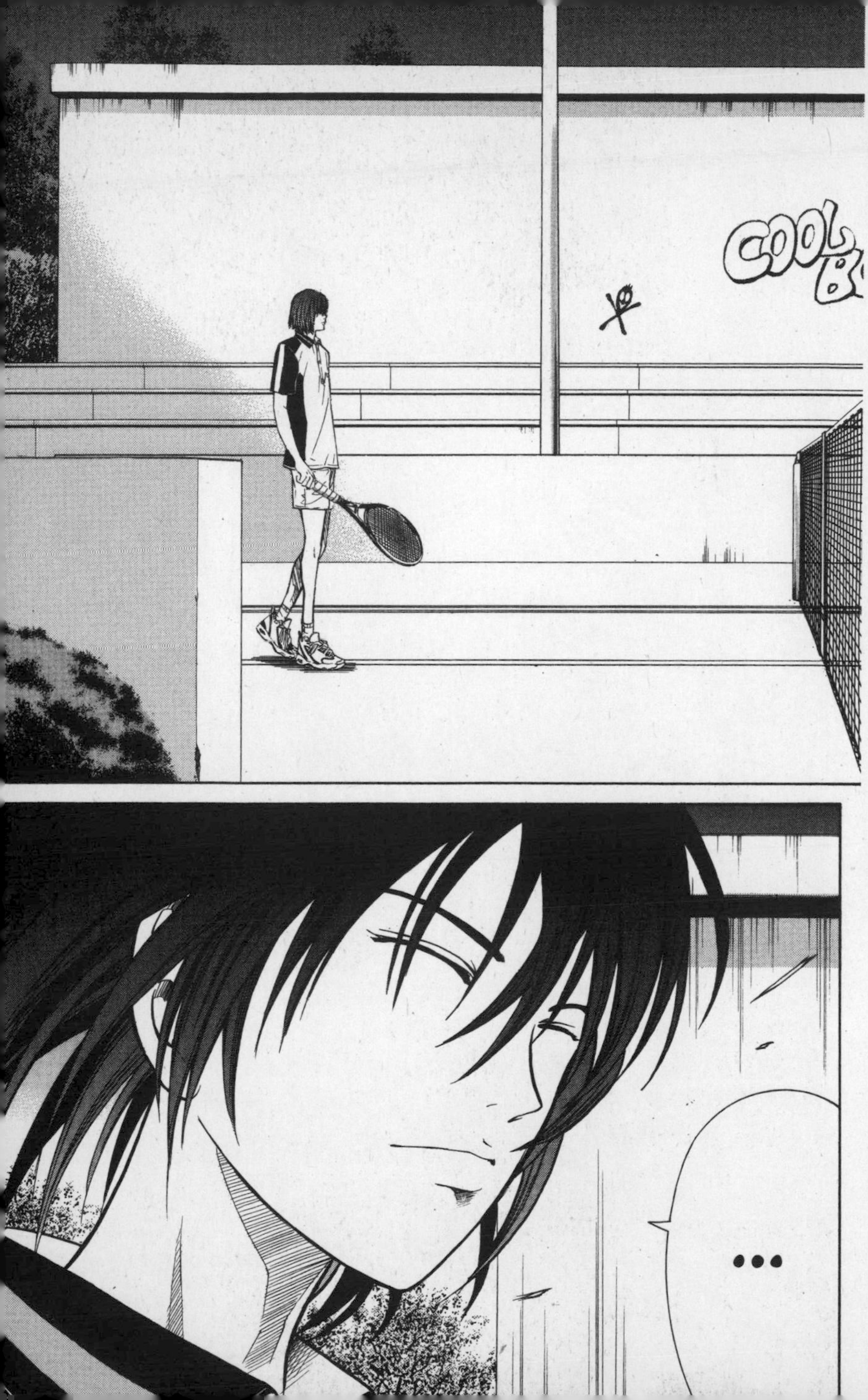
COOL
...

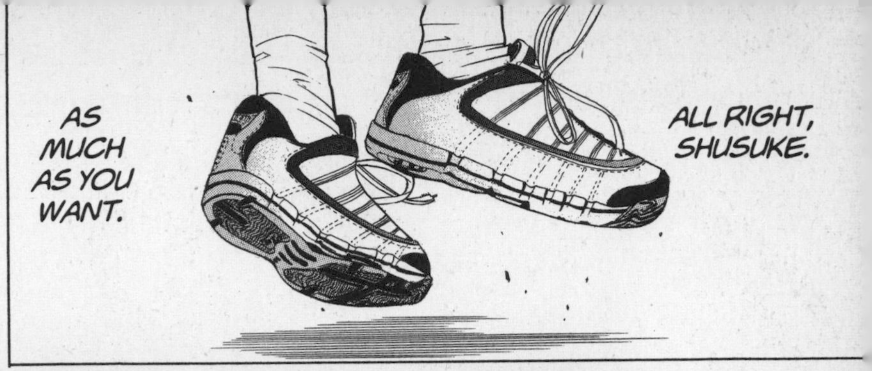
ALL RIGHT, SHUSUKE.
AS MUCH AS YOU WANT.

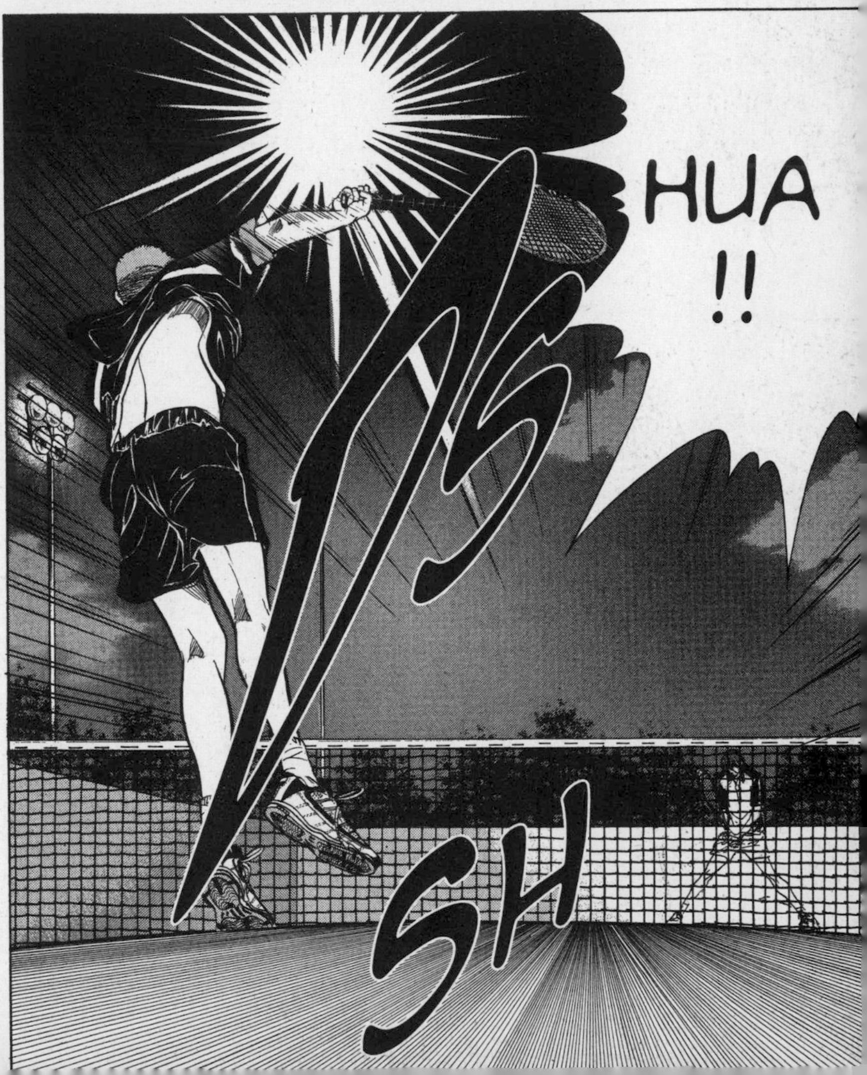
HUA!!
SH

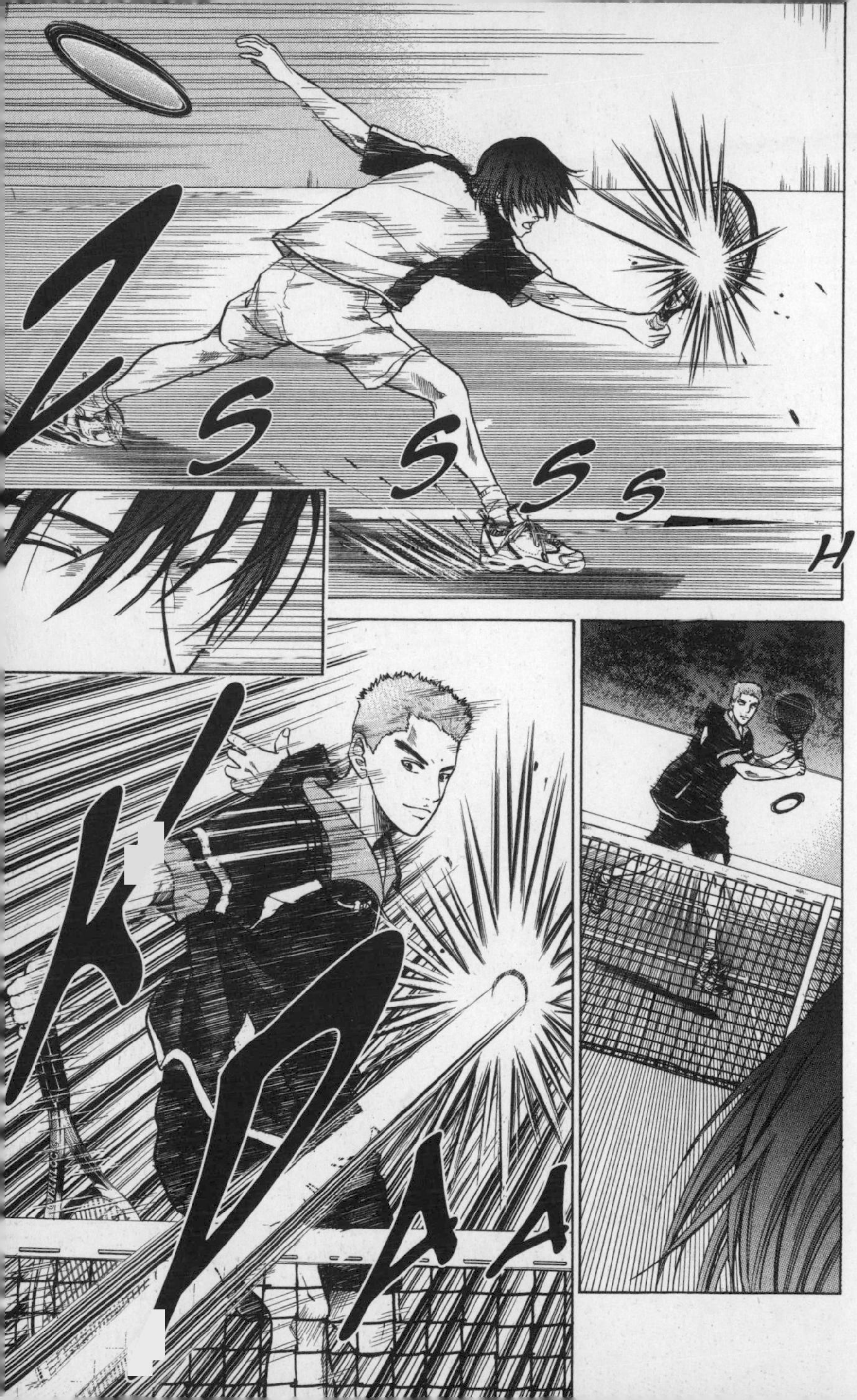
SSSSH
AA

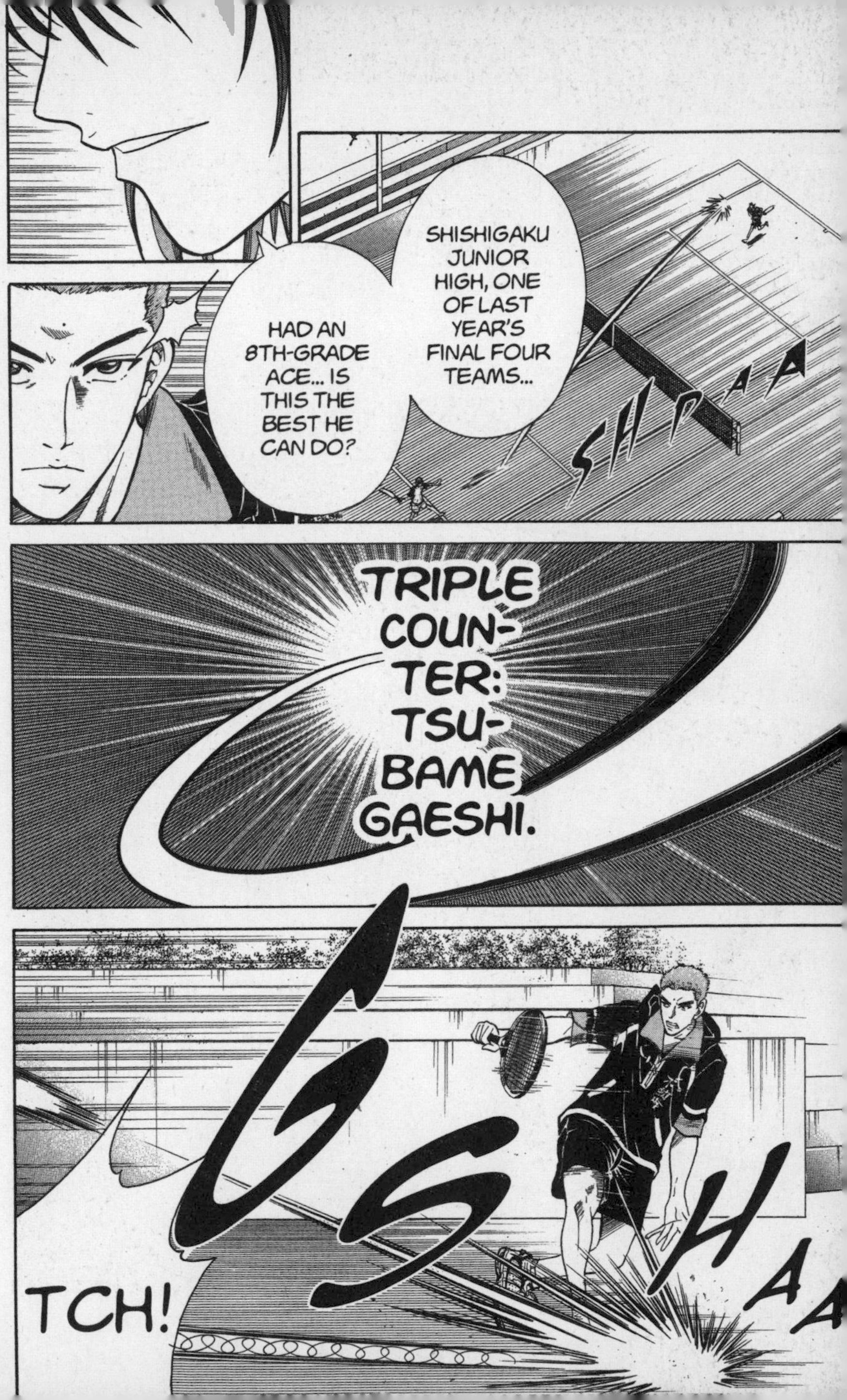
SHISHIGAKU JUNIOR HIGH, ONE OF LAST YEAR'S FINAL FOUR TEAMS...
HAD AN 8TH-GRADE ACE... IS THIS THE BEST HE CAN DO?
SHPAA
TRIPLE COUNTER: TSUBAME GAESHI.
GSHAA
TCH!

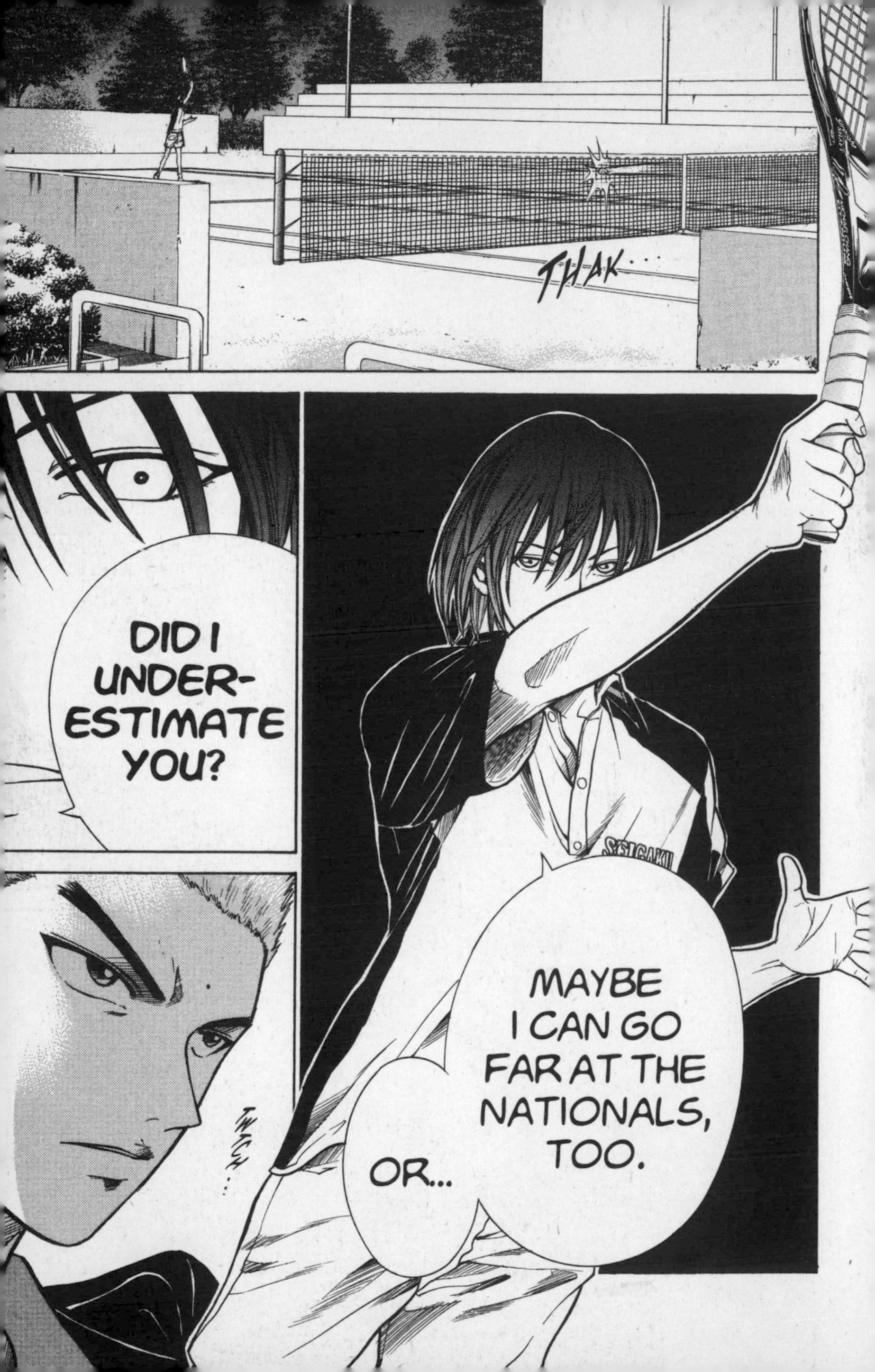
THAK...
MAYBE I CAN GO FAR AT THE NATIONALS, TOO.
OR...
DID I UNDER-ESTIMATE YOU?
TWITCH...

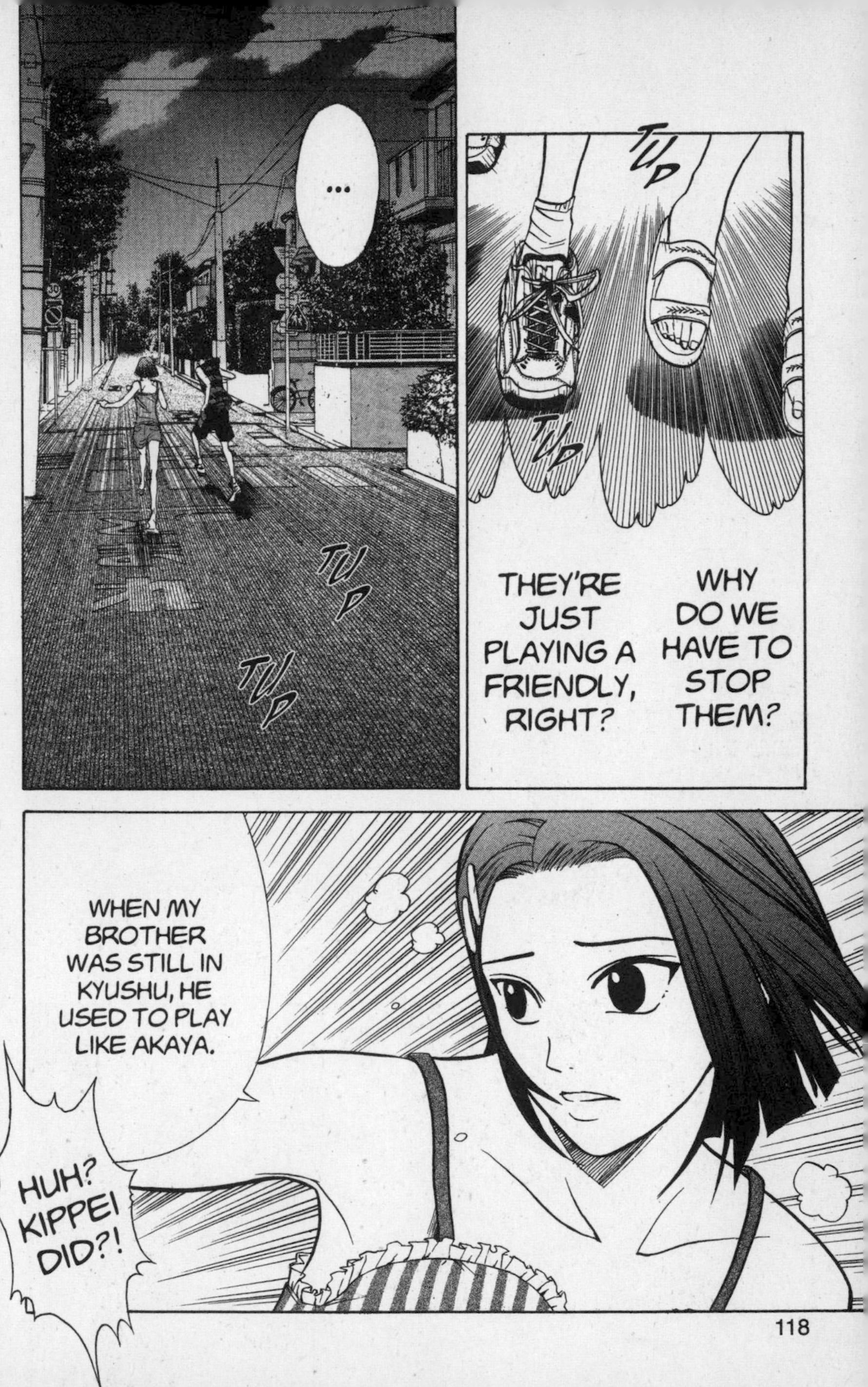
TUD
TUD
WHY DO WE HAVE TO STOP THEM?
THEY'RE JUST PLAYING A FRIENDLY, RIGHT?
...
TUD
TUD
WHEN MY BROTHER WAS STILL IN KYUSHU, HE USED TO PLAY LIKE AKAYA.
HUH? KIPPEI DID?!

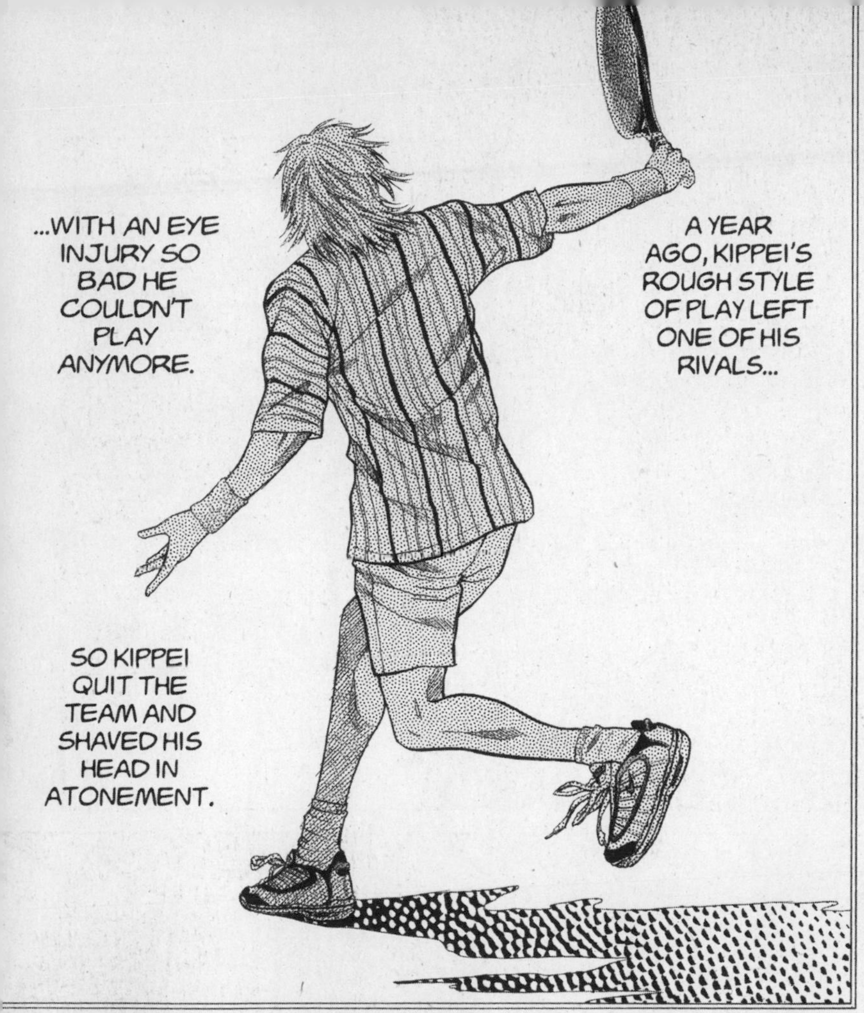
A YEAR AGO, KIPPEI'S ROUGH STYLE OF PLAY LEFT ONE OF HIS RIVALS...
...WITH AN EYE INJURY SO BAD HE COULDN'T PLAY ANYMORE.
SO KIPPEI QUIT THE TEAM AND SHAVED HIS HEAD IN ATONEMENT.
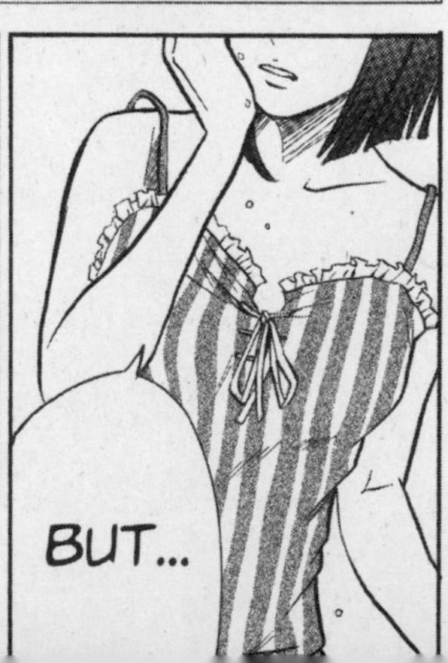
BUT...
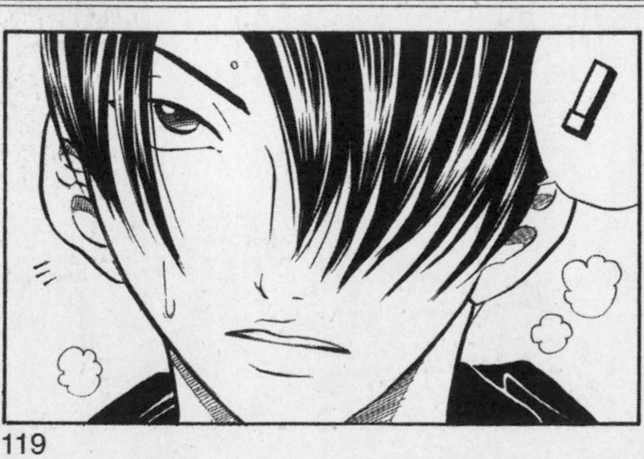

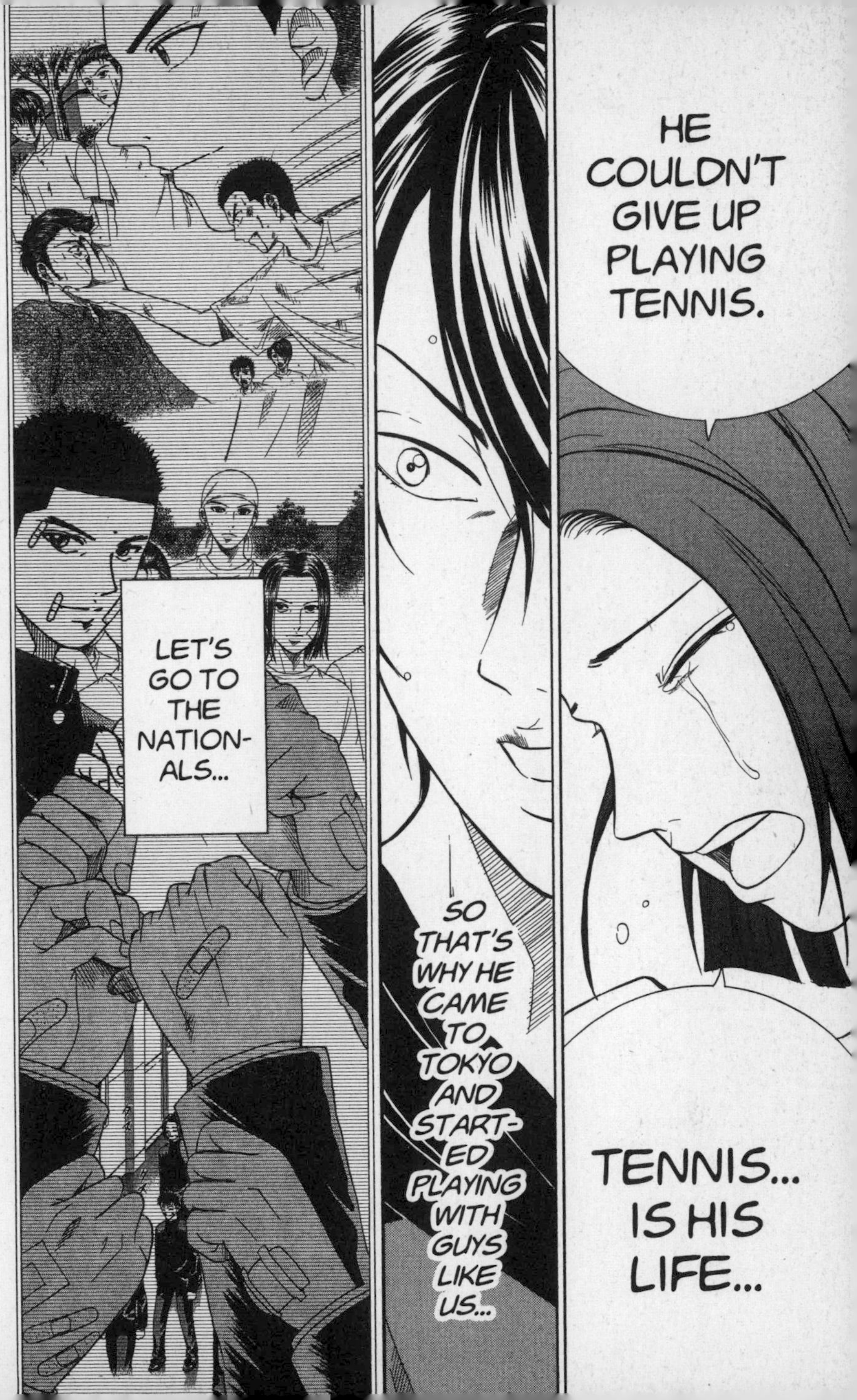
HE COULDN'T GIVE UP PLAYING TENNIS.
TENNIS... IS HIS LIFE...
SO THAT'S WHY HE CAME TO TOKYO AND START-ED PLAYING WITH GUYS LIKE US...
LET'S GO TO THE NATION-ALS...

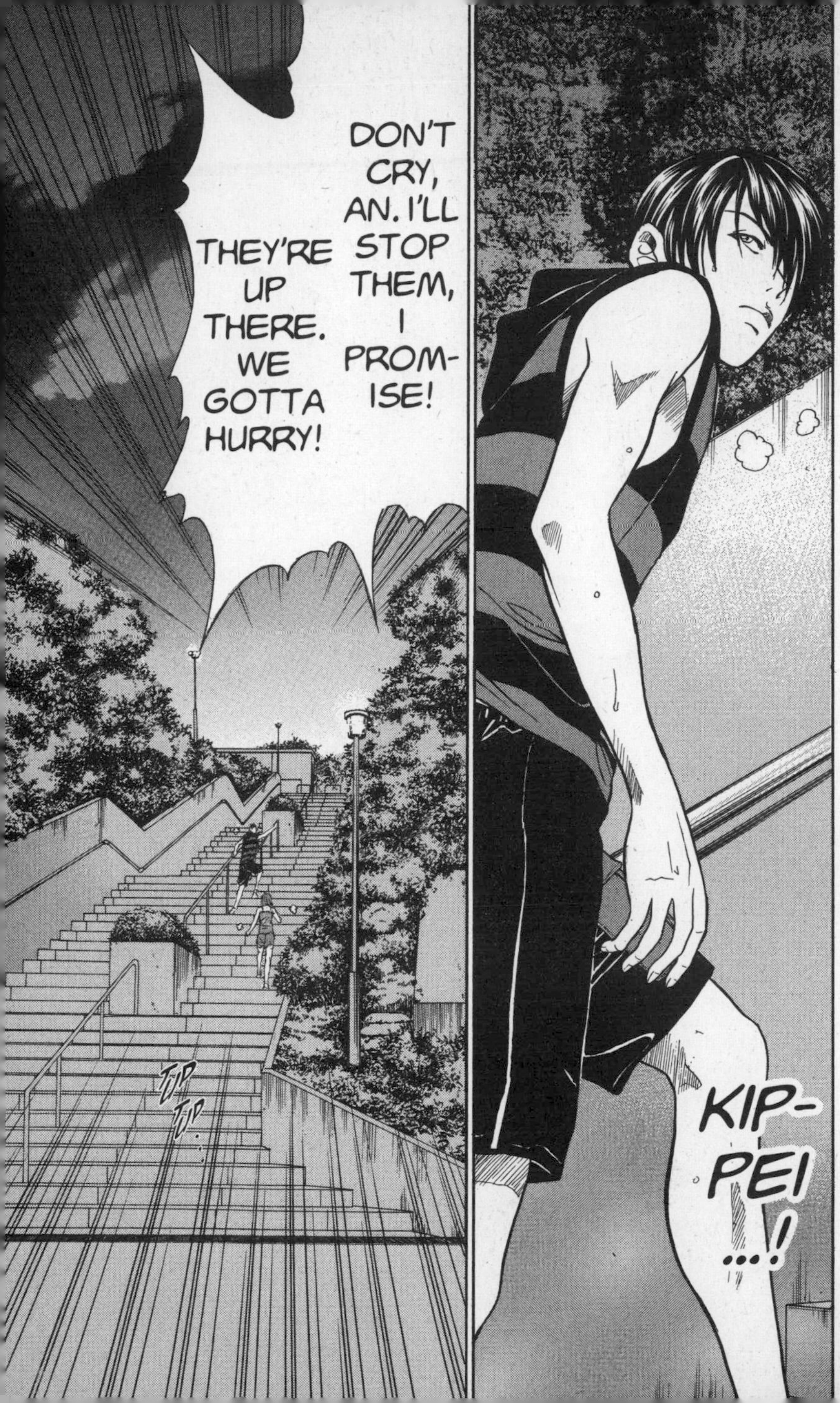
KIP-PEI...!
DON'T CRY, AN. I'LL STOP THEM, I PROMISE!
THEY'RE UP THERE. WE GOTTA HURRY!
TUP TUP..

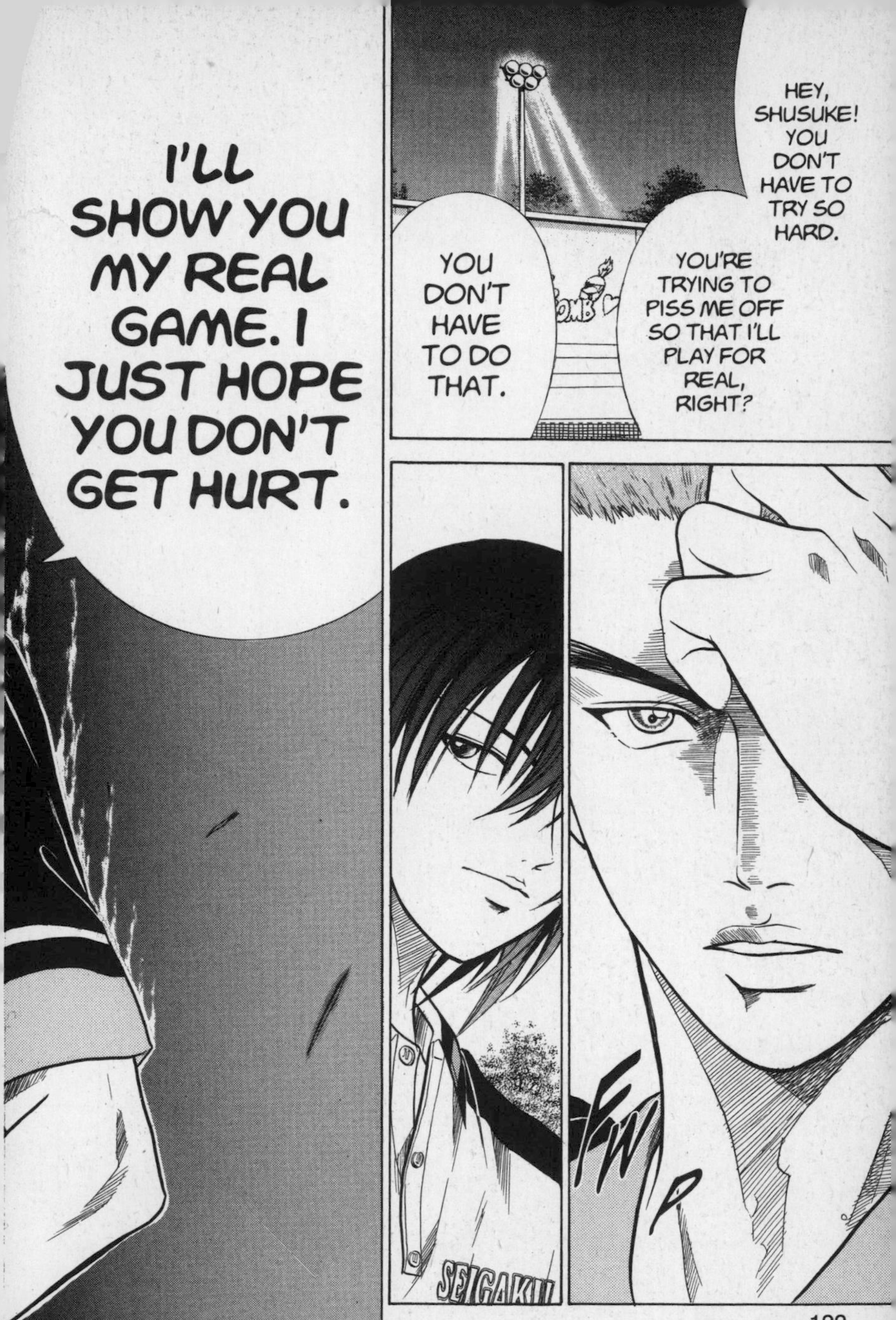
HEY, SHUSUKE! YOU DON'T HAVE TO TRY SO HARD.
YOU'RE TRYING TO PISS ME OFF SO THAT I'LL PLAY FOR REAL, RIGHT?
YOU DON'T HAVE TO DO THAT.
FWP
SEIGAKU
I'LL SHOW YOU MY REAL GAME. I JUST HOPE YOU DON'T GET HURT.

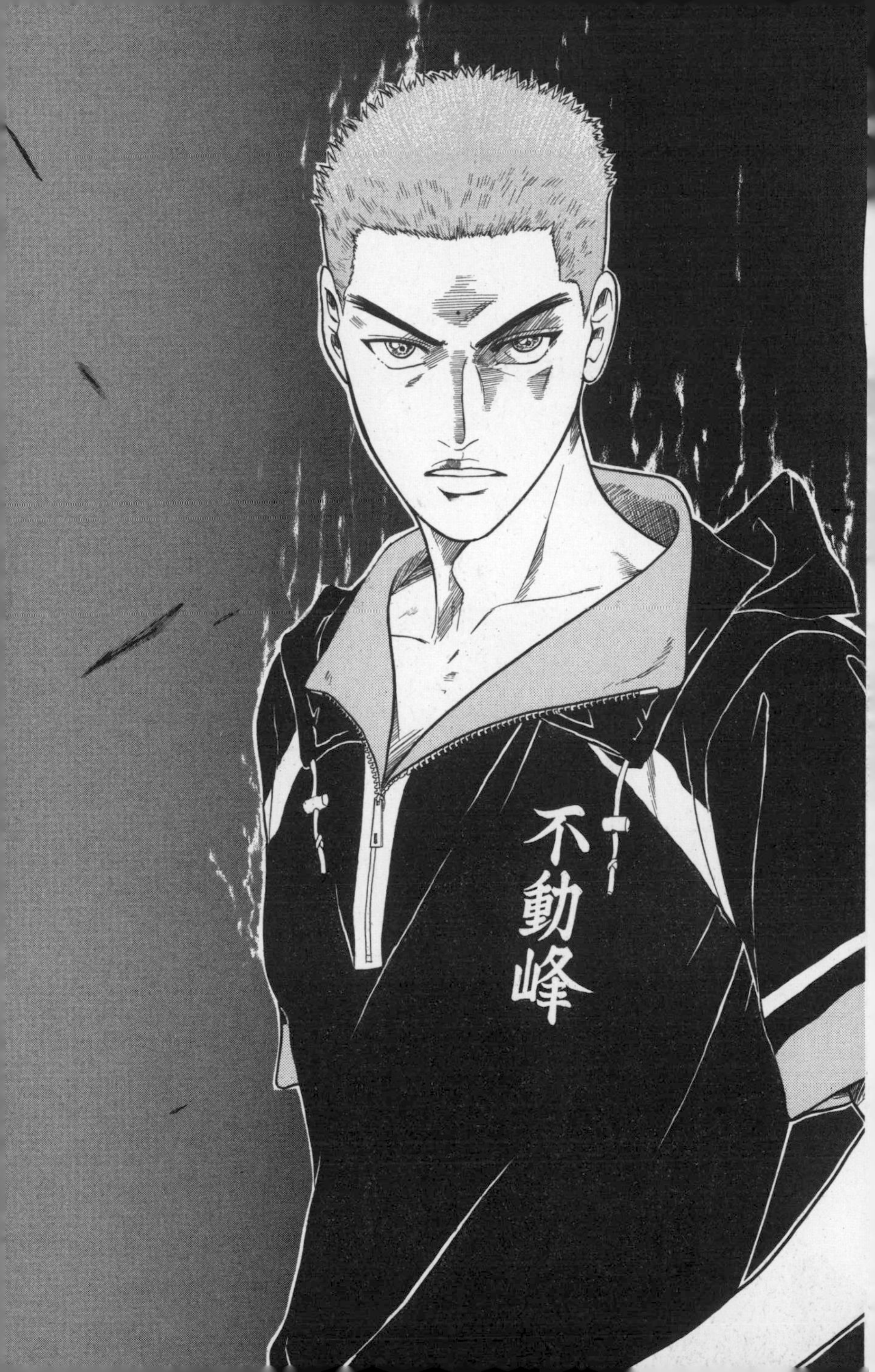
不動峰

不動峰
-FUDOMINE-

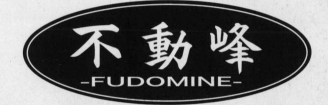

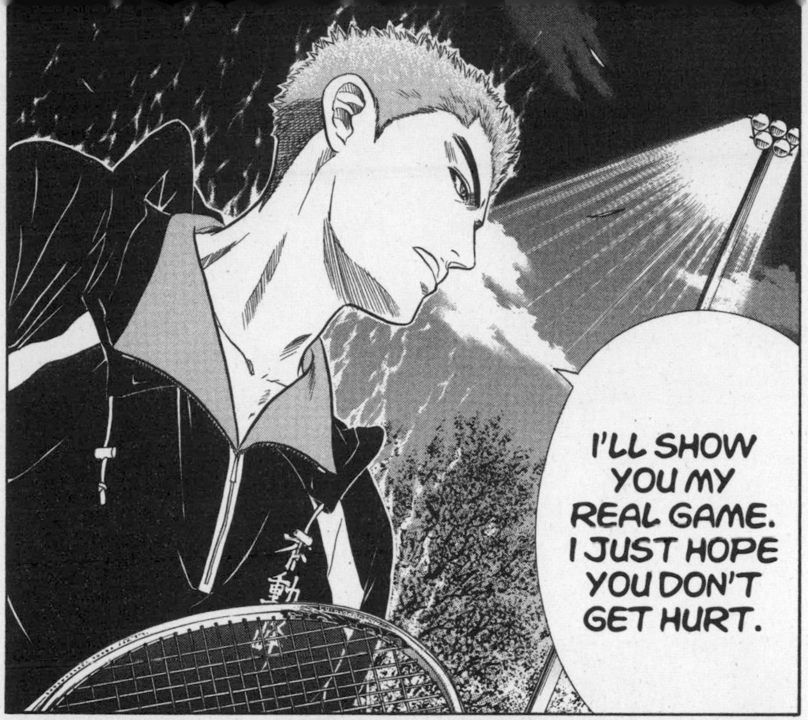
I'LL SHOW YOU MY REAL GAME. I JUST HOPE YOU DON'T GET HURT.

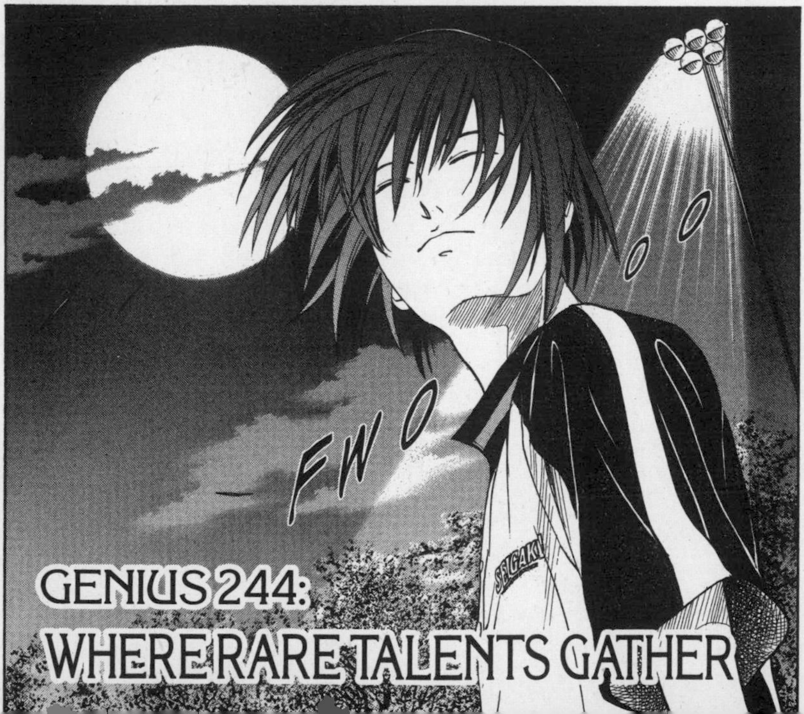
FWO
GENIUS 244:
WHERE RARE TALENTS GATHER

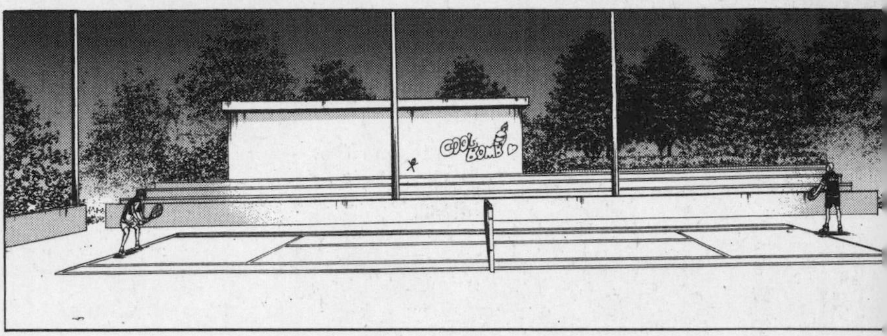
COOL BOMB

GENIUS 244

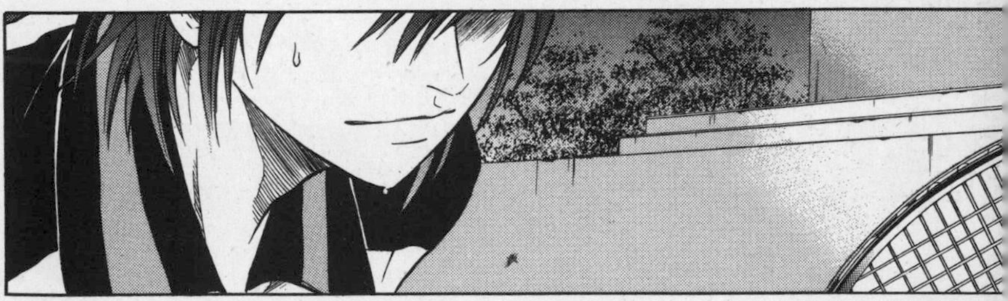

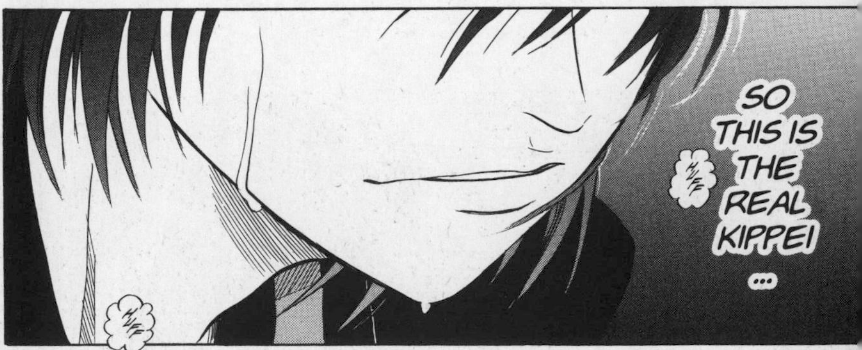
SO THIS IS THE REAL KIPPEI ...
HUFF

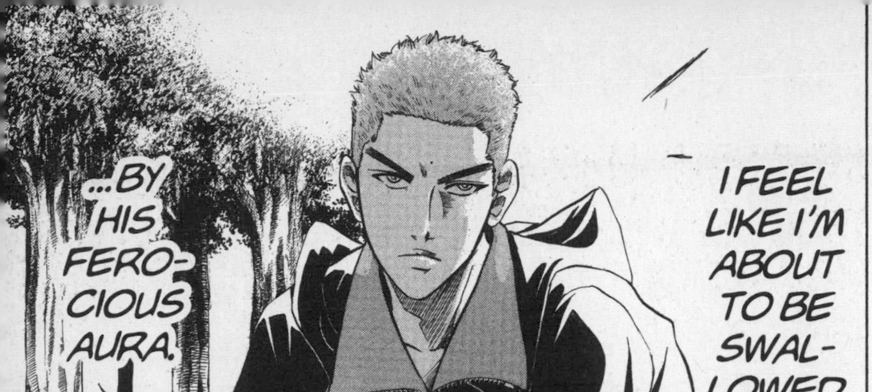
I FEEL LIKE I'M ABOUT TO BE SWALLOWED...
...BY HIS FEROCIOUS AURA.

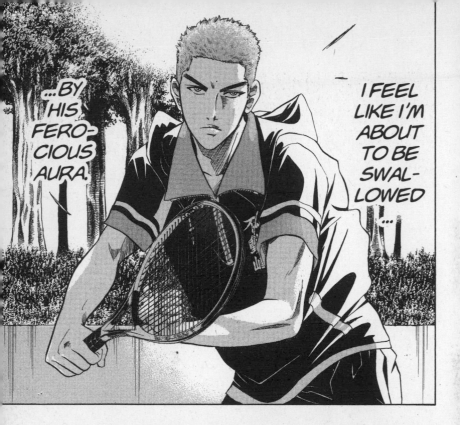

WHERE RARE TALENTS GATHER

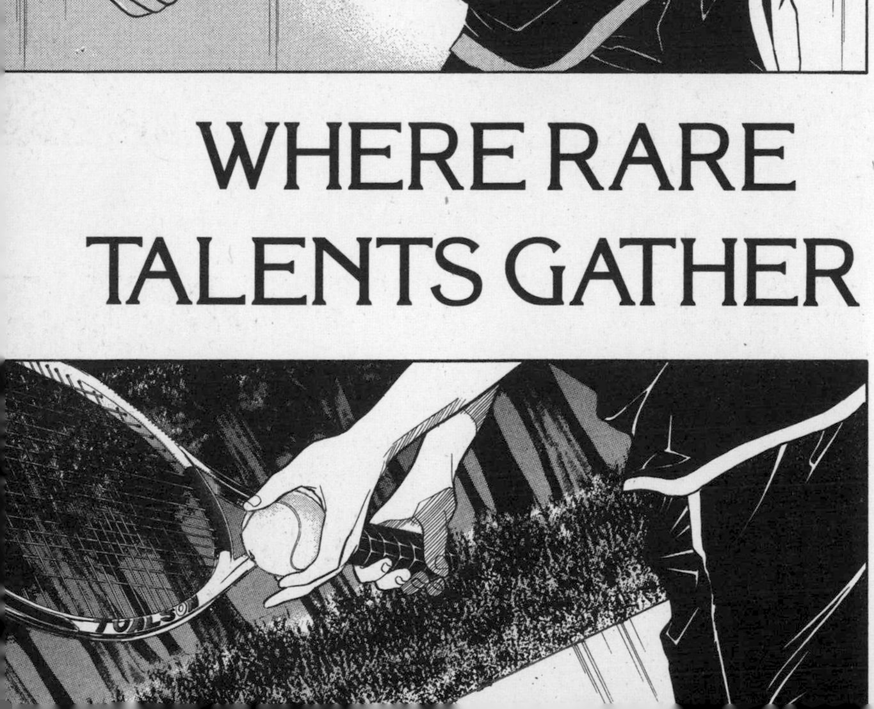

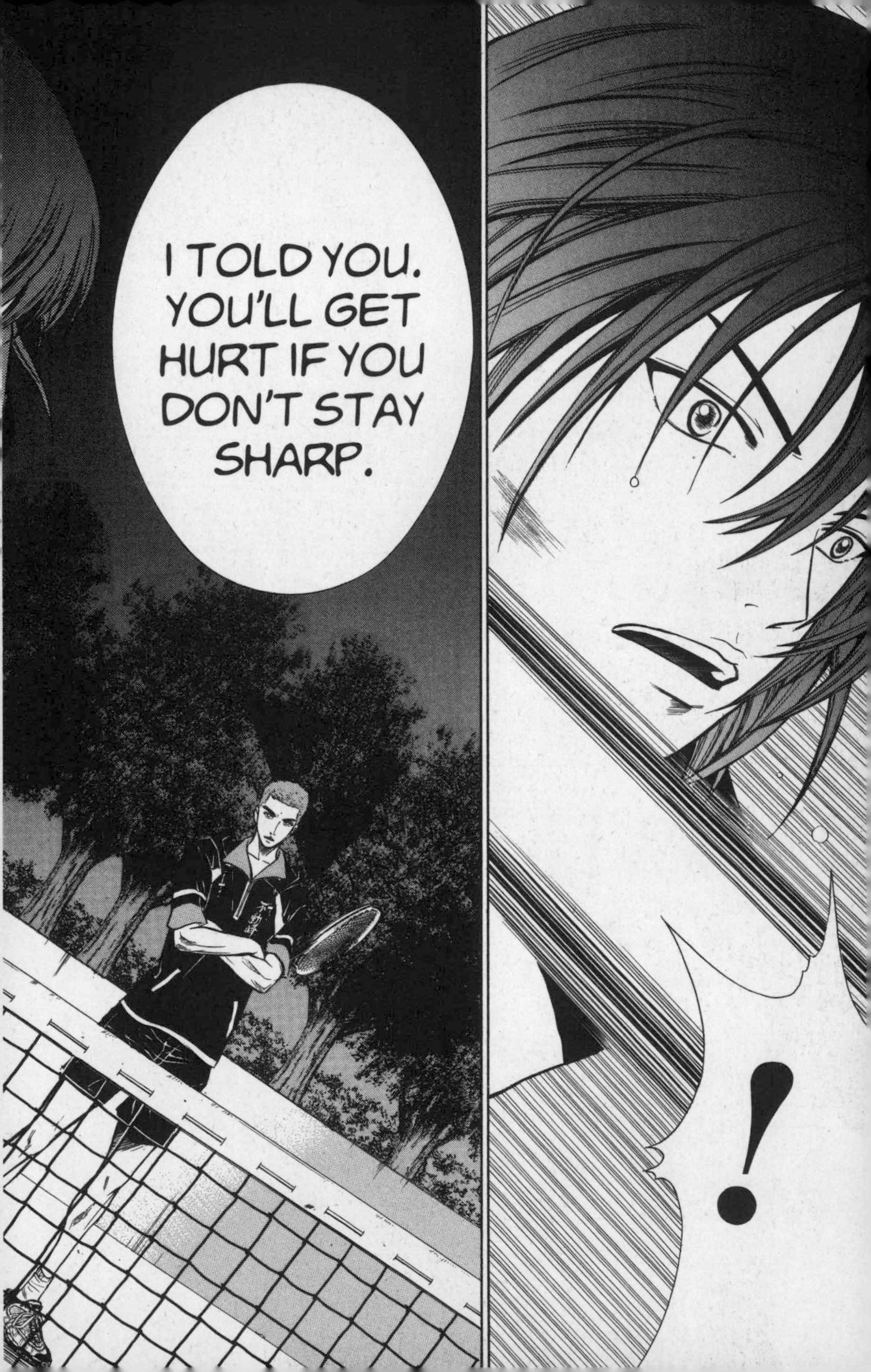
I TOLD YOU. YOU'LL GET HURT IF YOU DON'T STAY SHARP.
!

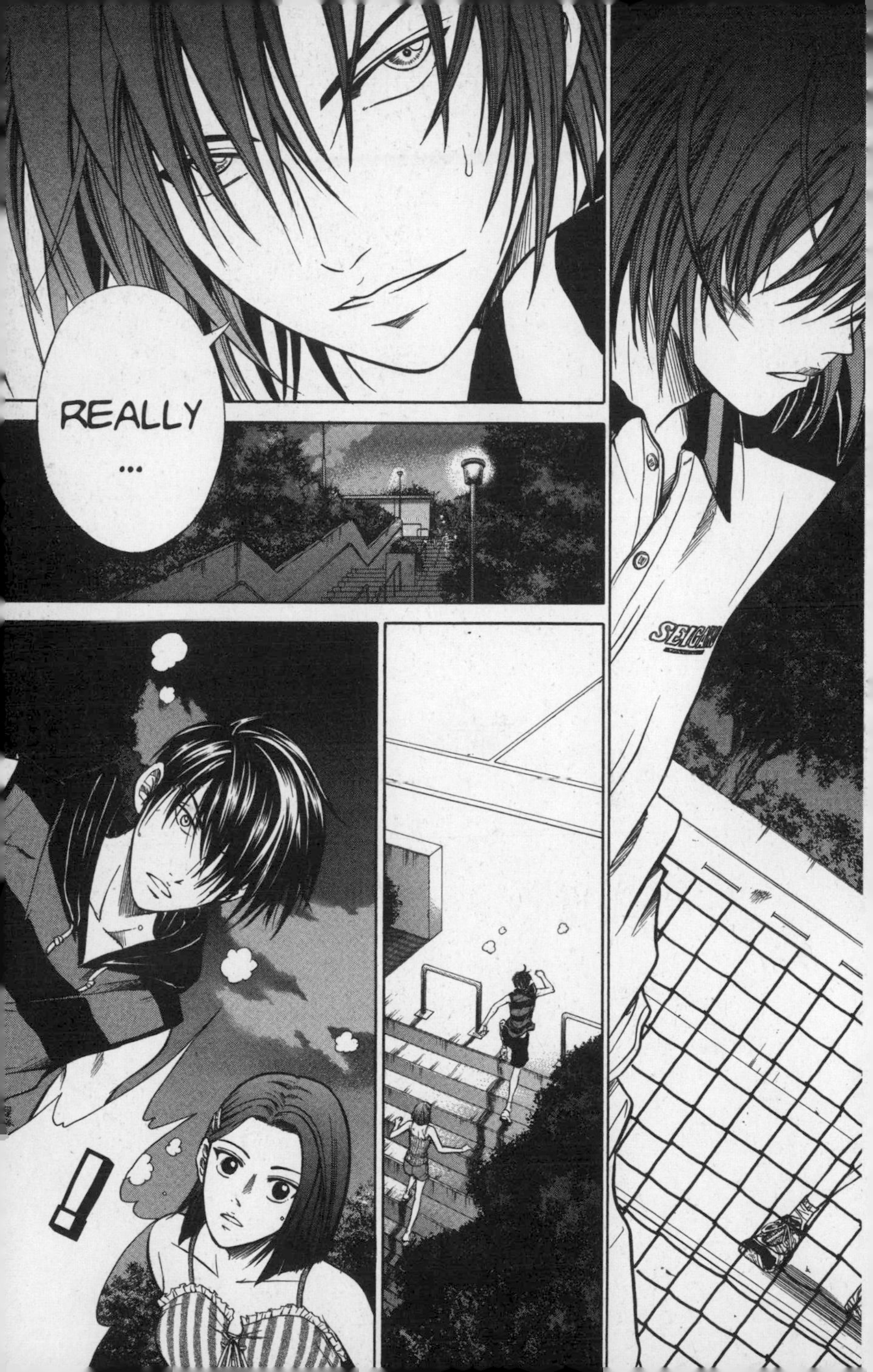
REALLY ...
!

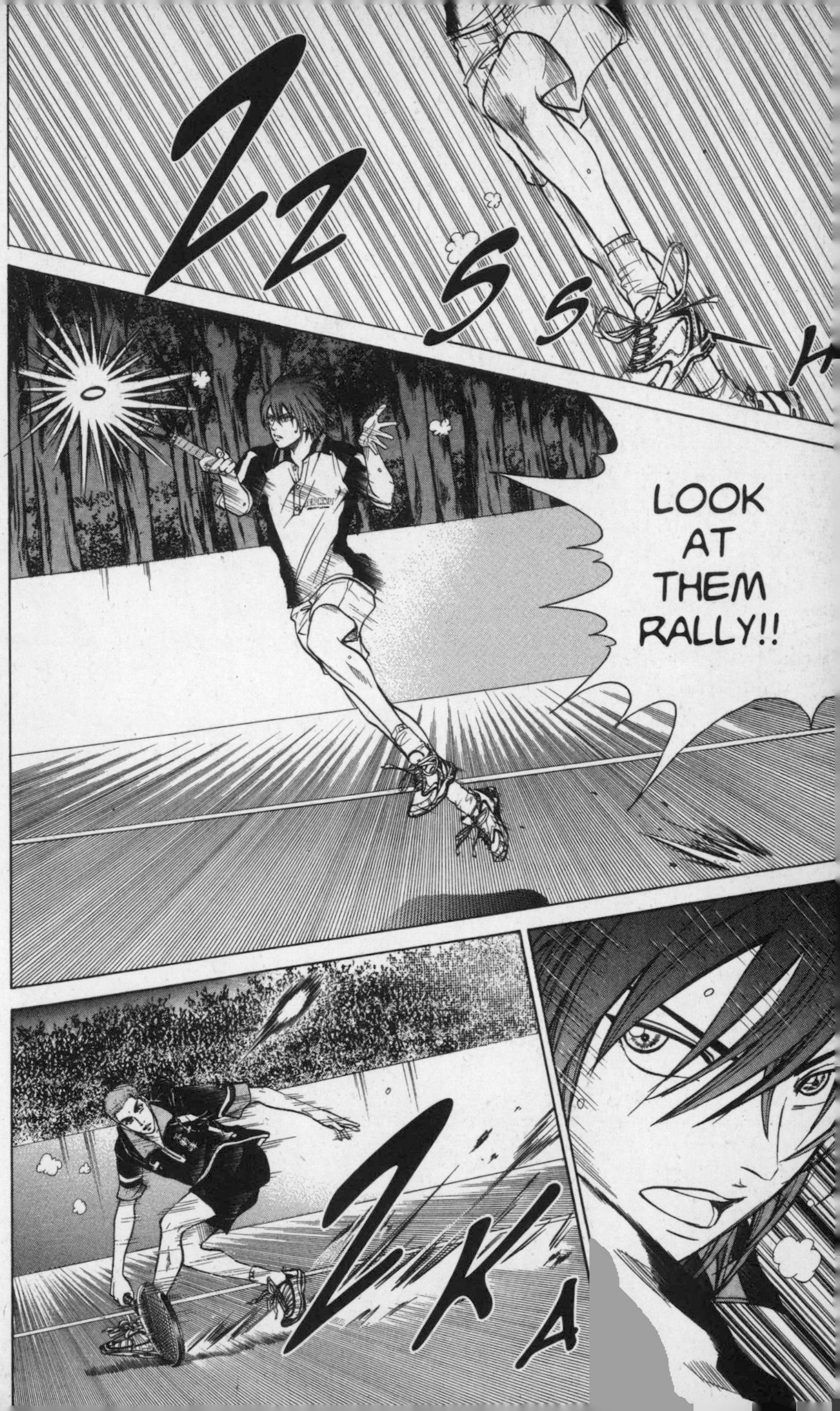
ZZSss
LOOK AT THEM RALLY!!
ZKA

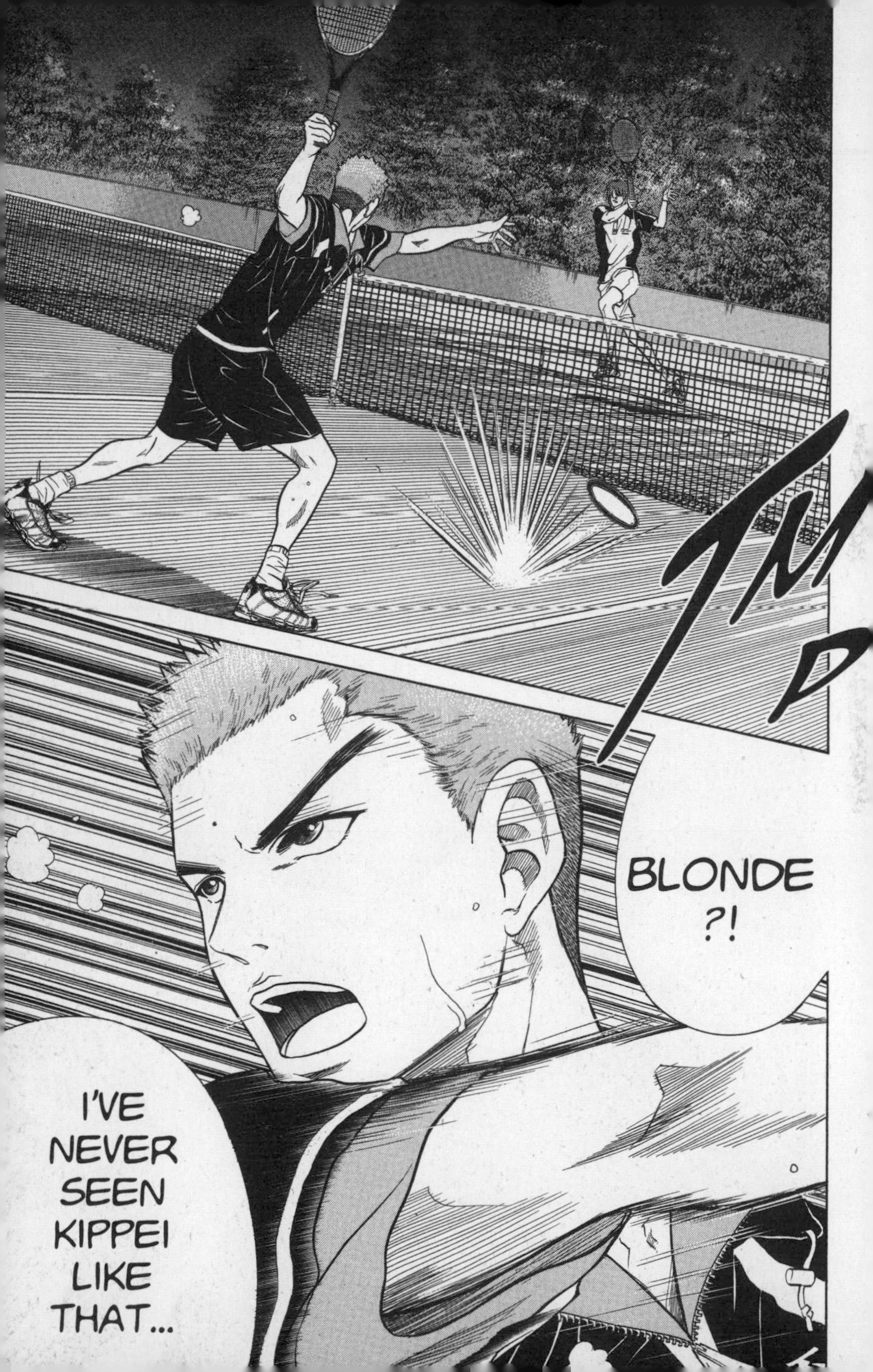
TMD
BLONDE ?!
I'VE NEVER SEEN KIPPEI LIKE THAT...

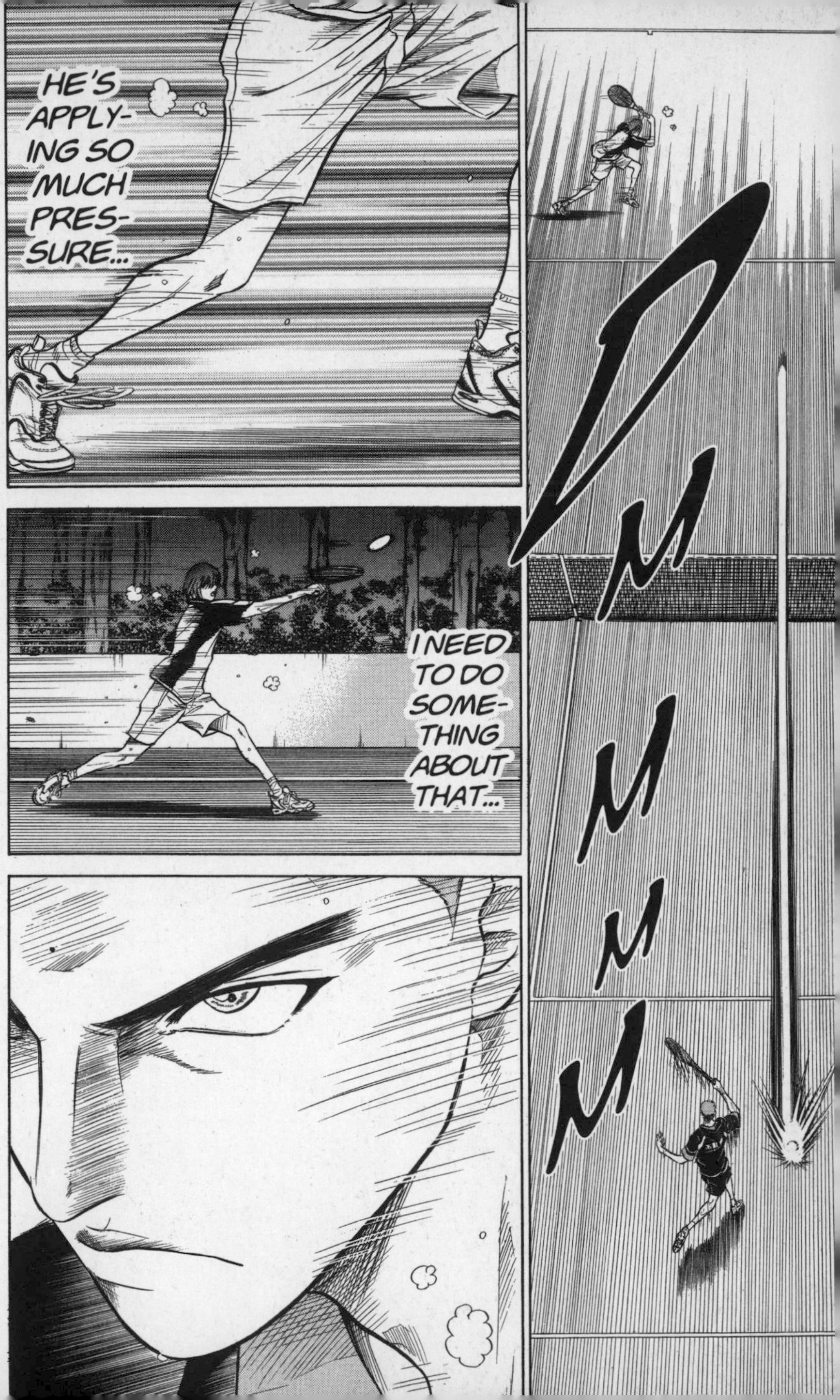
DMMMM
HE'S APPLYING SO MUCH PRESSURE...
I NEED TO DO SOMETHING ABOUT THAT...

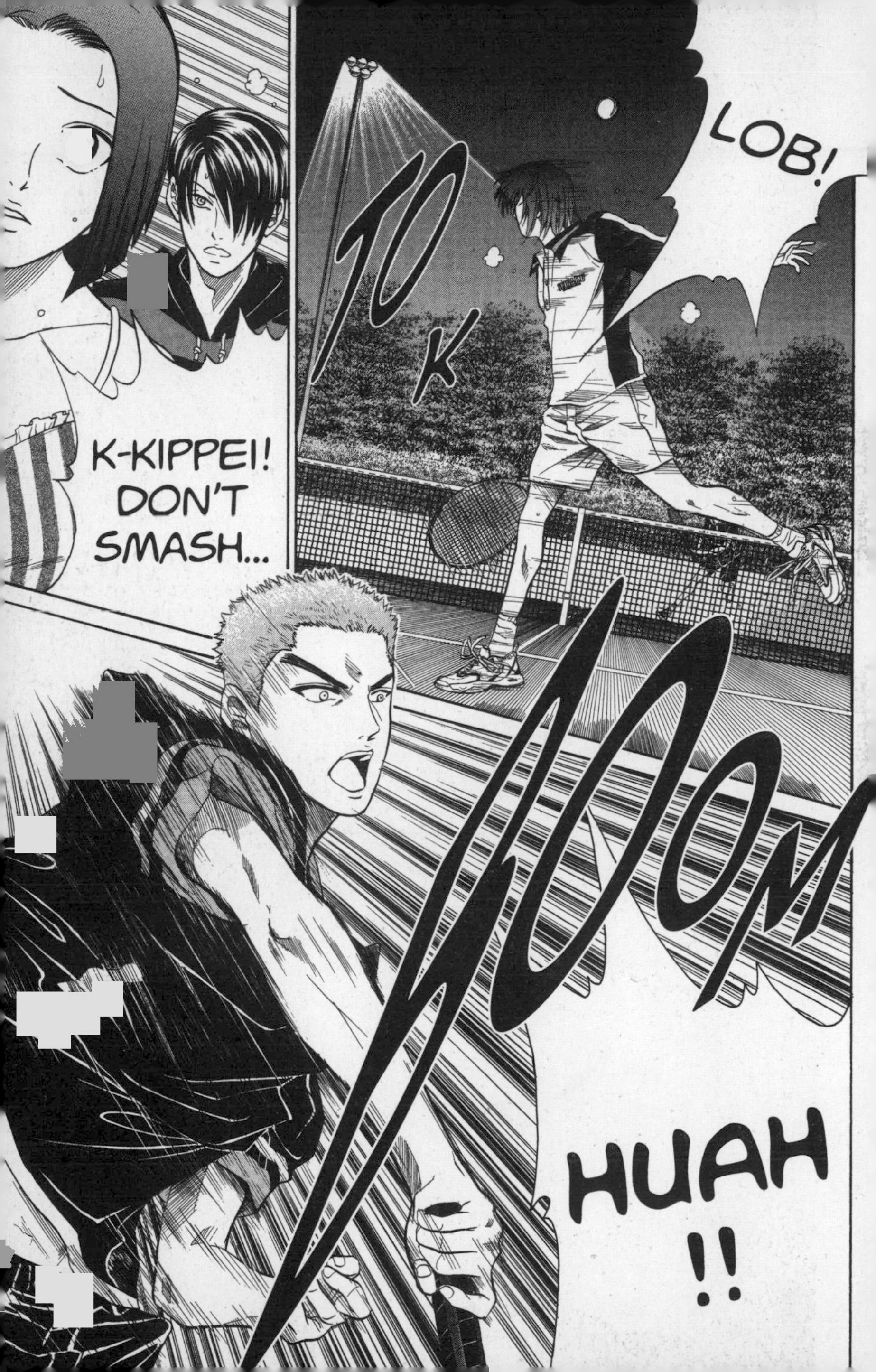
LOB!
TOK
K-KIPPEI! DON'T SMASH...
VOOM
HUAH!!

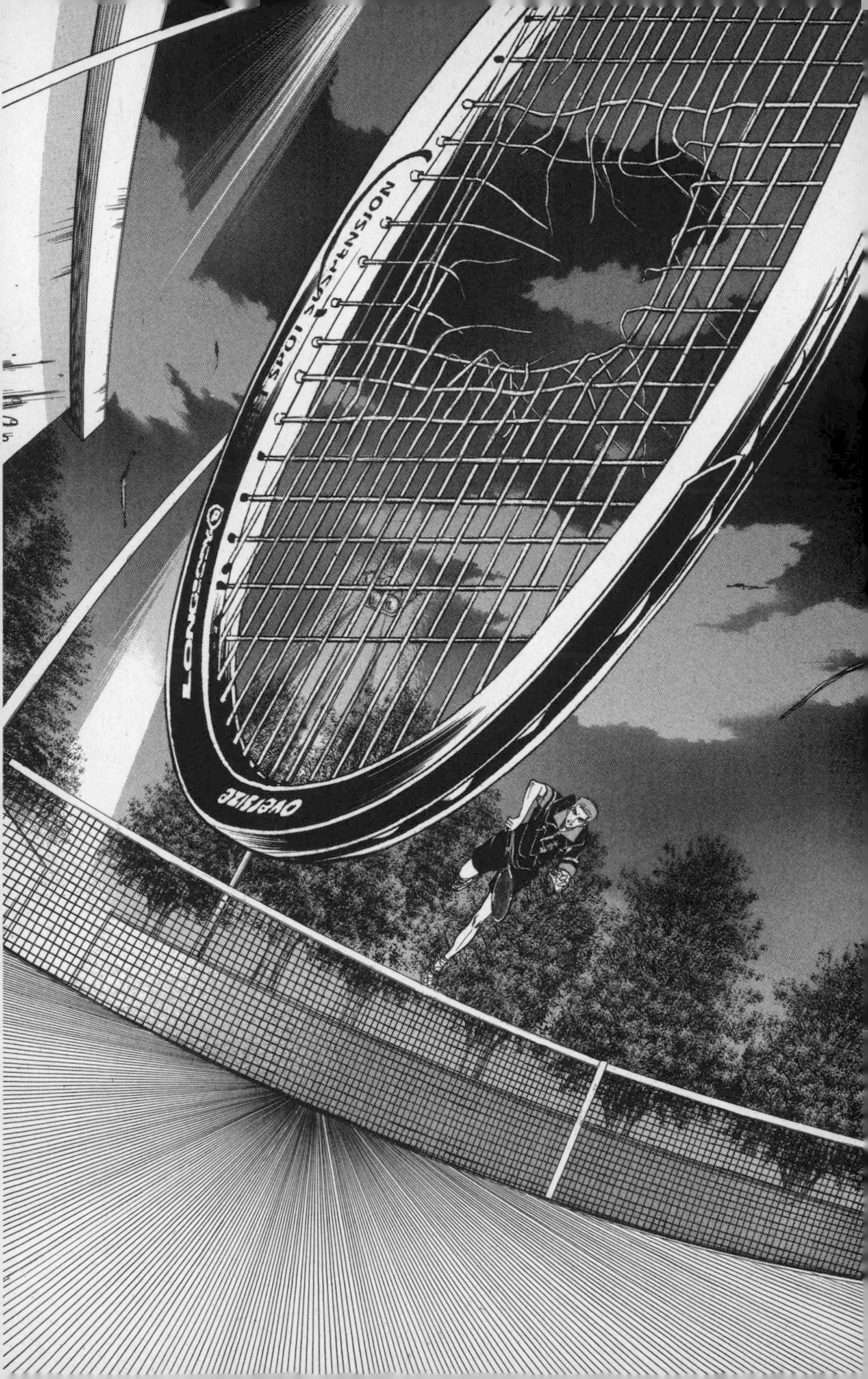
SPOT SUSPENSION

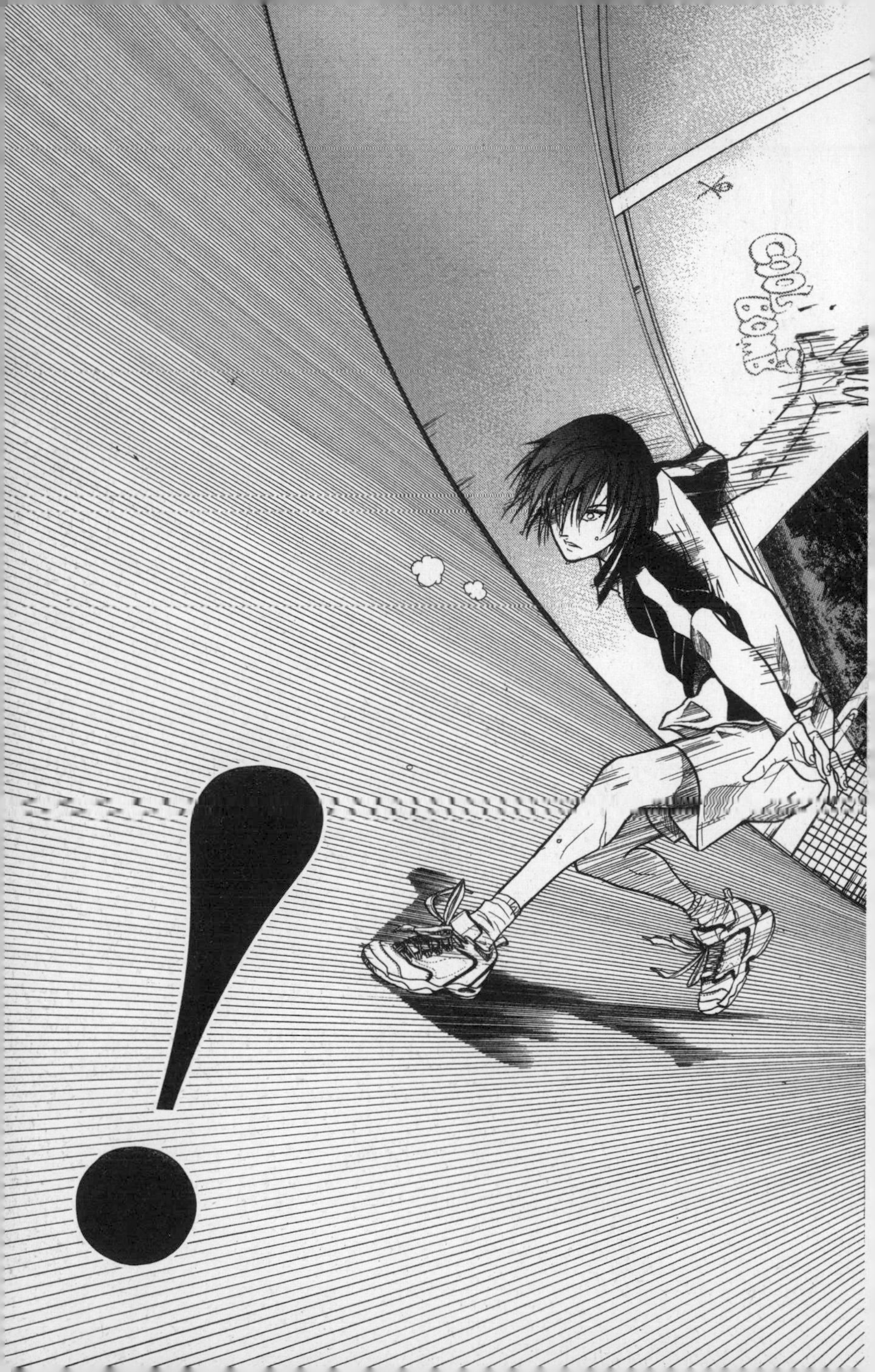
COOL BOMB
!

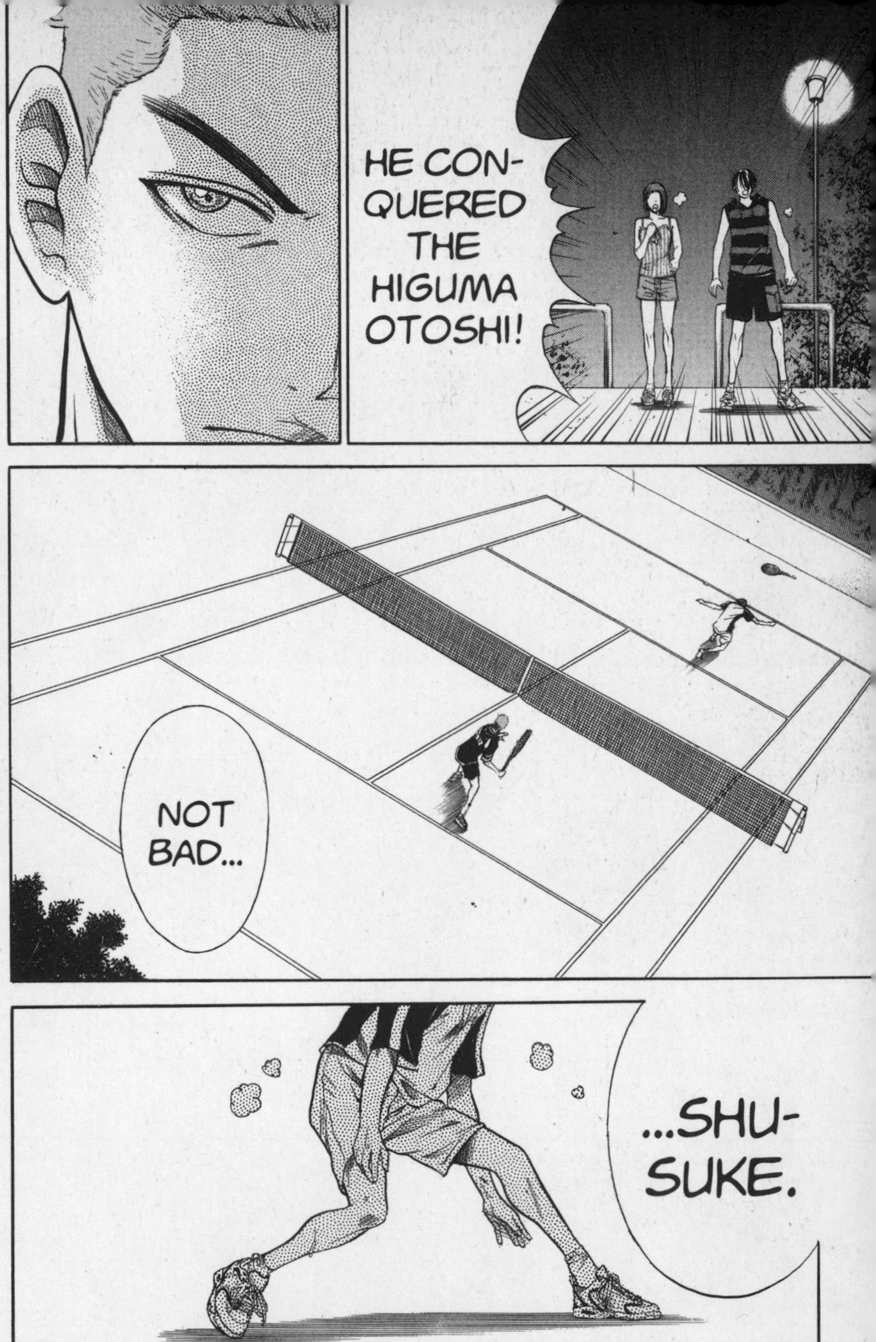
HE CON-QUERED THE HIGUMA OTOSHI!
NOT BAD...
...SHU-SUKE.

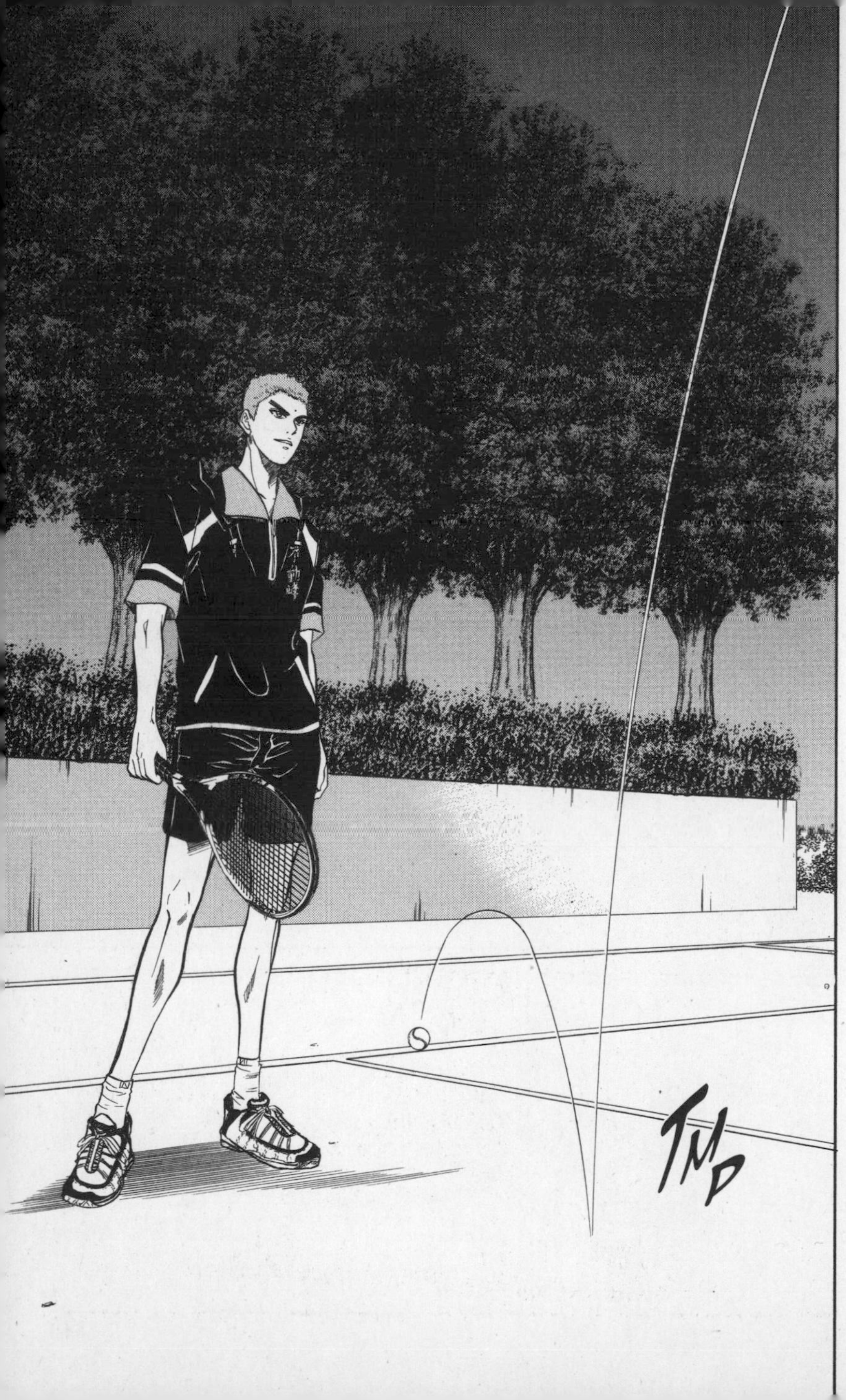
TMP

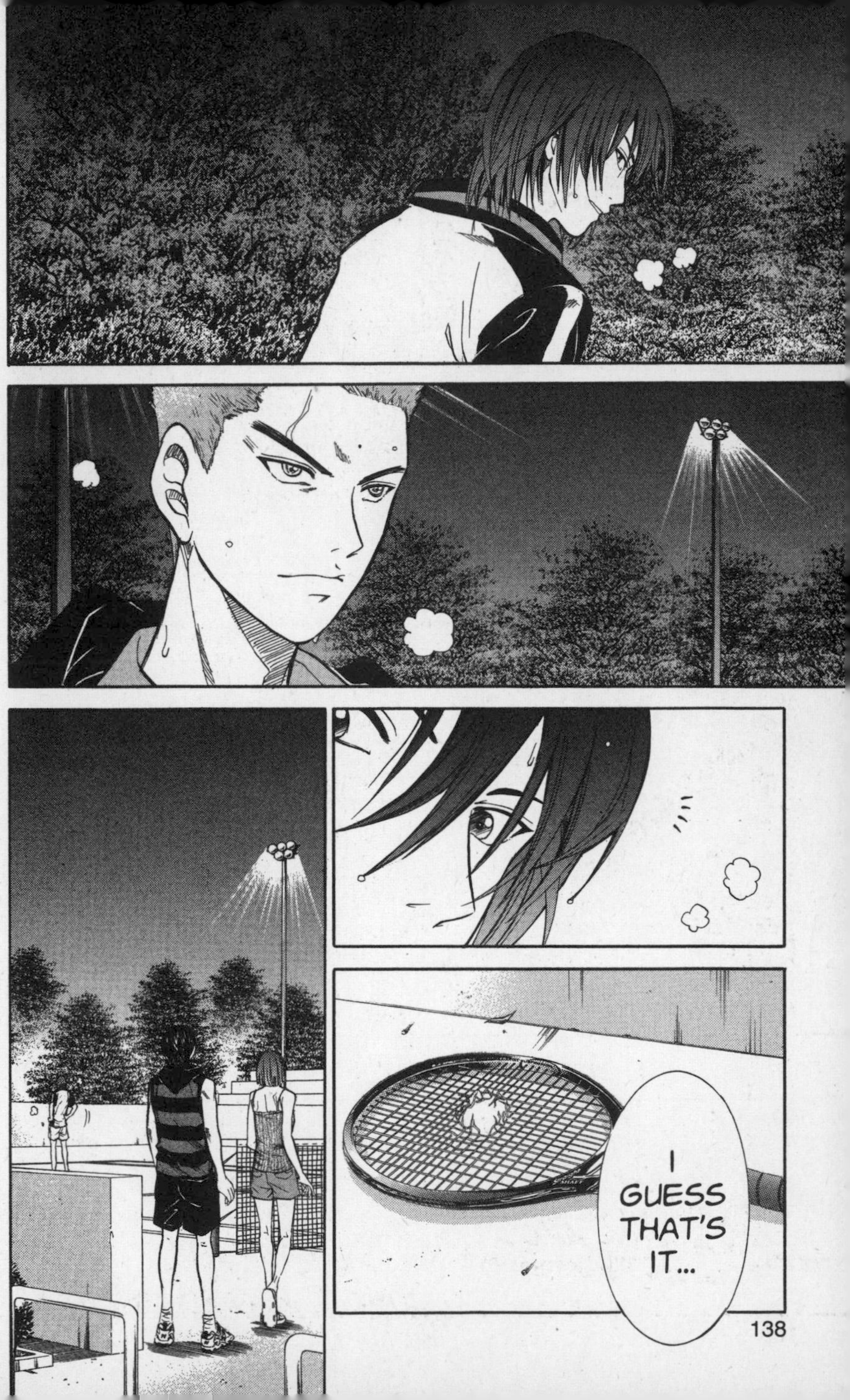
I GUESS THAT'S IT...

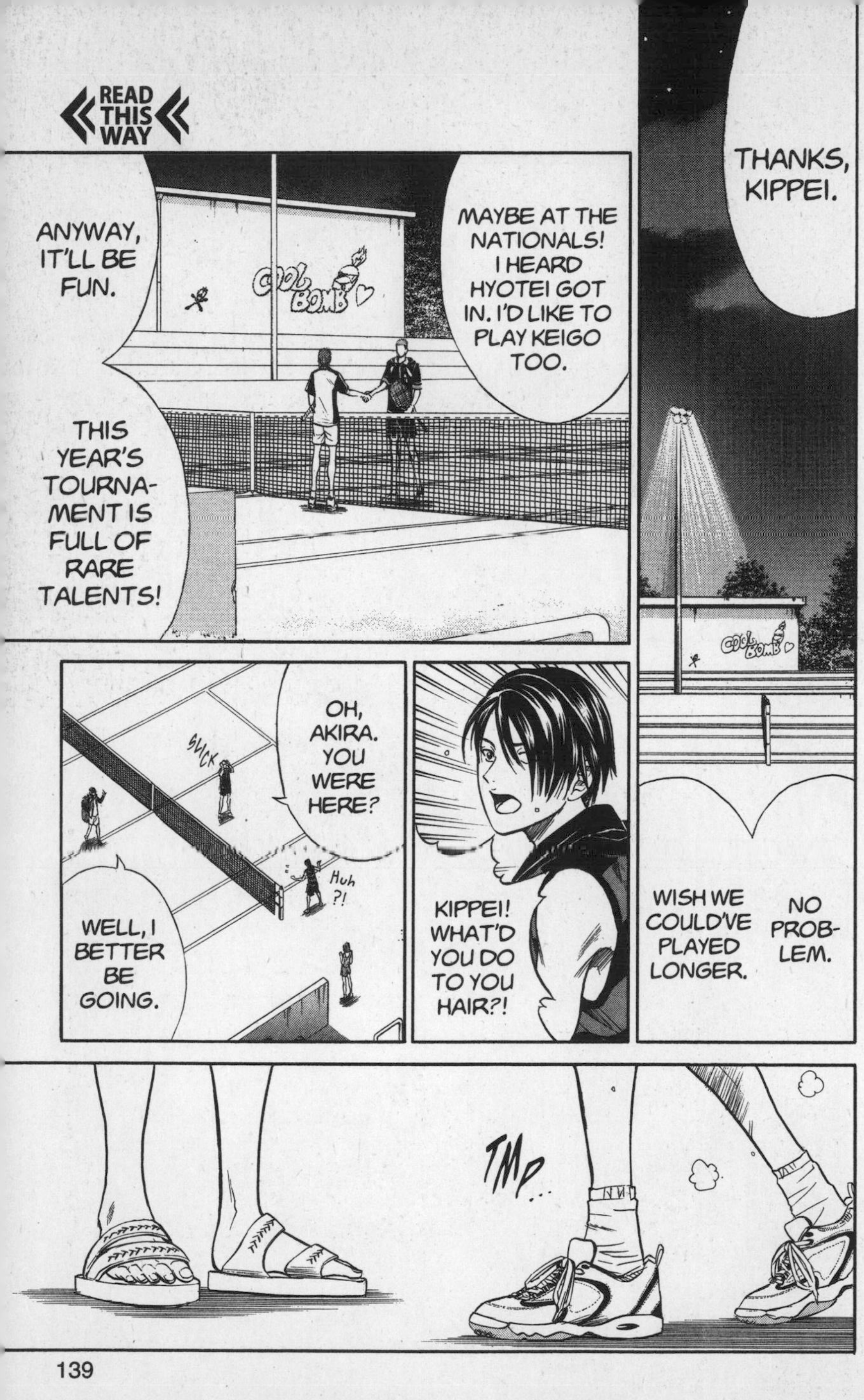
READ THIS WAY
THANKS, KIPPEI.
NO PROBLEM.
WISH WE COULD'VE PLAYED LONGER.
MAYBE AT THE NATIONALS! I HEARD HYOTEI GOT IN. I'D LIKE TO PLAY KEIGO TOO.
ANYWAY, IT'LL BE FUN.
THIS YEAR'S TOURNAMENT IS FULL OF RARE TALENTS!
COOL BOMB
KIPPEI! WHAT'D YOU DO TO YOU HAIR?!
OH, AKIRA. YOU WERE HERE?
SLICK
Huh ?!
WELL, I BETTER BE GOING.
TMP...

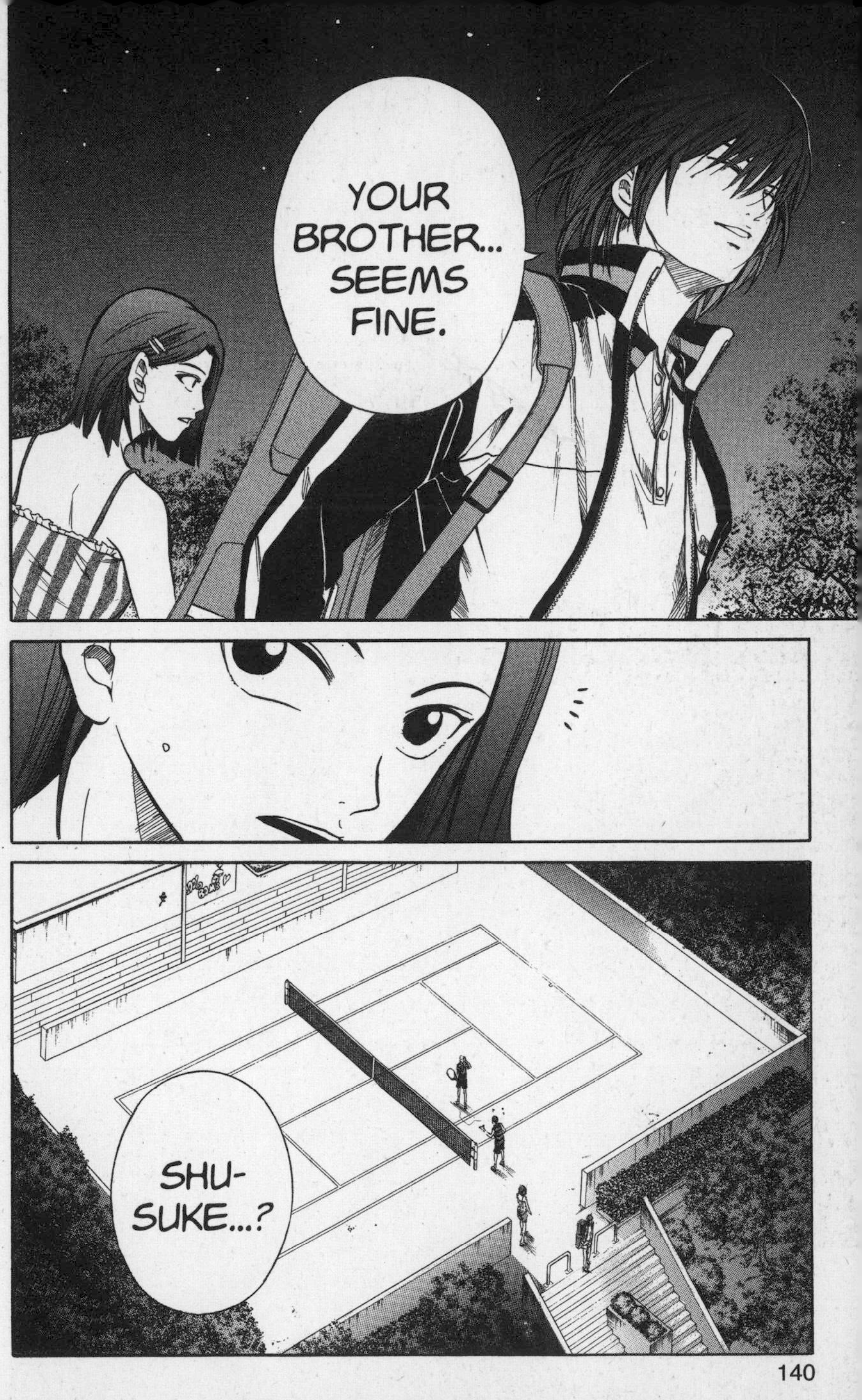
YOUR BROTHER... SEEMS FINE.
SHU-SUKE...?

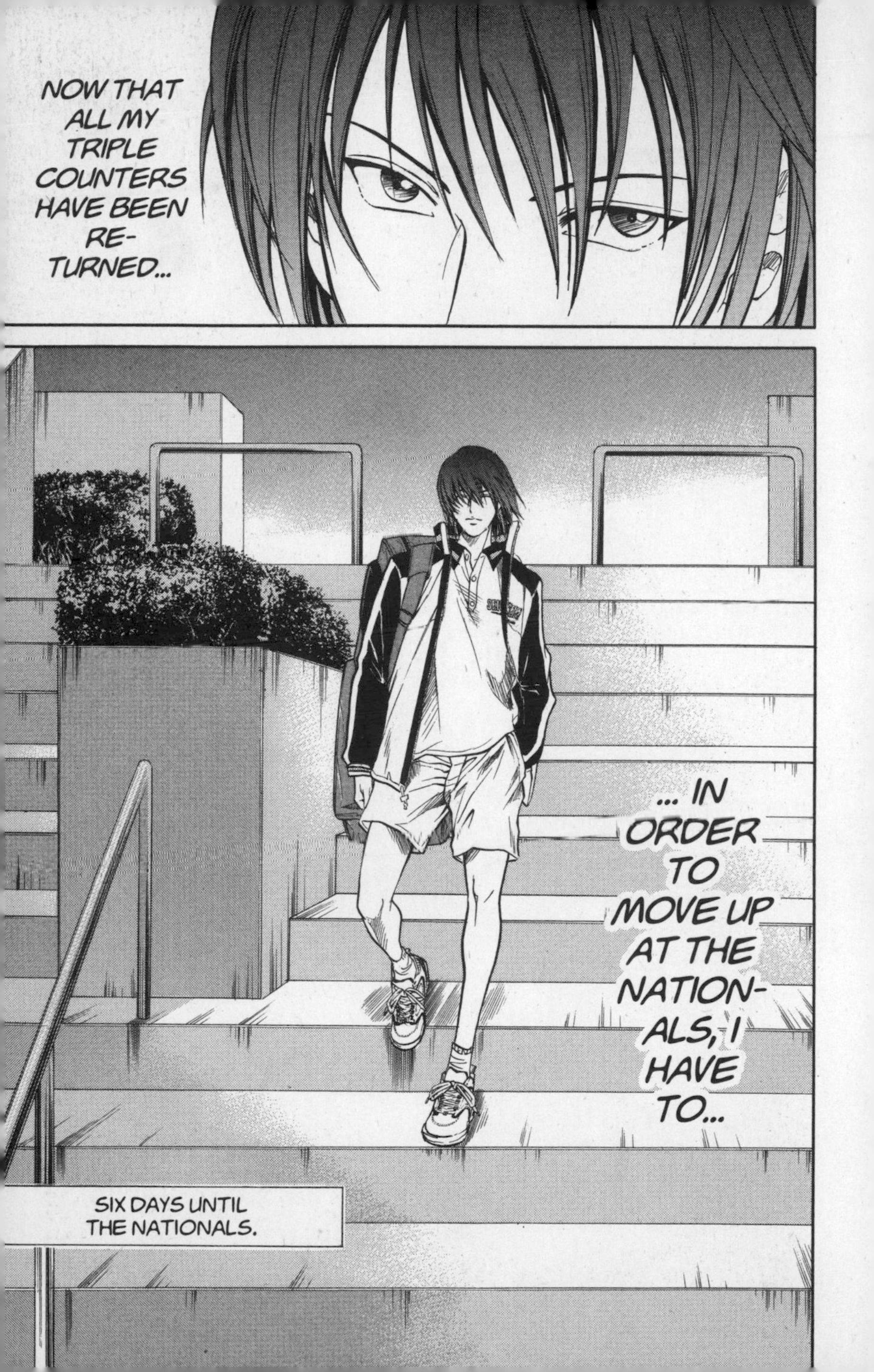
NOW THAT ALL MY TRIPLE COUNTERS HAVE BEEN RE-TURNED...
... IN ORDER TO MOVE UP AT THE NATION-ALS, I HAVE TO...
SIX DAYS UNTIL THE NATIONALS.

テニスの王子様

THE PRINCE OF TENNIS

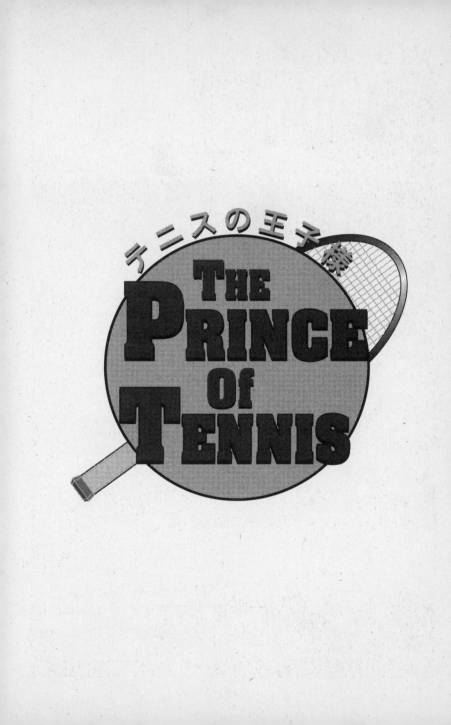

WILD 1: WILD CHILD

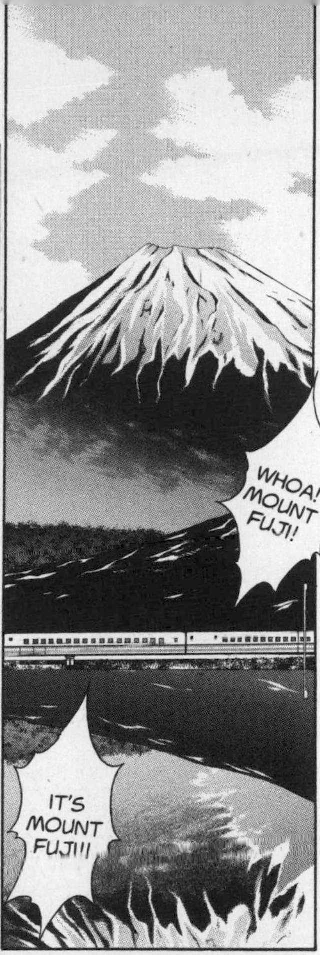
WHOA! MOUNT FUJI!
IT'S MOUNT FUJI!!

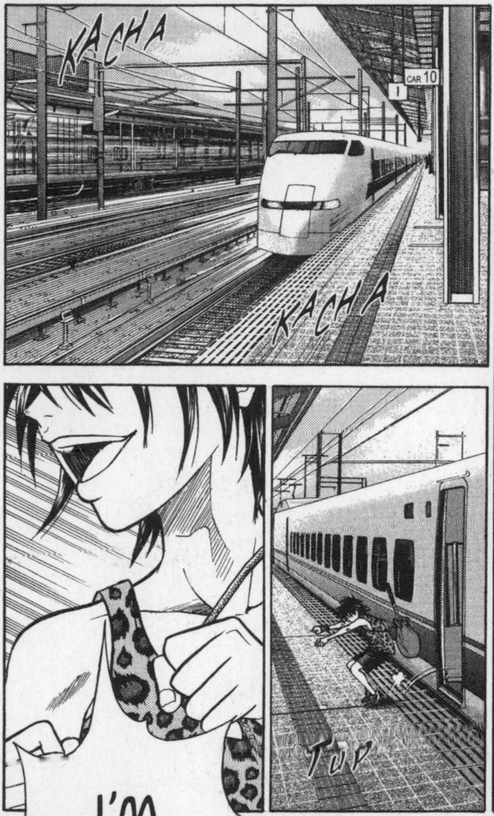
KACHA
CAR 10
KACHA
TUP
I'M HERE, TOKYO!!

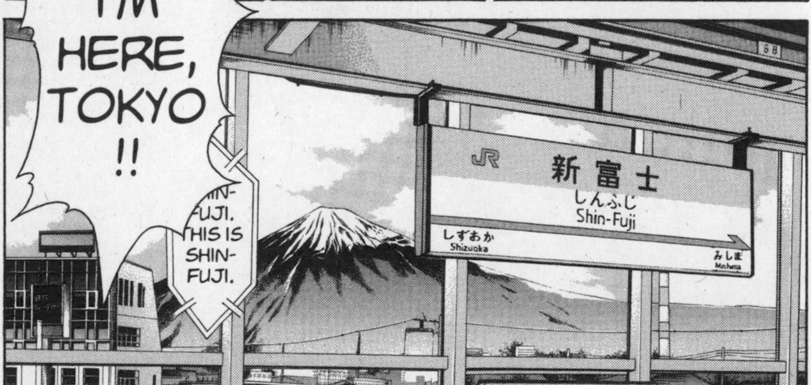
JR
新富士
しんふじ
Shin-Fuji
しずおか
Shizuoka
みしま
SHIN-FUJI. THIS IS SHIN-FUJI.

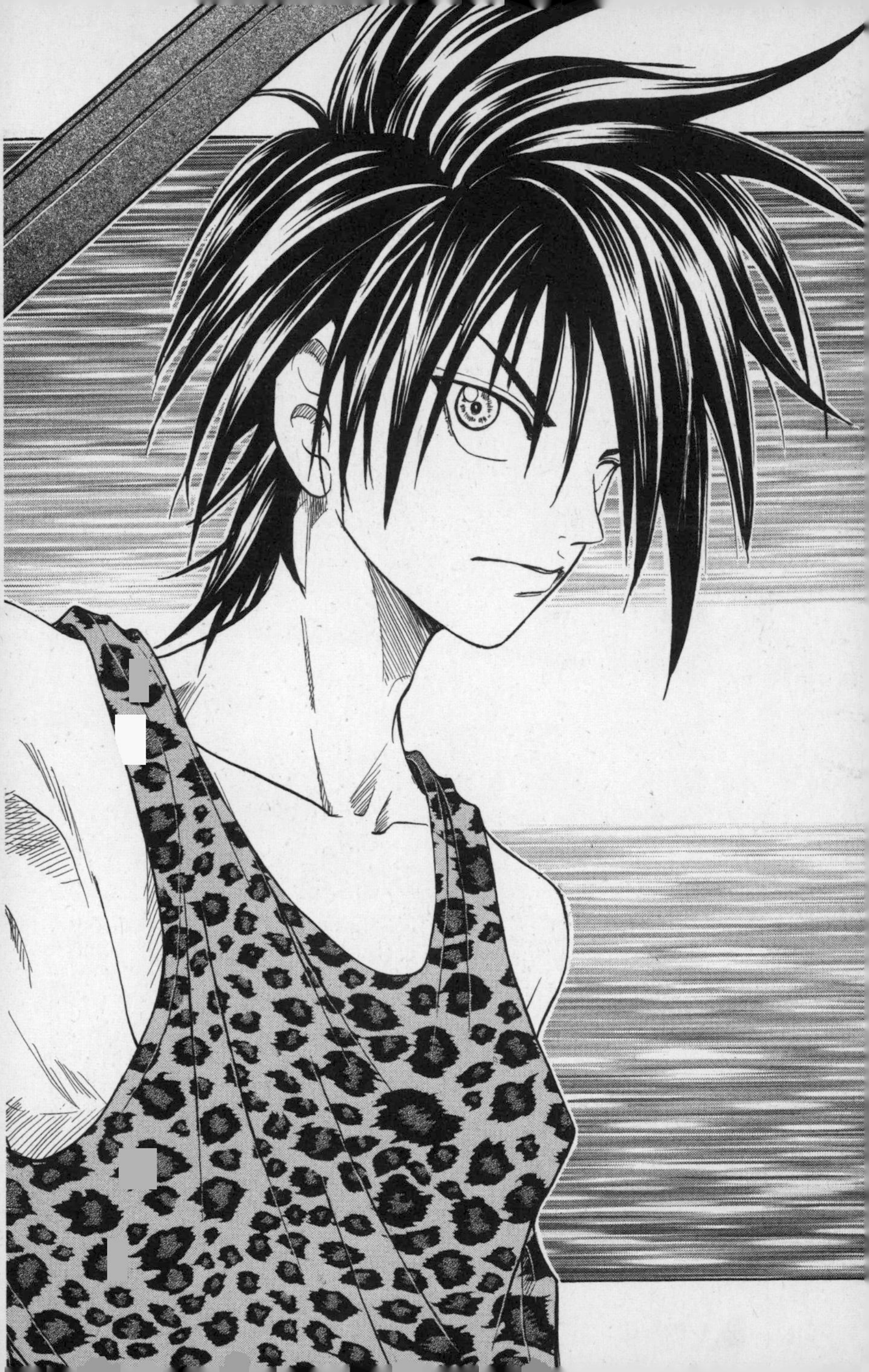

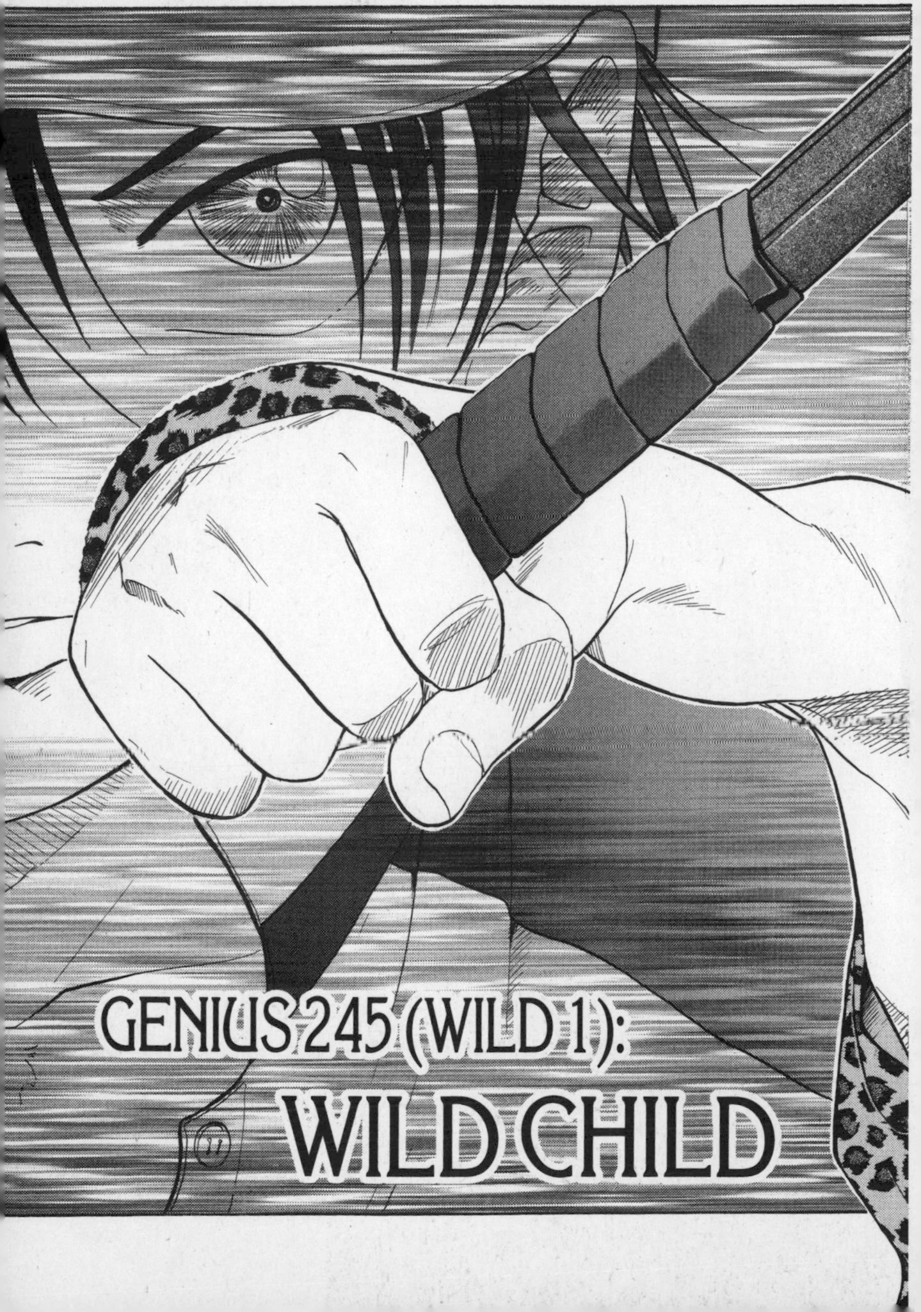
GENIUS 245 (WILD 1):
WILD CHILD

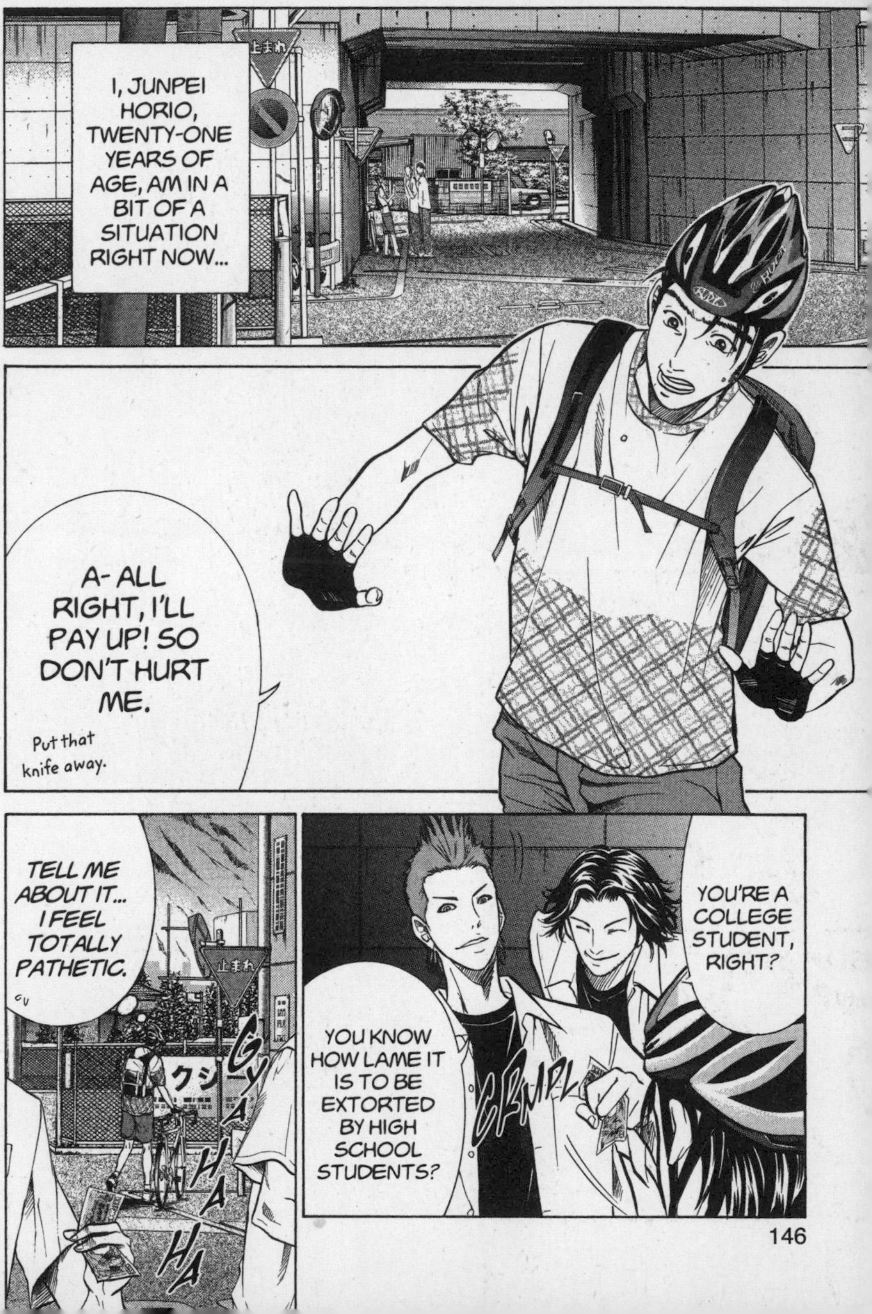

I, JUNPEI HORIO, TWENTY-ONE YEARS OF AGE, AM IN A BIT OF A SITUATION RIGHT NOW...
止まれ
A- ALL RIGHT, I'LL PAY UP! SO DON'T HURT ME.
Put that knife away.
YOU'RE A COLLEGE STUDENT, RIGHT?
YOU KNOW HOW LAME IT IS TO BE EXTORTED BY HIGH SCHOOL STUDENTS?
CRMPL
TELL ME ABOUT IT... I FEEL TOTALLY PATHETIC.
止まれ
GYAHAHAHA

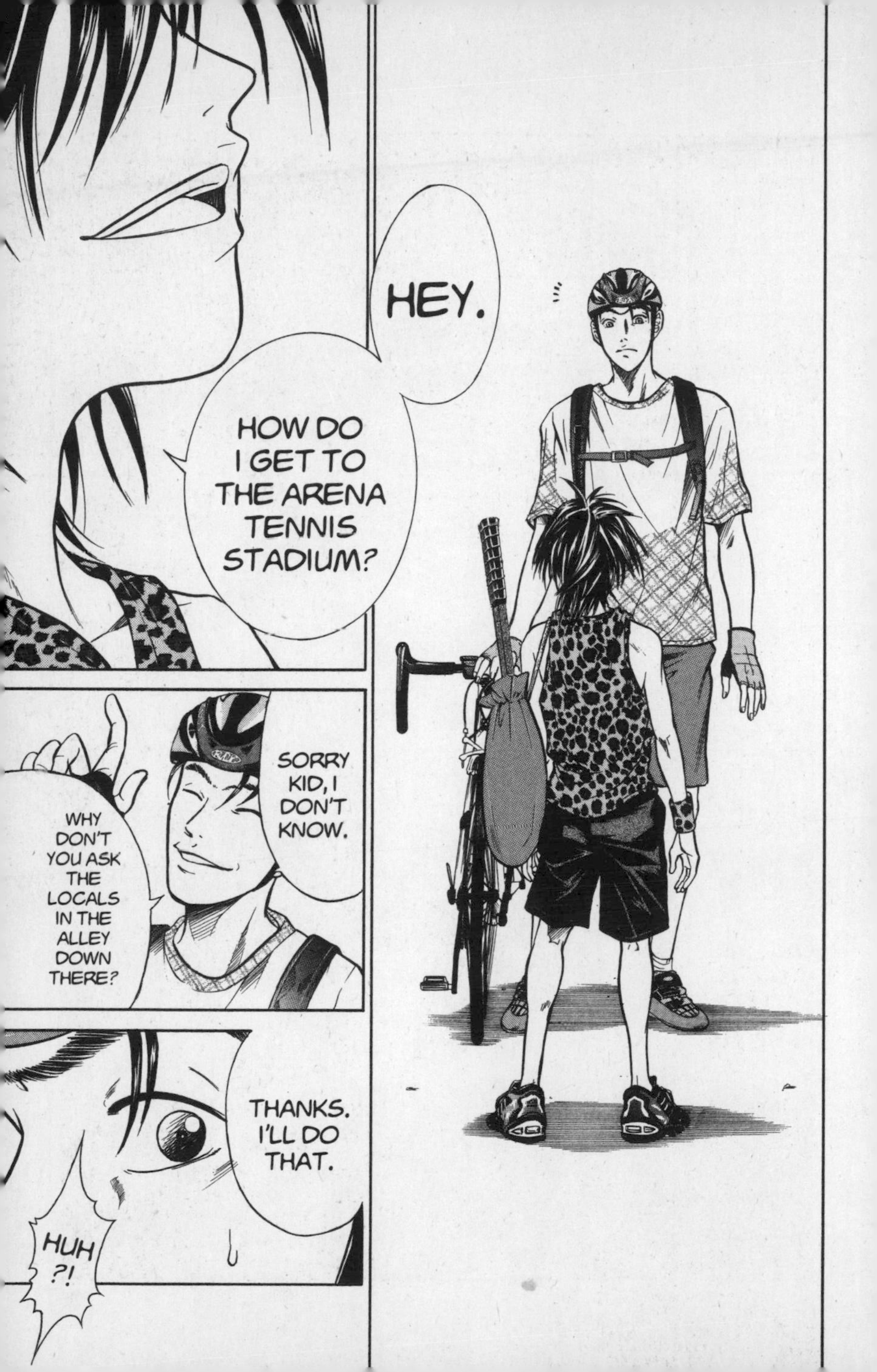
HEY.
HOW DO I GET TO THE ARENA TENNIS STADIUM?
SORRY KID, I DON'T KNOW.
WHY DON'T YOU ASK THE LOCALS IN THE ALLEY DOWN THERE?
THANKS. I'LL DO THAT.
HUH ?!

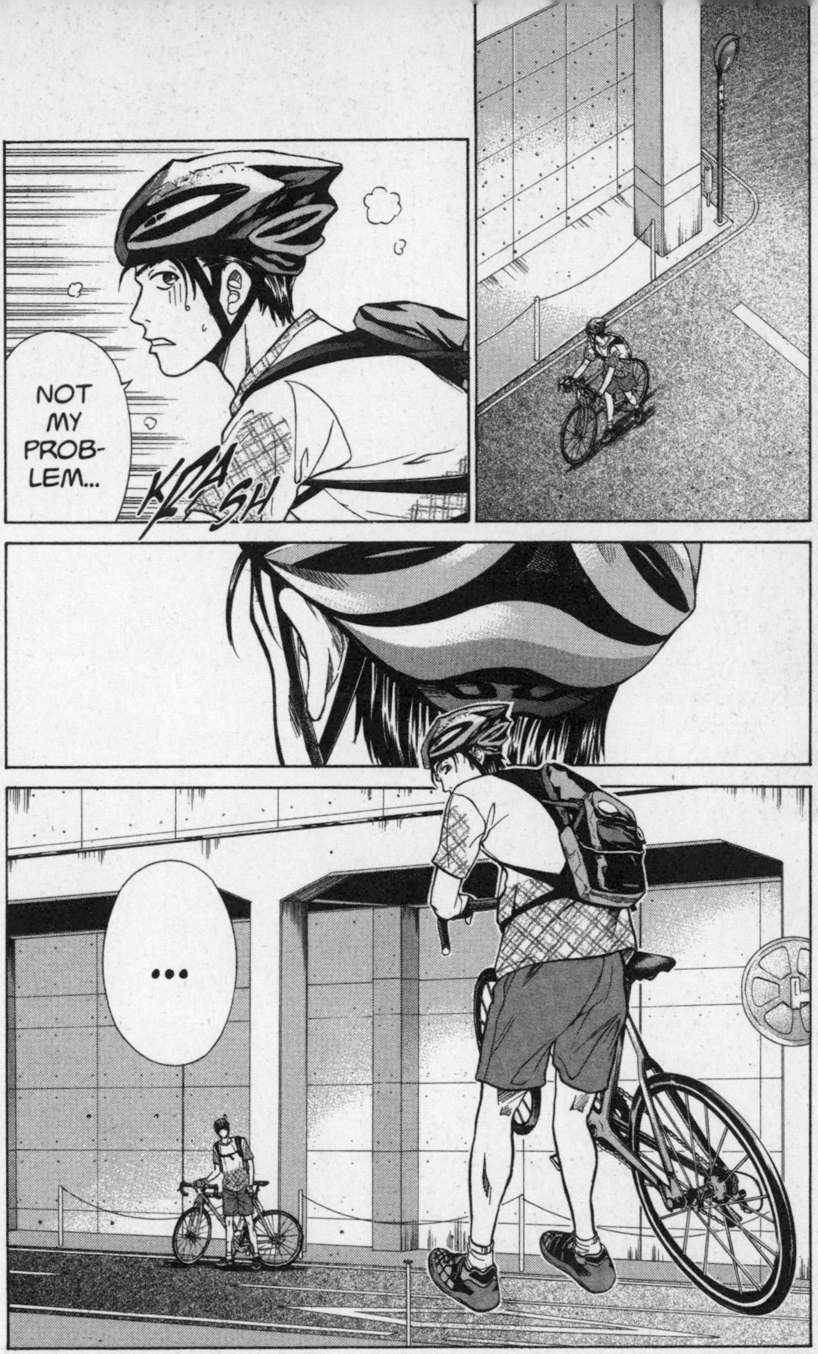
NOT MY PROB-LEM...
KLASH
...

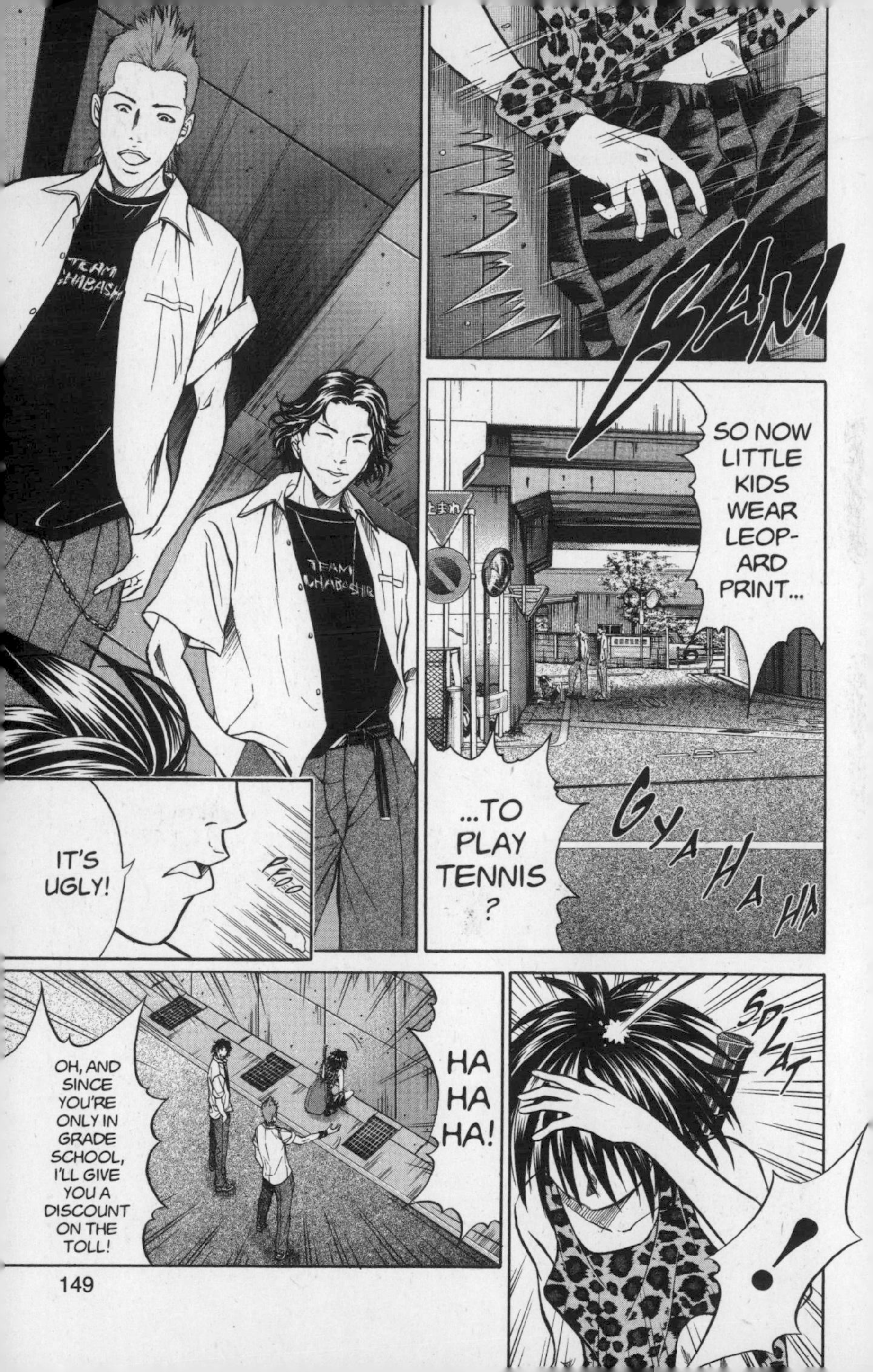
BAM
SO NOW LITTLE KIDS WEAR LEOP-ARD PRINT...
GYAHAHAHA
...TO PLAY TENNIS?
PFOO
IT'S UGLY!
SPLAT
!
HA HA HA!
OH, AND SINCE YOU'RE ONLY IN GRADE SCHOOL, I'LL GIVE YOU A DISCOUNT ON THE TOLL!

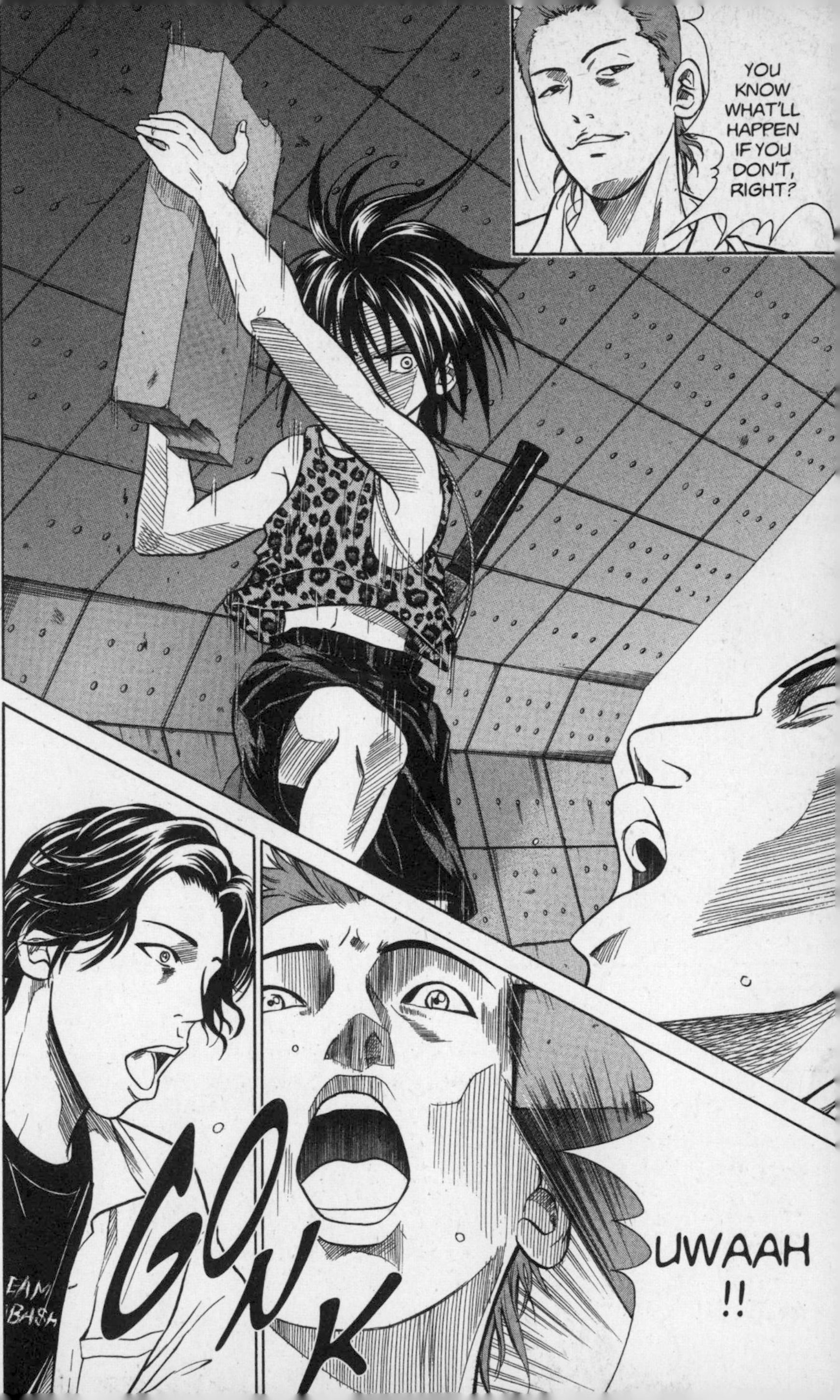
YOU KNOW WHAT'LL HAPPEN IF YOU DON'T, RIGHT?
GONK
UWAAH !!

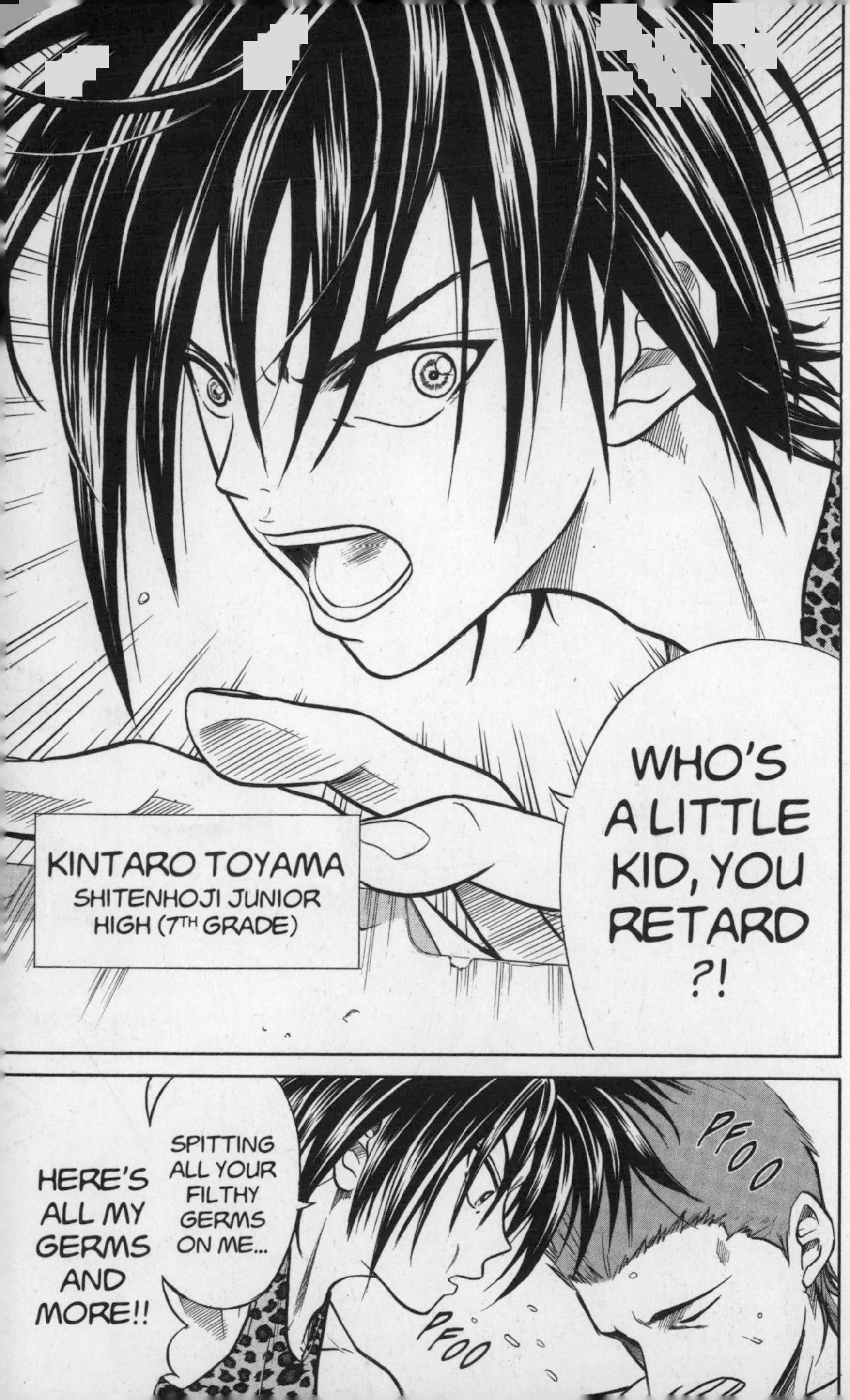
WHO'S A LITTLE KID, YOU RETARD ?!
KINTARO TOYAMA
SHITENHOJI JUNIOR HIGH (7TH GRADE)
PFOO
SPITTING ALL YOUR FILTHY GERMS ON ME...
HERE'S ALL MY GERMS AND MORE!!
PFOO

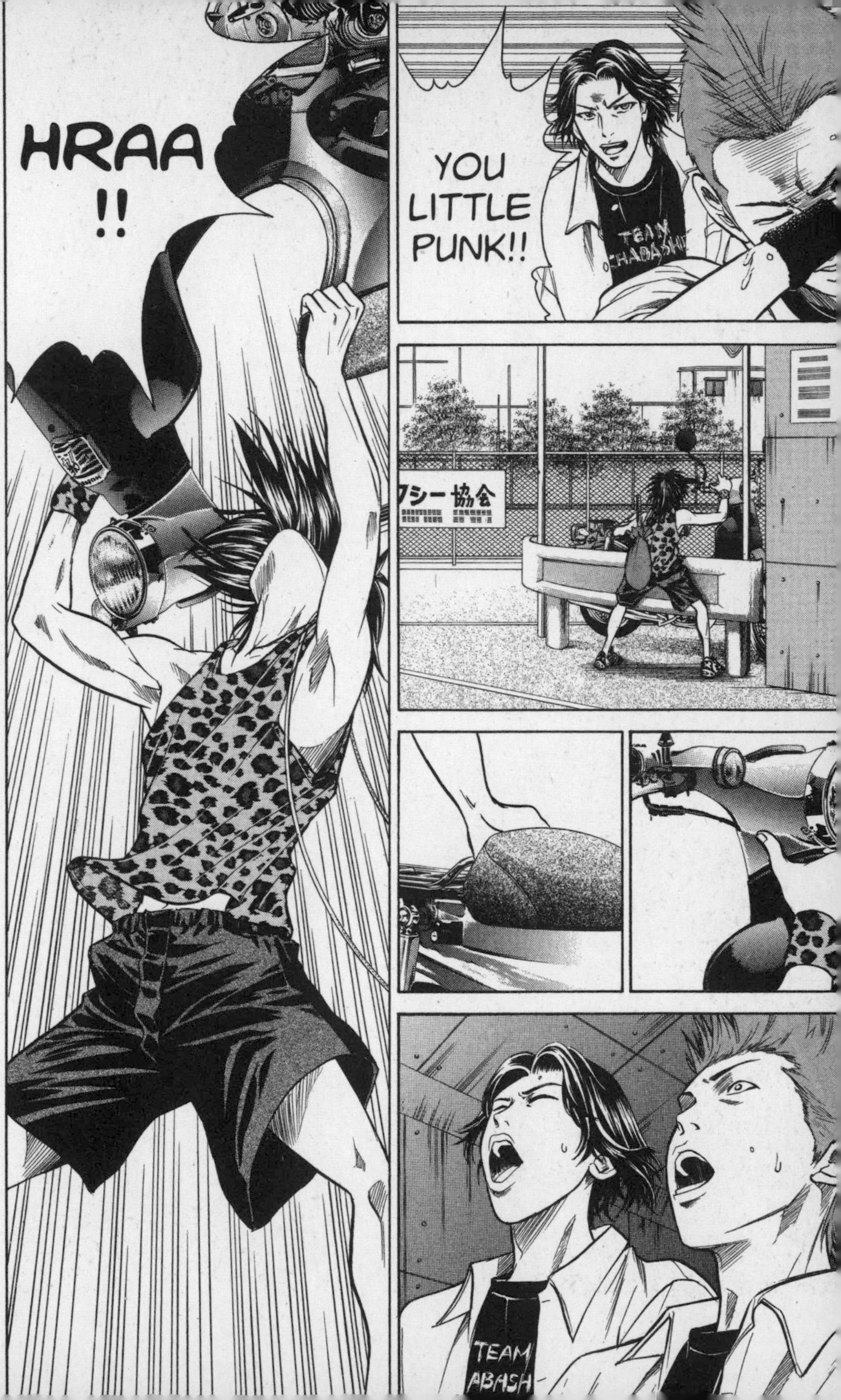
YOU LITTLE PUNK!!
TEAM
CHADASHI
フシー 協会
TEAM
ABASH
HRAA !!

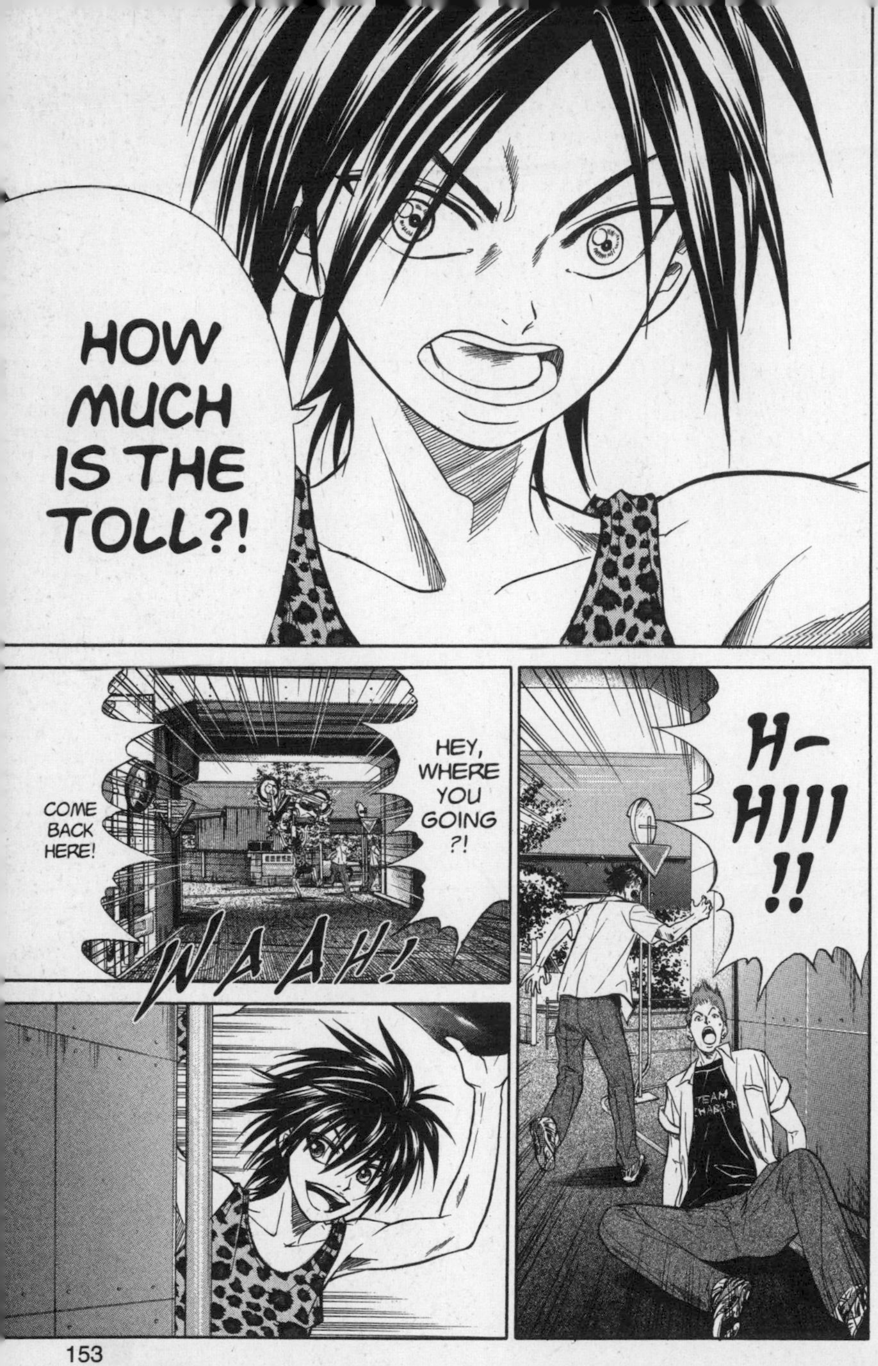
HOW MUCH IS THE TOLL?!
H-HIII!!
HEY, WHERE YOU GOING?!
COME BACK HERE!
WAAH!

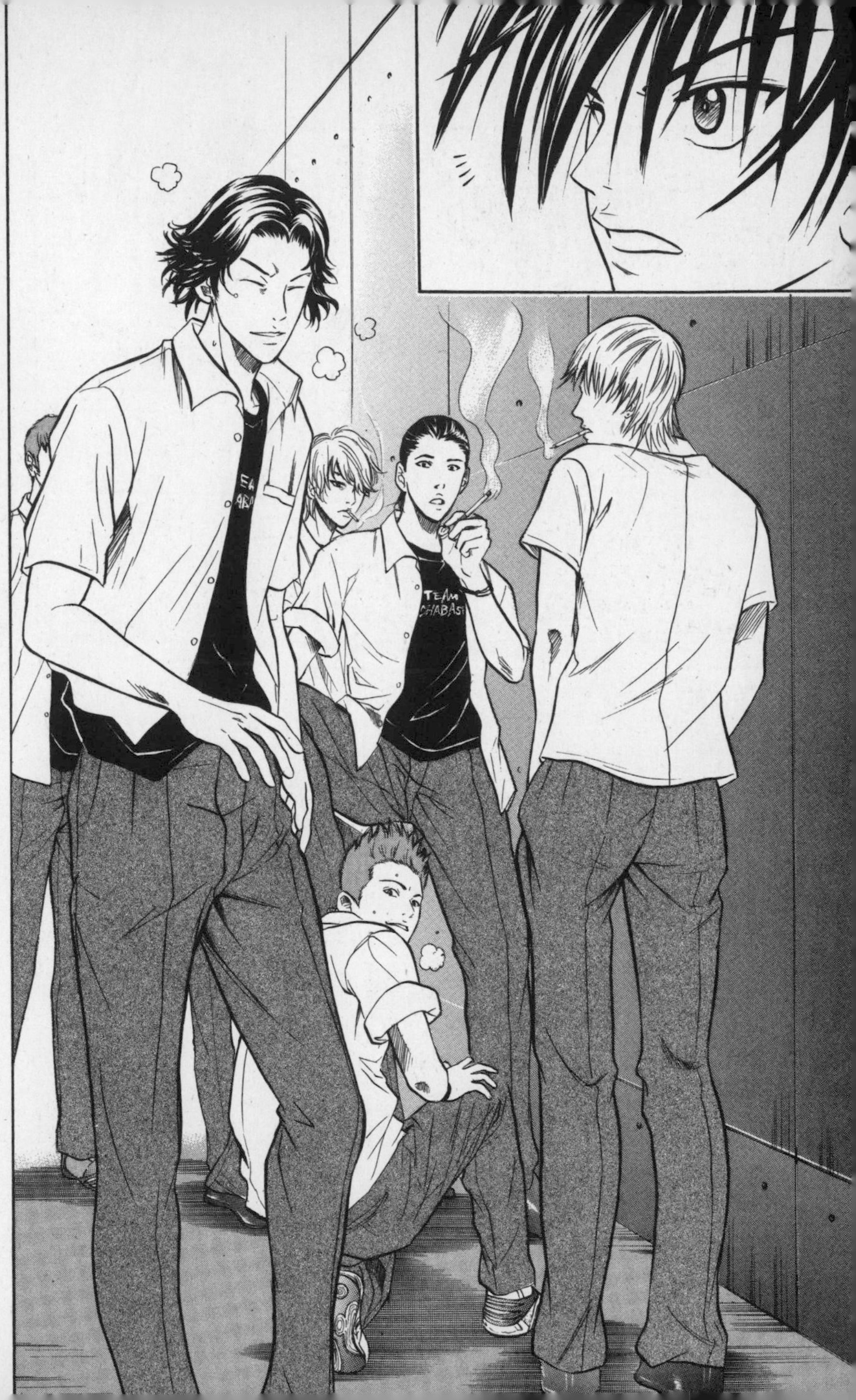
TEAM CHABAS

READ THIS WAY

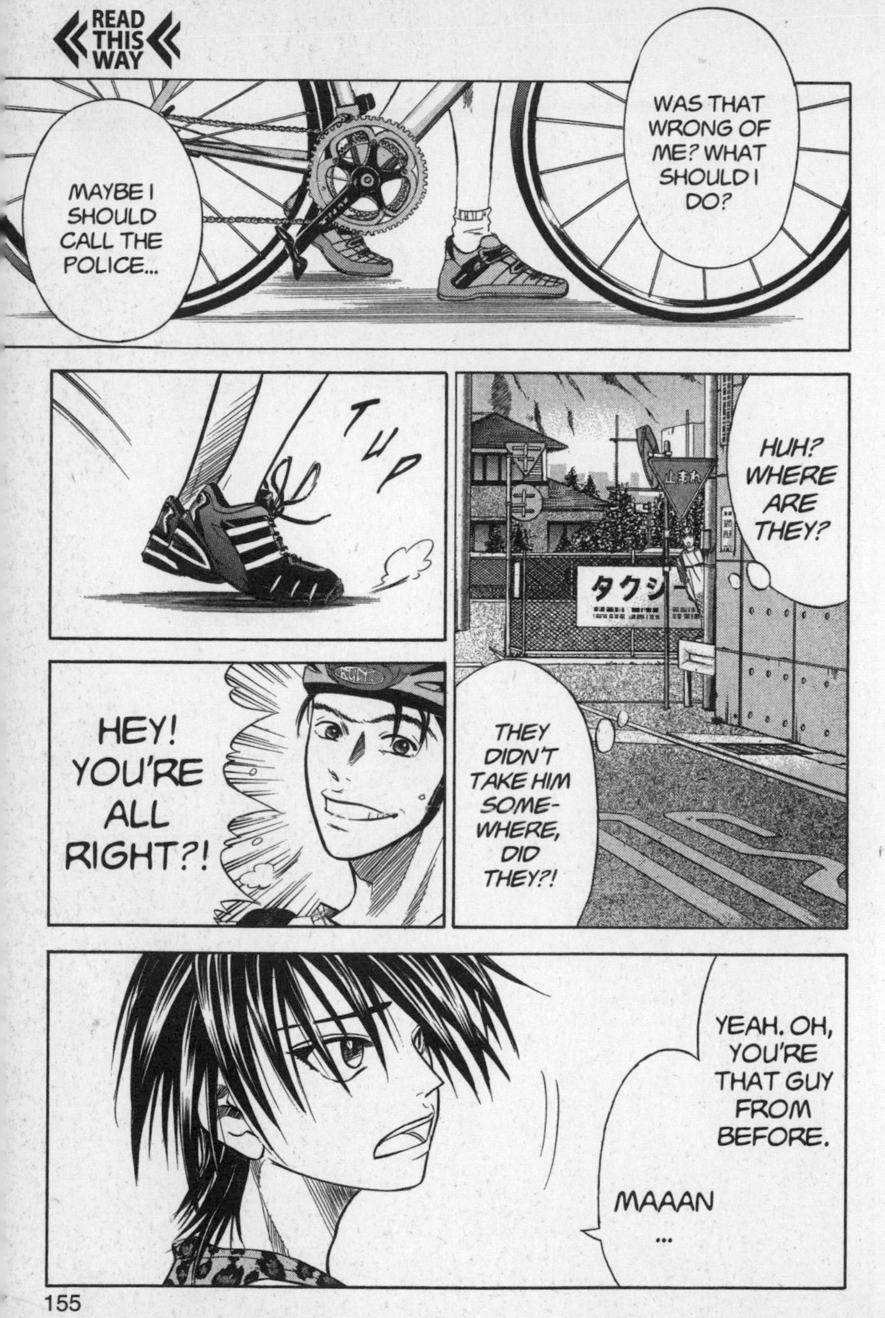

WAS THAT WRONG OF ME? WHAT SHOULD I DO?
MAYBE I SHOULD CALL THE POLICE...
HUH? WHERE ARE THEY?
タクシー
THEY DIDN'T TAKE HIM SOME-WHERE, DID THEY?!
TUP
HEY! YOU'RE ALL RIGHT?!
YEAH. OH, YOU'RE THAT GUY FROM BEFORE.
MAAAN ...

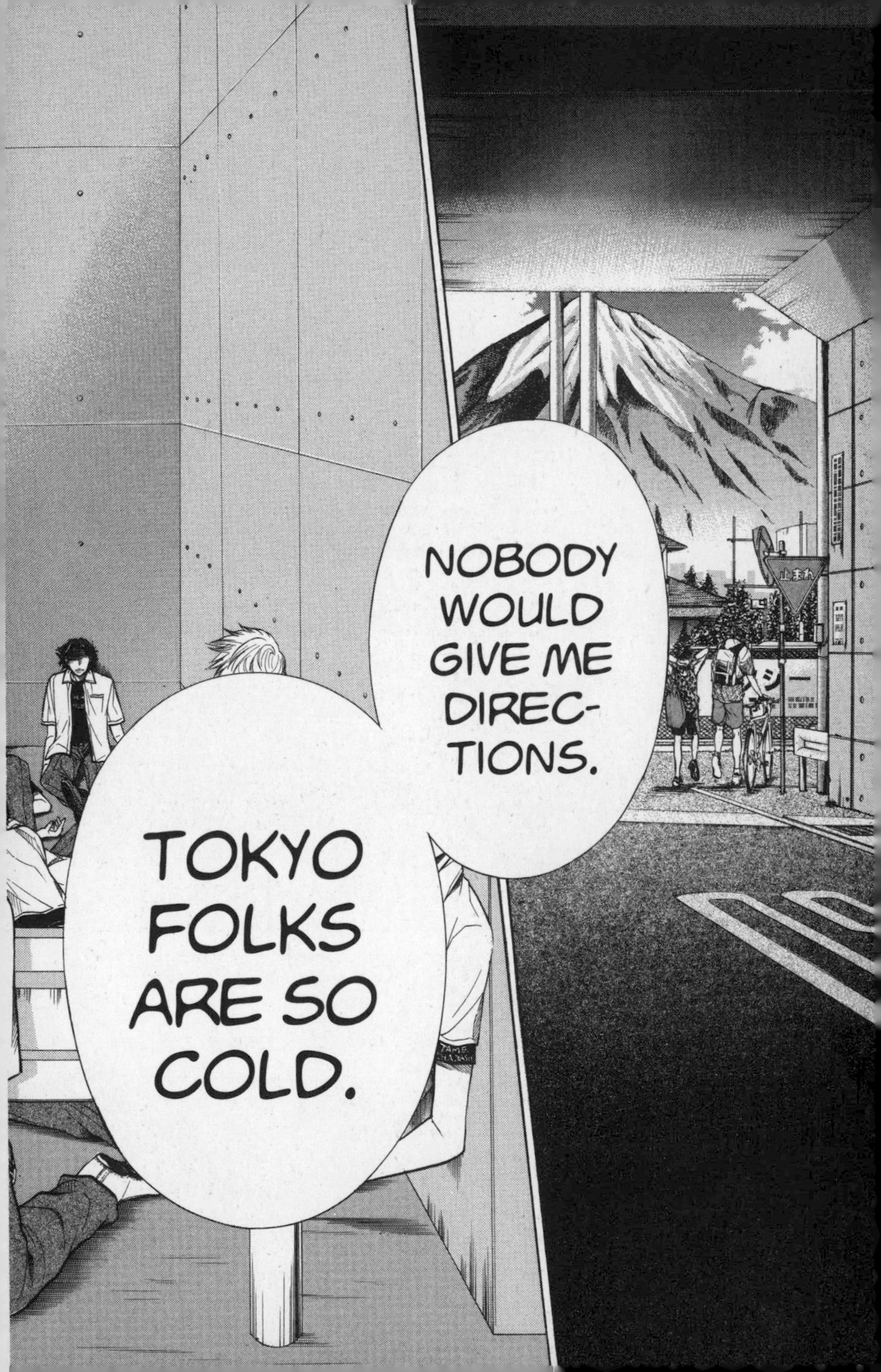
NOBODY WOULD GIVE ME DIRECTIONS.
TOKYO FOLKS ARE SO COLD.

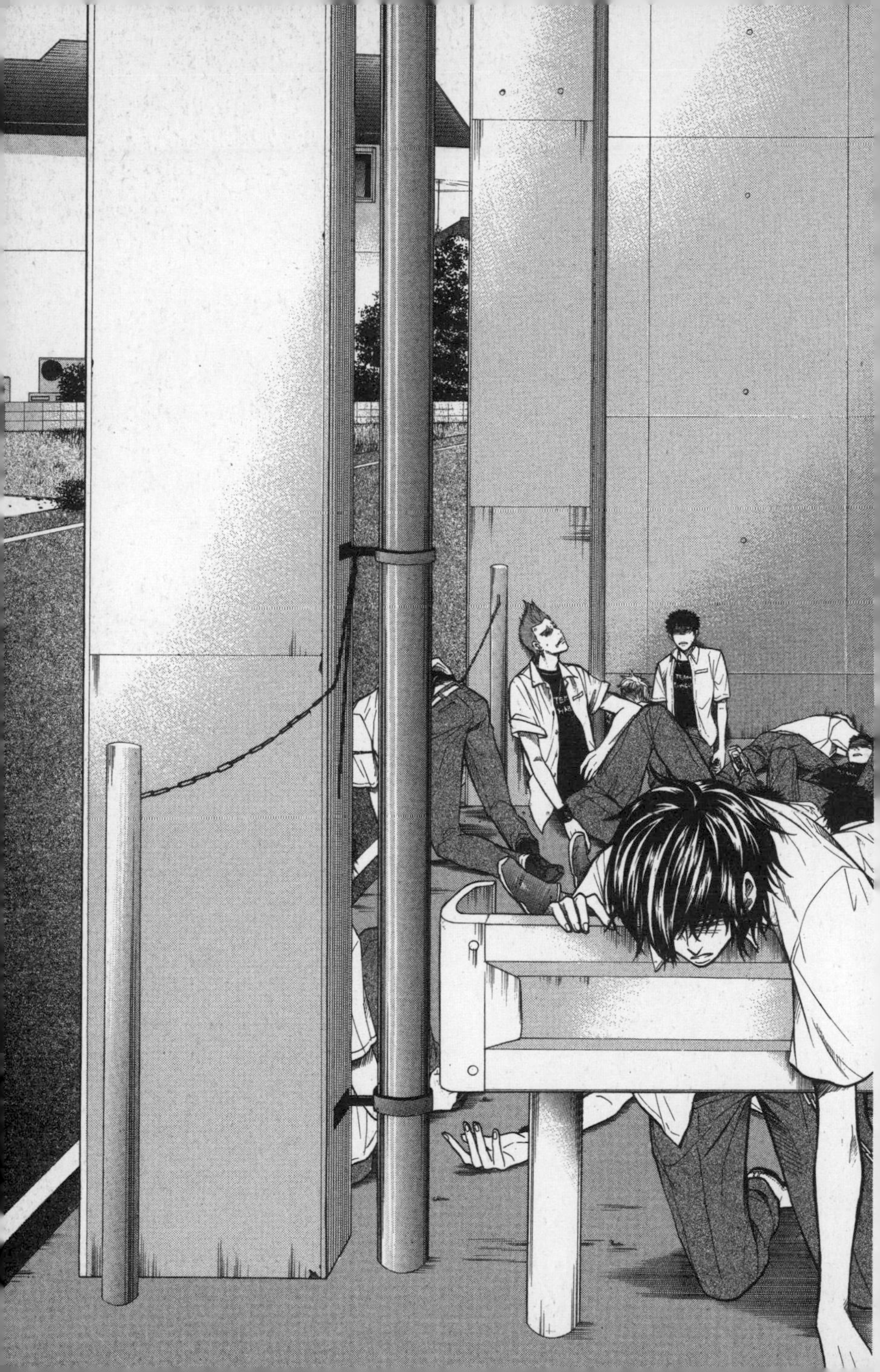

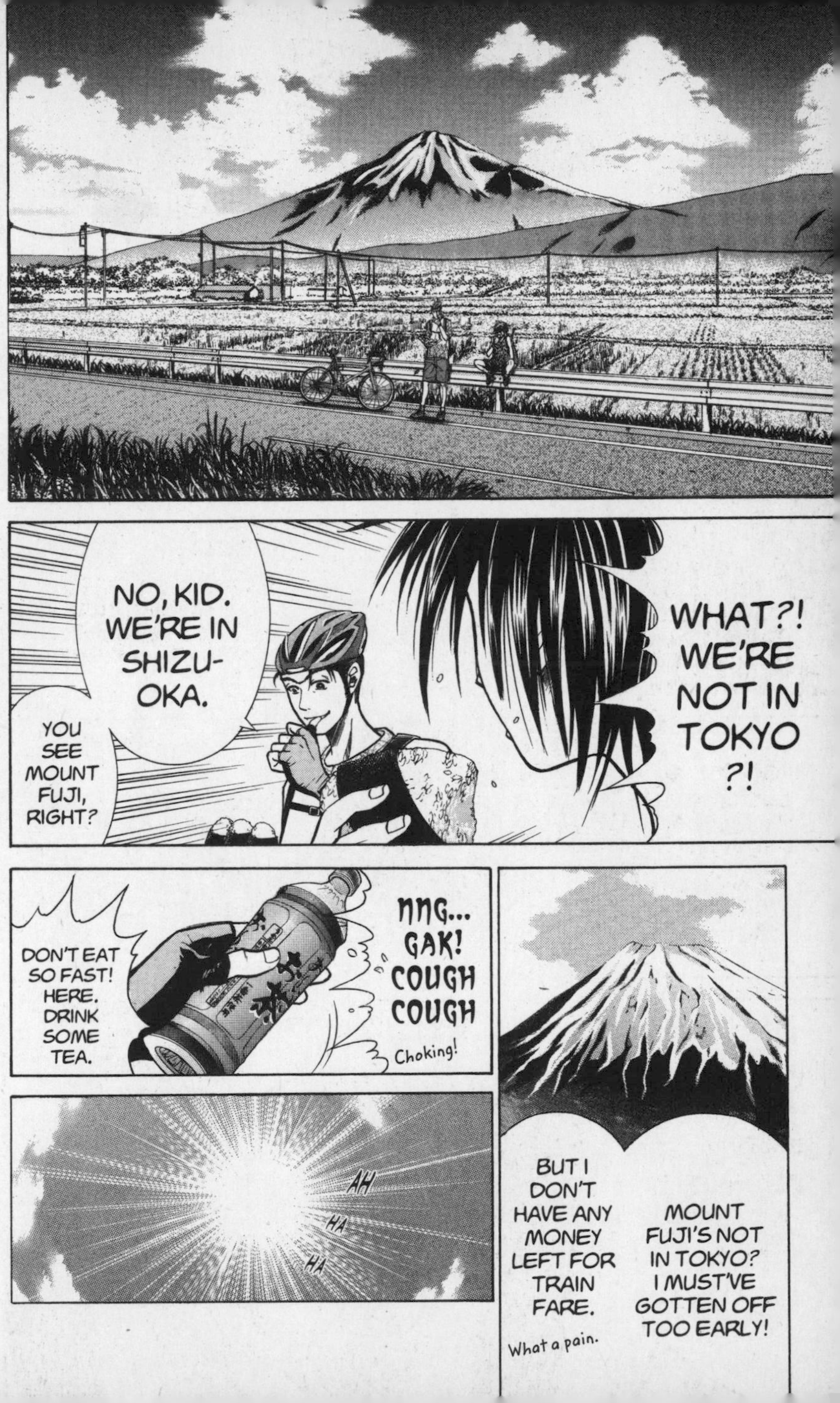
WHAT?! WE'RE NOT IN TOKYO ?!
NO, KID. WE'RE IN SHIZU-OKA.
YOU SEE MOUNT FUJI, RIGHT?
MOUNT FUJI'S NOT IN TOKYO? I MUST'VE GOTTEN OFF TOO EARLY!
BUT I DON'T HAVE ANY MONEY LEFT FOR TRAIN FARE.
What a pain.
NNG... GAK! COUGH COUGH
Choking!
DON'T EAT SO FAST! HERE. DRINK SOME TEA.
AH HA HA

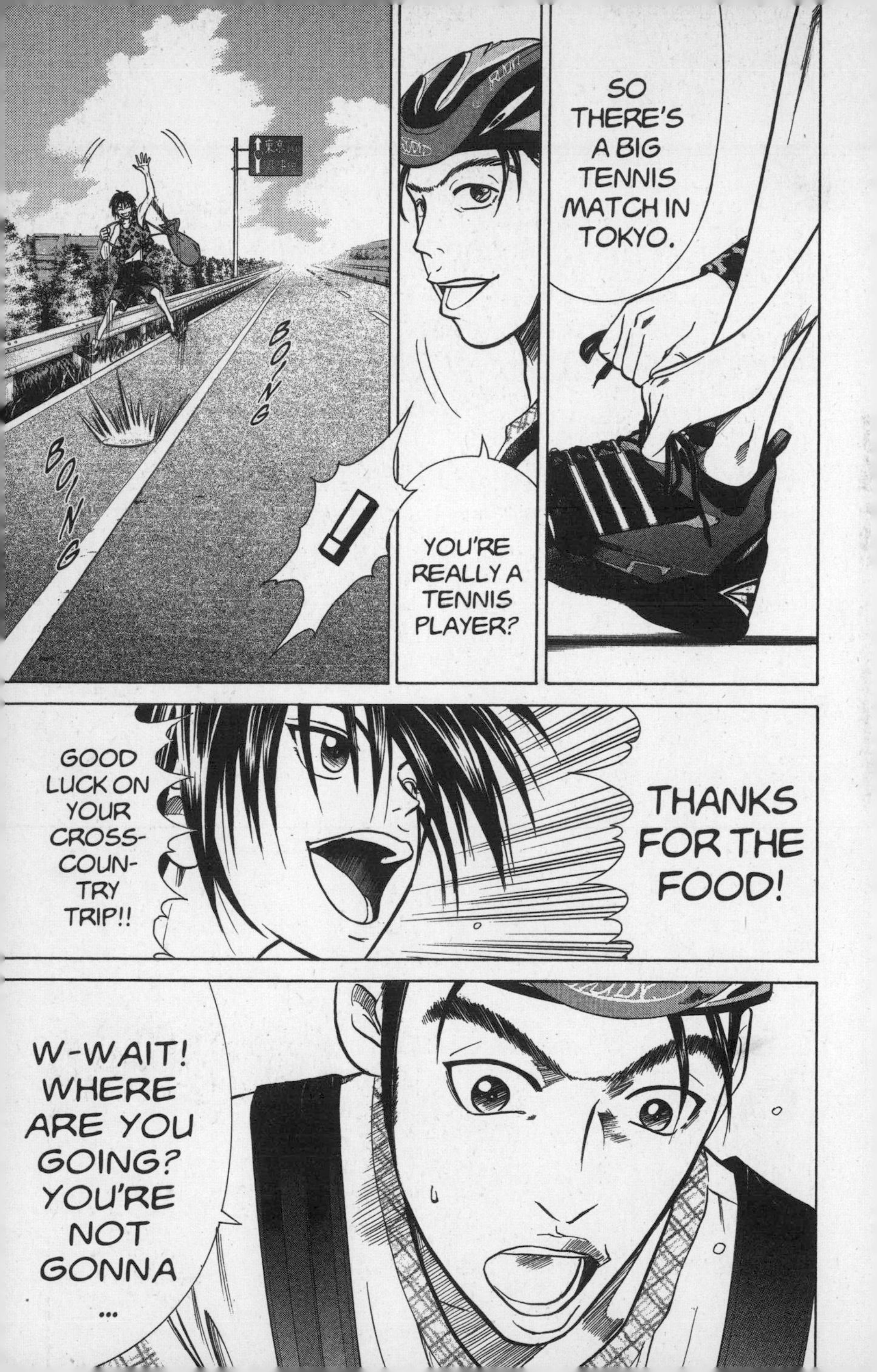

SO THERE'S A BIG TENNIS MATCH IN TOKYO.
!
YOU'RE REALLY A TENNIS PLAYER?
BOING
BOING
THANKS FOR THE FOOD!
GOOD LUCK ON YOUR CROSS-COUNTRY TRIP!!
W-WAIT! WHERE ARE YOU GOING? YOU'RE NOT GONNA ...

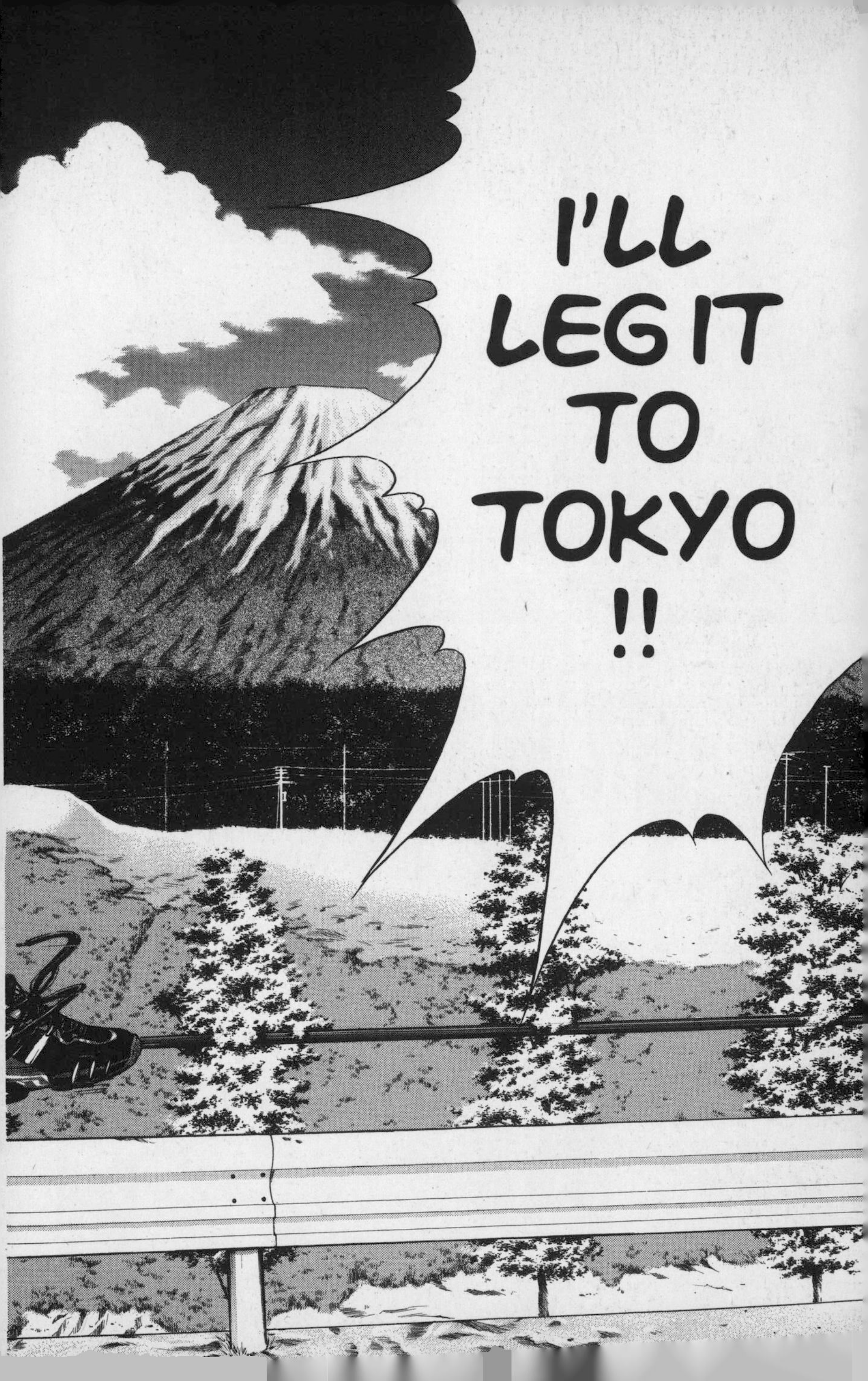
I'LL LEG IT TO TOKYO!!

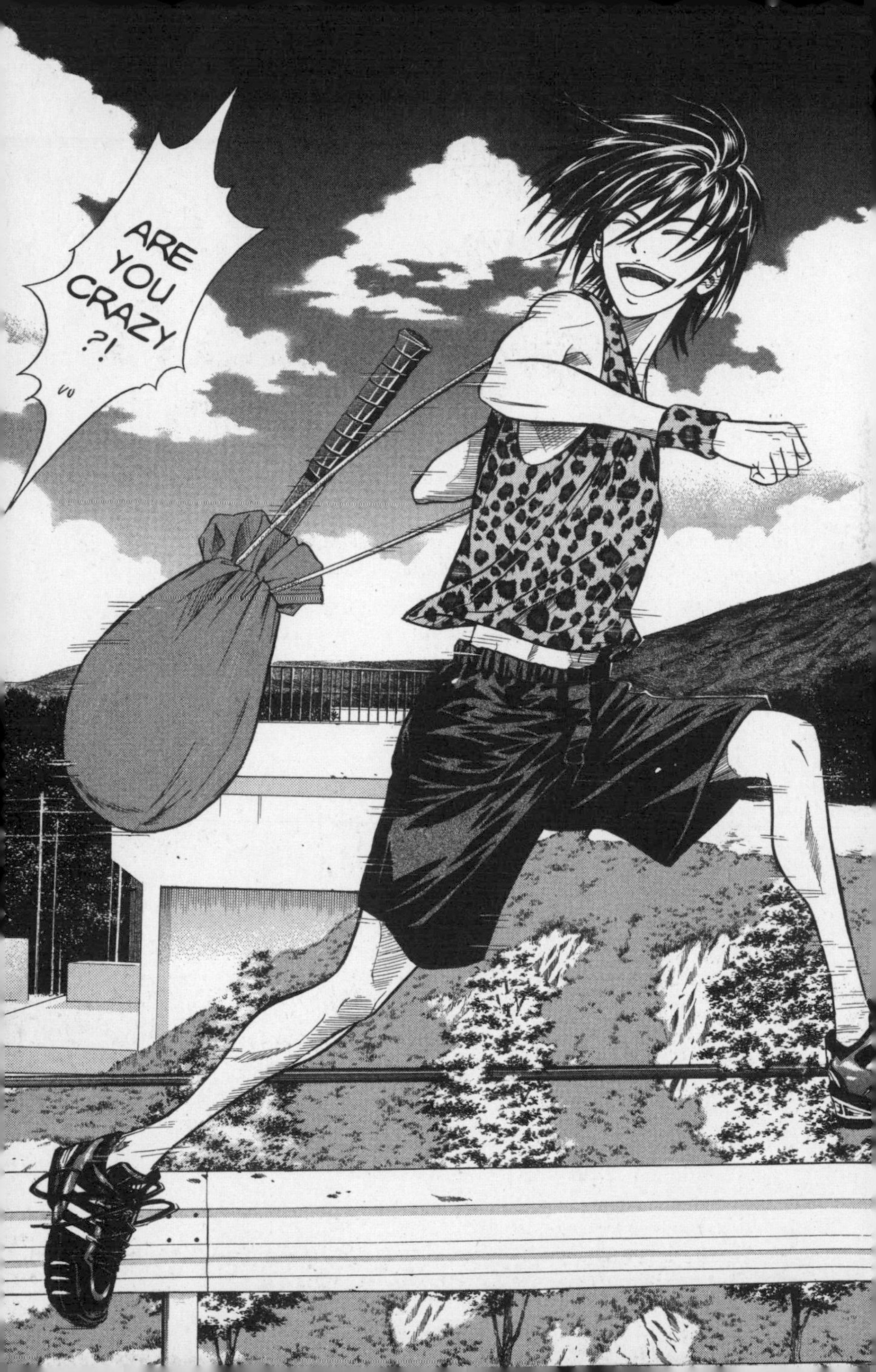
ARE YOU CRAZY ?!

テニスの王子様
THE PRINCE OF TENNIS

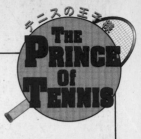

Thank you for reading *The Prince of Tennis*, volume 28.

I went to the wrap party for the movie and the TV series the other day. It was a huge success!! A band performed all the opening and closing theme songs from over the years, a raffle was held, and we even had a panel discussion. The TV anime series caught up to the manga, so it will temporarily go off the air. I'm really grateful to everybody who supported the series over the last three years. The good news is that, considering how much demand there is for a sequel, I'm sure we'll see the National Tournament story arc on TV soon. I'll keep working hard on the manga, so please keep up the support!! (You all want to see it don't you?! Higa, Hyotei, Shitenhoji...) I'll keep trying to convince the big shots [laughs]. Kattenguwa!* ⇐ Okinawa dialect

The manga is entering the Nationals arc! This is where the real *Prince of Tennis* begins! Keep your eyes open! I'll see you in the next volume.

P.S. Thanks to the two members of SCRIPT who came to the party despite having a show the next day. I hope to see you guys again at your next show!

There were so many Valentine's Day chocolates sent in that we couldn't count them all in time for this volume. So we'll be announcing the results in the next one!!

Haide!!

テニスの王子様
T. KONOMI
2005. 3. 10

Send fan letters to: Takeshi Konomi, *The Prince of Tennis*, c/o VIZ Media LLC, P.O. Box 77010, San Francisco, CA 94107

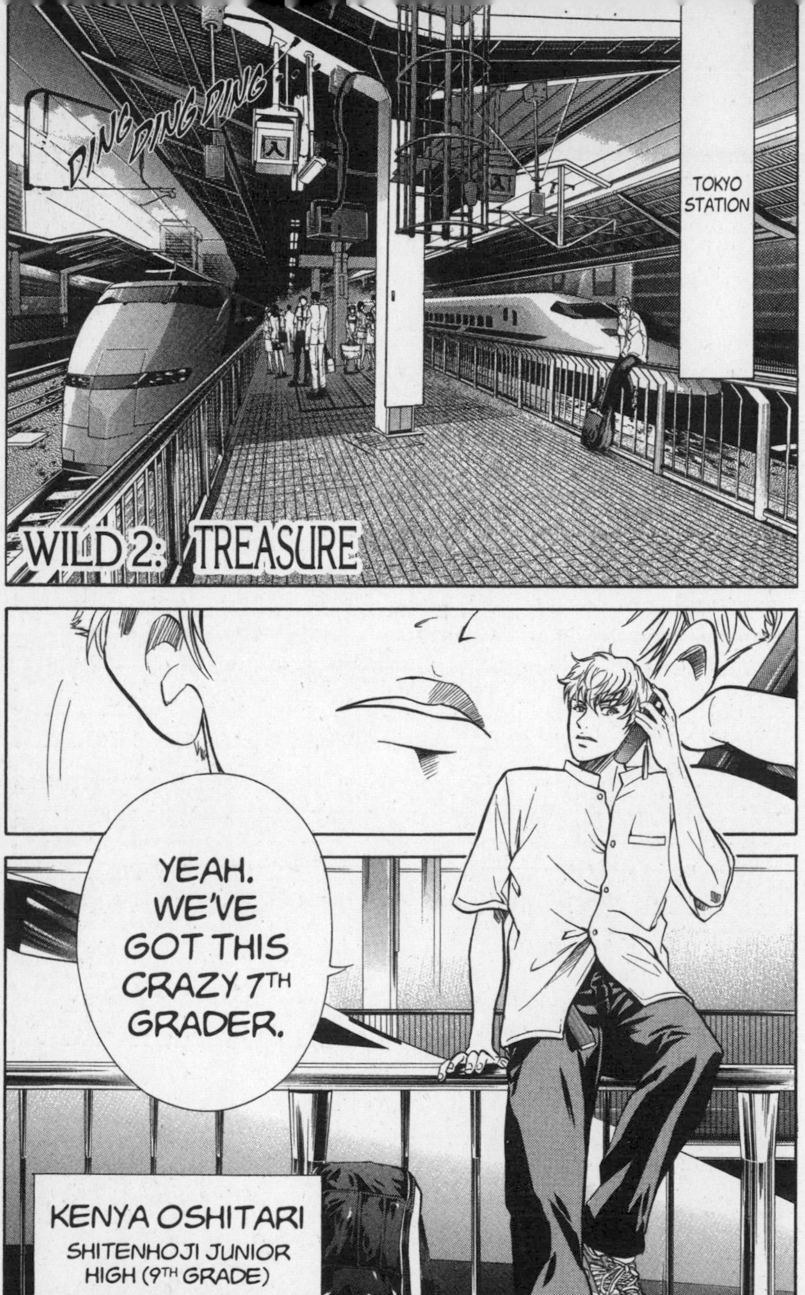
TOKYO STATION
DING DING DING
WILD 2: TREASURE
YEAH. WE'VE GOT THIS CRAZY 7TH GRADER.
KENYA OSHITARI
SHITENHOJI JUNIOR HIGH (9TH GRADE)

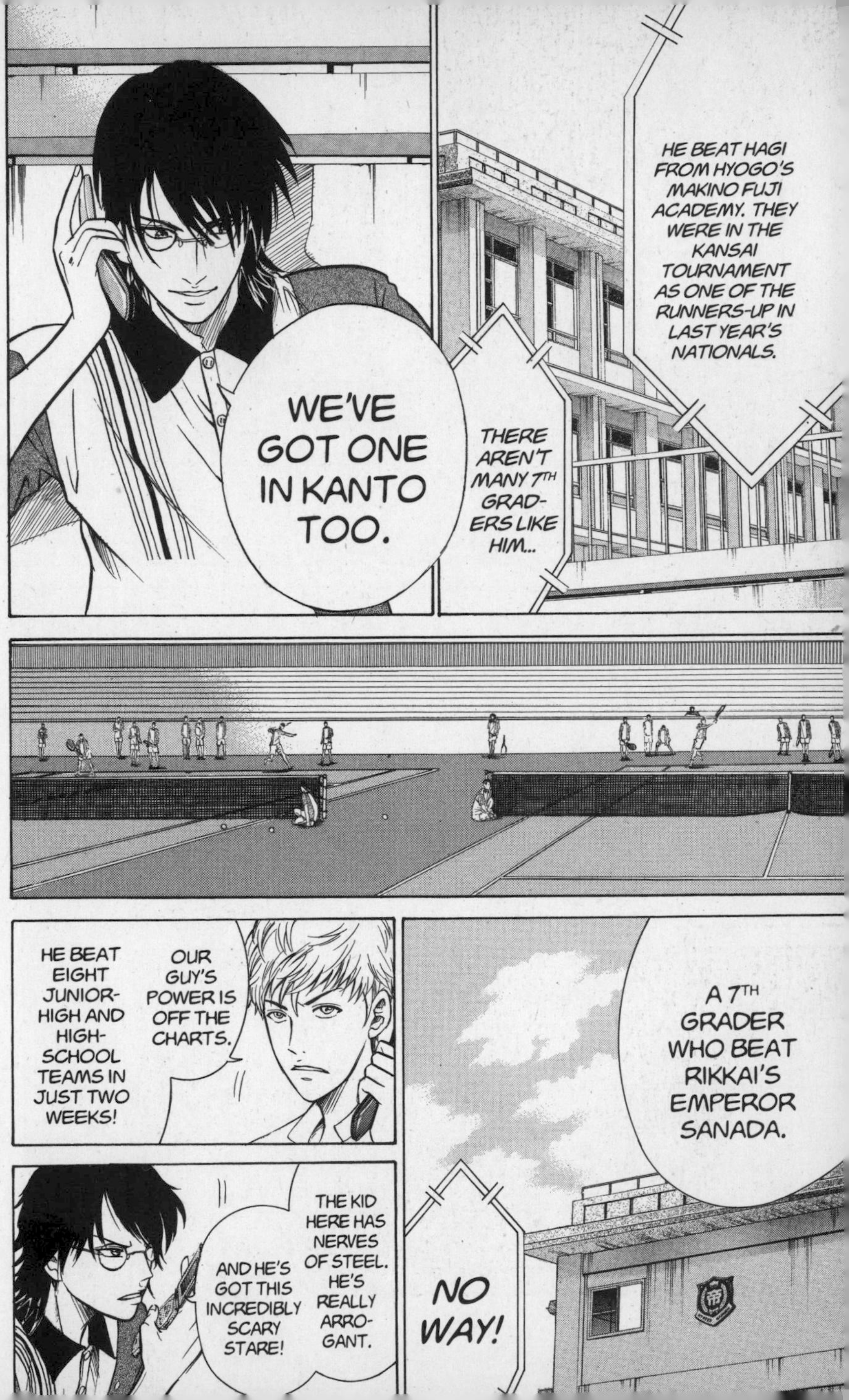
HE BEAT HAGI FROM HYOGO'S MAKINO FUJI ACADEMY. THEY WERE IN THE KANSAI TOURNAMENT AS ONE OF THE RUNNERS-UP IN LAST YEAR'S NATIONALS.
THERE AREN'T MANY 7TH GRADERS LIKE HIM...
WE'VE GOT ONE IN KANTO TOO.
A 7TH GRADER WHO BEAT RIKKAI'S EMPEROR SANADA.
NO WAY!
OUR GUY'S POWER IS OFF THE CHARTS.
HE BEAT EIGHT JUNIOR-HIGH AND HIGH-SCHOOL TEAMS IN JUST TWO WEEKS!
THE KID HERE HAS NERVES OF STEEL. HE'S REALLY ARROGANT.
AND HE'S GOT THIS INCREDIBLY SCARY STARE!

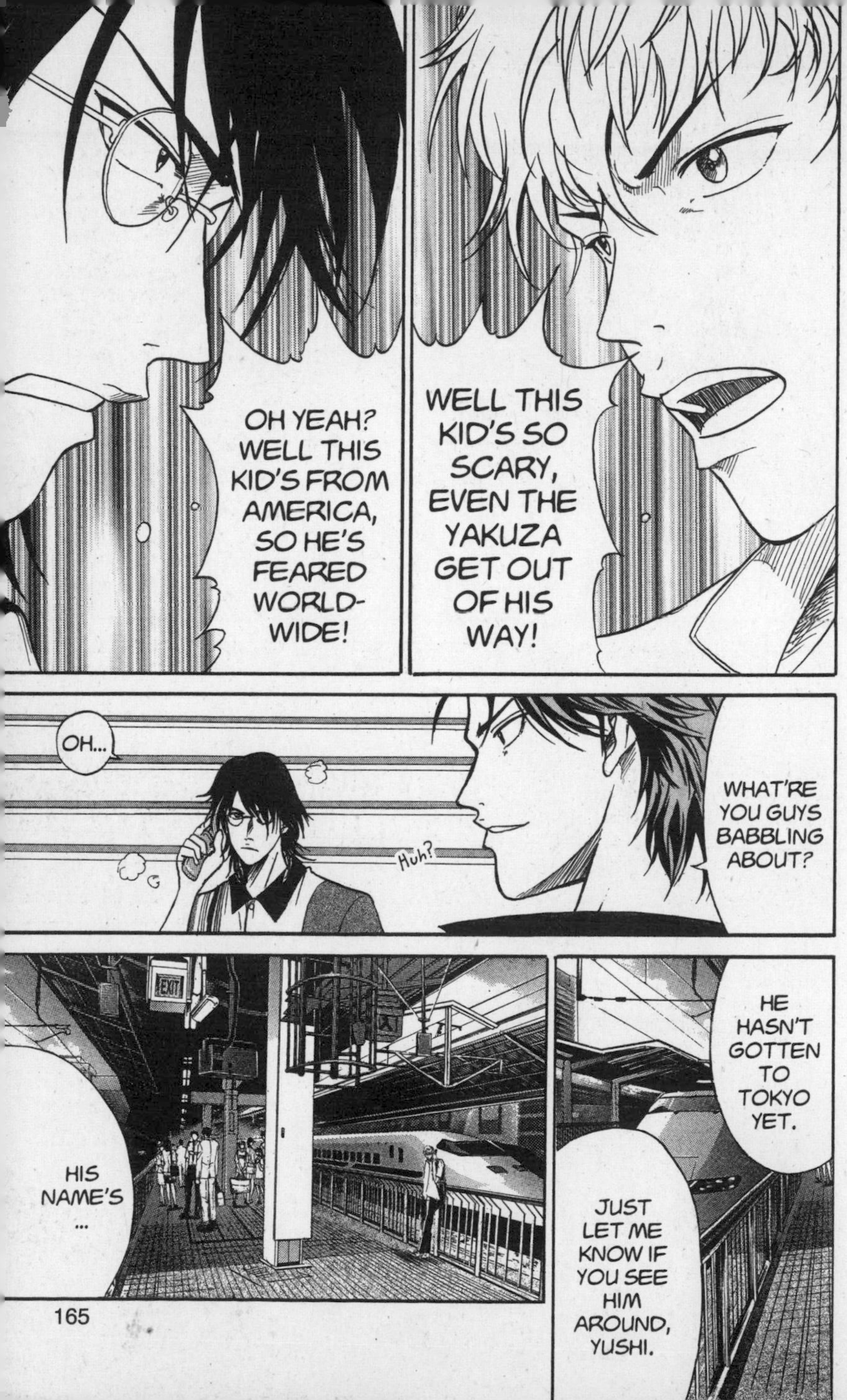
WELL THIS KID'S SO SCARY, EVEN THE YAKUZA GET OUT OF HIS WAY!
OH YEAH? WELL THIS KID'S FROM AMERICA, SO HE'S FEARED WORLD-WIDE!
WHAT'RE YOU GUYS BABBLING ABOUT?
Huh?
OH...
HE HASN'T GOTTEN TO TOKYO YET.
JUST LET ME KNOW IF YOU SEE HIM AROUND, YUSHI.
EXIT
HIS NAME'S ...

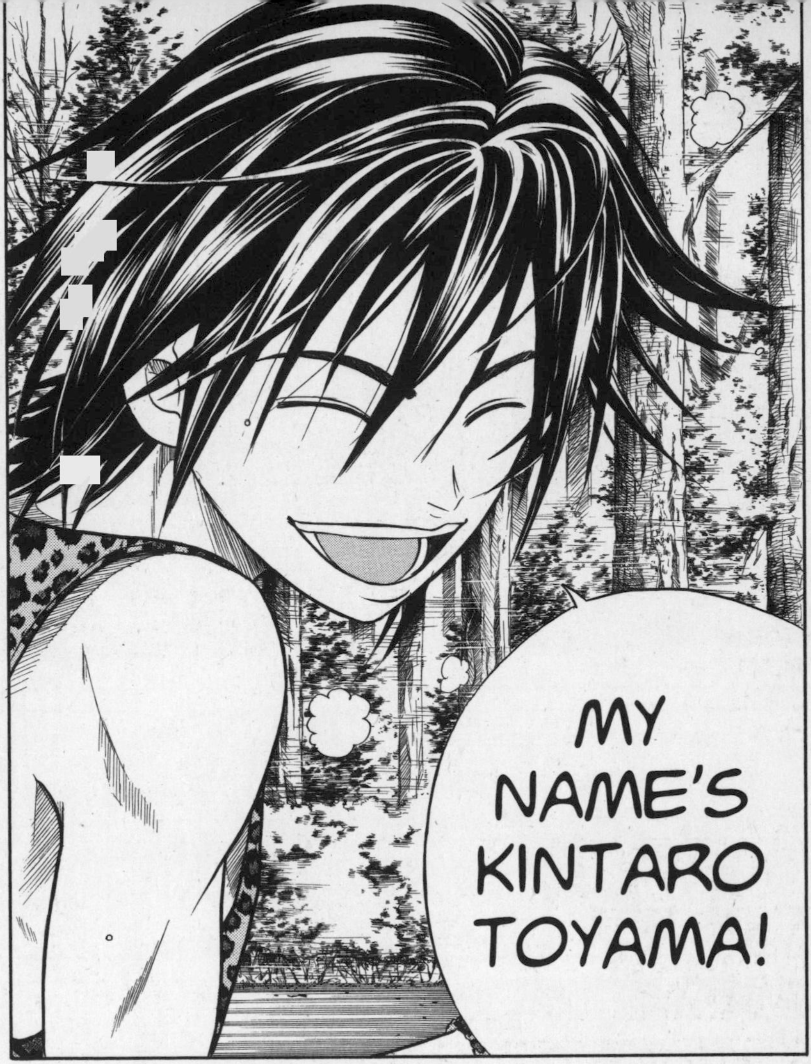
MY NAME'S KINTARO TOYAMA!

GENIUS 246 (WILD 2): TREASURE

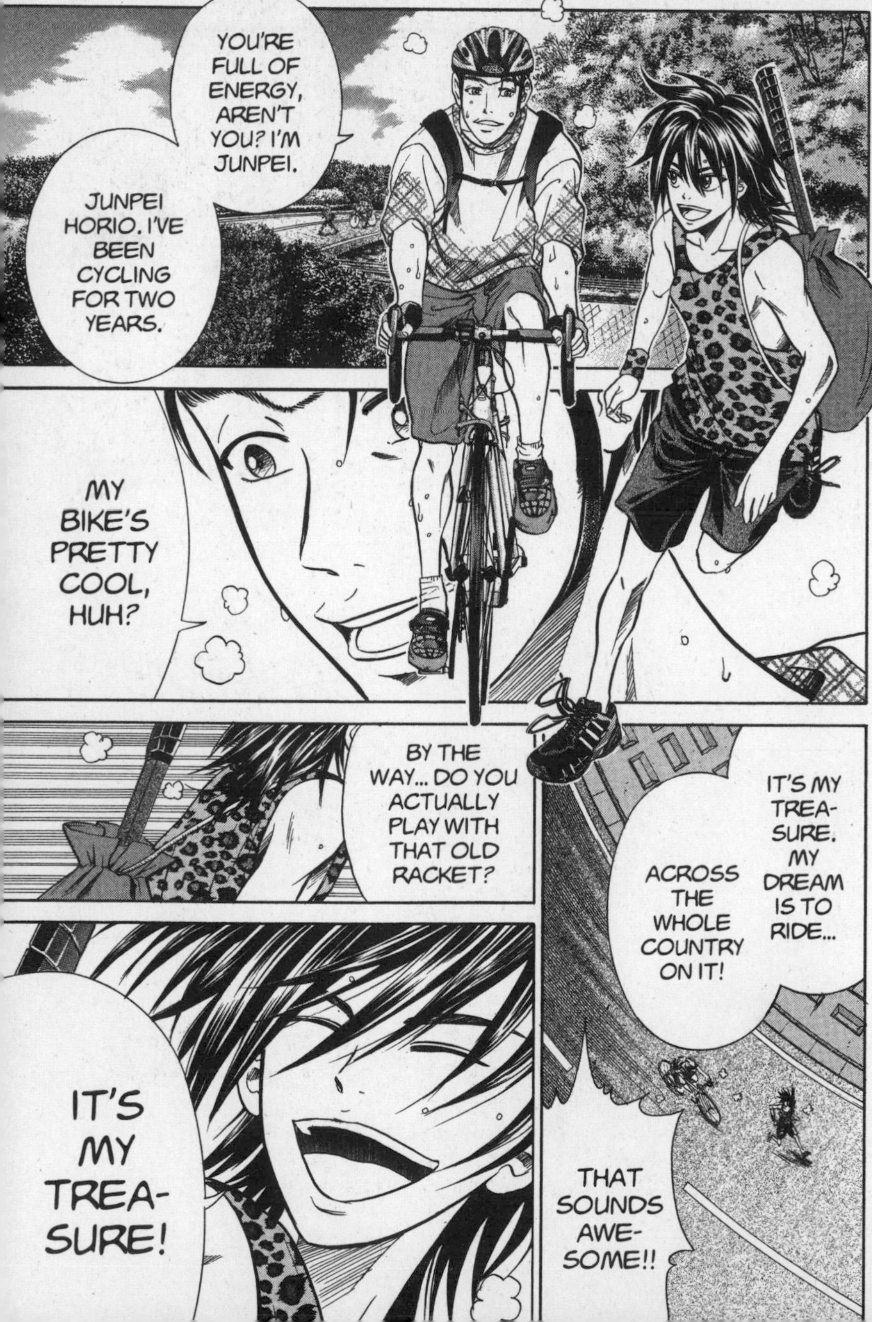
YOU'RE FULL OF ENERGY, AREN'T YOU? I'M JUNPEI.
JUNPEI HORIO. I'VE BEEN CYCLING FOR TWO YEARS.
MY BIKE'S PRETTY COOL, HUH?
IT'S MY TREASURE. MY DREAM IS TO RIDE...
ACROSS THE WHOLE COUNTRY ON IT!
THAT SOUNDS AWESOME!!
BY THE WAY... DO YOU ACTUALLY PLAY WITH THAT OLD RACKET?
IT'S MY TREASURE!

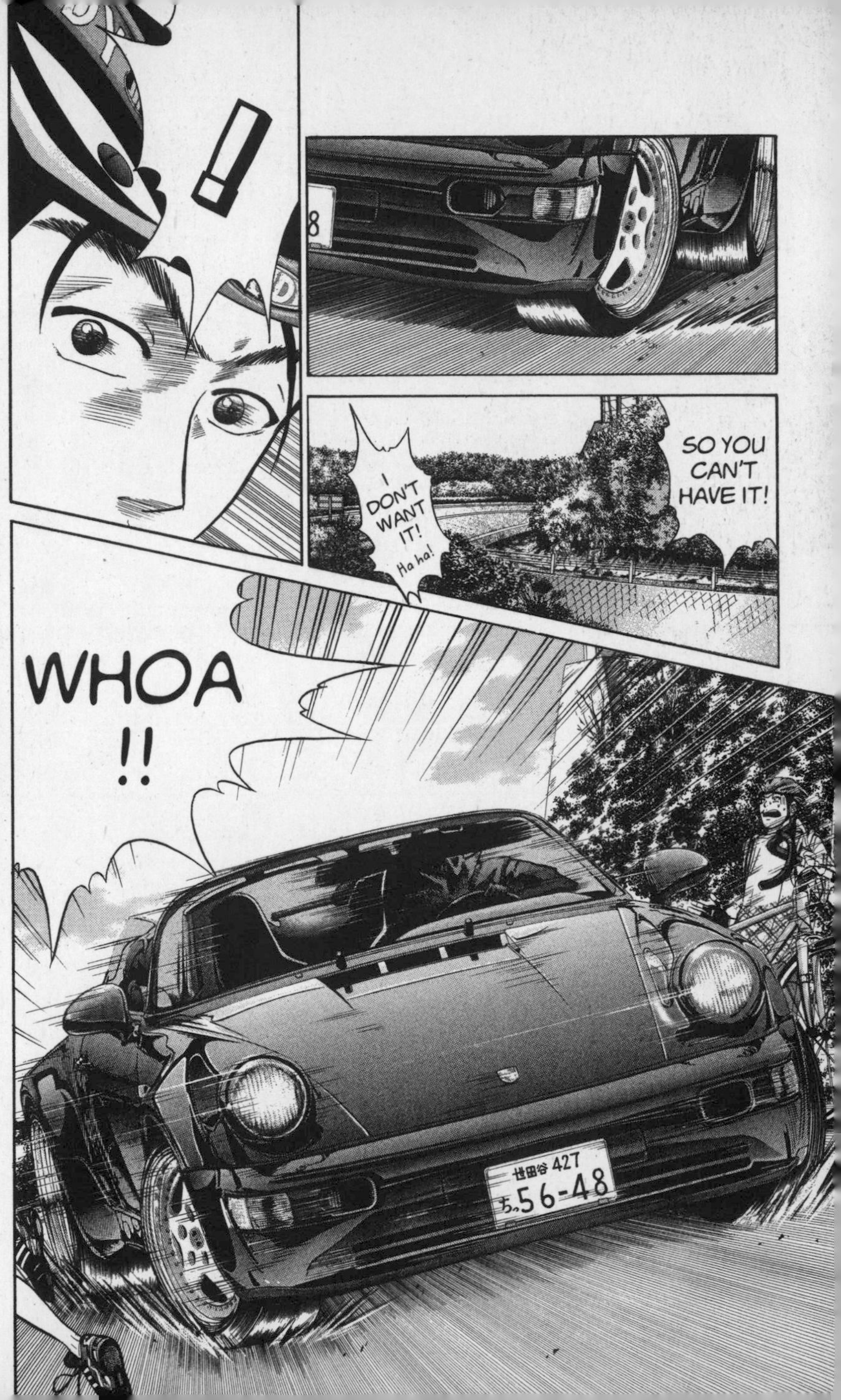
SO YOU CAN'T HAVE IT!
I DON'T WANT IT! Ha ha!
!
WHOA !!
世田谷 427
ち 56-48

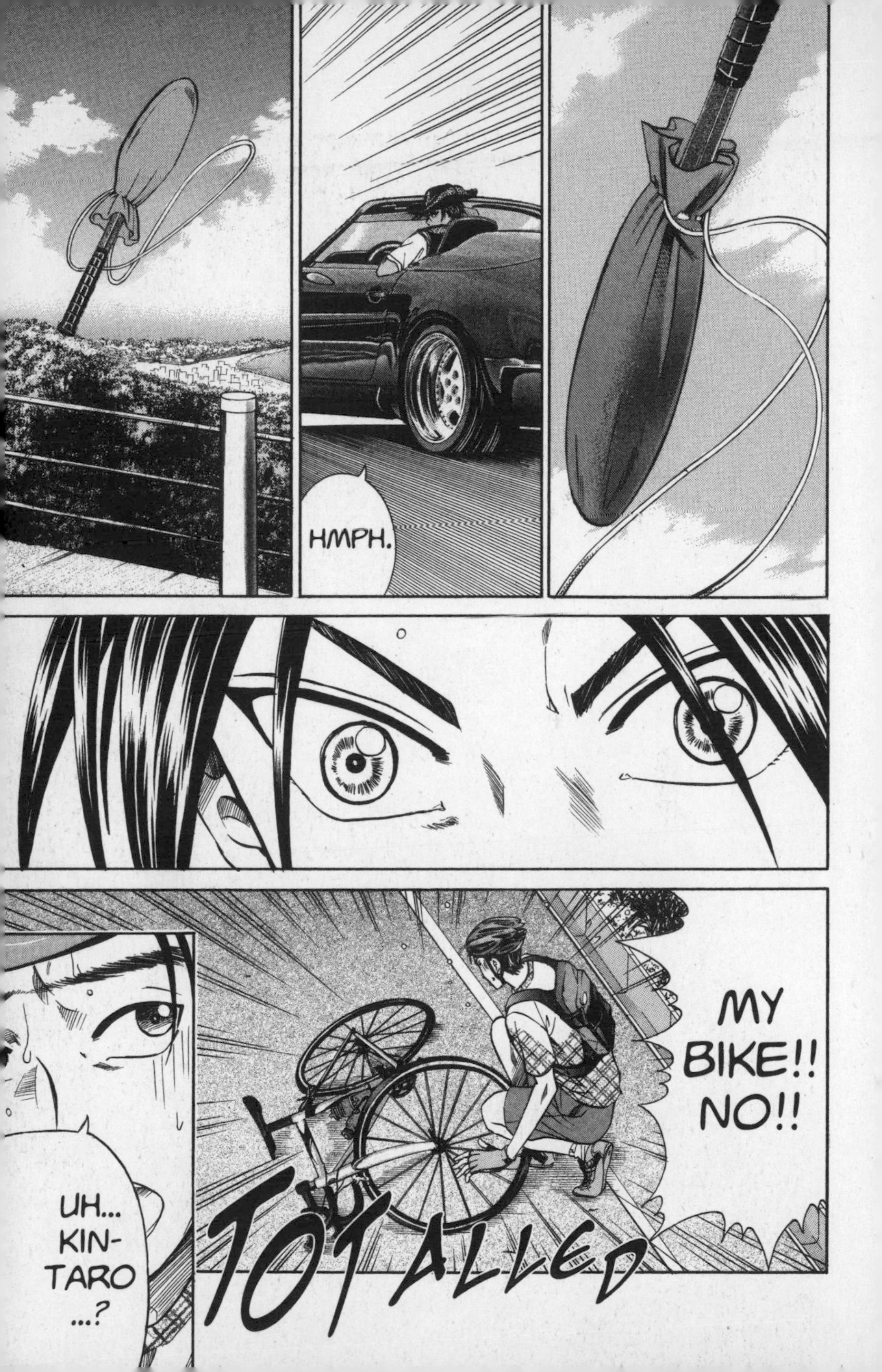
HMPH.
MY BIKE!! NO!!
TOTALLED
UH... KIN-TARO ...?

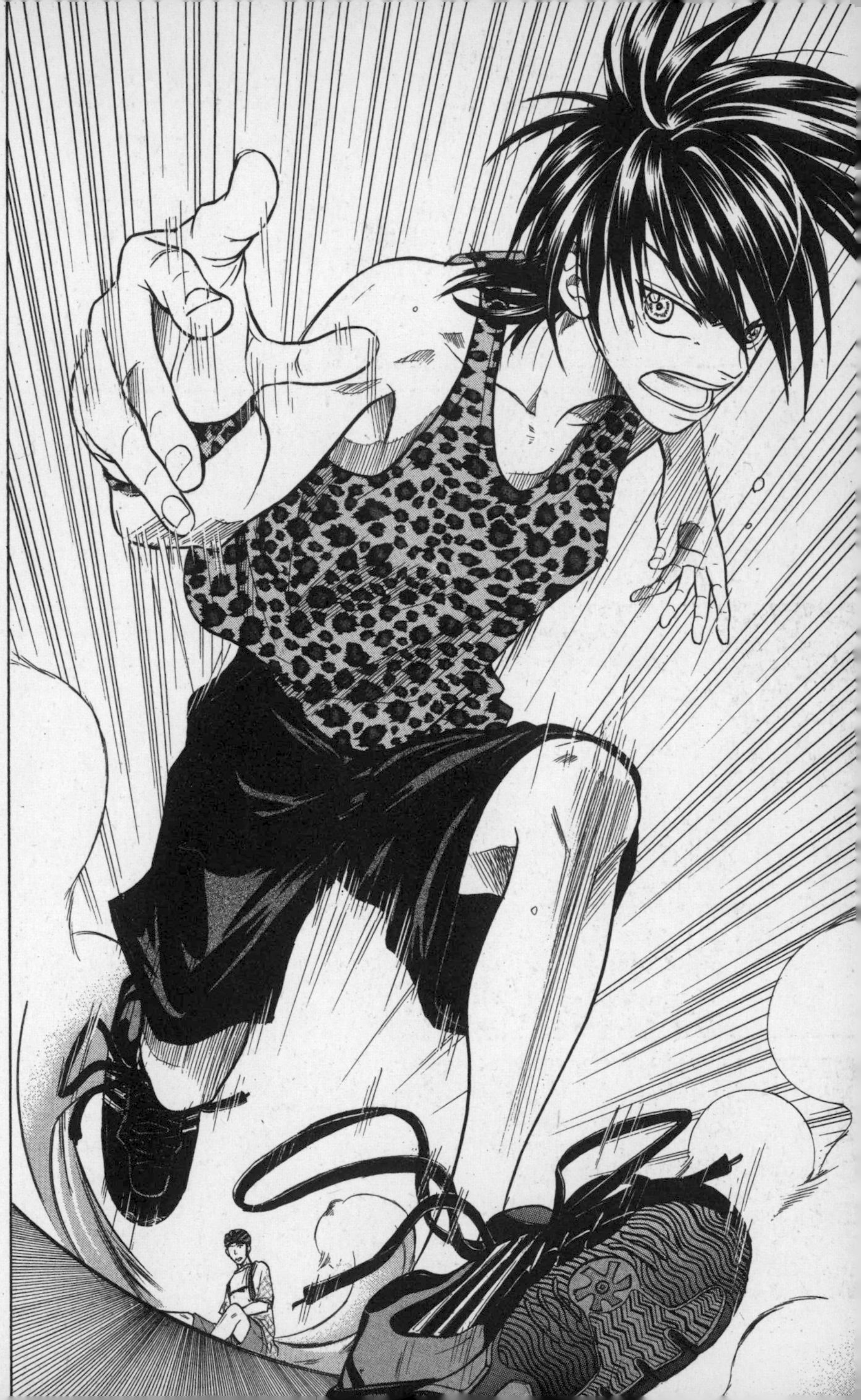

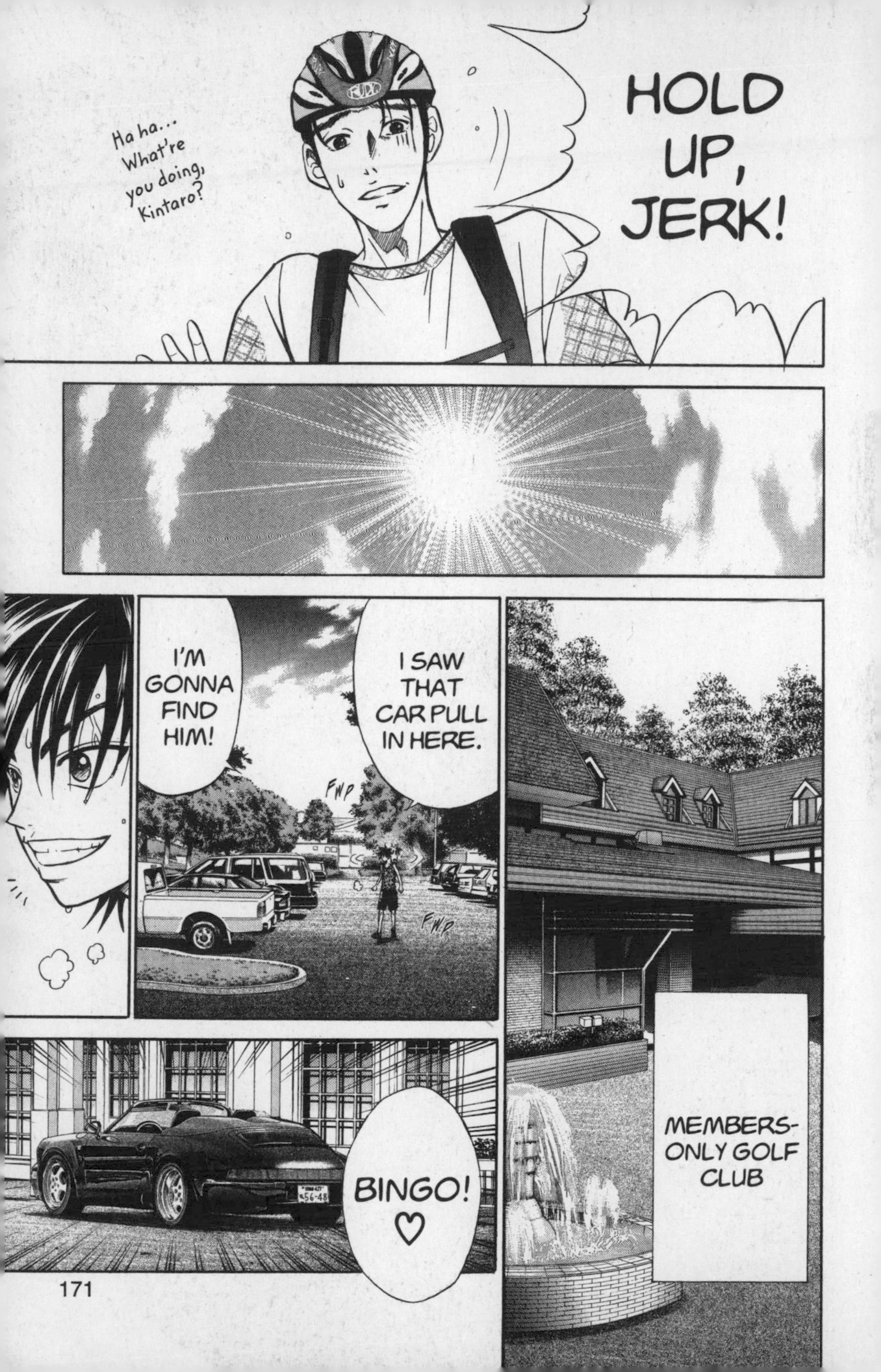

HOLD UP, JERK!
Ha ha... What're you doing, Kintaro?
MEMBERS-ONLY GOLF CLUB
I SAW THAT CAR PULL IN HERE.
FWP
I'M GONNA FIND HIM!
FWP
BINGO! ♡

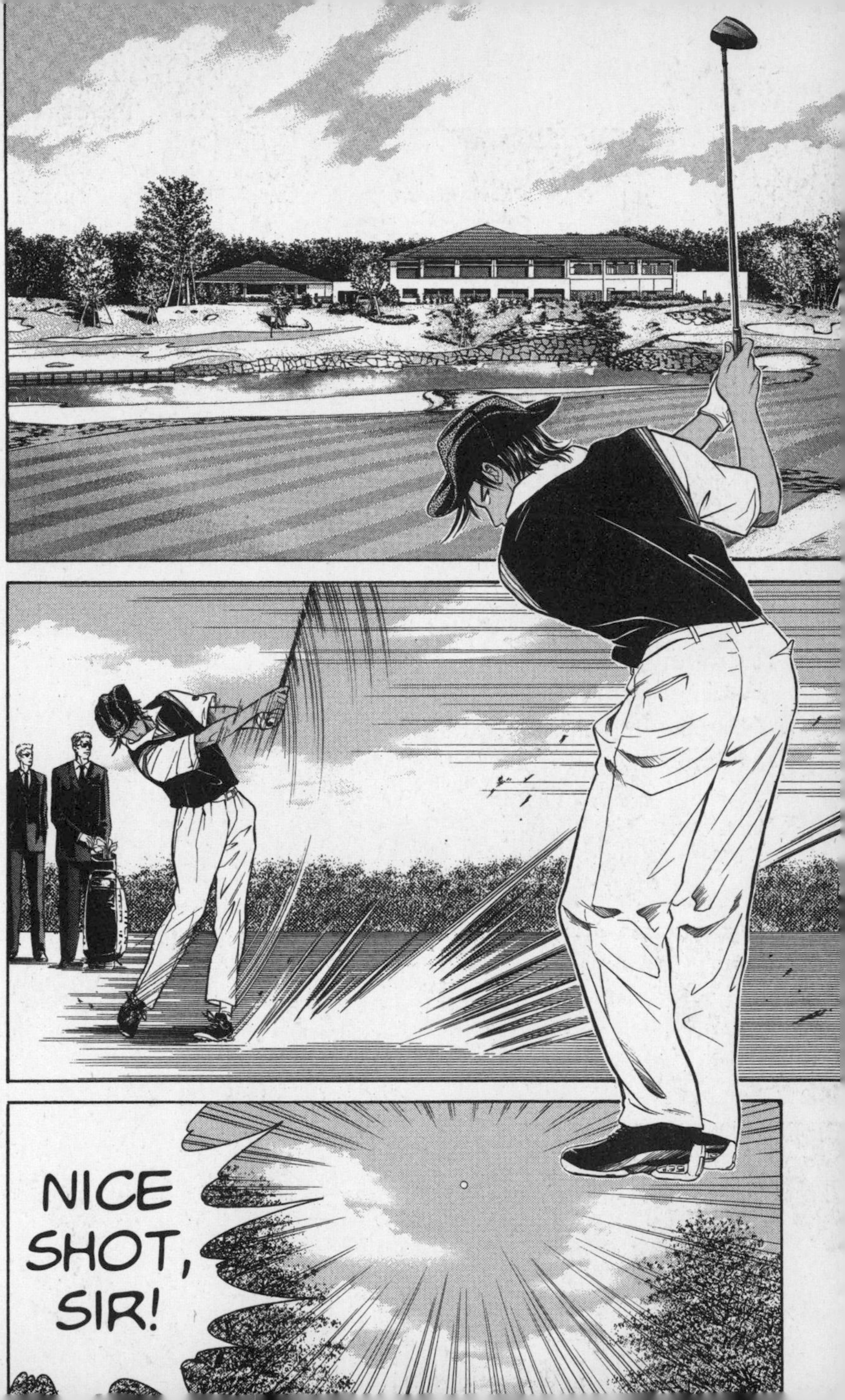
NICE SHOT, SIR!

READ THIS WAY

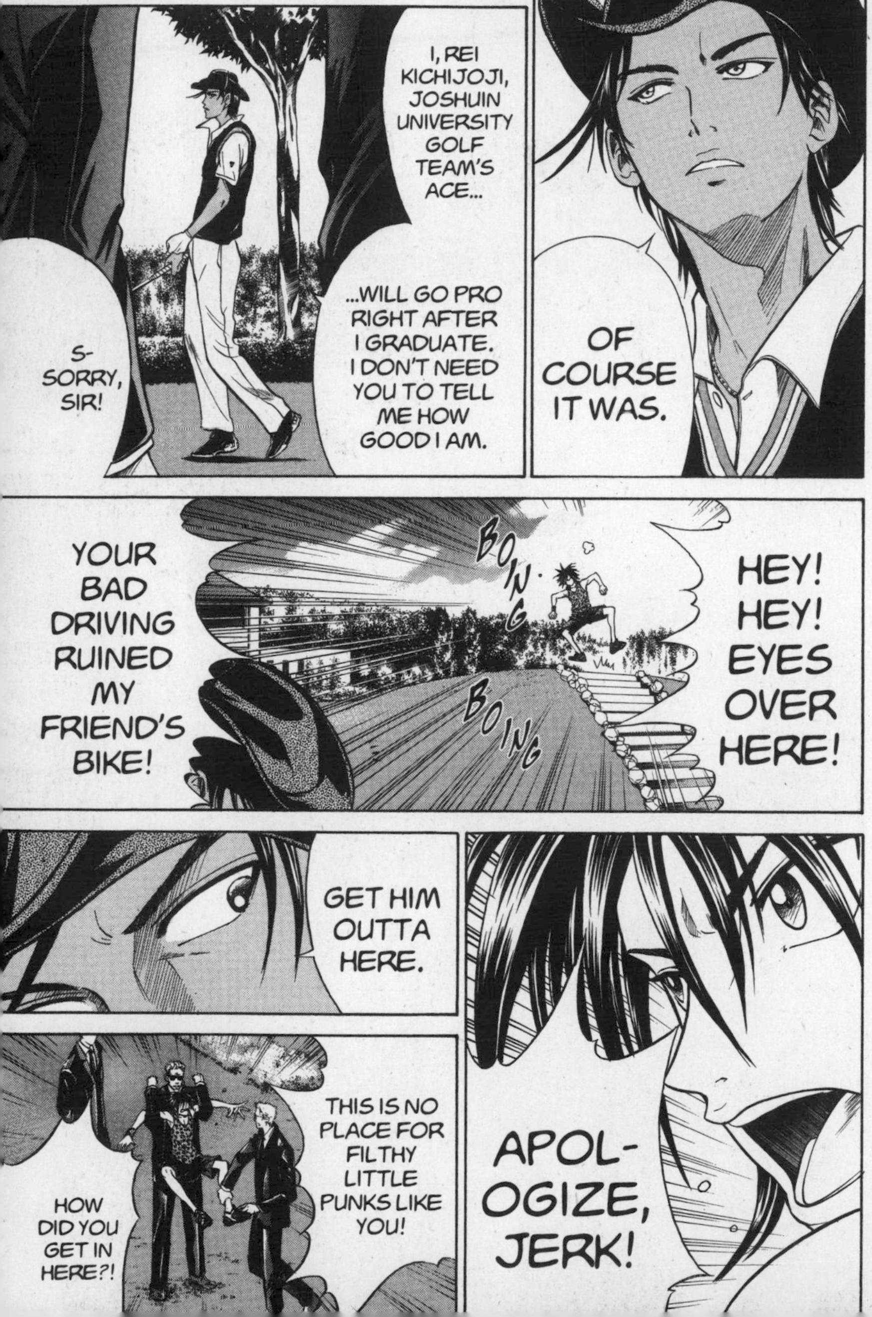
OF COURSE IT WAS.
I, REI KICHIJOJI, JOSHUIN UNIVERSITY GOLF TEAM'S ACE...
...WILL GO PRO RIGHT AFTER I GRADUATE. I DON'T NEED YOU TO TELL ME HOW GOOD I AM.
S-SORRY, SIR!
HEY! HEY! EYES OVER HERE!
BOING
BOING
YOUR BAD DRIVING RUINED MY FRIEND'S BIKE!
APOL-OGIZE, JERK!
GET HIM OUTTA HERE.
THIS IS NO PLACE FOR FILTHY LITTLE PUNKS LIKE YOU!
HOW DID YOU GET IN HERE?!

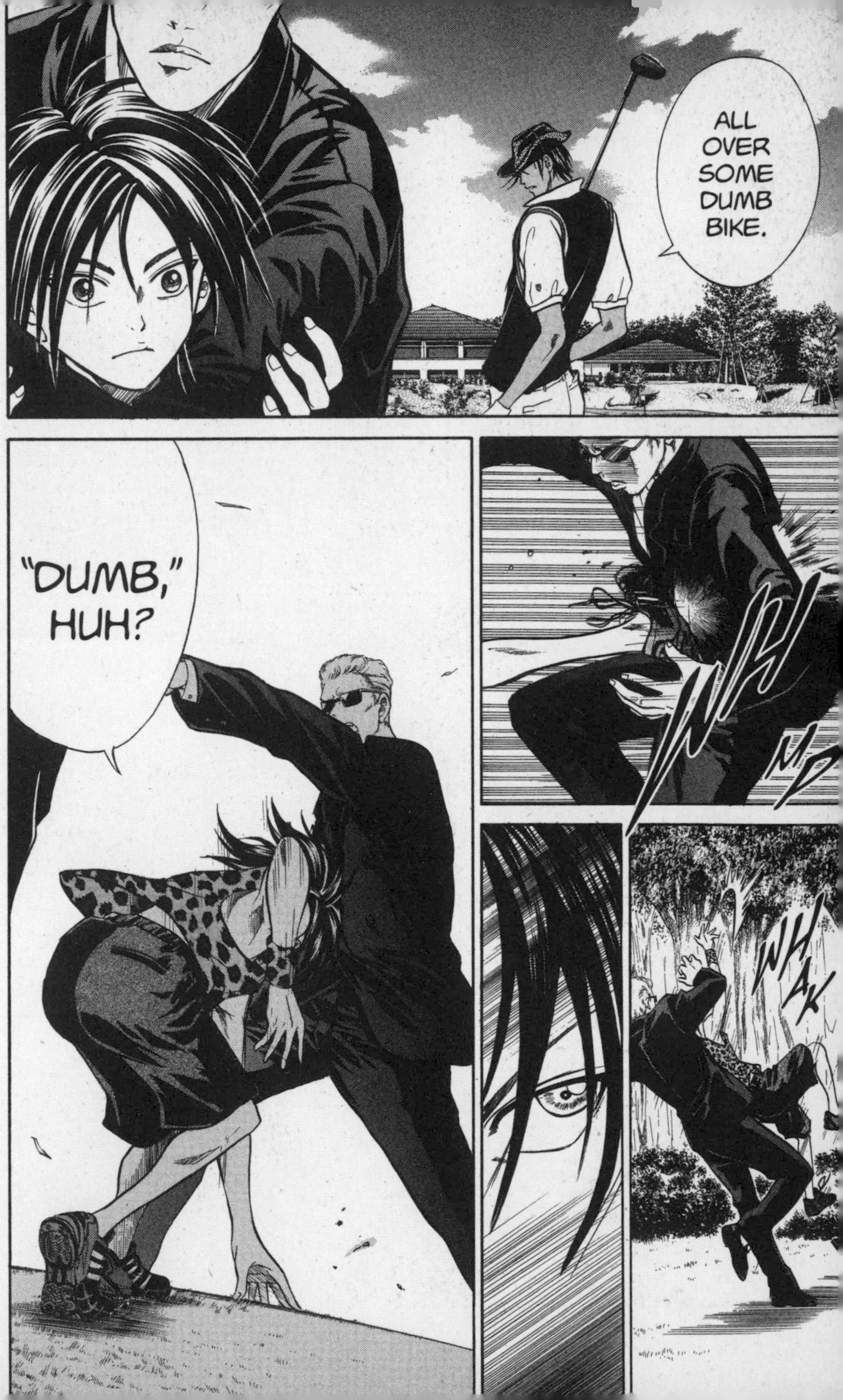
ALL OVER SOME DUMB BIKE.
WHAK
"DUMB," HUH?

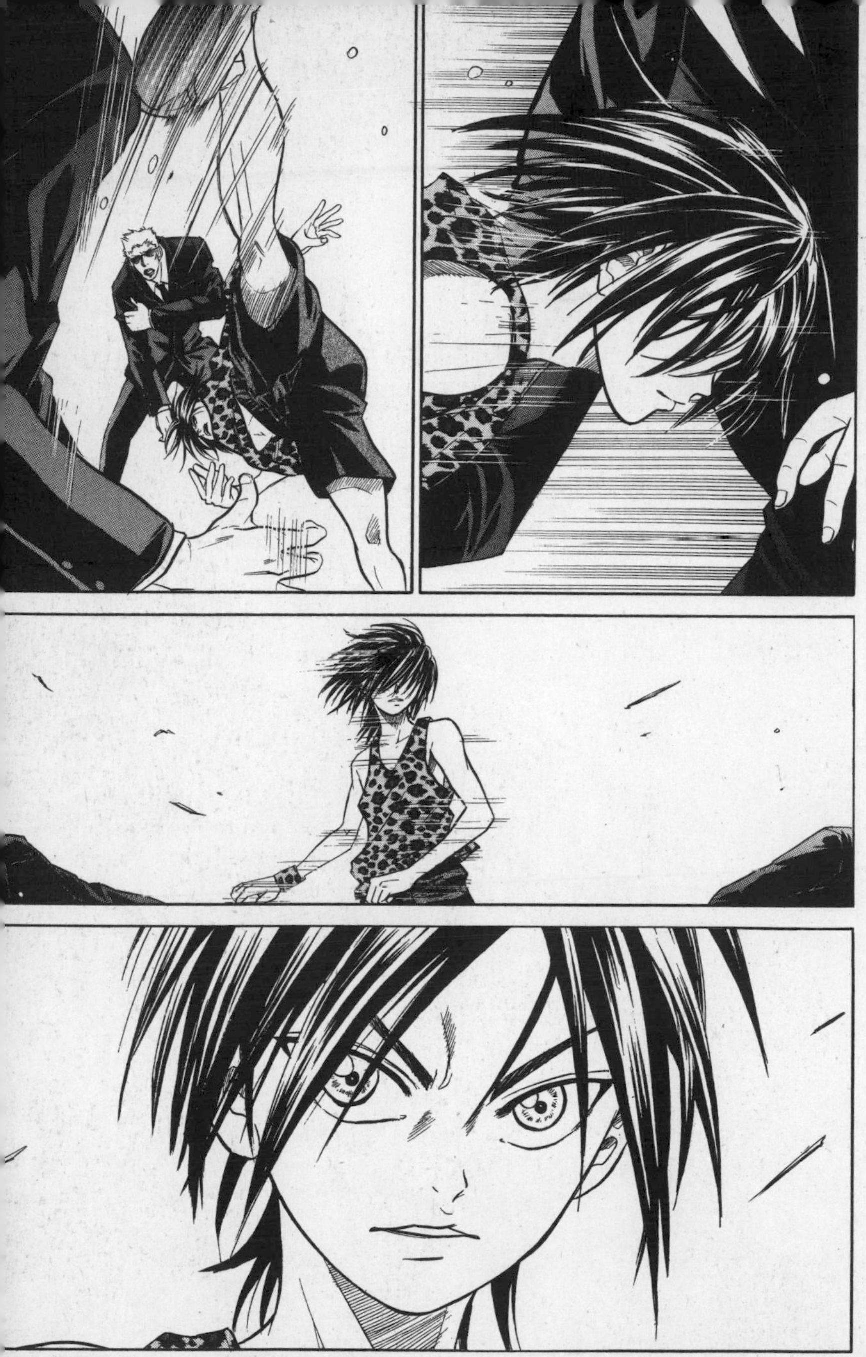

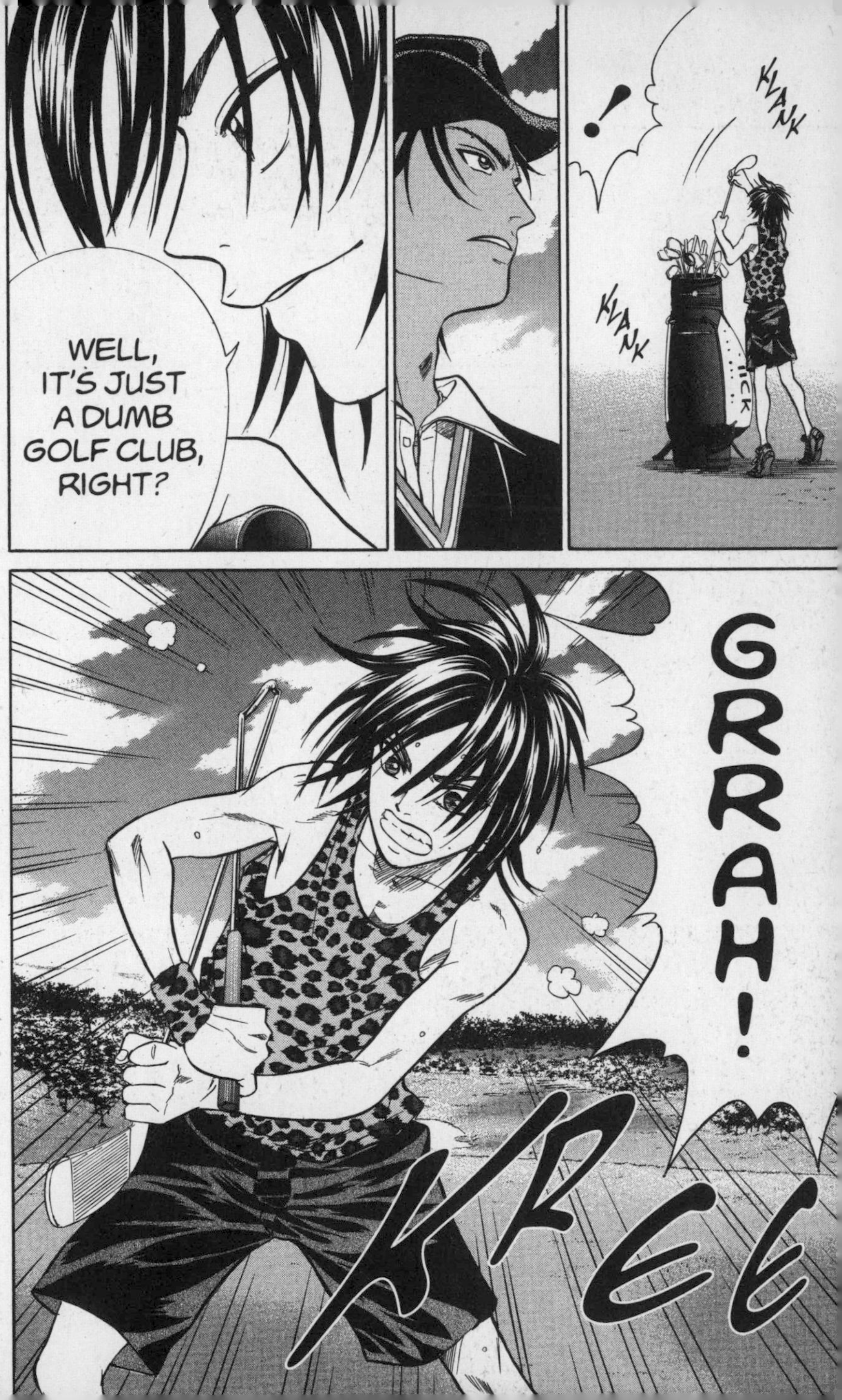
!
KLANK
KLANK
WELL, IT'S JUST A DUMB GOLF CLUB, RIGHT?
GRRAH!
KREE

READ THIS WAY

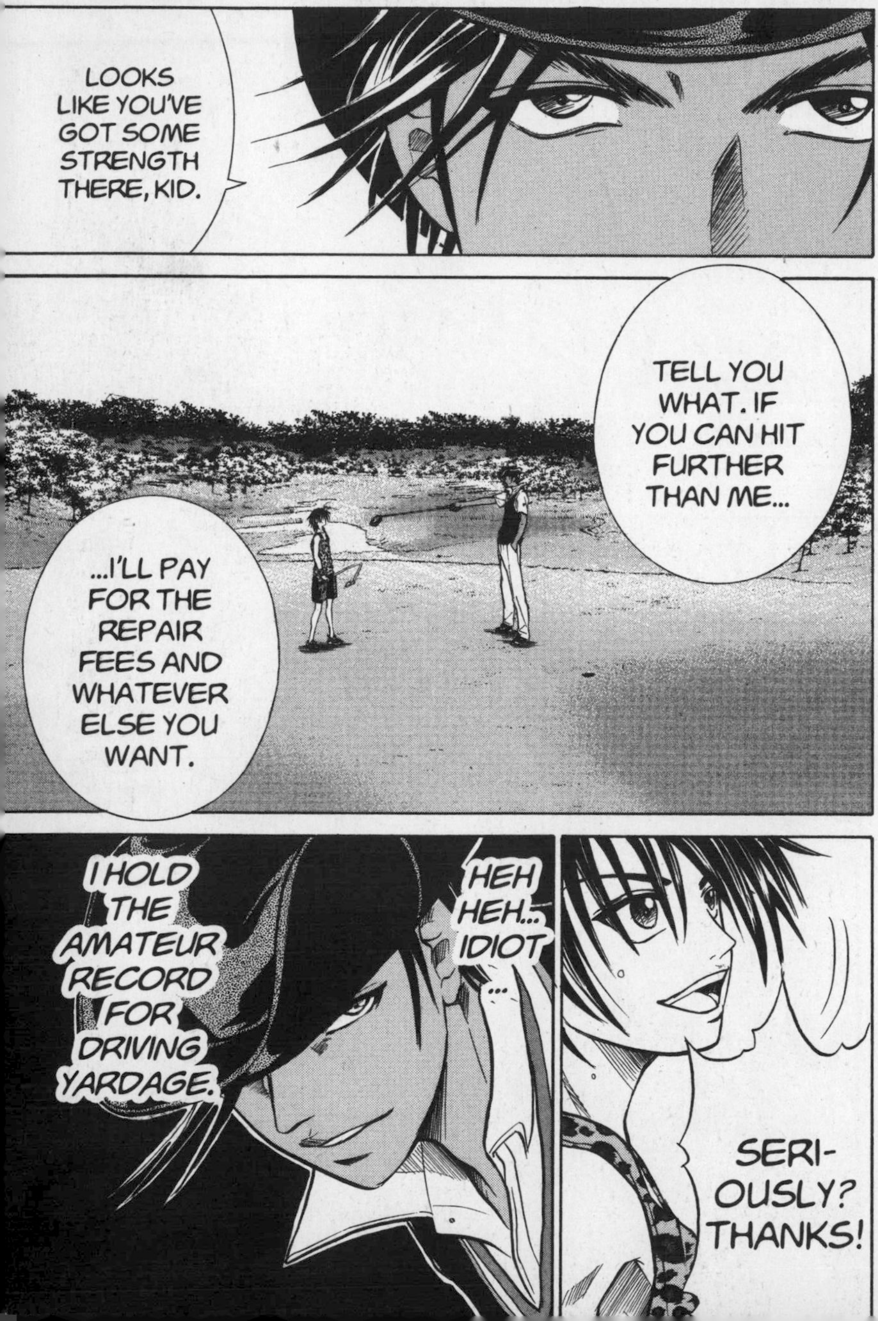
LOOKS LIKE YOU'VE GOT SOME STRENGTH THERE, KID.
TELL YOU WHAT. IF YOU CAN HIT FURTHER THAN ME...
...I'LL PAY FOR THE REPAIR FEES AND WHATEVER ELSE YOU WANT.
SERI-OUSLY? THANKS!
HEH HEH... IDIOT...
I HOLD THE AMATEUR RECORD FOR DRIVING YARDAGE.

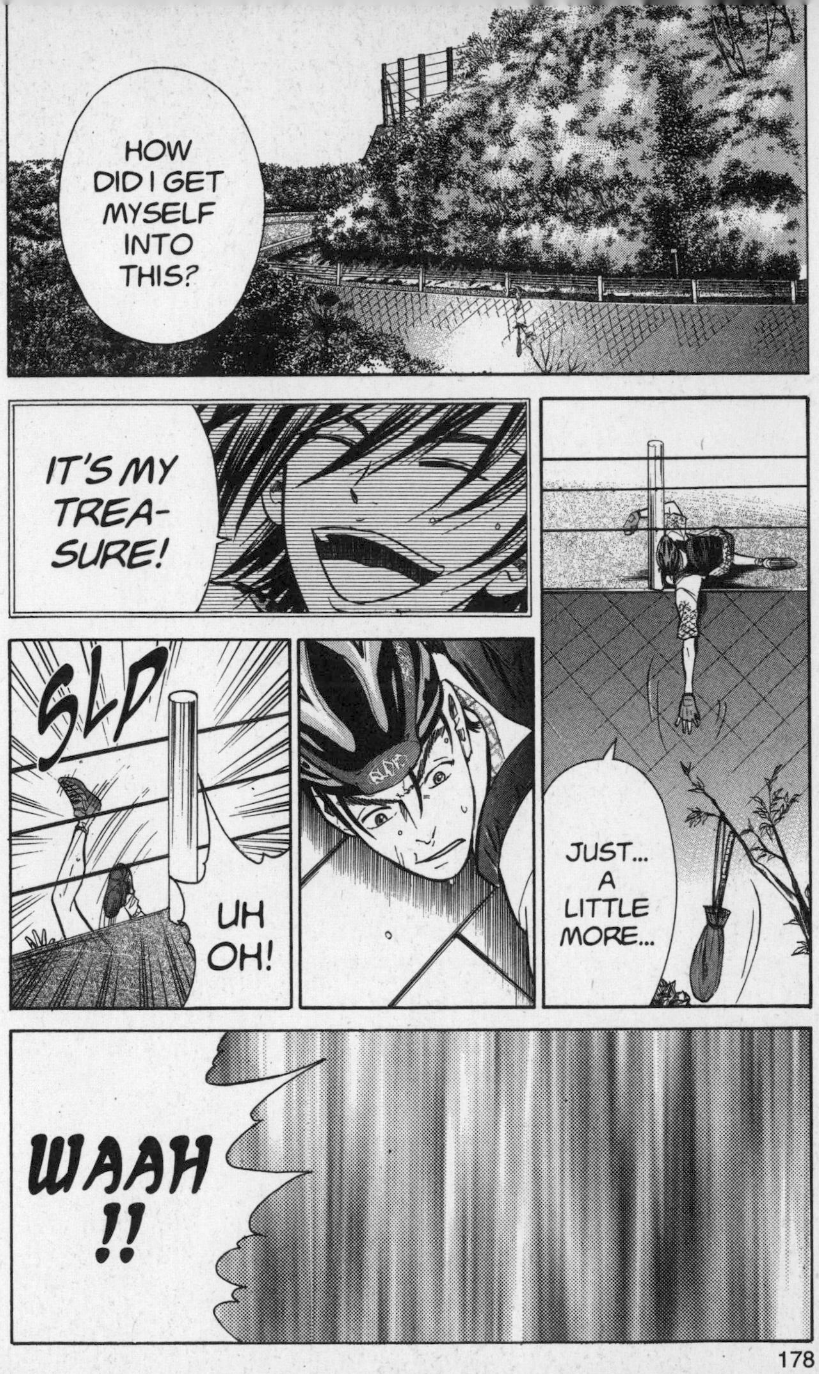
HOW DID I GET MYSELF INTO THIS?
JUST... A LITTLE MORE...
IT'S MY TREA-SURE!
SLD
UH OH!
WAAH !!

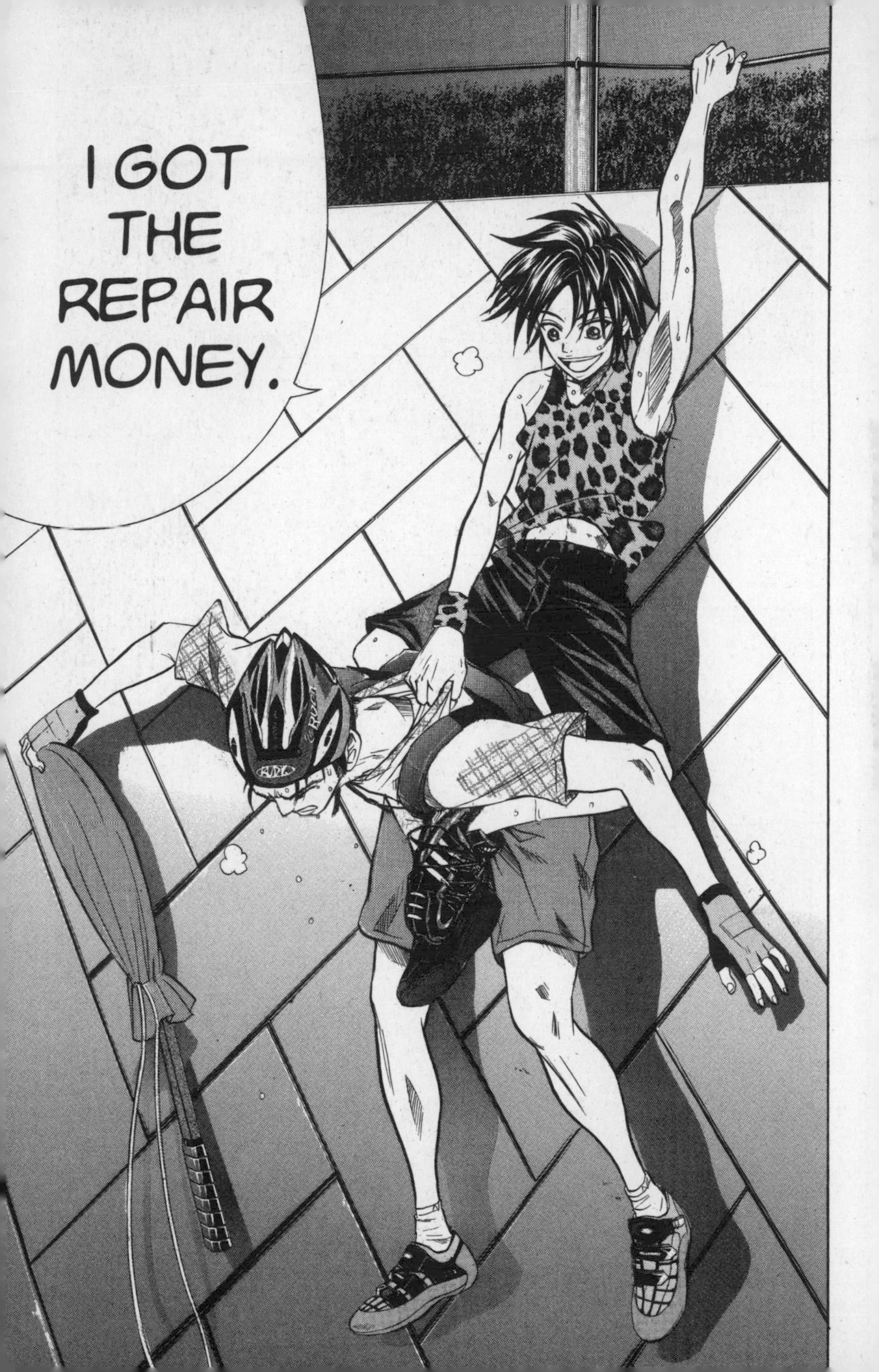
I GOT THE REPAIR MONEY.

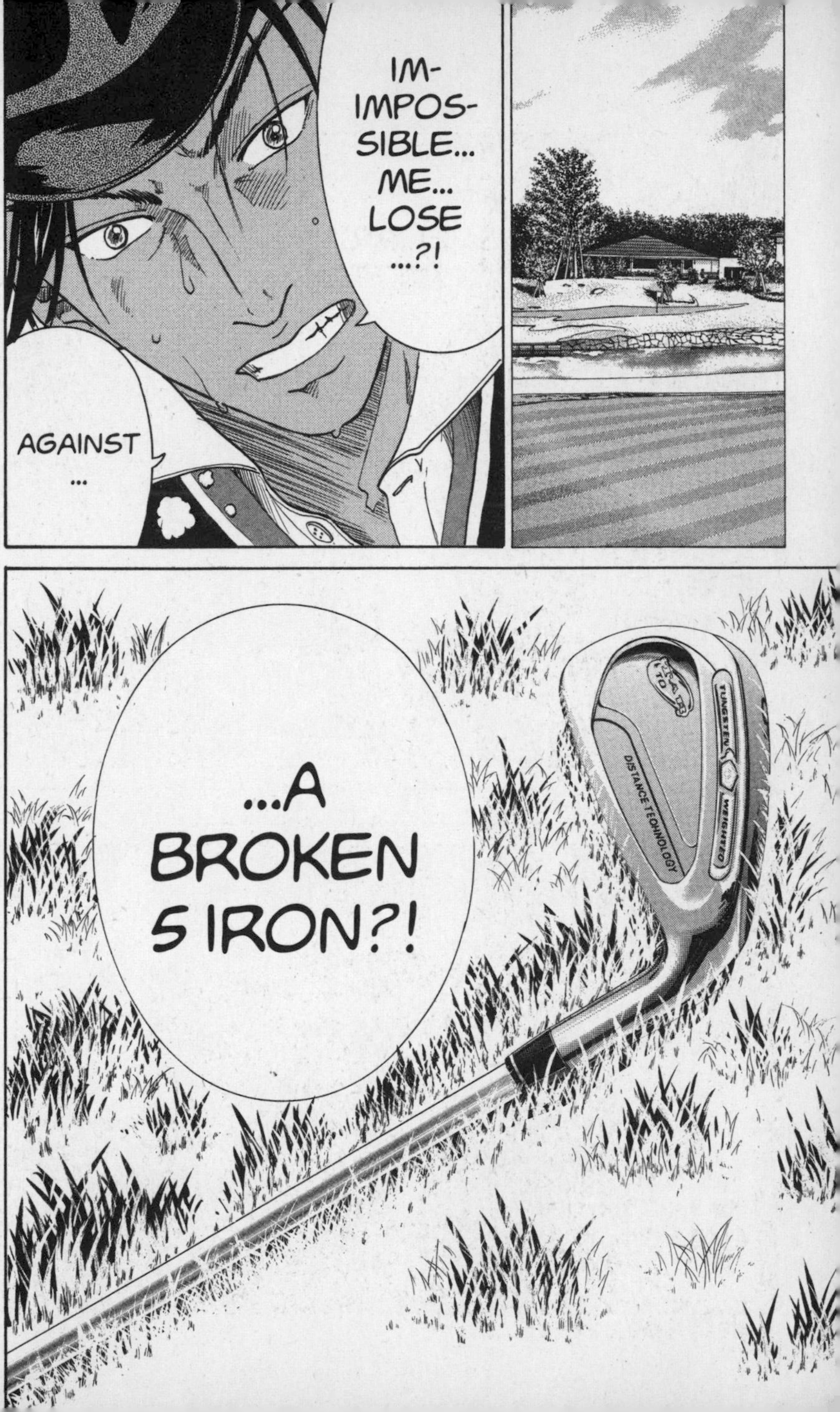
IM- IMPOSSIBLE... ME... LOSE ...?!
AGAINST ...
...A BROKEN 5 IRON?!
TUNGSTEN
WEIGHTED
DISTANCE TECHNOLOGY

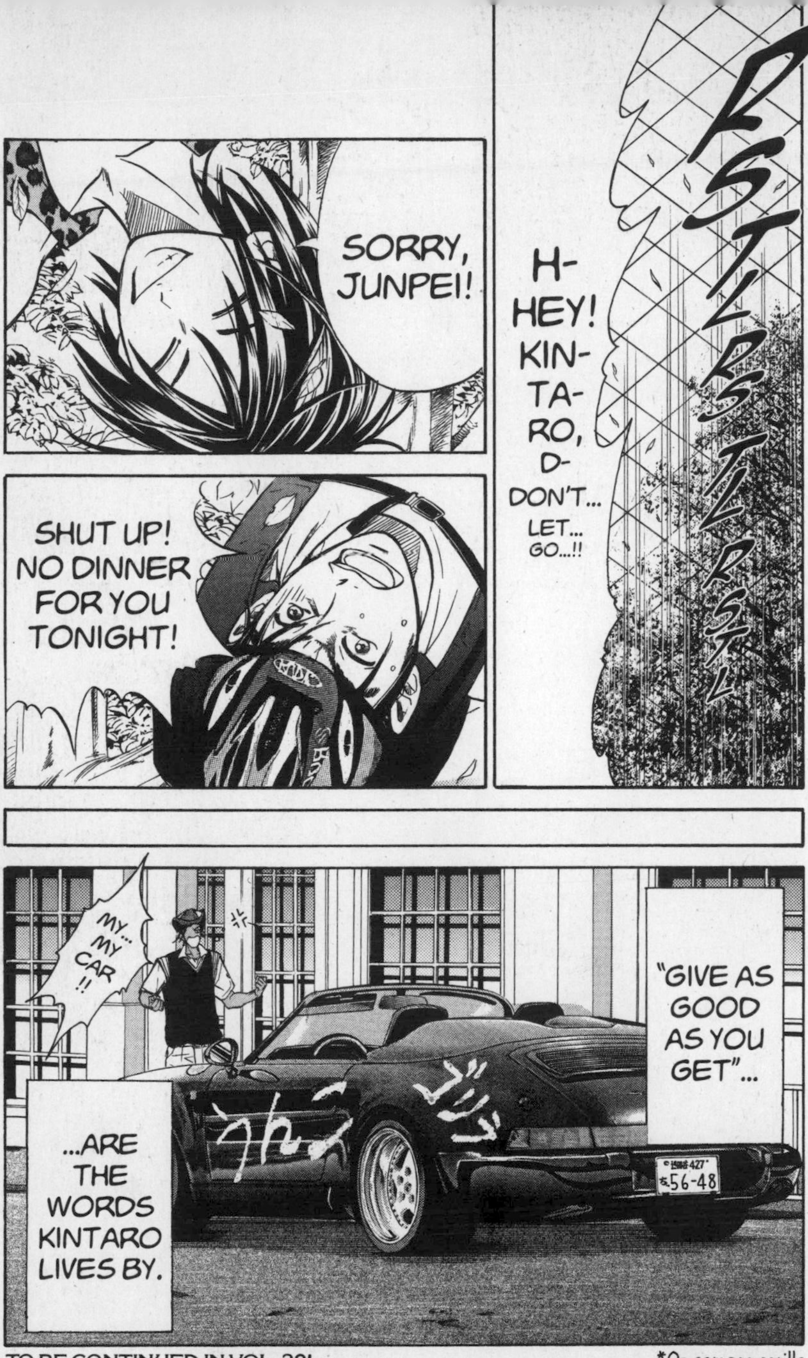
H-
HEY! KIN-TA-RO, D-DON'T... LET... GO...!!
SORRY, JUNPEI!
SHUT UP! NO DINNER FOR YOU TONIGHT!
"GIVE AS GOOD AS YOU GET"...
MY... MY CAR!!
...ARE THE WORDS KINTARO LIVES BY.

TO BE CONTINUED IN VOL. 29!

*On car: poo gorilla

In the Next Volume...

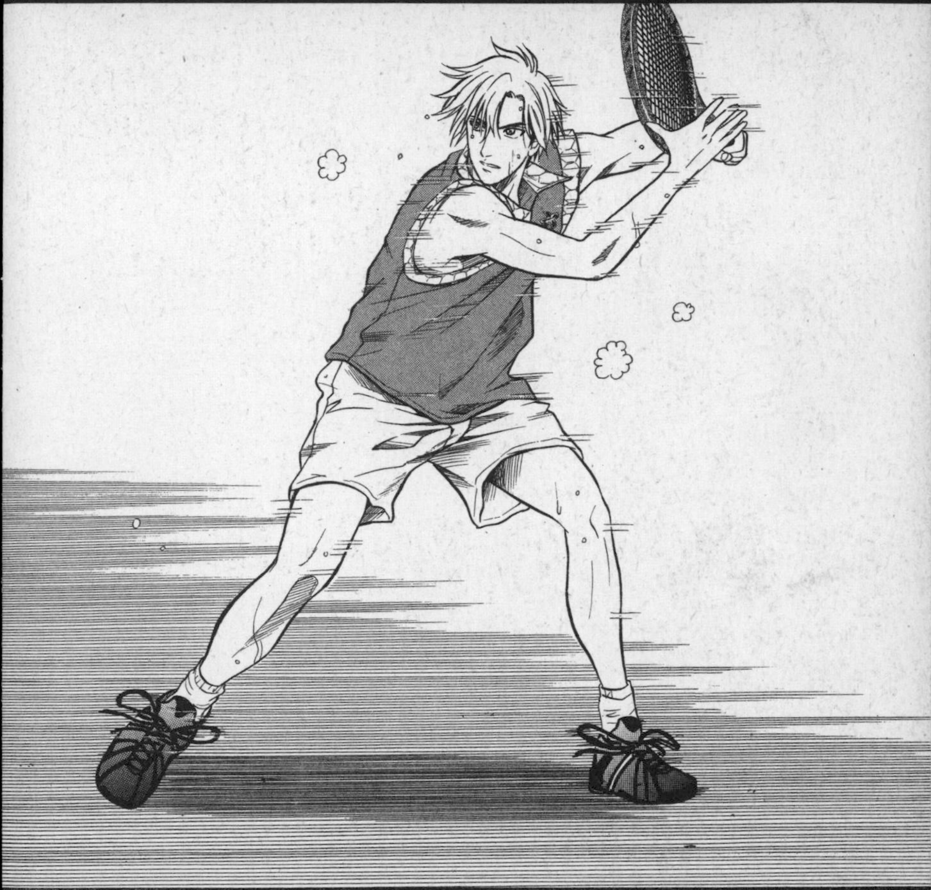

The Nationals Begin!

After watching Higa mow through their first-round matches, the Seishun players are taken aback by the team's dominance. But there's no time for doubt—the second round is starting, and it's Ryoma versus Higa's heavy hitter, the giant Kei Tanishi and his unreturnable "Big Bang" serve.

Available January 2009!